D1571848

Lorine Niedecker

Also by Margot Peters

Lorine Niedecker

A Poet's Life

Margot Peters

The University of Wisconsin Press

Publication of this volume has been made possible, in part, through support from
the **Anonymous Fund**
of the College of Letters and Science
at the University of Wisconsin–Madison.

The University of Wisconsin Press
1930 Monroe Street, 3rd Floor
Madison, Wisconsin 53711-2059
uwpress.wisc.edu

3 Henrietta Street
London WC2E 8LU, England
eurospanbookstore.com

Printed in the United States of America

Library of Congress Cataloging-in-Publication Data
Peters, Margot.
Lorine Niedecker: a poet's life / Margot Peters.
p.   cm.
Includes bibliographical references and index.
ISBN 978-0-299-28500-5 (cloth: alk. paper)
ISBN 978-0-299-28503-6 (e-book)
1. Niedecker, Lorine.   2. Poets, American—20th century—Biography.   I. Title.
PS3527.I6Z855   2011
811'.54—dc22
[B]
2011018267

Excerpts from Lorine Niedecker's letters, manuscripts, and other materials are reprinted by permission
of the Estate of Lorine Niedecker. Excerpts from Edwin Honig's "A Memory of Lorine Niedecker in
the Late '30s" are reprinted by permission of the National Poetry Foundation. Excerpts from James
Laughlin's *The Way It Wasn't* and other materials are reprinted by permission of New Directions
Publishing Corp. acting as agent, copyright © 2006 and 2011 by the Estate of James Laughlin. Excerpts
from Jerry Reisman's "Lorine: Some Memories of a Friend" and "On Some Conversations with Celia
Zukofsky" are reprinted by permission of the Reisman Family Trust.

For

Ann Engleman

Contents

Lorine Niedecker

Introduction

Life without poetry is, in effect, life without a sanction
Wallace Stevens

Lorine Niedecker, 1903–70, is usually classified as a modern twentieth-century American Objectivist poet. Modernism dates from the kind of poetry written by T. S. Eliot and Ezra Pound in the 1920s and 1930s. "Out of the blurry, putrid, excessive body of language," writes critic Daniel Tiffany, "emerged Pound's image, with its hardness and clarity and precision: an icon rising from the excrement of language." Admiring Pound for "really beating the hell out of flabby, sentimental writing," the Objectivist poet Carl Rakosi saw a way ahead cleared of deadwood: "We were free, for the first time, to be absolutely honest, absolutely sincere, and to write in exactly the form we wanted to write in. That's the big thing!"

Objectivists, then, were second-wave modern American poets writing from the late 1920s through the 1960s. They included William Carlos Williams, Louis Zukofsky, Charles Reznikoff, Carl Rakosi, George Oppen, the British poet Basil Bunting, and Lorine Niedecker. The Objectivists scorned imprecision, sentimentality, loose imagery, inflated language, grandiose subjects, and traditional forms. All major Objectivists had the integrity to pursue their craft whether the literati noticed or not; and every poet writing today owes an enormous debt to the Objectivists who, along with Eliot and Pound, shaped the poetics of the twentieth and twenty-first centuries.

Yet the Objectivists weren't even a group but an edgy mix of poets who shared intellectuality, left-leaning politics in their youth, a belief in Marxist historical materialism, and the poetic aim of clarity and precision. Or as the non-Objectivist Wallace Stevens put it, paraphrasing Pound, "Not Ideas About the Thing But the

Thing Itself." Many of them were Jewish and urban; except for Niedecker, all were male. Niedecker would seem to be the complete outsider, yet Carl Rakosi considered her the most thorough Objectivist of them all: "With her the external world, the object, is primary, it is most out front, and subjective is most subsumed, so Objectivist is appropriate for her."

But Niedecker's poetry is far more than depicted objects. In the 1930s she was strongly influenced by surrealism, dreams, and the subconscious—the internal world. Though she abandoned surrealistic writing, she never renounced an influence "that has always seemed to want to ride right along with the direct, hard, objective kind of writing." By the 1960s she was writing a "reflective" poetry that was as much about her memory/interpretation of the object as the object itself. But then, all Objectivist poetry is characterized by deviation more than adherence to the rule.

During her lifetime, Niedecker received perhaps more praise from her (chiefly male) colleagues than any other twentieth-century woman poet. William Carlos Williams, Basil Bunting, and Jonathan Williams considered her a modern Emily Dickinson—only better. She was compared to Williams himself, as well as to Catullus, Sappho, H.D., and the masters of haiku. She was ranked "in the company of literary adventurers such as Mina Loy and Jane Bowles." At her death, Allen Ginsberg praised her uniqueness: "one in the world."

Yet Lorine's greatest fear was that her poetry and name would vanish. Published only by small presses in limited editions and in esoteric literary magazines, so retiring as a poet she was known only to other poets and a handful of readers, she had real grounds for this fear. And for almost two decades after her death her work did seem in danger of disappearing from the canon.

The reasons for her obscurity, both during and after her lifetime, are compelling. First, she lived physically removed from other poets, on Blackhawk Island, four miles from the small city of Fort Atkinson, Wisconsin. As Mary Oppen, wife of the Objectivist poet George Oppen, said of the 1920s and 1930s, "The United States at this time was a place in which one did much better not to admit being an artist or poet or writer, especially if one believed in oneself." The solution was to find a community of artists, poets, and writers—that is, to live in New York, as did Objectivists Louis Zukofsky, Charles Reznikoff, Carl Rakosi, and the Oppens themselves. (William Carlos Williams was across the Hudson River in New Jersey.) Though she corresponded with Louis Zukofsky and eventually with Cid Corman in Japan, Niedecker had no community of artists available to her. She had no access to universities and lecture circuits had she wanted them—she did not appear on platforms in Millay's flame-colored gowns, Marianne Moore's tricornered hats, or May Sarton's feminist pantsuits. In fact, with one exception, she refused to read her poetry at all, believing that a poem must emerge from a silence shared by reader and work.

Then too she adopted a stance of militant self-effacement. "Wonder if there's a society for stray animals I can join," she wrote Zukofsky. "And I'd have to handle and sell books?" she asked Cid Corman, who wanted to publish a collection of her poetry. "*This I can't do.*" To a request to record her reading poetry: "A tape of, by, me? Nice of you to ask but I'm not sure my reading would be the best. (Altho' actually I say my verse to myself a million times, sometimes whisper it 'aloud' for moosic.) Hardly think I should, Bob." When a friend announced that her book *North Central* was in Brentano's on Fifth Avenue, she responded: "These moves to *push* me will always bother me a bit." The University of Wisconsin–Milwaukee asked her to give a reading, "but I fight shy of that kind of thing." The operative word is *fight*. She was as determined not to appear in public as she was determined to get her poetry into print. Much of that work, however, she cast in deliberately modest forms: modernist *Mother Goose* rhymes, ballads, and haiku. And she had far too keen a sense of humor to promote herself as Poet. At her boldest, she might announce, "I think I'm making a small insect buzz in this prairie grass . . . that may be heard in London."

Again, the Objectivists with whom she identified were largely ignored in their lifetimes. It was always "a glorious shock," Lorine wrote Cid Corman in 1968, to see his, her, or Zukofsky's names, "as so much of the literary world has gone on for so long without indicating that we exist." None of them began to get a fair hearing until the 1960s except William Carlos Williams, who, some twenty years older than the others, published first and dominated the spotlight. Angry at the lack of response to the Objectivist issue of *Poetry* that he edited in 1931, Zukofsky scolded a Gotham Book Mart audience: "the 'Objectivist's' number of *Poetry* appeared in February. Since then there have been March, April, May, June and July and we are now in the middle of August. Don't write, telegraph."

Western Union never called. Popular anthologies, edited by Louis Untermeyer, Conrad Aiken, and Oscar Williams, generally ignored the Objectivists, who were blackballed as cultural outsiders. William Carlos Williams was the exception, though he could write Zukofsky in 1946, "Eliot is still our enemy and ALL the universities without exception." Some Objectivist poets, like Carl Rakosi, stopped writing for decades. Niedecker did not, but worked steadily with a devotional faith in the validity of her calling. She is often compared to Emily Dickinson, who did not achieve real recognition until publication in 1929, forty-five years after her death.

Niedecker was further marginalized because poets who happen to be women have universally confronted prejudice from male colleagues and critics, if not the public. If they were recluses like Emily Brontë, Christina Rossetti, or Emily Dickinson, who didn't threaten the establishment, they were reluctantly accepted as eccentric phenomena. If they burned the candle at both ends—Edna St. Vincent Millay—or committed suicide—Sylvia Plath and Anne Sexton—the establishment granted them a certain iconic status. But Ezra Pound dismissed Amy Lowell's Imagistic poetry as "Amygism." Jonathan Williams called Niedecker "the best contemporary *poetess.*" James Laughlin called modern women poets "the ladies." Carl Rakosi dismissed most female poets as flabby, effusive, and sentimental. Most importantly, Niedecker lived in an age when anthologies were edited by men. Their selections, biased toward male poets, determined which poets were taught in colleges and universities—which ones survived or were buried.

Finally, Niedecker was compared in small but crucial scholarly circles to Louis Zukofsky—to her disadvantage. "However much Niedecker may have gained from her association with Zukofsky during her lifetime," wrote Niedecker scholar Jenny Penberthy in 1993, "she has, ironically, suffered from it since." Though their thirty-nine-year correspondence was the major output for both, scholars used to dismiss the relationship as mentor–pupil, partly because, in pruning her letters, Zukofsky retained material about himself. Scholars also ignored the fact that Niedecker critiqued Zukofsky's poetry and more often than not rejected his advice to her. Zukofsky did write much more poetry than Niedecker and ascribed to it a severe importance, wishing to be known as *the* modern poet. Niedecker thanked him repeatedly for his help, outwardly deferred to him (though her list of favorite Zukofsky poems is remarkably short). Her deference to Zukofsky, therefore, was partly responsible for scholars ignoring her original, independent body of work.

Considering all these factors, it is unsurprising, therefore, that the critic Rachel Blau du Plessis could write in 1990 of Niedecker's "intense marginality," or that in 2003 John Lehman titled his brief biography of Niedecker *America's Greatest Unknown Poet.*

In 2011, however, Lorine Niedecker is no longer unknown. The *Collected Works*, edited by Jenny Penberthy, was published in 2002. Her letters to Cid Corman and Louis Zukofsky appeared in 1986 and 1993. *Lorine Niedecker: Woman and Poet* and *Radical Vernacular*, collections of criticism, came out in 1996 and 2008. Most important of all, Lorine Niedecker is currently anthologized, which makes her work available to teachers, students, and general readers.

She is indeed, as she is commonly called, a poet of place (*not* a regional poet), but her work cannot be limited to that category. She is also a poet of people, from her vivid thumbnail portraits of Mr. Van Ess, Poet Percival, and Missus Dora to her later works about Thomas Jefferson, William Morris, and Charles Darwin. She is, as well, a thinking poet with a clear vision of the mutability of all material things and their primal bond.

Certainly Lorine Niedecker is a poet for these hard times. A humble person, except for her certain belief in her calling. A secularist who lived in her mind. A person of discipline and intellectual toughness. A poor person who knew that poverty can have advantage over property. An ironist whose wit cuts through sham and shibboleth. An antimaterialist who advised throwing "*things* / to the flood." A person in intimate touch with nature. An ecologist long before our contemporary passion for "going green."

> Scuttle up the workshop
> settle down the dew
> I'll tell you what my name is
> when we've made the world new.

Perhaps the world is made new enough now to recognize Lorine Niedecker's extraordinary gifts. This biography explores the life and work of a woman who, along with Emily Dickinson, Walt Whitman, Wallace Stevens, and William Carlos Williams, is one of America's unique poetic voices.

I

Carp-Seiner's Daughter

1903~1918

I grew in green / slide and slant / of shore and shade
"PAEAN TO PLACE"

Lorine Niedecker lived most of her life on Blackhawk Island in Jefferson County, three-plus miles west of the city of Fort Atkinson in southeastern Wisconsin. Even when marriage took her to Milwaukee for six years, she camped in apartments she never considered home.

Blackhawk Island is not an island but a peninsula accessible during Lorine's childhood by a single dirt road. On the north side, farmland gave way to frog swamp, then Mud Lake. On the south, farms sloped to the Rock River, which widened upstream, eating away at low banks until the peninsula became a point where the river flowed into Lake Koshkonong. Just as Blackhawk Island is not an island, Lake Koshkonong is not a lake but 10,460 acres of river spilling over its flood plain, at a maximum depth of eleven feet. A good fishing lake, it is also home to pelicans, egrets, herons, cranes, and geese.

When Lorine was born, Blackhawk Island was a woodland paradise edged by water. The tip of the peninsula was dominated by the Blackhawk Hunt Club, catering to sportsmen from Fort Atkinson and far beyond, courtesy of the Chicago and Northwestern Railroad. General Philip Henry Sheridan had patronized the island's elite establishment in the 1880s. Horse-drawn carriages collected hunters and fishermen at the Fort Atkinson train depot and drove them to the island's end, where staff poured whiskey, brandy, and Wisconsin beer to greet their arrival.

The Fountain House, named for a flowing well in the front yard, was also a major island establishment and dominated Lorine's early years. Her maternal grandparents, Gottfried and Louisa Kunz, owned the ten-guest hotel, residence, resort, bar, and restaurant. Lorine remembered:

> trees thick, great branches. Robins' nests allowed on the window sills on the store-room side of the house. Evenings the red-wings, the wind died down, the little river still. The birds gathered close in a song of settling down . . . over two hundred acres . . . owned by the family—
>
> The moss green Morris Chair. The shadows plush green in the water. Pictures of afternoons of those days: women in their chairs, the mild, wild lowland, excessively beautiful, willows, ease-ness, drooping health, the ladies with long, flowing skirts, their handkerchiefs in their laps.

If one didn't mind mosquitoes and the occasional snake in bed, Blackhawk Island was a shifting, watery paradise. Evidence ten thousand years old survives of hunting and fishing on the island, to which Chief Black Hawk, pursued by General Henry Atkinson, fled briefly during the Black Hawk War of 1832.

Soft maple, elm, ash, alder, and weeping willow flourished. Calls of bitterns, mallards, Canada geese, and sandhill cranes surpassed human noise except in hunting season. Iridescent dragonflies darted in the reeds; monarch butterflies paused in late summer sun. In winter, rabbit, muskrat, mink, and fox prints patterned snow. Musing on the riverbank, Lorine watched blue kingfishers skim the water, sunlight dance on the undersides of willow branches.

Theresa Henrietta Kunz Niedecker gave birth in the Summer House at W7528 Blackhawk Island Road. She and her husband had been living with her parents until they bought the Summer House in preparation for their child. Lorine Faith Niedecker's birth certificate states that she was born at 1:30 a.m. on Monday, May 11, 1903, as do the doctor's notes. Yet she celebrated her birthday on May 12, an unsolved contradiction. Dr. Frank Brewer, who had established a hospital in Fort Atkinson, delivered the baby, and the Niedeckers named her Lorine after his wife.

Theresa's parents, Gottfried and Louisa Kunz, were second-generation German immigrants. Theresa's grandmother, Caroline Kunz, owned considerable island land. She gave acreage to Theresa at the time of her marriage, but it was signed over to her husband, so that Theresa had no money of her own, and her older sister Ida had to help her out from time to time.

Lorine's father, Henry Niedecker, was a voluble, energetic man whom people either liked or distrusted. He was born in Sutter, Sacramento County, California, in 1879, to Charles and Emelia Niedecker. After a flood washed away his crops and cattle, the widowed Charles Niedecker returned to the Fort Atkinson area with his children Charles, George, Emma, and Henry. Henry and Theresa met at the Black Hawk Country School, where they competed fiercely to be top readers. Henry was the kind of man who successfully sported white suspenders, white shirt, and black tie when he wasn't wearing waders. Generally he was calm, but his anger could explode.

Theresa Niedecker was called Daisy. "She was tall!" said friends in wonder. Her husband reached her shoulder. In photographs she appears stoic. After Lorine was born, Theresa began to lose her hearing. Doctors connected her increasing deafness to the birth of her only child.

Lorine took after neither of her parents particularly, though shown a photo of Daisy taken in 1900, a friend exclaimed, "I see Lorine!" Lorine was small, pretty, and blonde with large, deep-blue eyes shaded at the corners by heavy lids—though "No one remembers her without thick glasses which required her to tilt her head to bring into focus any thing or anybody not on eye level." By photographic testimony, Lorine was a happy child. She was shy—but never shy of herself—kind, bright, and passionately taken with the world around her.

Henry Niedecker made money and spent it. During Lorine's childhood he ran (ineptly) the Fountain House for the Kunzes; owned the *General Atkinson*, a trim launch carrying forty sightseers when not pulling barges; made money as a hunting and fishing guide; and developed Daisy's property until he owned, in 1911 when he had the land platted, twenty-six Blackhawk Island lots.

He also co-owned the Niedecker-Thompson Fish Company that in 1908 was shipping three thousand pounds of *cyprinus carpio* east every week. Republican governor William D. Hoard had introduced carp into the area to cater to the taste of its German immigrants. Gefilte fish, at that time most commonly made from carp, was also a staple of New York Jews. Between 1920 and 1930 thirteen commercial fishermen operated on Lake Koshkonong. Men packed the catch (carp could measure up to four feet long) into two-hundred-pound boxes, loaded them into steel tanks, hoisted the tanks into freight cars, pumped them with air and ice, and expressed the carp to New York via rail. For the Hanukkah season thirteen carloads hauling 429,000 pounds of fish left for New York City every week. At Peck Slip Fish Market in south Manhattan, rabbis passed the cargo as Kosher.

Daisy stayed home. She washed, ironed, sewed Lorine's frocks, darned stockings, scrubbed floors, cooked, and pulled weeds, all the while looking "neat as a pin."

Living yards from mud and rotting fish carcasses, with a husband who emerged daily from the river in stinking waders, she suffered the torments of the obsessively clean. She fought Blackhawk Island another way, demanding that Henry clear trees so she could plant sunflowers, daisies, hollyhocks, and zinnias. Daisy is the mystery in Lorine's life, a vital woman whose deafness drove her into solitude and resentment.

Lorine's second cousins, Adeline and Arvella Hartel, remembered Daisy as "a very lovely person, very very deaf, who never seemed to go any place. She always had her dog with her, rather large, long-haired, reddish. At times it seemed as though she could lip-read." Lorine later told a friend that her mother had "Indian heritage." Photographs don't contradict her.

Photographs document Lorine's otherwise unnoted years. Lorine sitting on Henry's lap in white dress and black stockings, her arm around his neck. Lorine in a horse-drawn wagon. Lorine in Indian garb with a bow and arrow. Lorine reading a book or playing a ukulele on the banks of the Rock River. Lorine grinning atop a haystack. Lorine in the river, hair tied up in a kerchief. Lorine with girlfriends in a canoe.

A photograph of Lorine and her mother suggests a story, the two seated apart in an open shed. Mother and daughter gaze into the distance, Lorine with her hair in a blonde pigtail topped by a white bow. Daisy, narrow-belted waist, furrowed brow, gazes bleakly into the distance. It may mean nothing, but Lorine leans away from her mother as though they may not be going in the same direction. Though Daisy, according to her daughter, was a "descendent for sure of Mother Goose" who spoke "whole chunks of down-to-earth (o very earthy) magic" that Lorine greedily drank in.

As a small child Lorine played around the Fountain House, talking with guests or observing with awe an Eagles' annual picnic attended by nearly seven hundred people. She loved Grandfather Gottfried Kunz, "head thrown back . . . such great smiling wrinkles around his eyes . . . braided my hair and told me nursery jingles. . . . There *were* three *crows* sat *on* a *tree*. . . . And if he saw me at a distance outdoors he'd hold out his arms wide."

She shrewdly observed her elders. Grandmother and aunts made their own cheese, bread, and sausages that they hung from rafters in the upper hall of the Fountain House. They canned vegetables harvested from the big garden. They cleaned house like Furies, cooked, washed, and sewed, never thought their men worked hard enough. They considered energy their virtue. They spoke an easy, unconsciously poetic vernacular.

Too easygoing for his wife, Gottfried Kunz enjoyed being a hotelier, and was untroubled about money owed him by cheesemakers who came from Milwaukee to vacation at the Fountain House—cheapskates, hauling their own Limburger and barrels of beer. Kunzes and Niedeckers were generous and politically liberal. Their convictions were simple: money was bad and inevitably corrupted the person who owned it. Industries adopting new machines that threw people out of work were bad. Cities in general were bad. They were country folk who loved the land and wouldn't cut trees for profit. "Trees are the best things a man can have," said Gottfried, "that little while he lives."

Neither Kunzes nor Niedeckers were church people. Said Lorine, "I always thought the people were really good."

Lorine loved school. She went first to the one-room Black Hawk Country School at the junction of Highway 106 and County J, transported in a wagon or Henry's horse and buggy. A boy from the island, Ernest Hartwig, noticed Lorine: "[A] cute little girl, always quite shy, with weak eyesight and thick lenses."

But driving Lorine took up Henry's valuable time and anyway roads were often impassible in deep winter or spring flood. Few people owned cars in the first decade of the twentieth century, so neighbors couldn't give Lorine a lift. She was absent so often—and so hated being absent—that in 1910 the entrepreneurial Henry persuaded the Kunzes to sell the Fountain House. To Lorine's sorrow, her grandparents Gottlieb and Louisa Kunz retired to Long Lake in northwestern Wisconsin. (In 1917, Gottlieb would be found in a woods, dead, his back against a tree, a fitting end.)

With his four-thousand-dollar share—Daisy's, in reality—Henry had a fine house built at 1000 Germany Street with ten rooms, oak woodwork, and a spacious screen porch facing Rock River. He established Niedecker & Anthes, "All Kinds of Farm Implements, Also Bicycle Repairing." Shortsightedly, he geared the store to horse-drawn farm equipment. Lorine walked to Barrie School on Robert Street for second to fourth grades and to Caswell School for fifth and sixth, a little over a mile.

Florence Dollase, who lived nearby on the corner of Sherman and Jackson, also attended those schools. She and Lorine became mates. Lorine shyly told Florence about the wonders of Blackhawk Island, and Florence was invited to a birthday party for Lorine given by Daisy: "My, she was tall!" Florence wondered why, in all the years they were school pals, Lorine never mentioned her mother. As for Lorine's father, Florence borrowed the opinion of her uncle Art, an area trapper who knew him well: "Uncle Art *never* had a kind word to say about Henry Niedecker."

Florence was a serious, plainspoken child with straight eyebrows and dark hair. Though opposites, their independent minds drew them together. Florence was good at math, while Lorine loved books, writing, and music. In fourth grade Lorine sang the part of the Fairy Godmother in the operetta *Cinderella* with true pitch but not a solo voice. She also took piano lessons from Miss Mattie Snell and played very well.

Lorine's cousin Edna was also a childhood friend. "Lorine and I lived on [Germany Street] . . . and spent many early mornings bird-watching along Rock River," said George Neidecker's daughter. Charles Niedecker Sr., who had married Mary Brandel in 1883, lived at 516 Germany Street. Recalled Edna: "Our mutual grandparents lived next to Lorine and whenever we saw them Grandmother always had a 'candy treat' in a pocket of her apron. Our parents played cards. Aunt Daisy would get so excited. Her hearing was a sad thing and difficult for both Uncle Henry and Lorine. . . . A fun time was the family reunions. . . . I will never forget the huge pleasure launch Uncle Henry had—spent many hours taking people on Rock River and Lake Koshkonong. He rented duck-blinds to many Chicagoans and would entertain them. He and Lorine adored each other."

Niedecker & Anthes failed because engines prevailed over horses, something Henry might have predicted when he bought himself a snappy touring roadster in 1912. ("A hummingbird can't haul," said Daisy.) He sold 1000 Germany Street (speedily renamed Riverside Drive after World War I broke out in 1914) for $4,800, and the Niedeckers gave up town luxury for the island in 1916. Lorine didn't seem to mind. She could lose herself for hours outdoors among "redwinged blackbirds, willows, maples, boats, fishing (the smell of tarred nets), tittering and squawking noises from the marsh." Or rock in the riverbank glider, nose deep in a book. She was a passionate sighter of red-tails, green herons, orioles, and migrating warblers. Doves woke her on summer mornings, river-wash lulled her to sleep.

Still, Lorine joined the Opoponopokuk Campfire Girls for hikes, nature study, and cookouts. The girls lashed tin cups to their belts and wore lace-up boots. In 1914, for the best bird notebooks, the Ingleside Club awarded Lorine and Charlotte Hagemann leather-bound copies of *Land Birds East of the Rockies.* Lorine admitted that with her poor eyesight she could only see birds in flight; she became expert by studying bird books, memorizing birdsongs, and using binoculars. Lorine was elected club secretary, earned her Torchbearer rank, and over the years "took many honors, especially in nature study . . . and enjoyed spinning yarns around a camp fire."

In fall 1916 Lorine began seventh grade. Henry Niedecker's carp-seining business was flourishing, so her parents arranged to board her with their friends Charles and Barbara Bowen at 506 Riverside Drive at the corner of the Robert Street Bridge. Calling for her, Florence would spot Lorine in the Bowens' bay window.

Lorine would skip down the front steps, and the two set off for Fort Atkinson High School, which also housed grades seven and eight. Freezing or sweating, they hiked the twenty-eight blocks round trip as a matter of course.

They shared few classes, though in Domestic Science they were cooking partners. Making rice muffins one day, Lorine accidently doubled the sugar. "We had the sweetest, best muffins of the whole class," said Florence grudgingly. She considered Lorine "vague, ill-responsive and off in another world . . . not forthcoming, a loner. Kids took advantage of her." The adult Florence would never understand how absent-minded Lorine "managed to succeed so well in the poetry world," nor would she really understand the books of poetry Lorine faithfully inscribed to her. To Florence, as to most people, Lorine was a mystery.

2

High School

1918~1922

Only let me feel young and willing to work / I'd not grudge the
failure, nor would I shirk.

"Reminiscence"

I n August 1918 the bloodiest war in history ended, and that fall
Lorine entered Fort Atkinson High School as a freshman.

The school's *Tchogeerrah* yearbooks chart Lorine's progress through the next
four years. Avoiding the Tennis Association and Poultry, Garden, and Canning
Clubs, she is photographed with the girls' glee club, taught by Lydia Cocke, who
wore pince-nez and string of pearls. The girls wear white middy blouses lashed
with dark scarves; Lorine alone wears plaid. In freshman year photos, she's always
at the end of a row. She takes off her glasses for the photographer, looking lost or
just blind. By end of first term she had earned a 93 in English, 86 in algebra, 92 in
Latin, and 83 in domestic science.

"She had a visual disability which required her to wear glasses specially ground
for her," said her friend Juanita Schreiner, a smart, heavy girl with a beautiful singing
voice, "but still it was necessary for her to carry a hand magnifying glass in order
to read print easily read by others. There was a birdlike quality about her, a quiet
voice, and she walked with quick light steps. She was a very good student but
required much time to study because of her impaired vision. Her dry sense of
humor always amazed her friends but we always knew it was in fun because she
had a shy twinkle in her eyes."

As a sophomore, shy Lorine went out for debate. Behind a retiring exterior she was passionate about ethical and political issues. Winning third place, she is photographed, blonde hair shining, at the end of the back row. Glee club photograph that year, Lorine last row. Alone.

The crowd, led by Glenn Downing, *A* student and athlete, plunged on without her. Couples dancing to "Hinky Dinky Parlay Voo" and "Dardenella" didn't miss her. She didn't attend Valentine parties, weenie roasts, or pep rallies. She didn't picnic at Crabtree Point or meet the crowd after school to dance at Olin's Confectionary—though she might, if she had a nickel, have a soda at the Crystal Cafe after school with her best friend Anna Ramsey. She was unaware that her Blackhawk Island had become the petting place of choice.

But Lorine was there.

A skilled debater, she argued to a tie the negative side of "Resolved: that all immigrants, with the exception of near relatives of citizens of the United States or of those who have experienced a desire to become such, shall be excluded from the U.S. for a period of one year." She sang in choirs. She was a model student. Daisy Lieberman, an English teacher with a warm smile and catching love of poetry, particularly inspired her. Lorine felt bereft when Miss Lieberman left after her sophomore year.

Enter Ernie Hartwig, Lorine's classmate at the Black Hawk School resurfacing from Lutheran elementary school, one of the few students who knew Lorine from the island. He remembered a "cute little girl, fine boned, always very refined," with blue eyes magnified by thick lenses. "She never went out on the water, didn't like it in the boats, never went out in the big tug her father built for his seining. From the time she was a little girl she was a naturalist . . . watched birds for hours." Now he became one of her few male friends. "I always spoke to Lorine in the halls. Her best friend was Anna Ramsey, a good student like Lorine and also quiet." He noted that Lorine always clutched a clean handkerchief to her chest.

Unlike the Hartwigs, Lorine's parents had not taken her to church, though she'd been baptized at St. John's Community Church. "I was not made to go to Sunday school or church sessions as a child," she would write a friend, "and I can say now like Henry James and William who didn't go either; I didn't have so much to unlearn when I grew up. I wouldn't discard the Bible, tho, by any means." Lack of church affiliation widened the gulf between her and the folk of Fort Atkinson.

Ernie remembered her parents:

> Henry was never coarse, always polite. He was soft-spoken, calm,
> but when he got angry he got really angry. Me and my brother
> Frank knew Henry real well and we both worked for him as high
> school boys at his seining business to make money. . . .

Daisy, she was an extremely fastidious housekeeper. She kept the wood floors of their house polished and never let anybody into the house. Lorine told me that she and her mother could sit in the same room for a whole evening without passing a word. Even her father did not usually sleep in the house, but stayed in a quonset-like building next to the house, where he kept his seining gear and where the men were fed who helped him seine carp. This building was about three doors downstream from The Fountain House, where Henry later also allegedly kept his lady friend who is said to have parted him from his money.

By Lorine's high school years, Henry and a neighbor, Gertrude Runke, twenty-one years younger, had become lovers, using a Quonset hut with tin roof and windows near his house for their meetings. Henry had grown weary of his bitter, deaf wife who hated his waders on her clean floors.

Gertrude Runke was three years older than Lorine. In 1920, when Gertrude was twenty, she gave birth to a daughter whom she named, flagrantly, Lorrine. Henry remained good friends with Gert's husband, Otto, who did handyman work at the Fountain House, but Daisy loathed Gertrude. Lorine watched as her abandoned mother retreated into silence; and the more silent she became, the more in atonement and fury she scrubbed, laundered, planted, weeded, and cooked for her husband's carp-seining crew in the hut she knew was his trysting place. Lorine agonized for her mother, yet was drawn to her father:

> My father
> thru marsh fog
>   sculled down
>   from high ground . . .
> bore the weight of lake water
>   and the cold—
> he seined for carp to be sold
> that their daughter
>
> might go high
> on land
>   to learn
> Saw his wife turn
> deaf
>
> and away. . . .

Henry may perhaps be forgiven for wife-cheating but not for cheating his family. Early on, Gertrude Runke hog-tied her lover with demands. Frontage by frontage foot, lot by lot, Henry signed over his ownings on Blackhawk Island to Gertrude's husband, Otto, in exchange for his wife. What this common enchantress offered, besides sex, was laughs and conversation, appealing enough to extract a good deal of Henry's cash and half his property. Otto took Gert out for Friday fish fries to celebrate her contribution to their income. Most people believed he "put Gert up to" getting Henry into bed.

Lorine would write:

> What a woman!—hooks men like rugs,
> clips as she hooks, prefers old wool, but all
> childlike, lost, houseowning or pensioned men
> her prey. She covets the gold in her husband's teeth.
> She'd sell dirt, she'd sell your eyes fried in deep grief.

By 1921, her junior year, Lorine was on the yearbook staff and continued girls' glee club, mixed glee club, and debate, in which she partnered with Glen Bell, a solemn senior in wire-rimmed glasses. She crammed *Political Philosophy* by Wisconsin's famous Progressive Robert La Follette to bolster her arguments: "From the first sentence to the last the league of nations is a sham and a fraud. It pretends to be a league to preserve the peace of the world. It is an alliance among the victorious nations of Europe to preserve for themself the plunder and the power they gained by the war." Lorine had already become a progressive populist. She was also a pacifist, agreeing with La Follette that "the present congress will pass a military program that will impose upon the people of the United States the greatest tax burden for an alleged preparedness against an alleged danger that has ever been known in any country at peace with all the world."

In spring she went to the prom with Anna Ramsey, Juanita Schreiner, and Harriet Westphal, who had played Cinderella to Lorine's Fairy Godmother in grade school. Ernie Hartwig drove her home. "He was crazy about Lorine but didn't think he was good enough" for the shy, intellectual, poetic girl. In the senior yearbook, Ernie would be described as "heart-whole," meaning that he hadn't given his heart to anyone else.

As a junior Lorine scored 86 in plane geometry, 92 in English, 94 in stenography, and 90 in French. The *Tchogeerrah* featured her long poem "Reminiscence":

> The light of day is growing dim,
> And fires, the western skies illume,

From bays and creeks, the blackbirds call,
Oh, Canadian honker, we know 'tis fall.

Lorine has almost mastered iambic tetrameter; "dim" and "illume" is a felicitous near-rhyme, "Oh, Canadian honker" is bad (though Wallace Stevens would address swans in 1923 as "O ganders"). The poet goes on to mourn how "grey and sere has Nature grown," pleading

Turn backward, years that are flying along,
To-night all to youth does surely belong.

Nothing like reaching the vast age of seventeen for feeling that life is passing you by.

That June she wrote in her friend Juanita Schreiner's *Tchogeerrah*: "It is not necessary to remind you of the unearthly hour we spent together before school pouring [*sic*] over geometry, etc. Thank you for your kind assistance on the Annual. Juanita, your spirit is one to be envied. Good luck, Lorine."

And in Harriet Westphal's book, in large, bouncy handwriting: "Well, Harriet, the shark in *Geometry*, the main room whisperer, the best sport in the world. I always think of you on a reception committee. Well—best wishes from an ambiguous classmate. L. F. N."

Lorine returned to Blackhawk Island for the summer, where she threw herself into helping her mother with housework, cooking, and gardening. When she could, she escaped to wander the island, peering into trees, ponds, and swamp, bird book in hand.

Most important, she had discovered poetry—first with Daisy Lieberman, then for herself with a copy of Wordsworth that she took out with her that summer, "rowing a boat or walking the woods and reading him—o my!" She was also writing poetry, conscious how much had changed since the days of Keats and Emily Dickinson, searching for a form, a style. She showed some of it to Ernie, and to pretend he understood, he teased that one word "just doesn't seem right."

"It took me *two months* to think of just the right word for that line," said Lorine indignantly.

Looking back, she would recognize that her serious interest in poetry began that summer when she was eighteen.

In the fall of 1921 Lorine returned to Fort Atkinson for her senior year, staying at 800 Riverside Drive with Henry and Bertha Meyer and their daughters Avis and Lucy. The apparent ease with which Lorine accepted boarding out (she also stayed in town with her Niedecker grandparents) indicates toughness as well as relief in escaping tensions at home.

As a senior Lorine came into her own. In glee club and debate photos, she was no longer at the end of the row and was confident enough to face the camera wearing glasses. She took American history, physics, French, English, debate, and passed gym with a B+. She easily made the honor roll, the girls' debate team won "affirmative" on "Disarmament," and the Debate Club sent eight teams to the state finals.

Still, she impressed most classmates as an introverted loner. Clarence "Cal" Langholff, a sophomore, met her in debate class. The smallest boy in his class, he knew something about shyness and recognized in Lorine a sympathetic soul: "A smart girl, a book worm, studied a lot. Calm, very pleasant, very polite. Not very popular, never went with any boys."

Instead of dating, Lorine was writing another poem for the *Tchogeerrah*, a sarcastic requiem for the murder of "refined speech" by slang. Everybody these days was a "crook," "tough bird," "wild woman," or "guy." Everybody exclaimed mindlessly, "That's a cinch!"

> I tell Tom of the quake that made Mexico shake,
> "Well, ain't that the berries?" quotes he.
> When describing a quail or a sunset or whale—
> They're "wonderful!"—each of the three.

For the young poet who spent two months searching for an exact word, communicating with her slang-spouting classmates was the poem's title: "Wasted Energy."

The class of 1922 chose for its motto "Not How Long You Live, But How." Its colors were red and white, its flower an American Beauty rose. Lorine's senior-class photo shows a blonde and very pretty young woman with an inward gaze. She chose as her motto Longfellow's "The love of learning, / the sequestered nooks, / And all the sweet serenity of books." Throughout the *Tchogeerrah* she was very present—snapshots, "Class History," her poem, and a mention in the "What If" column: "What If—Lorine never asked questions." But no student could match class president Glenn Downing's long list of achievements.

Lorine wrote in Juanita Schreiner's yearbook: "I have been in every one of your classes and I'd have to forget some to forget you. If you wanted to know the nice things I think about you and how I wish I could borrow your mind sometimes—And how we have enjoyed many a laugh. Well, school will soon end and our friendship won't of course. Lorine Faith 'Squeaky.'" And to Florence

Dollase she wrote: "[W]e came up from the depths together, so to speak. And I planned on Whitewater—I am not planning for Beloit—so maybe this will turn out. Hope you don't type all the rest of your life, but hope you get a good position and enjoy pounding those 'rattlesome' keys. . . . Write to me next year."

Presided over by Principal Frank Bray, commencement exercises for seventy students were held on Thursday evening, June 8, at the high school auditorium. Each girl's shining hair was topped by a huge bow, while boys smiled stiffly above starched white collars. As the fiftieth commencement, the ceremony had an air of importance. As Secretary of the Class Night Committee, Lorine took the stage with the glee club to sing "Rosebuds" and again with the senior girls' glee club to sing "Carmena" and "Oh, Fort Atkinson High, we're leaving you." President Silas Evans of Ripon College held forth on "The Rules of the Game." Relatives and friends surged forward to congratulate.

The class of 1922 would be remembered as exceptional. Particularly remarkable were the numbers of girls going on to colleges, not only Milwaukee Downer, Whitewater Normal, Milwaukee Normal, Milton, and Lawrence—but out of state: Northwestern, Oberlin, the Chicago Schools of Music and Nursing, Pennsylvania College for Women, Women's College Downeast.

Therefore, that post-graduation shock of being tossed into the real world didn't affect Lorine and her friends. She had applied to a private liberal arts college, Beloit: "My favorite studies are English and French, and my favorite activities literary, aesthetic dancing and dramatic." Her proposed occupation: teaching. Meanwhile, relatives were clucking that Lorine's going to college was "a very *unusual* thing to do."

Lorine decided to attend the summer session for students trying to complete college in less than four years. Seventy-six dollars paid for entrance fee, tuition, room and board, and three courses for six weeks. She submitted her fine blonde hair to a cut and a perm and packed her clothes and books, primed for the adventure.

3

Beloit College

1922 ~ 1924

Feign a great calm; / all gay transport soon ends.
"When Ecstasy is Inconvenient"

That summer of 1922, when she was nineteen, Lorine traveled twenty-five miles south to Beloit, where she met her Rock River in more civilized mood. She had a room in Chapin Hall, a men's dorm given over to freshmen women, directly across the spacious green from Middle College, the heart of the campus. One imagines her going down to dinner that first evening in her best dress, shy, but not crushed; too curious to be daunted. She would quickly discover the excellent Carnegie Library and the campus Indian turtle mound, Beloit's unofficial mascot.

She found herself in an institution molded for its first thirty-six years by Rev. Dr. A. L. Chapin (Yale, class of 1937): "If I were seeking in the whole West for a young Yale, I should go at once to Beloit." More progressive than Ivy League schools, Beloit College had gone co-ed in 1895. When Lorine entered as a freshman, the gender battle was at high pitch, though she would have accepted as normal the ratio of faculty and administration—thirty-two men, seven women. As for the ratio of women students to men, Beloit foresaw that women would account for "about forty per cent of the total attendance." In 1928 President Eaton would admit that the presence of women "has affected a moderate but appreciable lifting of the average of scholarship, they having furnished somewhat more of their share of the best scholars and considerably less than their share of the poorest."

Two faculty members were currently agitating for women's rights on campus. Dean Katherine Adams was firm: "[W]omen are in Beloit College to stay. . . . We need a women's dormitory unit, large and modern, near Emerson Hall, on the 'Women's Campus.'" Also needed: a women's union, full college curriculum for women, methods of teaching that would meet the needs of women, scholarships, endowments, and a wholesome social life. "It is a great desire of ours to help our women to understand themselves, with insight and with power."

Another faculty member pressed as hard. Mabel Lee, author of *Memories of a Bloomer Girl*, was a dynamic women's physical education instructor who went toe to toe against the male Athletic Department for the right of women to use the Buccaneers' gym and outdoor facilities, to wear uniforms—to exist at all. The only other solid contribution women had so far made to Beloit was the gift of the chapel, "intimately associated with its higher life."

Beloit was on the quarter system—tuition $75 per—which, with incidental fees, came to $231 for the year. Board and room cost $125 per quarter. Lorine's 1922–23 year, therefore (with summer school), cost Henry $432, the equivalent of $2,295 in 2008.

A retrospective article in the Beloit College *Round Table* of 1991 says that "Niedecker was a model high school student, but her academic performance dissolved while attending Beloit College."

Not quite.

Many gifted students, faced with a liberal arts curriculum, experience a grade drop in their freshman year. At Beloit after the first trimester, Lorine had earned *C*s in botany, history, and (oddly) public speaking. Economics was an unqualified disaster: *F*, with many absences from class. But by the end of the third trimester, 1922–23, she had earned one *C*, six *B*s, and three *A*s—hardly an academic dissolve.

By early 1923 Lorine had adapted Beloit to her interests. She was taking English courses right and left, some from the head of the department, Professor George Clancy. She joined the women's debate team formed only a year earlier, and in June was elected secretary–treasurer. A debate was held with Rockford College on Saturday, February 17, after the basketball game, in the chapel, judged by Professor A. T. Weaver from the University of Wisconsin–Madison. With Helen Wallace and last-minute substitute Margaret Calland, Lorine argued the negative side of "Resolved That Child Labor should Be Prohibited by an Amendment to the Federal Constitution"—Beloit's case being that child labor is best taken care of by the several states.

The event was a disappointment, not only because Beloit lost but because the chapel was almost empty. Scheduling the debate after a basketball game was a mistake; still, the lack of student support reflected the marginal interest in a women's team. A letter to the school newspaper—"Beloit women can debate. They have proved it"—was some comfort.

Earlier that month Lorine had gone eagerly to chapel to hear Harriet Monroe, editor of the new magazine *Poetry*, lecture. Despite a heavy academic schedule, Lorine was writing and in May was invited by the poetry society Ka Ne to read along with four other freshmen. "Lake Koshkonong" and "Fever" apparently do not survive; however, the *Round Table* of May 26 reported that the poems "showed ability and originality in every instance. It was noticeable that the trend was away from the beaten path and a venture into more modern subjects and methods of treatment." And she pursued her passion for music, performing in a piano recital Lavelle's "Le Papillon."

As a sophomore Lorine moved into Stowell Cottage, a comfortable campus house for eighteen women. Harriet Westphal, her Fort Atkinson high school friend, was also on campus, singing first soprano in the glee club and vesper choir. Lorine did not join either group, though she received *B*s and *A*s in Music. That academic year she took three quarters of philosophy with John Forsyth Crawford, Beloit's "best read and most widely informed teacher," who had a close understanding with his students "akin to nothing on campus."

She was active again in the forum club, which debated Knox College at Beloit on February 29, 1924, this time with the riveting topic: "Resolved: That all penal institutions in the United States should be administered according to the central plan introduced by Thomas Mott Osborne at the United States Naval Prison at Portsmouth." Lorine wasn't present: "The Beloit team was hampered considerably by the fact that a few days previous to debate Miss Lorraine [*sic*] Niedecker, who was to be the second speaker on the affirmative team, was taken ill."

When did Lorine know that she would not be returning to Beloit after her sophomore year? Perhaps by the distribution of the 1924 *Codex*. Her inscription in Ella Barton's yearbook in large, agitated handwriting, is uncharacteristically emotional, almost incoherent:

> My dear No I'm not too busy to sign my John Hancock or whatever you call it, but gosh, El. I'm busy these last few moments. And I remember in all the rush one Sunday night when we talked and talked and I remember most what you said about the physical weakness after an emotional strain regarding such work as you and I are doomed to dabble in or survive emotionally successful and physically weak and mentally unstable—but it's life, old girl—isn't it? Lorine

It's said that Lorine left Beloit to care for her ailing mother. But Daisy was only forty-six in 1923 and not physically ill, though she was becoming more withdrawn and strange. Unlikely too that Daisy would demand such a sacrifice from her only daughter. Nor would have Lorine so longed for Blackhawk Island that she would have left Beloit voluntarily. She'd established a firm footing at the college, made friends, was comfortable living away from home, and adored learning.

But Henry needed a live-in companion for the deeply depressed wife he'd rejected, as well as for someone to help serve meals to his carp crew. More crucially, he could no longer pay Lorine's college fees.

In 1922 Henry had decided to erect, at his expense, a Blackhawk Island Club House and Social Center "for the purpose of relaxation and sociability on the Island." At the January 1923 opening of the Gothic-style building, he treated twenty-four guests to a banquet that "made the feast of Belshazzar look like a free lunch." Music was led by violinist A. R. Hoard, Charles "Fred" Bowen (with whom Lorine had boarded) led the dancing, and Barbara Bowen prepared the feast. Henry expected membership dues to more than repay his investment. This did not happen. Strapped to pay builder and upkeep, while feeding Gertrude's greed, Henry was forced to remove his daughter from Beloit College. "To bankers on high land / he opened his wine tank," Lorine would write, mild criticism for the folly that ended her college education.

That summer of 1924, therefore, Lorine was back on the Island with silent Daisy, and her father and Gert next door. In August she and Anna Ramsey spent a week at Lake Waubesa with former Campfire Girls; yet apart from this adventure, the debater, public singer, and pianist who had made close friends and planned on teaching went underground. She could set her future course neither by her free-wheeling father nor her reclusive mother. Truly, she faced a "blunted female destiny."

4

Searching

1924~1931

Have you been married? Yes, I've been attacked.
                                "Stage Directions"

G randfather Gottlieb advised her to learn a trade; Henry wanted
   her to work in a bank. But Lorine had one calling and pursued
it. She wrote poetry and she read it: Shakespeare, Christina Rossetti, Whitman,
Eliot, Pound, H.D., Marianne Moore, E. E. Cummings, and William Carlos
Williams. Her copy of *Selections from Byron, Wordsworth, Shelley* was her bible,
with hundreds of notations.

In prose she sought out dissent and radicalism: George Santayana's *Scepticism
and Animal Faith*, Havelock Ellis's *The Dance of Life*, and George Brandes's *Jesus, a
Myth*, which argues that eliminating what cannot possibly be historic from the
New Testament would be like peeling away Peer Gynt's onion to find nothing at
the center. She marked a passage from Upton Sinclair's *Mammonart* that cites
Coleridge's "Kubla Khan" as a prime example of the artist in denial:

> There is no such place as Xanadu; and Kubla Khan has nothing to
> teach us but avoidance. His pleasures were bloody and infamous,
> and there was nothing "stately" about his "pleasure-dome." There
> never was a river Alph, and the sacredness of any river is a fiction of
> a priestly caste, preying on the people. There are no "caverns
> measureless to man"; while as for a "sunless sea," a few arc-lights
> would solve the problem. . . . From the beginning to the end, the
> poem deals with things which are sensual, cruel, and fatal to hope.

These books honed Lorine's instinctive distrust for the splendid, endowed, fantastical, and untrue—as they were honing a new realistic poetry. She slipped a passage of Tolstoy between the pages of *Mammonart*:

> The artist of the future will understand that to compose a fairytale, a little song which will touch, a lullaby or a riddle which will entertain . . . is incomparably more important and fruitful than to compose a novel or a symphony, or paint a picture which will divert some member of the wealthy classes for a short time, and then be forgotten. The region of this art of the simple feelings accessible to all is enormous, and it is as yet almost untouched.

It is probable that after Beloit she continued to write poetry in the modernist vein. Yet no private writing from these years survives—no letters, no jottings, no journals.

She missed friends, Ella Barton among them. She and Florence Dollase had parted ways, Anna Ramsey was attending nursing school in Chicago, and Harriet Westphal had transferred to the New England Conservatory of Music in Boston. Everyone seemed to be moving on except Lorine, stuck in swamp and swale. Yet she possessed, and was possessed by, a calling. Meanwhile she got the island even deeper under her skin on solitary walks to the point, and dealt with Daisy, "tall, tormented, darkinfested":

> Well, spring overflows the land,
> floods floor, pump, wash machine
> of the woman moored to this low shore by deafness.
>
> Good-bye to lilacs by the door
> and all I planted for the eye.
> If I could hear—too much talk in the world,
> too much wind washing, washing
> good black dirt away.
>
> Her hair is high.
> Big blind ears.
>
> I've wasted my whole life in water.
> My man's got nothing but leaky boats.
> My daughter, writer, sits and floats.

Guilt at floating spurred her to apply to the Fort Atkinson Public Library as an assistant librarian in May 1928. Again, she solved the problem of getting into town from the island by staying during the week with her first cousin Roland Hartel and his wife, Maude, and walking home on weekends if she couldn't get a lift. Maude and Roland had two daughters, Arvella and Adeline. Some fifteen years younger than Lorine, they fled to their bedroom after supper: "She was *very* different. . . . She always sat there with her little notebook."

As a low-paid assistant librarian, Lorine was comfortable shelving books and stamping cards at the Fort Atkinson library. By June she was writing "Library Notes," a column for the local *Jefferson County Union* in which she encouraged patrons to explore new books on science, child care, history, travel, psychology, philosophy, music, local politics, and gardening.

She also urged patrons not to ignore classics like Olive Schreiner's *The Story of an African Farm*, Lytton Strachey's *Queen Victoria*, Carl Sandburg's *Abraham Lincoln*, Willa Cather's *My Antonia*, and Edith Wharton's *Ethan Frome*. Bernard Shaw was a favorite, particularly *Saint Joan* and the "incomparable preface" to his play *Heartbreak House*. Emil Ludwig wrote "a brilliant history" of the life of Goethe. "Not enough can be said of the beauty of 'Swords and Roses' by Joseph Hergesheimer." Heywood Broun was the "supreme columnist, outstanding in clear thinking, humor and fair play."

She cheerleads for reading itself: "A book in the hand is worth ten on the shelf," she advises, or, "It is said that no man is ever quite the same at the close of a book as at the beginning." She quotes Voltaire: "It is reading alone that invigorates the understanding; conversation dissipates it; play contracts it." Behind the initials "L.N.," she obviously enjoyed giving Fort Atkinson a piece of her mind.

That year too, 1928, she had two short poems published. Both "Transition" and "Mourning Dove" illustrate the precision that would characterize her later work: in "Transition," an image of autumn leaves "like gorgeous quill-pens / in old inkwells / almost dry"; in "Mourning Dove," the felicitous vowel play of "dee round silence / in the sound" of them. Yet in "Mourning Dove" she gives up Imagism almost before she's begun: "Or it may be I face the dull prospect / of an imagist / turned philosopher."

During these years she met a man who attracted her. He and his brother worked off and on for Henry Niedecker, seining carp. The man was Frank Hartwig, the older brother of Ernest, who had liked Lorine in high school.

The Hartwigs had a thirty-acre farm on both sides of Blackhawk Island Road, two miles townward from the Niedeckers, where they raised Holsteins. The Hartwig stead was attractive, with narrow white clapboard siding, apple trees shading the west side, and a large garden outside the kitchen door. Silo and barn, outhouse, milk house, chicken house, and machine shed were well maintained. Grazing land sloped to the Rock River.

Born on May 31, 1899, Frank was four years older than Lorine, the middle child of Friederich and Rosina Hartwig, who'd emigrated from Germany about 1890. Frank had dropped out of high school after his junior year: he liked outdoor work like farming or construction. He was dark, slim, and handsome, like the young Henry Niedecker but without Henry's bravado. Frank was a loner, less outgoing than Lorine, never one for small talk. He was sensitive and didn't like "killing pretty ducks."

They started to date. Frank would pick her up in his Model T truck and they'd rattle into Fort, where silent stars like John Gilbert and Garbo hypnotized them at the local movie house. After the film, perhaps they ventured into Olin's Confectionary for a chocolate soda. More probably, Frank packed a pint to tipple on the way home.

Frank brought Lorine to the farm. She admired the Holsteins, the handsome big white barn, the tree-shaded house. Rosina adored her—such a sweet, shy, down-to-earth girl. Frank's father called her "a doll." Yet Frank told no one that Lorine had agreed to marry him.

"What? You?" Ernest responded, disbelieving when Frank told him on November 28 that the wedding was the next day. "Frank never went with any girl for very long. He said he'd never marry. He was by himself an awful lot. . . . [I]t didn't seem like they were in love or anything. . . . It must have been a hidden love affair."

At five o'clock on Thanksgiving Day 1928, Lorine and Frank were married by Rev. Palmer Janke in the parsonage of St. Paul's Lutheran in Fort Atkinson. Lorine was twenty-five, Frank twenty-nine; occupations assistant librarian and road contractor. Ernest Hartwig and Anna Ramsey were best man and maid of honor. After the ceremony the four had a quiet dinner at the former Fountain House, now the Riverside Guest House. The occasion was too quiet for Ernie: Where were parents, friends? "It was odd. Anna and I talked about it afterwards." They concluded that Lorine, rather than Frank, had preferred to soft-pedal the event, almost as though she were denying the union.

According to his niece Lois Bielefeldt, Frank bought a Buick and had a small house built for his bride at 311 Garfield, a quiet street north of Fort's business district. If true, their wedding plans dated from summer 1928, when the house was under construction. As a road contractor, Frank was confident of making a good living: the automobile had arrived, speeding up the tempo of living and invading a once-remote Blackhawk Island. Every week the *Jefferson County Union* headlined stories about killed pedestrians and dead drivers hanging from trees. Frank's gravel was in demand, though it was less safe than dirt on deep-ditched, shoulderless roads.

The estimation of how long Lorine and Frank lived as husband and wife ranges from one night to two years.

"Lorine's marriage lasted one night," said Nathalie Kaufman Yackels, a confidant in later years. "She didn't know *anything* about sex." "If that's all it amounts to in marriage," Lorine told Anna Ramsey soon after the wedding, "it's not for me." Lorine seems to have looked upon Frank as a friend, a fellow loner. If he was as sexually inexperienced as Lorine was naive, intercourse could have been a disaster. As for providing her with companionship: Frank had bought three trucks on credit and rented three gravel pits. He hauled, crushed, and laid road gravel all day and "at night repaired his machinery. He didn't have many hours to be with Lorine, he worked very hard."

The marriage baffled Florence Dollase: "*Why?* She wasn't a housekeeper! She *never* liked to cook." Years later, Lorine's friend Cid Corman, poet and publisher, expressed equal mystification. Lorine must have been pregnant or thought she was pregnant; why else would she have married a farmer? This was also the suspicion of some people at the time. And a bizarre rumor circulated that she and Frank had stillborn twin daughters.

(There is another possibility. Frank never dated a woman before Lorine, Ernest was incredulous that he married, he never dated a woman after Lorine, he accepted the failed marriage without protest, and he never blamed Lorine for leaving him. If Frank Hartwig were homosexual it would put an entirely different slant on Lorine's reported, "If that's all it amounts to in marriage, it's not for me.")

They are together on June 29, 1929, photographed at Anna Ramsey's marriage to John Grover. Frank is identifiable as the best-looking man at the gathering, wearing a light suit with plaid tie and standing behind Lorine, the only guest looking away from the camera. She appears rueful, almost suffering: her smile is strained.

On October 29, 1929, Black Thursday initiated a series of stock market collapses that would usher in the Great Depression. The *Jefferson County Union*, for which Lorine was still writing "Library Notes," ignored the disasters, only reporting a spate of area bank robberies and burglaries without analyzing the phenomena. No one knows when Lorine walked out on Frank, but not too long after Black Thursday, Frank was wiped out when he couldn't make payments on the house and some thirty thousand dollars owed in road equipment. Frank's father died in 1929; he necessarily moved back to the farm to help Rosina. Lorine alternated staying with the Hartels in town and her parents on the island.

For Frank the marriage was a financial, emotional, and sexual disaster. He retreated into himself, galled by the hopelessness of Rosina's repeated attempts to get the couple back together by inviting Lorine for dinner. If she came—she and Frank were friends enough that she did—Ernie drove her home. Frank never spoke against her to anyone, never explained the breakup, never remarried.

One can say that the marriage failed because of the Depression. Not that Lorine was one to quit in hard times, but the only alternative Frank offered her was life on the farm, unpalatable because she was a water, not a land, person. She might have been content working on her poetry while Frank ran his business: Frank's relatives vigorously deny that he would have interfered with his wife's writing. But life as a farm wife would have interfered. She'd seen Daisy worn down by endless housework: "Hatch, patch and scratch, / that's all a woman's for." She was not domestic; she wanted to write. Yet the reasons Lorine left him possibly go deeper.

There is Frank's physical similarity to Henry Niedecker, the father Lorine was extremely close to; perhaps this created an attraction to Lorine at first, then an unconscious source of guilt and shame. There is the line in "Stage Directions," a poem Lorine wrote in 1934: "Have you been married? Yes, I've been attacked"— and the panicky revulsion she expressed to at least two friends. There's the claim of Daniel Billet, whose father owned a resort on Blackhawk Island, that "Frank had drinking problems. Doesn't everybody in Wisconsin?" Years later Lorine told a friend that Frank "drank and was mean to her." Then there's the reason that Lorine gave later in life when a friend asked why she (again) was marrying an apparently unsuitable man: "He's the only man who ever told me he loved me." Frank never told her he loved her. Reason enough for Lorine to go her own way.

Lorine was blamed for walking out on Frank: "Not many people in Fort liked Lorine after she dumped her first husband." Rumors spread that she was "loose." Betrayed Frank got the sympathy.

With businesses laying off, Lorine hung on at the library, continuing to write her column, which made the front page of the *Jefferson County Union* eight times. On May 23, 1930, however, the newspaper introduced a lively new "Books on Parade" feature by Craig Rice, pseudonym of twenty-two-year-old Georgiana Ann Craig, who would become semifamous as a detective writer and locally infamous as an alcoholic who passed out on the best sofas in town.

More ominous, the *JCU* announced on August 8, 1930, the hiring of Harriet Chamberlin from Philadelphia's Drexel Institute as an assistant librarian. With the economy worsening day by day, Lorine's position was in jeopardy. The *JCU* was running Craig Rice's "Books on Parade" more frequently. On December 12, Lorine's last column appeared. Before Christmas the head librarian informed her she was fired.

At the same time, Henry Niedecker's seining business was in trouble. Originally imported from Germany as a sport fish, carp had multiplied out of control, stripping Lake Koshkonong of vegetation. Duck hunters, boaters, and recreational anglers hated carp fishermen. The State of Wisconsin investigated; by 1934 carp seining would be under its control. Henry was forced to advertise: "Lake Koshkonong. Famous Fishing Grounds. Well wooded. Quiet. Private. Paved Highway. Excellent Fishing. Lots, all-year homes for sale. Take 106 out of Fort Atkinson to fork. Take left fork bearing to river four miles. See name Henry Niedecker on mailbox." But he wouldn't make half the money catering to sportsmen as he had seining carp.

Lorine returned to Blackhawk Island, where folks were still coping with clean-up from the big flood of 1929. No poems survive from 1929, but her restless, half-articulated gift would not permit her to sit and float. The touted American poets— Edna St. Vincent Millay, Carl Sandburg, and Robert Frost—only confirmed her impatience with received form. Robinson Jeffers was too romantic, pessimistic; Wallace Stevens too elegantly abstract. Even Marianne Moore and the eccentric E. E. Cummings weren't daring enough for a poet to whom the unconscious had always been important.

At twenty-seven she was again dependent as a child on her father for support; not divorced, not married; the morose Daisy with her aching, cotton-stuffed ears her chief companion; the Depression deepening everywhere. Her desperation is reflected in the 1930 poem "When Ecstasy is Inconvenient":

> Feign a great calm;
> all gay transport soon ends.
> Chant: who knows—
> flight's end or flight's beginning
> for the resting gull?
>
> Heart, be still.
> Say there is money but it rusted;
> say the time of moon is not right for escape.
> It's the color in the lower sky
> too broadly suffused,
> or the wind in my tie.

Know amazedly how
often one takes his madness
into his own hands
and keeps it.

5

Finding

1931~1933

I went to school to Objectivism.
Niedecker to Clayton Eshleman

In February 1931 Lorine checked out the Fort Atkinson library's current issue of *Poetry Magazine*. It turned out to be guest-edited by a twenty-seven-year-old New York poet, Louis Zukofsky. Zukofsky had selected the poets and provided a discussion of what he called Objectivism: the poet's "[d]esire for what is objectively perfect, inextricably the direction of historic and contemporary particulars." What is objectively perfect can be a thing or an event: an Egyptian fish-shaped bottle or a performance of Bach's *Saint Matthew's Passion*. The Objectivist poet must bring the thing or event into resonant focus.

Zukofsky chose for the issue works by Carl Rakosi, Robert McAlmon, Charles Reznikoff, Norman Macleod, George Oppen, Kenneth Rexroth, Basil Bunting, Whittaker Chambers, and Arthur Rimbaud, among others. Perhaps the poem that most simply illustrates the goals of Objectivism is the minor poet S. Theodore Hecht's "Table for Christmas":

> The little Christmas tree
> Which she moved,
> The white bread which she set
> Down: so there were
> The Christmas tree,
> The white bread,
> And in each corner of the table,

Four in all,
Little wine bottles,
Pink ribbons tied about their necks.

Hecht's aim is to describe ordinary objects like a Christmas tree and white bread through vital particulars that evoke a particular scene and moment. He eschews conventional devices of rhyme, strong rhythms, alliteration, metaphor, personification, and symbolism for the observed truth of the woman's actions. It is a poem born, like Objectivism, from the Depression: spare, terse, muted. Yet it conveys emotion. As Zukofsky said, "The emotional quality of good poetry is founded on exact observation."

Still, a problem. Besides the impossibility of herding highly individual poets into an Objectivist pen, Zukofsky admits that only Ezra Pound's poems are consistently objective. This leads him to distinguish between Objectification and "Sincerity," which he defines as a preoccupation with accuracy of detail, exemplified (often) by Reznikoff, though Reznikoff can be Objective as well. The way grows darker because, apart from citing examples, it's impossible to discuss the perfect object in abstract terms. Criticizing "the woolliness of what Zukofsky threw together as the group's manifesto," Carl Rakosi offered his own streaming definition: "[Objectivist] conveyed a meaning which was, in fact, my objective: to present objects in their most essential reality and to make each poem an object, meaning by this the opposite of vagueness, loose bowels and streaming, sometimes screaming consciousness."

Actually, the *Poetry* magazine issue of February 1931 was not Zukofsky's idea. "Ezra Pound had been hammering away at Harriet Monroe in letter after letter that the once-great *Poetry* was dying on its feet," said Rakosi, "and had cajoled and wheedled and shamed her into accepting Zukofsky as the bright new talent who could put life into the old rag."

But Zukofsky never intended to define Objectivism, believing it impossible. He chose the term under pressure as a flag for second-wave Modernist poets. Rakosi commented, "Zukofsky foiled Harriet Monroe, was thumbing his nose at her." Chosen to launch a new movement, he "just wanted to get by." Not quite: Zukofsky saw Monroe's offer as an opportunity to spotlight both himself and poets he admired. But he was really no more interested in categorization than the evasive T. S. Eliot:

[O]bjectivism—I never used the word; I used the word "objectivist," and the only reason for using it was Harriet Monroe's insistence when I edited the "objectivist" number of *Poetry* . . . Well she told me, "You must have a movement." I said, "No, some of us are writing to say things simply so that they will affect us as new again."

"Well give it a name."

"All right, let's call it 'Objectivists.'" . . . I wouldn't do it today.

Ignorant of the politics behind Zukofsky's *Poetry*, Lorine immediately felt the importance of the Objectivist creed. Briefly: (1) "clarity of image and word-tone"; (2) "thinking with things as they exist, and directing them along a line of melody"; (3) "economy of presentation"; and (4) the poetic rendering of current speech. Here, she felt, "*was the center of literature in this country and in the world.*"

Lorine had undergone an epiphany crucial to her art. Reading Wordsworth her eighteenth summer, she'd realized how great he was, yet how dated. Objectivism offered fresh criteria that fit Lorine's intellectuality: clarity, economy, rendering of current speech, thinking with things as they exist.

Still charged six months later, she conquered her shyness and wrote Zukofsky in care of *Poetry*. Her letter came at the right time: Zukofsky was bitter about the limited reaction to "the 'Objectivist's' number" (which was to become the most famous *Poetry* issue ever published).

While working on the Objectivist issue, he'd had an appointment at the University of Wisconsin, which he dismissed as a cultural wasteland except for one promising student, Martha Champion. Here was a letter not from Madison but from the deeper abyss of a place called Fort Atkinson. Yet Lorine was an engaging, quirky letter writer, passionately interested in his ideas. (Zukofsky would tell her that her letters were her best writing.) Despite close relationships with Ezra Pound, the British poet Basil Bunting, and William Carlos Williams, Zukofsky was pursuing a lonely course in poetry and was judged "beyond the reach of most critics and readers." He answered Lorine's letter. She wrote back. He liked her poetry.

"Dear Miss Monroe," she wrote November 5, 1931, "Mr. Zukofsky encourages me to send some of my poems to you." Harriet Monroe, founder of *Poetry* in 1912, accepted one. Lorine replied:

> I am very much in need of money but I understand that "Poetry Magazine" has also that need. I suggest you keep whatever will be coming to me for my poem "When Ecstasy is Inconvenient" merely sending me 2 copies of the issue in which the poem will appear.
>
> Very truly yours,
> Lorine Niedecker
> (Mrs. Frank Hartwig)

Objectivism had immediately appealed to Lorine, yet Surrealism was in the air. André Breton's *Le Manifeste du Surréalism*, first issued in France in 1924, claimed that "We are still living under the reign of logic . . . But in this day and age logical methods are applicable only to solving problems of secondary interest." Lorine read *transitions* magazine, sent to her by Zukofsky, in which she discovered Gertrude Stein and James Joyce's *Finnegans Wake* in progress. Though drawn to both Objectivism and Surrealism at this point, perhaps because so many aspects of her life seemed surreal, she felt a strong urge to explore levels of consciousness. In January 1933 she sent *Poetry* three poems "tending toward illogical expression." She explained the 189-line "Progression" thus:

> 1st section—simple knowing and concern for externals; 2nd section—the turn to one world farther in; 3rd section—the will to disorder, approach to dream . . the individual talking to himself, the supreme circumstance.
>
> I had sketched my theory thus: Poetry to have greatest reason for existing must be illogical. An idea, a rumination such as more or less constantly roams the mind, meets external object or situation with quite illogical association. Memory, if made up of objects at all, retains those objects which were at the time of first perception and still are the most strikingly unrecognizable. In my own experience sentences have appeared full-blown in the first moments of waking from sleep. It is a system of thought replacements, the most remote the most significant or irrational; a thousand variations of the basic tension; an attempt at not hard clear images but absorption of these. Intelligibility or readers' recognition of sincerity and force lies in a sense of basic color, sound, rhythm.

Lorine's theory pushes beyond both Imagism and Objectivism. It is the mind's illogical association with image or object that gives it significance. Lines like "At the Capitol, cheese legislation only sets silk hats / tipping, rats divine, toward feline waistbands" contain plain concrete words—cheese, silk hats, rats, waistbands. Confused by syntax, however, a reader is uncertain about their association in the poet's mind and must rely on the poem's color, sound, and rhythm for its logic.

Monroe rejected "Progression," accepted "Promise of a Brilliant Funeral," and would publish it with "When Ecstasy is Inconvenient" in September 1933.

Meanwhile Lorine and Louis were corresponding at least once a week. Zukofsky was writing for the Communist publication *New Masses* (though he never officially joined the party), stimulating Lorine's own radical, populist, and Objectivist bent.

But while at this point Lorine believed expression of the subconscious was as important as Objectivism to poetry, Zukofsky, like William Carlos Williams, considered it a dead end. Still, he encouraged Lorine's experiments, and she awaited installments of his experimental "Thanks to the Dictionary," convinced she was in touch with genius.

None of Lorine's letters to Zukofsky from this early period survive; the few of his that do are affectionate, intimate. She would call him Zu, Zukie, Zum Zum, or ZuZu, the latter, when she pronounced it, an erotic buzz on her tongue. She used the word *suzz* often and only with him; it meant, variously, *hmmn*, *sigh*, *gosh*, *sheesh*, *wouldn't you know*. *Suzz* was almost Zu backwards. (Or Zeus, as those who believe Niedecker considered Zukofsky a god might argue.) A variant of *suzz* was *suzzle*, close to *nuzzle*. He initiated the empty brackets [ ] they both began to use to express affection.

After two years of letters, they made plans for Lorine to come to New York.

6

Zukofsky

1933~1934

Jesus, I'm going out and throw my arms around.
"NEXT YEAR OR I FLY MY ROUNDS,
TEMPESTUOUS"

Having saved little from her library assistant pay, Lorine had to ask Henry for bus fare east. As word spread of her plan, relatives and friends objected, noting that Lorine's going to New York was "a very *unusual* thing to do." It is evidence of Henry's love for his daughter that he gave her the money with few questions asked and some nostalgia: Peck's Slip in lower Manhattan had been the destination of his prosperous carp hauls.

Knowing Daisy's zeal, she would have packed Lorine's Beloit suitcase with freshly ironed clothes, disapproval evident in her tall back, and said good-bye with admonishments to keep herself neat and clean and not speak to strangers. Lorine carried a batch of recent poems to show Zukofsky. Her determination to fulfill her literary and emotional ties with him was astonishing.

In late fall 1933 she took a bus from Fort Atkinson to Chicago, an adventure in itself, but nothing like the experience that lay ahead. The Greyhound rolled east across Indiana, Ohio, and Pennsylvania, a lurching ride with endless stops. Pinched for money, she got off only to use the restroom and buy a five-cent hot dog or apple. Finally, after crossing New Jersey, she glimpsed the New York skyline before the bus plunged into the Holland Tunnel, emerging at Canal Street, then making its way uptown. Clutching her suitcase, Lorine stepped out into the Forty-Second Street bus terminal. Louis probably met her; neither could afford a taxi.

Louis had not expected someone quite so petite (Lorine stood at most five feet two inches), so fine-boned and blonde, so neat and modest. Her full, sensuous mouth denied a voice light as a girl's. She spoke with an accent he'd heard without love his year at Madison: *aunt* pronounced *ant*, *tomahto* as *tomayto*, a hard *r* in words like *near* and *Harvard*. Midwestern talk, unsophisticated talk. Her deep blue eyes disconcerted him as she peered up to bring him into focus through pebble lenses.

Lorine had not expected Louis. A Lithuanian Jew from an Orthodox Lower East Side immigrant family that spoke only Yiddish, Louis at twenty-nine was tall with an equine face, Groucho Marx eyebrows bristling above dark eyes, a skull thatched with black hair. His emaciated grace reminded people of Fred Astaire, his imitation of the Chinese actor Mei Lan-Fang's female impersonations sent friends into hysterics. He enchanted people with his "voluble, mercurial, ceaselessly inventive talk." He was a hypochondriac who chain-smoked, kept all windows closed, and considered a short walk exercise. He'd been something of a child prodigy, hearing only Yiddish until he entered grade school and writing his first poetry in English at twelve. His favorite writers were Lucretius, Aristotle, Plato, Aquinas, Spinoza, Wittgenstein, and Charles Sanders Pierce. He wished to be reincarnated as a student of Bach. He didn't know what color his mother's hair was because she always wore the Jewish Orthodox wig. On a recent visit to Italy, he and the "sexually predatory" Ezra Pound had gone to bed together.

Zukofsky's young literary protégé and sexual partner Jerry Reisman was present at their meeting. "[S]he and Louis exchanged shy greetings and Louis introduced her to me," said Reisman, who claimed he'd read all of Lorine's letters to Louis and his to her.

In Greenwich Village, Zukofsky's apartment at 41 West Eleventh Street proved to be one room between street and basement, two windows at sidewalk level. There was a bathroom, clothes closet, table, phonograph and stack of records, a desk under one window, and a double bed.

"Later," explained Reisman, "when [Lorine] began to unpack her things and Louis saw what she had brought—an ironing board and an iron, for example—he concluded that she was prepared to stay a long time. He looked a bit worried. He had not planned to have a long-term live-in relationship with Lorine." Evidently, Lorine had. After all, he'd invited her to come a thousand miles to New York to stay in a one-room Village apartment.

Though a man of "relentless intellectual abstraction," Zukofsky was also a virile man who conducted sexual affairs. "I don't think Louis loved anybody," Reisman said. "He liked sex. Women thought he was sexy. He was very charming when he wanted to be." Louis's friend William Carlos Williams knew about the sex. "Hope you don't catchum syphilis after all," he'd written him the previous year, *not* in regard to Lorine. "It takes six weeks you know to develop, not 30 days. The treatment is very effective—and painful and disgusting." Reisman says Louie and Lorine became lovers immediately. Again Louie consulted Williams, who was also a doctor; Reisman is sure Lorine met Williams at that time. Williams "cavalierly" prescribed a gel, but "a gel is only a spermicide, why didn't he tell her to use a diaphragm?" wondered Reisman.

Though he hated leaving his apartment, on this first visit Louis may have taken Lorine to matinees (he adored Chaplin, and Sergei Eisenstein's films), art museums, and the apartments of friends. He introduced her to bargain drugstores and five-cent White Castle hamburgers. The thronging streets and honking horns, the towering new Empire State and Chrysler Buildings—the contrast between elegant storefronts and closed banks, women in furs and men like her father wiping windshields for a tip—shook her. New York streets, she said, "frightened me as much as not having money."

Louis had no money, working as a soda jerk and at the post office because, though qualified, he'd rather put a bullet to his head than teach again in a public high school. They spent much of their time in Louis's apartment writing, Zukofsky working at his desk on "Thanks to the Dictionary," short prose pieces chosen by tossing dice to open to an inspirational dictionary page. His offbeat experiment matched Lorine's bent. She avidly and critically read the pages he handed her.

She met the violinist and composer Tibor Serly and the designer Russell Wright and his wife, Mary. She also met Charles Reznikoff, chief example of "sincerity" in Zukofsky's Objectivist essay in *Poetry*. In 1934 the Objectivist Press would publish three works by Reznikoff, including the first installment of his major poem *Testimony*. "Rezy, yes," Lorine remembered, was the "gentlest soul possible, afraid he might intrude, afraid to leave his umbrella out in the public hallway and afraid to bring it dripping into the room. . . . What lovely poetry."

On weekends Zuk and Lorine were joined by Jerry, living in the South Bronx with his parents, majoring in physics at the City College of New York, and working on a scenario of Joyce's *Ulysses* he hoped to sell to Hollywood. Louis had been Jerry's English teacher at prestigious Stuyvesant High School, where Jerry cut classes regularly. Zukofsky had sensed talent and steered him into physics, but also inspired Jerry to write:

> A weekend visitor would have been likely to find me doing my
> homework on a folding card table in the center of the room, Louis

working at his desk in a corner near one of the windows, and Lorine working at the table under the light from a table lamp. Sometimes we'd work for hours in deep silence. Once, Lorine's pen was scratchy and Louis suddenly screamed at her to stop the noise. Lorine was frightened and hurt by his outburst. . . .

Lorine was shy and unworldly, but she was lively and talkative when with people she liked. Her sense of humor sparkled in conversation as it does in her poetry and sometimes she was surprisingly uninhibited. She almost worshipped Louis, who was a phenomenal teacher, by far the best I ever knew, and Lorine was eager to learn. They both recognized each other's literary worth and uniqueness very early in their careers.

Lorine, added Jerry, was "honest, affectionate, the most naive person I've ever met. If I had to find one word to describe her character it would be 'pure.' That sounds corny. I mean she came to people without ulterior motives."

Lorine stayed on with Zukofsky in his one-room Village apartment, Christmas approaching. Both dismissed the holidays as "Hollowdays." Louis had repudiated his father's Orthodox Judaism at an early age, and Lorine did not believe. Still, he asked: "Will you write me a Christmas poem?"

"Will I!" Lorine exploded seventeen stanzas deploring America's "Gay Gaunt Day," addressing Zukofsky's alienation as a Jew:

> You are wrong to-day
> you are wrong to-day,
> my dear. My dear—

Her final lament: "Christ what a destiny / What a destiny's Christ's, Christ!" Zukofsky called the poem "Written at Lorine's umbilical."

But Louie became restive with Lorine's presence, so sometime early in 1934 she packed her ironing board and returned to Blackhawk Island. Letters again flew back and forth. They still used [ ] to convey a love never spoken on his part.

Lorine had boldly gone to the man she'd fallen in love with through his words. Now, undeterred by Zukofsky's distrust of surrealism (though he considered dreams important), Lorine continued to explore the irrational, automatic writing, and the absurd—thumbing a nose at conventional language and thought. Much as she realized that Objectivist principles had the potential to discipline her work, she wanted something more: she was not merely Zukofsky's pupil. In February 1934 she sent *Poetry* three sense-defying poems set side by side on the page:

Canvass	For exhibition	Tea
Unrefractory petalbent	for round	dilemma
prognosticate	of or	my suit, continuous
halfvent purloined	in the young beautiful of life	dear hind button off . . .

Lorine explained:

> An experiment in three planes: left row is deep subconscious, middle row beginning of monologue, and right row surface consciousness, social-banal; experiment in vertical simultaneity (symphonic rather than traditional long line melodic form), and the whole written with the idea of readers finding sequence for themselves, finding their own meaning whatever that may be, as spectators before abstract painting. Left vertical row honest recording of constrictions appearing before falling off to sleep at night. I should like a poem to be seen as well as read. Colors and textures of certain words appearing simultaneously with the sound of words and printed directly above or below each other. . . . It means that for me at least, certain words of a sentence,—prepositions, connectives, pronouns—belong up toward full consciousness, while strange and unused words appear only in subconscious.

"Utter mystification," replied Monroe. Lorine did not give up: "Would the enclosed 'Eleven Month Stare' and 'Almanac Maker' be 'utter mystification?' . . . If it would not be hurrying you too much I should appreciate hearing by April 21st so I may know whether to take them with me to New York."

Without Monroe's verdict, Lorine returned to New York that April 1934, again staying in Louie's West Eleventh Street apartment, where Jerry Reisman was still working weekends on his screenplay of *Ulysses* and Louis deep in his planned magnum opus "A." Though she'd started four days earlier than planned, she missed an anticipated event: Gertrude Stein and Virgil Thomson's form-bending opera *Four Saints in Three Acts* with an all-black cast. She did inspect an exhibit of Salvador Dali's surrealist paintings at the Museum of Modern Art, comparing his work on canvas to hers on the page. At the New York Public Library she read D. H. Lawrence's *Fantasia of the Unconscious* because the subject interested her, though she probably took Lawrence's "blood-consciousness" and "lower centers" skeptically, as she must have queried his "Most dreams are purely insignificant."

This time, she met the Objectivist poet George Oppen and his wife, Mary. (Lorine was never impressed by Oppen's poetry, saying that "there are times I've felt he's down in the grass as an insect (singing from his knees), all angular, a kind of constipated grasshopper.") On his part, Oppen would credit her with "an acerbic bravery," though he considered some poems "barely audible." Four years younger than Zukofsky, the Oppens had migrated from the West and were living in Brooklyn Heights. In France they had established, with Zukofsky, the press To (The objectivists), and published An "Objectivists" Anthology. They were intimate with Zukofsky and Reisman.

"They were wonderful company," said Mary Oppen, "very funny and bright together, flying kites, riding on the merry-go-round. Louis elegant, funny, a splendid actor, mimic, Louis and George working together on George's poetry. Louis, George and I would sleep together, I making sure I was in the middle. We laughed together all the time."

They invited Lorine to dinner without Zukofsky, "and after waiting for her until long after dinner-time, we ate and were ready for bed" when they heard a timid knock at the door. Lorine.

"What happened to you?"

"I got on the subway, and I didn't know where to get off, so I rode to the end of the line and back."

"Why didn't you ask someone?"

"I didn't see anyone to ask."

"New York was overwhelming," says Mary, "and she was alone, a tiny, timid small-town girl. She escaped the city and returned to Wisconsin. Years later we began to see her poems, poems which described her life; she chose a way of hard physical work, and her poetry emerged from a tiny life. From Wisconsin came perfect small gems of poetry written out of her survival, from the crevices of her life, that seeped out into poems."

Mary Oppen is patronizing. Keen for adventure, she and George had sailed their own catamaran through the Great Lakes down the Hudson to New York, and had just returned from a year in the south of France. They had money and interesting friends, were urban and a couple. To Mary, Lorine could only be a tiny girl with a tiny life—though Lorine was a gritty thirty-one and would not *choose* a life of hard physical work.

By May 4 Lorine had returned to Blackhawk Island to find Monroe's rejection of "Eleven Month Stare" and "Almanac Maker" with the comment, "Too witty or not witty enough."

Lorine replied, "[M]y head might pour out at the eyes except for having been told some nice things by a nice person (Louis Zukofsky) in New York. I should like to tell you, but I realize it would come better from him than from me. And I feel I shall be meeting you and talking with you within the coming year, perhaps this fall. I ought to warn you, however, that I'll have to appear with lines like these, the most spontaneously automatic I've been able to achieve."

On May 31 she sent "Three Poems," another "experiment in planes of consciousness [that] will probably disturb you even more than it does me." The following week she left again for New York, stopping this time in Chicago to pay Monroe a visit. Monroe was still mystified. Lorine argued that her poems were abstract paintings: readers could take what they wanted from them. But Monroe had come away empty-handed, unlike William Carlos Williams, who exclaimed when Zukofsky read him "Synamism": "This is new, would publish it first thing if we had a press."

Eventually Zukofsky sent all six of Lorine's experiments to Ezra Pound, who accepted them for his issue of *Bozart-Westminster* in 1935.

"Glad you agreed with me as to the value of Lorine Niedecker's work," wrote Zukofsky, "and are printing it in Westminster."

Pound replied testily: "Surrealism (meaning the yesteryear variety) is a painter's show / what fahrtin literature has it got? . . . I don't think yr / Niedecker is so hot. . . . It got by because I printed one tadpole on each recommendation of qualified critics."

"There's no use wasting yr time calling me down about surrealisme," Zukofsky shot back. "Nor have I swallowed Miss Niedecker's mental stubbornness. However, her output has *some* validity, *some* spark of energy, which the solipsistic daze-maze of Mr. Kummings hath not."

Pound also accepted Lorine's "Stage Directions" and a brief play, *Domestic and Unavoidable* (which Jerry Reisman turned into a screenplay). Some lines between the Young Man and the Young Girl resonate with the current poetic differences between Lorine and Zukofsky, as well as with her sense of a deeper divide:

> YOUNG MAN—She's unconscious. It must be her strong will
> that does it.
> YOUNG GIRL—And corners are precarious beasts. They put a
> wall of weeping between us, suffering, the technologic
> absolute.
> YOUNG MAN—(*Shifting in his chair*) My dear, I have other
> affiliations. It's been penciled and ruled. My life is elsewhere.
> (*Confused murmur begins off stage.*)
> YOUNG GIRL illumined —Oh, I shouldn't want you to be
> faithful to me alone.

Lorine had also begun to write overtly propagandistic poems, on terms she explained to Monroe:

> I am enclosing "Communism or Capitalism" for consideration. . . . The effect of propaganda in poetic (?) form has the effect on me of swearing that I as a writer will portray my epoch and truthfully evoke life in its totalities only as I am able to make magic, magic of dream and deep subconscious and waking isolation thick unto impenetrability. One's fear is people—going social—but now I have another fear: it has been hard to sell magic—will the time come when it can't be *given* away?

Convinced that propaganda could never be poetry unless it tapped the subconscious, she still had been "going social[ist]": mixing with leftists, typing Zukofsky's highly political "A"-8, reading issues of the *New Masses* and the *Daily Worker* he sent her, meeting Zukofsky's radical friends.

The Kunzes and Niedeckers were liberals, but in New York she had met leftists united by their hatred of the unchecked capitalism that had created the Great Depression. Equally disturbing to leftists was the rising power of Fascism in Europe. George and Mary Oppen briefly saw affiliation with the Communist Party as the only way to fight Hitler's anti-Semitism, forced into law in 1933. Topics at Bickford's Restaurant were the looming Loyalist conflict with Spanish Fascists, the questionable liberalization of America under Roosevelt's New Deal, socialism, and the movies of Charlie Chaplin. Lorine didn't need a big shove toward the Left; dissent was intrinsic to her nature. More persuasive than her *Handbook of Marxism*, she had witnessed the Depression in New York: bread lines, shuttered doors, families tossed out with their furniture onto New York streets.

But Lorine's experiment with propaganda was short-lived; she later looked back on "Proletarian (God forbid) poetry" with a shudder. Though he edited a *Workers' Anthology*, Louis advised her not to submit "God Slain by Troops" and "No retiring" to *Poetry* because doctrine would put off Harriet Monroe, but Lorine herself did not think doctrine could pass for poetry unless transformed by the alchemy of "magic." She was searching for a poetic form that would express not only dissent but her sense of the wonder of everyday experience.

Mary Hoard, a library board member, had lent Lorine Amédée Ozenfant's *Foundations of Modern Art*. Thanking her, Lorine explored her reaction. She dismisses the author's allegiance to universal laws, yet his book opens up "ideas I should have known long ago. Objects, objects. Why are people, artists above all, so terrifically afraid of *themselves*? Thank god for the Surrealist tendency running side by side with Objectivism and toward the monologue tongue. It is my conviction that no one yet, has talked to himself. And until then, what is art?"

She confides to Hoard that sometimes she writes in trance: "It is my belief objects are needed only to supplement our nervous systems. . . . [T]he most important part of memory is its non-expressive, unconscious part. . . . We remember, in other words, a nerve-sense, a vibration, a colour, a rhythm. . . . I conceive poetry as the folktales of the mind and us creating our own remembering . . . and to me, that means, inchoate thought, the Self association of nervous vocables coloured by the rhythm of the moment. . . . [T]his would be of course what no one else has written—else why write?"

However inchoate her intuition, she was fighting Objectivism even while calling it "the center of literature in this century and in the world." When she argued the Unconscious with Zukofsky, he would reply, "Is it logic?" Which, said Lorine, "he *would* say."

All her life, Lorine would be torn between feeling and logic. Intuitively, she bent toward flow and free association, yet her rational mind fought instinct. In turning toward Objectivism, Niedecker admits that her inner impulses could terrify her. Her conflict would produce some of the most reined-in yet emotionally loaded poetry of the twentieth century.

7

Loss

1934~1936

this going without tea holds a hope of tasting it.
"Promise of Brilliant Funeral"

Lorine was in love with Zukofsky against her better judgment. Late in 1934, she bought a calendar with sunny platitudes for each month of the year. Over these she pasted her own terse lines: "Her understanding of him is more touching than intelligent; he holds her knees without her knowing how she's boned" . . . "Don't send steadily; after you know me I'll be no one" . . . "I like a loved one to be apt in the wing" . . . "All night, all night, and what is it on a postcard." She laced the calendar pages together with orange ribbon and sent "NEXT YEAR OR I FLY MY ROUNDS, TEMPESTUOUS" to Zukofsky for Christmas. Her January entry—"Wade all life backward to its source which runs too far ahead"—is profound.

She returned to New York in 1935. This time she met Jerry Reisman's first cousin Edouard Dechar and his wife, Diane, who had married that year and "lived in a garret on West Eighth, not far from Louis."

"I met Lorine several times while she was staying with Louis Zukofsky," says Diane Dechar. "She was lovely and somewhat withdrawn with visitors, it seemed to me. I did like her very much."

Diane remembers hours of elbow-to-elbow talk over coffee in the submarine glow at Bickford's, debating the New Deal, communism, writers, musicians, and the benighted indifference of the establishment to the Objectivist Movement. (In the 1950s and 1960s Jack Kerouac, Allen Ginsberg, Andy Warhol, Woody Allen, and William Styron would make Bickford's their unofficial headquarters.) Though Lorine may have been quieter than the rest, she was passionate and informed.

Near the end of this prolonged visit, Lorine discovered that she was pregnant. She was dismayed and elated. Louis was appalled. William Carlos Williams protested that his instructions had not been followed thoroughly.

"I want to keep the child," Lorine pleaded. "I'll have it in Wisconsin, raise it on Blackhawk Island, and never bother you for support money or anything else."

But Louis was adamant: Lorine would not bear his child. An abortionist must be found, and money raised immediately to pay for the operation. Lorine was forced to ask her father for cash to terminate the child she wished to keep.

"Now, as for the person who did help Lorine when she needed a woman's support and warm friendship," says Diane Dechar, "this was Pauline Glenn, sister of Jerry Reisman. She did have the knowledge and time for Lorine and was a source of comfort and assistance. . . . Lorine was in good hands with Pauline."

Jerry Reisman remarked: "One of my cousins recommended a fine female [Russian émigré] doctor. Her fee was $150—a lot of money in those days. Lorine obtained the money from her father."

Abortion "was the most common form of birth control then," said Mary Oppen. "Women were pretty matter-of-fact about abortions; it was accepted, but hidden." The fastidious Zukofsky, who, Carl Rakosi claimed, was "inhibited, terribly inhibited" and "very very fearful of women," distanced himself from the whole business; Pauline and Jerry were Lorine's companions in the difficult weeks following. According to Reisman, Lorine was not matter-of-fact about the abortion: "After the operation the doctor revealed that her patient had been carrying twins. Lorine ruefully named them 'Lost' and 'Found.' Physically, she recovered quickly; but I think she must have ached for her twins all the years of her life."

Jerry claimed that after the abortion, "Lorine and I had become such close friends by now that Louis urged us to become intimate. We needed no further encouragement." It seems unlikely that Lorine would have wanted sex after her traumatic experience; there is no confirmation of Reisman's statement. And though she may have "ached for her twins all the years of her life," raising them as a single parent would have severely challenged the poetic career she was bent upon.

Other new-made friends urged her to stay in New York and find a job, but "In NY it seemed too absolutely difficult to even *try* for a job." Emotionally, too, she needed to get back to Wisconsin.

"We all felt sad when Lorine went back home," says Diane. But Zukofsky was impatient for her to leave.

Back in Wisconsin, Lorine continued to type Zukofsky's major poem "A" ("Three carbons, please") and send him her poetry. Little survives that reflects the trauma she suffered in New York, except perhaps these lines from the political poem "News":

> To wit, the lover said.
>
> As a young woman
> I saw that
>
> done
>
> no child
> no enlightenment.

"The lover" is Niedecker, confirmed when she tells Zu she may omit the phrase since "I'm no longer in depression [ ]." Twenty-nine years later, in 1964, Lorine wrote the poem "Who was Mary Shelley?" a meditation on the poet's wife working on her masterpiece *Frankenstein* while the important poets Shelley and Byron talk the night away downstairs. The concluding stanzas might be called "Who was Lorine Niedecker?"—

> Who was Mary Shelley?
> She read Greek, Italian
> She bore a child
>
> Who died
> and yet another child
> Who died.

—but at this Objectivist point, Lorine scorned confessional poetry. The personal was there, masked.

As for Louis, his militant need for privacy prevented his committing emotion to paper. He did write, "I remember last year, but *ver novum*," and tried to comfort her by telling her she was better off away from him: "[Y]ou know how difficult I can be at times, so something makes up for that gap of distance. I'm really nicer in that gap, more understanding by [ ]."

Still, Zukofsky missed Lorine. In September 1936 he and Jerry took the train to Chicago, then bused to Fort Atkinson. For their visit Lorine moved out of her parents' house into one of Henry's cabins, where Louis and Jerry also stayed. Louis was tense, unsure how much Lorine's parents knew about their relationship, but Henry gently and kindly put him at ease. Jerry thought her father "[w]arm and friendly, he liked to talk about national and world politics and he let me have two of his guns for target practice."

Daisy was another matter: so upset about Lorine "living in sin" with Louis that she was rigid in his presence. "Lorine avoided her mother as much as possible," said Reisman, "because of the tension between them which apparently had existed for years." Louis avoided her more assiduously. "Mercifully," said Reisman, "I don't think she ever suspected that Lorine was having a relationship with both of her visitors."

Fascinated, Jerry watched the Niedecker soap opera. The bitter, hostile, deaf mother. Gertrude Runke next door. Lorine seething as her father signed away assets to Gert. Henry purposefully introducing Jerry to Lorrine Runke, "a very attractive girl" whom, Jerry suspected, might be sleeping with Henry. (In 1944 Lorrine would write Reisman asking to be his live-in housekeeper. He refused. Two years later, at twenty-six, she was dead.)

"In New York I was impressed with Lorine's courageous wish to return home from her visit, willing to confront her stern mother and a very conservative community with the fact that she was pregnant and unmarried," said Reisman. "Now I felt that if she had done so, it would have been just another development in an ongoing drama."

As a diversion for Jerry, Louie encouraged his former Madison student Frank Heineman to visit the island. Frank was Jerry's age and, like him, a physics major. The four of them tore about in Frank's rented Ford, explored Indian mounds, and rowed on Lake Koshkonong. And while Jerry and Frank shot at targets or slid down haystacks in a barn, Lorine and Louie talked poetry and made love.

Back in New York, Louis complained to Bill Williams about "domestic difficulties." Williams replied, "I wish to God you could break loose and—what, I don't know."

Which domestic difficulties is unclear since Zukofsky was involved with another woman. In January 1934, when he was hosting Lorine for the first time, Louis had met Celia Thaew (pronounced Tave) while working on several Civil Works Administration projects at the Teacher's College of Columbia University.

Celia was dark haired, handsome, nine years younger than Zukofsky, and Jewish. Passing her desk, he'd spotted a copy of Bill Williams's *In the American Grain*. He asked to borrow it, then returned it the next day with anonymous pages of his poem "A." She handed them back, approving their musical structure. They struck up a friendship.

She was a musician, a pianist. She invited him to concerts when she had tickets; occasionally he sent her his work. They saw each other infrequently, then more often: their intellectual friendship deepened gradually over the years into love. By 1937, according to Celia, they were going steady.

Louis introduced Celia to his circle. "She was not as popular as Lorine," says Diane Dechar. "Louis and Celia were not very nice together." Celia says she decided quite early she would not interfere with Louis's literary friends: "I'd rather mind my own business." She also dismissed as irrelevant the "hundreds" of women who visited Louis from Wisconsin—hundreds meaning Lorine and perhaps Martha Champion. "There were other women," she knew.

It would be years before Lorine knew that Zukofsky the lover was lost to her.

8

Folk Magic

1936–1938

I must possess myself, get back into pure duration
"Progression"

In 1935 and 1936, before Celia Thaew grew serious about Zukofsky and he was still addressing Lorine in letters as "My Lady Fair," Lorine was abandoning her surrealist explorations in poetry. Still, when Zukofsky recommended she be included in a new anthology, *Poetry Out of Wisconsin*, she sent the editors "Stage Directions," "Domestic and Unavoidable," "The President of the Holding Company," and "Fancy Another Day Gone." Though Frederick Larsson accepted "Stage Directions," his coeditor August Derleth vetoed: "No, STAGE DIRECTIONS by Niedecker won't do: I am not and have never been taken in for one second by Dadaism, Surrealism, or any other cracked and half-baked ism foisted on the world by unbalanced and adolescent creative minds." (Years later Lorine dismissed Derleth too severely as "prolific" and "tripe.")

Lorine had also sent "When Ecstasy is Inconvenient," but "I'd rather not have [this poem] from POETRY included—written back in 1930." Yet in the 1937 anthology Lorine was represented solely by "Ecstasy." Zukofsky, whom Derleth balked at including at all as a Wisconsin poet, merited five poems, "though," said Derleth, "I must confess that I have seen mighty little of Z's work that is not gibberish." Yet Zukofsky's "gibberish" was printable, Niedecker's not. To underscore the imbalance, Zukofsky received a complimentary copy of *Poets Out of Wisconsin*, but had to request one for Lorine.

In December 1935 Lorine sent thirteen poems to Zukofsky in a new folk style inspired by reading the Objectivist issue of *Poetry*. He read them to William Carlos Williams and Robert Allison Evans, a radical poet published in *New Masses*. Williams praised her forms; Evans kept exclaiming, "Now what do you think of that! That's good! You say she's a woman, I never saw a woman with a mind like that."

She had chosen to modernize *Mother Goose*—why? Chiefly because Grand-father Gottfried's and Daisy's folk-talk rang in her ears, demanding release. As she must celebrate water, she must celebrate her verbal heritage. But *Mother Goose* rhymes were also Objectivist as well as politically subversive—simplicity under-mining established authority. She saw the form as a weapon against privilege, property, and politics:

> Apples are high—
> that shows they're scarce,
> still the stores always seem to have plenty.
> Can't get a price
> the farmers say—
> I guess it's because there're too many.

Encouraged by Zukofsky, Lorine announced her new project to Harriet Monroe: "Looking around in America, working I hope with a more direct consciousness than in the past, the enclosed Mother Goose." As she'd told Mary Hoard, "I conceive poetry as the folk tales of the mind." Her thirteen *Mother Geese* are political, subversive, playful, and deadly, "Niedecker's knife buried to the hilt before you know it's drawn."

> O let's glee glow as we go
> there must be things in the world—
> Jesus pay for the working soul,
> fearful lives by what right hopeful
> and the apse in the tiger's horn,
> costume for skiing I have heard
> and rings for church people
> and glee glow glum
> it must be fun
> to have boots for snow.

Niedecker contrasts the Haves with their skiing outfits and rings against the Have-Nots, the fearful and hopeless whom Jesus, not the State, must save; though when the poor enter the church apse in search of Him, the horned tiger of capitalism gores them. The "poemness of the poem," to quote poet-critic I. A. Richards, confirms Niedecker's sympathies: three lines for the rich, seven for the poor, the mournful vowels of the last three lines shaming the high glee of the first.

Equally playful and sinister is Niedecker's miniature Boschean hellscape of madness, need, and greed:

> She had tumult of the brain
> and I had rats in the rain
> and she and I and the furlined man
> were out for gain.

What turned Niedecker away from surrealism and automatic writing to "a more direct consciousness"? Chiefly fear of her own subconscious: she embraced Objectivism as a floating plank rescuing her from drowning in surrealistic dreams. And she wanted to be published, known. *Poetry* and *Poets Out of Wisconsin* had rejected her surrealistic writing, and Pound accepted it only on Zukofsky's recommendation. She did not want to be published only on Louie's recommendation.

She had also fought through seven years of personal and professional turmoil during which the surreal had seemed a natural form to express "waking isolation thick unto impenetrability." She had weathered that stretch, emerging with a clearer understanding of where her strengths lay. Writing to Harriet Monroe early in 1936, for example, she signed herself for the first time "Lorine Niedecker" with no parenthetical "Mrs. Frank Hartwig"—a new claim to identity. And, though FDR could not meet every election promise, by 1936 his New Deal had "yielded a legacy of commonality and community that filtered down to the local level."

Though still and always a loner, Lorine sensed this change. It encouraged her to express more commonality and community in her poetry. And what more commonly communal than the Mother Goose rhymes of childhood that she'd been rereading, along with Lewis Carroll's *Alice in Wonderland*, Zukofsky's essay on Carroll, and Alfred Jarry's proto-Absurdist drama *Ubu Roi*. She remembered Tolstoy valuing a song, lullaby, riddle. She could play that game, relying on a reader to know Mother Goose disaster rhymes (cradle falling, cows in the corn) to give this Depression poem extra punch:

> O rock my baby on the tree tops
> and blow me a little tin horn.
> They've got us suckin the hind tit
> and that's the way I was born.

Language she had heard from childhood was the idiom for the new genre. Henry was a storyteller; Daisy's pithy talk emerged almost as complete poems. "Time for BP [Bean Pole, Lorine's name for Daisy] to write me a poem," she'd write Zukofsky, who envied her gold mine. "My mother was a kind of Mother Goose, straight out of the people . . . told me this just as it is":

> The museum man!
> I wish he'd taken Pa's spitbox!
> I'm going to take that spitbox out
> and bury it in the ground
> and put a stone on top.
> Because without that stone on top
> it would come back.

Memories and a quick ear for local speech gave Lorine many voices to choose from: "I'm a different character in a different drama with almost every poem I write." With irony and wit, she would refine the idiom of common speech to essence. Though "Poet's Work" was written in 1962, it reflects the course Lorine set herself with the poems of *New Goose*:

> Grandfather
>   advised me:
>   Learn a trade
>
> I learned
>   to sit at desk
>   and condense
>
> No layoff
>   from this
>   condensery

Behind the simplicity of the lines lie pride and a declaration of independence. She had taken Grandfather Gottfried's advice: she had found a trade. There was no layoff from *this* condensery—no employer could lay her off; neither could she lay off her calling.

Lorine sent twelve "Mother Goose" poems to Harriet Monroe on February 25, 1936. "Nay Nay," replied the distinguished, but by now weary, editor of *Poetry*.

Monroe was seventy-five and would die seven months later in Arequipa, Peru, far from the American poetry scene she had done much to foster. Fortunately, a new champion of modern poetry and prose would launch a publishing company that year in a barn on his aunt Lelia's estate in Norfolk, Connecticut.

In 1933 James Laughlin IV, inheritor of a Pittsburgh steel fortune, had taken a break from Harvard after his freshman year, sailed to Paris to meet Gertrude Stein, then motored on to Italy to seek out Ezra Pound. But Pound, who'd been reading Laughlin's poems for months, "ruled them hopeless. He urged me to finish Harvard and then do 'something' useful."

Pound introduced the eighteen-year-old Laughlin to Zukofsky, in Rapallo on a traveling gift from Williams, the Oppens, and Pound. Six foot five and deeply tanned, Laughlin impressed Zukofsky as "a young god . . . very handsome, strikingly handsome." Laughlin was equally impressed with Zukofsky: "What an intense mind! But he was not at all impressed with me. We had little conversation. I simply listened to him talking to Pound. I think he thought I was a parasite."

Laughlin returned to the States, Pound's suggestion humming in his brain. "Something useful" turned out to be New Directions Press, its mission to print the best current experimental poetry and prose. *New Directions in Prose and Poetry*, Laughlin's first venture, featured twenty-five writers, including Pound, Williams, Elizabeth Bishop, E. E. Cummings, Marianne Moore, Wallace Stevens, Jean Cocteau, Henry Miller, Zukofsky, and Niedecker.

Having sent Laughlin his poem "Mantis," Zukofsky may have urged him to recruit Lorine for his anthology. Impressed, Laughlin accepted two brief surrealist plays, "The President of the Holding Company" and "Fancy Another Day Gone" for the first volume of *New Directions in Prose and Poetry*, published in 1936. Encouraged, she sent him an expanded seventeen-poem "Mother Geese" series and "Uncle": "This is my story and I enclose return postage in case I have to stick to it."

"I think your story is a fine piece of writing," Laughlin replied, "and am happy to accept it for NEW DIRECTIONS 1937. It has the sprawl of life. Also patches of beauty, without working for them." He offered her five 1936 *New Directions* copies to distribute, but she could think of no one but her Beloit philosophy professor, John Crawford, who might want one.

In his preface to the 1936 *New Directions*, Laughlin stressed Niedecker's originality. Not acquainted with "orthodox Parisian Surrealism," she "lives in Wisconsin and her ideas are all her own. Among her most interesting experiments were the poems written on three levels of consciousness which appeared about a year ago in the Wilson-Drummond 'Westminster' Anthology." He would continue to publish her. "I'm sorry," he said later, "that I never actually met Lorine Niedecker. From her many letters over the years I think of her as an old friend. She was an original in the best sense, hoeing her own row in poetry with complete disregard to literary fashion."

Although Laughlin accepted fifty-six pages of "A" in 1938, it was the only time he published Zukofsky: "Zuk was eager to have New Directions become the regular publisher of his books, I wish we had, but a small publisher can't do everything. And I realized that he might be difficult and demanding. So there was a cooling of what had never been exactly warm." Though Zukofsky may not have resented Lorine's ongoing appearance in *New Directions*, he highly resented Laughlin's dropping him and would write sarcastically to Lorine of "James IV."

Lorine still knew nothing of Celia Thaew. Zuk continued to write regularly, urging her to see Charlie Chaplin's subversive epic, *Modern Times.* He would send "silver" if she couldn't afford the movie, but best to get Henry and BP to take her; he'd reimburse them. He'd watched a protest parade of Work Progress Administration people and Communists, with Carl Rakosi marching in the ranks. Despite the hoopla, he didn't think the world was in a hurry for change.

A superb critic, he praised her new Mother Geese. "Ash woods," a poem in memory of her grandfather Gottfried Kunz, struck him as quite Hardyesque, her "little grandma" poem ("Just before she died") very close in meaning to William Blake's "The Chimney Sweeper," the first two stanzas of "Grampa" ("Grampa's got his old age pension") magnificent. "Seven years" ("Seven years a charming woman") was "poifick." He considered primal Niedecker her Henry and Daisy poem, "My man":

> My man says the wind blows from the south,
> we go out fishing, he has no luck,
> I catch a dozen, that burns him up,
> I face the east and the wind's in my mouth,
> but my man has to have it in the south.

Much as he praised, he urged her to strive for a balance of speech and *song.* Yes, she is necessarily intent on getting speech and thought down on the page, but eventually "*speech must sing*" as it does in the original *Mother Goose.* The best thing Pound ever said to him was "Look into thine ear and write." He likes her weather poem—"I hear the weather / through the house / or is it breathing / mother"—for its "fugue of *r*s." He suggests that, like Shakespeare, she establish a number of syllables per line but vary the beats: freedom restrained.

Another poem became *echt* Niedecker in its philosophy:

A monster owl
out on the fence
flew away. What
is it the sign
of? The sign of
an owl.

Originally she'd written "The sign of / an owl I guess." Drop the qualifier, Zukofsky urged. Lorine agreed. For her the natural world does not embody a supernatural. An owl is an owl—not an avatar, omen, or manifestation of divinity. Animals, birds, trees, she would insist all her life, are meaningful *in themselves*. "A monster owl" encapsulates Niedecker's materialist philosophy.

She continued to critique Zukofsky's work. He loved her wacky, dead-on comments: "The meaning the lines have even if they haven't" and "A derangement of the mind under terrific strain that makes everything clearer." She was typing his radio broadcast for the New York station WOR and fifty pages of "A"-8. She sent the deprived New Yorker a book on bird songs and "2 small victrola records." She may have visited him in New York in 1937; no record survives.

Zuk kept writing lover-like. They played "illiterate" in letters (as did Pound and Williams)—*wuz, poifect, youz, sumpin'*. A mix of comic strip, Yiddish, Hollywood, and Wisconsin rural, the jargon playfully displayed their linguistic versatility. Zu tells her he's moved again but the new place is right because he can write her late at night, alone, in dark silence. He wishes he, Basil Bunting, and Jerry could get away from New York to Wisconsin to stretch their hearts and senses. And then there's the dog. Will Lorine accept shipment of Jiffy, a neighborhood stray? Louie will pay half the five-dollar shipping charge. Lorine is their only hope. Zuk apologizes for his sentimentality, but then he'd wept when a duck, rescued from a Hudson River ice floe, refused food and died.

Lorine declined Jiffy, but anticipated Zuk's visit in July 1938 to Blackhawk Island: "Cold clear morning. Water rising here, heavy rains. Has rained ever since February 14, since beginning of high water in spring. Beautiful heavy growth tho everywhere and gardens (mine enehows!) prizeworthy. If continues to rain can't tell but what we'll be flooded but we sit on our thumbs and hope. Allus sit, here. Sit on the land even when it turns to water. As long as there's a road will be especking youz."

Instead, Zukofsky went with Jerry and Edouard and Diane Dechar to upstate New York near Lake George. And though he wrote that he would rather be a thousand miles west, her road had been open and he hadn't come.

9

Federal Writers' Project

1938–1942

Let's play a game. / Let's play Ask for a job.
"Let's play a game"

Headquartered in Madison, the Wisconsin Federal Writers' Project provided jobs for unemployed professional and white-collar workers. Lorine qualified.

She took the bus to Madison sometime in 1938, and rented a room close to the university campus. Thanks to two reminiscences written by Works Progress Administration friends, Federal Writers' Project records in the Wisconsin Historical Society, and a cranky but entertaining account of the project by WPA veteran Harold Miner, these years aren't a total blank. But a main source of information about Lorine's life is missing.

Only one complete letter and three fragments to Zukofsky between 1931 and 1944 survive. This is because Lorine and Louis destroyed virtually a decade of their correspondence.

A private person, Lorine agreed to the destruction, but it's questionable whether she initiated the idea. It would more likely have been the obsessively private Zukofsky who wanted to obliterate a past that had become an embarrassment. And how like modest Lorine not to protest, not to demand her letters back, though the words legally were hers. A substantial number of *his* letters survive from the 1930s because she didn't destroy them as ordered. *Her* reactions to their affair, her pregnancy and abortion, his work, his critiques of her poems, his increasing involvement with Celia Thaew (if he confided it) are destroyed.

According to Celia, she and Louis became more and more intimate until marriage was inevitable. Jerry Reisman's view differed:

> What she omits is that she pursued him relentlessly during those years and even used her bank account as an inducement to get him to propose. Finally, Louis said he'd date her if she'd go to bed with him. She insisted that he marry her first. Louis replied that marriage was out of the question. Celia held out for a long time, but in the end she gave in. Perhaps four or five months later, she began an intimate relationship with me as well. . . . Celia continued to press Louis on the issue of marriage and he continued to refuse. . . . [I] urged him to take the plunge. Finally, he agreed. Celia was ecstatic.

Mary Oppen says that Carl Rakosi urged Louis to marry Celia. Marriage would "protect" him, preserve the Jewish tradition, and erase his previous homosexuality. As for Lorine, "Louis would never have married a Gentile: he was too afraid of 'The Other.'"

Zukofsky hadn't necessarily falsified affection in his letters to Lorine. He didn't particularly want to marry. He never told Lorine he loved her; Celia (despite his beautiful love poems to her) would accuse him of the same crime. Two very different women wanted him. Lorine: a soul mate and his advocate in poetry, midwestern, formidably gifted, poor. Celia: urban, persistent, capable, on the spot, and earning seventy-five dollars a month.

In August 1939 Lorine drove in an old De Soto with Edwin Honig, his fiancée Charlotte, and coworker Joe Gary to New York. Lorine stayed with Louis: "When we arrived in Brooklyn," Honig recalls, "Louis Zukofsky was there to help Lorine take her bags from the trunk of the car." Louis and Celia were married on August 20, 1939, in Wilmington, Delaware, rather than New York because Zukofsky refused the required Wasserman (syphilis) test and did not want family or a religious ceremony. Startlingly, as a letter confirms, *Lorine was with Louis and Celia on their wedding day*: he reminds her on August 19, 1946, that tomorrow will mark seven years since they've seen her. Zukofsky was precise about dates.

This means that Lorine either arrived or left the day he married, more probably left, since Reisman doesn't mention Lorine in his account of taking the train to Wilmington with Louis and Celia. Logically, too, Zukofsky would date his last seeing Lorine from the day they said good-bye, which means that Lorine waved Louie and Celia off on their wedding trip—a singularly masochistic gesture.

There is no record of Lorine's feelings, but it is likely she felt both intrusive (as Celia must have felt *her*) and excluded, if not devastated. Zukofsky provides a clue in a letter dated October 30, 1939, when—guessing Lorine's impulse to drop silently out of his life—he begs her not to go underground. Ultimately, she did not. Zukofsky was too important; she could not bear the almost total isolation from the world of poetry that withdrawal would bring. She embraced the marriage to keep a lifeline flowing, smothering her romantic and sexual love for him.

She would deny she ever loved Zukofsky the man: "In after years if they talk about me and ask 'Was she ever in love,' they'll have to say, 'Yes, she was in love with Zukofsky's words.'" About Zukofsky, Lorine—usually so clear-headed—was a prime sublimator.

Thanks to Celia, Lorine escaped Zukofsky. He would still be her best critic. But as he'd warned, he was nicer personally in the [ ].

The Federal Writers' Project had gotten off to a rocky start in Madison. Headed by incompetents, seventy workers had produced only "a large accumulation of inaccurate and inane material, all elaborately filed and cross-indexed." In 1937 John Lyons turned the project around. When Lorine reported to the office at 149 East Wilson Street, she found a miscellaneous group of forty-eight employees— "distraught housewives, clerks, and displaced librarians," in one cynic's view— united by a terrific esprit de corps. Though everyone lived in fear of Congress terminating their jobs, their dicey futures bonded them more tightly.

On September 1, 1939, as Hitler's troops overwhelmed Poland, Britain and France declared war on Germany. That same day the WPA workers' fear became reality. With Republican gains in Congress, GOP attacks on the "Commie" WPA prevailed. The Federal Writers' Project was abolished.

Harold Miner notes:

> It is true that there were Communists on some of the Arts Projects; Communists often found it impossible to obtain private employment. . . . But it is untrue that the Communists were permitted to inject their Communism into Project work. Not only would any sane Project supervisor guard most vigilantly against anything of the sort, but all the rules requiring manuscripts to pass the approval of the Washington office, the co-sponsor, and outside authorities were designed to impose a check upon such a possibility.

Victim of a Commie scare, Lorine lost her job and returned to the island. But she was one of the lucky ones. In November the university decided to sponsor state arts projects and asked Lorine to join the renamed Wisconsin Writers' Project.

Edwin Honig knew Lorine best in 1938 and 1939. A penniless poet from

Brooklyn, he'd been drawn to Madison by "what was widely known as the most progressive university in the country." The nineteen-year-old managed to be hired by the Writers' Project as a junior writer at eighty-four dollars a month:

> There I met and quickly became friends with Lorine (she was a senior writer, making perhaps ninety-two a month!) on the basis of our interest in poetry.
>
> A slight, almost frail woman, she walked with quick short steps. Bifocals made her milky blue eyes seem larger than they were. Her hair was ashen blonde and wispy; the thickness of her lips made them look large as well. Her laugh was spontaneous and sudden, but quickly suppressed with one hand clapped over her mouth, her head averted. She had a good wit, a high-pitched girlish voice and a strong sense of the incongruous, which made her a good storyteller.

Among the project's many undertakings, the *Wisconsin Guide* and an encyclopedia of influential Wisconsinites dominated. Ninety-five percent of the laborious work was submitted anonymously: besides a paycheck, only camaraderie and feeling that they were contributing to history kept morale alive. Lorine didn't contribute to the *Wisconsin Guide*, but fourteen signed check sheets for biographies of state leaders like Steven Faville (dairy pioneer), Jason Downer (Downer Seminary and College), and Increase Lapham (naturalist) survive. Surprisingly, considering her poor eyesight, Lorine's typed check sheets are by far the neatest of those submitted. Portions of her work would be published in 1960 as the *Dictionary of Wisconsin Biography*—unsigned.

Harold Miner recalls: "Those who could not be taught to write well were used for research assignments or for checking manuscripts for accuracy against the sources shown in footnotes. Many learned to take adequate notes from which others (usually myself) wrote biographies." Lorine checked manuscripts for accuracy, but was hardly someone "who could not be taught to write well." She wrote her share of the two thousand unsigned biographies.

On the project, Lorine became close friends with Vivien Morgan, a writer who married the project's photographic supervisor, Harold Hone, in 1939. Hone's studio at the edge of the university campus became a gathering place for the Left—that is, for most project workers: "Much of the official chit chat revolved around the *Wisconsin Guide.* . . . But many of the unofficial hours were turned to radical politics. Like many young Americans who saw their own nation foundering, [they] looked to Russia as savior. Lorine was caught up in the web."

"Although Lorine was a Marxist," said Edwin Honig, "her strongest sympathies were for human beings, their talk and expressions, and not much for ideological argument." Ideology of any kind was antithetical to Lorine's subtle mind, though she heavily underlined her *Handbook of Marxism.* Yet she could not resist Party momentum at its height. She attended meetings; obeyed a summons to the Student Union Rathskeller to hear *New Masses* writer and cartoonist Bob Minor, survivor of a coal miners' strike and a Kentucky jail, declare, "Comrades! I've just come back from the last battle in the class struggle!" Honig was thrilled: Lorine was impressed by Minor's naiveté.

One aspect of being a female Leftist disturbed Lorine. "If you don't go to bed with me," fellow workers told her, "you're not a Comrade." Disillusioned, Lorine fled to Vivien Hone: "I cannot remember just when the pale blonde Lorine, frail at best, came to confide in me but confide she did: that party members considered it her duty to sleep with them and also to carry large bundles of propaganda pamphlets from door to door. Never a party member, I suggested 'no' on both counts: her frailty should forbid such heavy carrying and sleeping with a man should be done as a matter of her choice and affection."

Lorine may not have taken Vivien's advice. The camaraderie among project workers could have slipped into sex; Honig said that he and Lorine "might have become lovers"—except for the fact that he was engaged.

Instead, Lorine and Edwin became friends, researching side by side at long tables in the university library or the State Historical Society; lunching in the dark Union Rathskeller where a nickel bought "an endlessly refillable cup of coffee"; in warm weather eating bag lunches on the terrace overlooking a Lake Mendota dotted with white sailboats. Honig had a room near the library on State Street. Lorine often joined him evenings, drinking cider while he drank wine and did portraits in pastels. Honig heard a great deal about the Objectivists.

She took the bus home every weekend and often invited him along; she always wanted good friends to share her island. Edwin recalled: "Lorine's mother was awesomely gaunt, tall and silent; her father, an easygoing hunter-fisher-farmer, not regularly employed, was a good story-teller. I remember suppers of collard greens, rutabaga, potatoes, and mud hen. We were good friends."

Vivien Hone also met Henry and Daisy: "He lived in a modest house on the banks [of the Rock River]. Lorine's mother lived in an adjoining house and never spoke to her husband. The cause of that silent civil war was never made known to me, but what a hostile environment for [Lorine] the child." Vivien liked Henry "because there seemed to be a great bond of affection between daughter and father."

One Thanksgiving Lorine invited twelve of her favorite project people to dinner, including Vivien and her husband. Before eating, they took a long walk along the marshes of the river and Lake Koshkonong. According to Vivien, "The dead grasses, threatening yet beautiful dark skies, the honking of wild geese—all this elated us. I like to think that all of us were happy then, Depression or not, surrounded by friends, free and young."

Lorine had reserved a room at a private hunt club on Lake Koshkonong, closed for the season but with a resident cook. Vivien commented, "God knows how many dollars out of her modest project salary went into producing that soup-to-nuts holiday feast with all the trimmings: one duckling a piece for her guests, the traditional pumpkin pie and plum pudding and finally topped off with unexpected Norwegian pastries."

Vivien's account belies Niedecker's famous shyness, a mask she wore to avoid some people, rather than an affliction. Honig thought she was neither shy nor reclusive: "She was courteous, friendly, a good attentive listener, and quick to express her concerns, both personal and political, but never gabbed on about anything."

On one thing she and Honig disagreed. Lorine felt intimately tied to the British poets Basil Bunting, Ronald Duncan, and Hugh MacDiarmid—the Pound school. Honig didn't like Pound and distrusted her bond with Zukofsky: "She assiduously exchanged letters with him, and I was much impressed with the degree that she counted on his words as a source of living sustenance." He concluded that Lorine's ideas about poetry, politics, music, philosophy, and science came straight from Pound-Zukofsky; he was not a follower. But Honig couldn't know how grounded in philosophy and politics Lorine was, how deeply she researched; how it was she who typed Zukofsky pages of notes from her reading, not vice versa; how she had always remodeled Objectivist practices to suit her own poetry.

One letter from Lorine to Zukofsky survives from the Wisconsin Writers' Project years, an ebullient account of a May Sunday spent with Jane Tuttrup and Elinor Price, who came to Blackhawk Island to meet Angie Kumlien Main, bird authority and daughter of the famous naturalist Thure Kumlien:

> If you had been with us last Sunday maybe you'd remember it all your life. [ ]. . . .
>
> After dinner we went over across the lake by auto to the spot where Kumlien settled when he came to this country from Sweden in 1843. It was that kind of clear, spring, blue and yellow-green day that sometimes shines through the Anews and after we had driven through somebody's cow pasture there it was, the lilacs in bloom

and the planters' pines, nothing else to show a home had been there, except when you looked in the high grass, some rotting logs that were probably part of the foundations of the log cabin.

While exploring the old Kumlien property, they heard a rare western meadowlark: "I used to think the brown thrasher was the most beautiful singer of all birds I knew, but it sang there . . . as if the leaves of the trees were singing in every direction, a little flute-like but soft and many tones. . . . Maybe this past week has been the best of my three years in Madison, especially last Sunday. [ ]."

Lorine identified intimately with birds. So nearsighted she could not drive a car, she knew their calls. Angie Kumlien Main "always had to *see* the birds to appreciate 'em whereas I knew by their sound what they were and knowing what their colors were in my mind, was happy enough." Many people have called Lorine bird-like, not a bad comparison. Like a bird, she was small, often invisible among the trees, singer of a distinctive song. Perhaps she identified most closely with the sora rail, a hen-like marsh bird of secretive habit and mysterious voice, more often heard than seen. But she could also say "I'm just a sandpiper in a marshy region" and, famously, "I was the solitary plover / a pencil / for a wing-bone." Or, searching for an elusive new poetic form, she could describe herself as experiencing the pain and fear birds feel before migration.

Back in Madison Lorine looked up Thure Kumlien at the State Historical Society and read again about Chief Black Hawk, "who lost his women and children in the swamps where I live so the white army wouldn't find 'em. . . . Then Black Hawk was captured and taken on a trip over the east, shown to the President, and he dictated his life to a Frenchman and that's one of my great books." J. R. Paterson's *The Life of Black Hawk* inspired a taut, decisive *New Goose* poem:

> Black Hawk held: In reason
> land cannot be sold,
> only things to be carried away,
> and I am old.
>
> Young Lincoln's general moved,
> pawpaw in bloom,
> and to this day, Black Hawk,
> reason has small room.

She was writing poetry in the evenings. From her research for a biography of Increase Lapham—author of the first book published in Wisconsin; pioneer mapmaker; expert on effigy mounds, native trees, and grasses; and friend of the foremost American botanist, Asa Gray—Lorine distilled three lines:

Asa Gray wrote Increase Lapham:
pay particular attention
to my pets, the grasses.

The sibilants of *Asa*, *Increase*, *pets*, and *grasses* are like wind parting grass, while the *g*s of *Gray* and *grasses* book-end a poem punctuated by the plosives of *Lapham*, *pay*, *particular*, and *pets* and echoing the repeated vowels of *Lapham* and *grasses*. A small but perfect example of Niedecker making speech sing.

Fellow workers knew Lorine wrote poetry, said Edwin Honig, and "kidded her about being another Emily Dickinson, but she brushed this aside." As usual, she preferred to blend into the crowd. But the enormous amount of research she did in Madison fed her poet's mind. History and biography ignited her imagination.

Three months before *Wisconsin: A Guide to the Badger State* was published in March 1941, Harold Miner left for Washington to clean up the federal program mess. He wrote emotionally: "I want to pay tribute to the most gallant group of people I have ever known. I mean the Project's staff. . . . They bore poverty, opprobrium, and the recurring strain of the quota cuts and shake-ups without losing their self-respect, their respect for one another, or their keenness for and belief in what they were doing. There existed among them a gay, almost tender fellow-feeling which I find it impossible to define or describe. . . . They were truly a family." Lorine and her friends Elinor Price and Jane Tuttrup were among "the gallant group" still in the Madison office when he left.

Miner was succeeded as supervisor by Alice Foster. Foster, said Marie, friend of a project worker, had "a positive genius for handling WPA workers; she kept most of them in perpetual rage and hate. . . . And once she threatened Lorine, who was complaining about her supervision, with a transfer to the sewing project. Ain't that something?"

Perhaps Alice Foster was the reason that Lorine transferred to the Radio Scripts division. Though her work can't be identified—scripts were signed only by the director, Marcus Ford—she dramatized some of the project biographies for the *Wisconsin Men and Women Series*, produced weekly between May 15, 1940, and May 28, 1941, on Madison station WIBA.

The project staggered on. The attacks at Pearl Harbor on December 7, 1941, ended Depression subsidizing as the United States launched into military production and the economy boomed. Lorine survived severe personnel cuts made in April 1942, but on June 3, a scorchingly hot day, she called on Marie: "Lorine dropped in at three. Her certification has been cancelled and she's being dropped on the 23rd."

Project workers scattered like leaves, though Edwin Honig and Vivien Hone would later blow back into Lorine's life. She had tasted four years of congenial work, modest economic independence, comradeship, and liberty.

No coincidence, then, that when she returned to Blackhawk Island she at last initiated proceedings against Frank Hartwig, whom she'd never divorced. On September 3, as plaintiff, she appeared with Henry and her lawyer, William Rogers, at the Jefferson Country Court House.

From the Clerk of Court records:

> Q. When did you separate?
> A. Well by separating you mean the last time we saw each other?
> Q. Yes.
> A. In the fall of 1934.

Rogers wanted more detail:

> Q. Have you lived with the defendant or seen very much of him since Oct. 1, 1934?
> A. No, not lived with him and I have seen him only once.
> Q. Since that time?
> A. Yes.
> Q. Can you tell us what the reason is for your separation at that time?
> A. Well, the immediate reason was four years previous to that we lost the house in Fort Atkinson and were depossessed in Fort Atkinson and each one of us went to live with our parents and saw each other once [or] twice a week until the fall of 1934, when I went to New York and we agreed not to see each other any more.

So the mystery of how long the marriage lasted is solved, or is it? Lorine and Frank separated in 1930 but "saw each other" until fall 1934.

The law means "how long did you co-habit sexually?" Does Lorine take the question to mean that October 1, 1934, was last time she and Frank met? No: she says she hasn't "lived with" Hartwig since that date.

Since the timing is linked to New York and Zukofsky, with whom she'd fallen in love, it may be that she and Frank saw each other sexually twice a week until she announced she was going to New York to stay with Zukofsky. Then what about Lorine's reported revulsion on her wedding night?

There's Ernest Hartwig's testimony that he always took Lorine home from her farm visits and that Lorine and Frank were just friends. But Ernest seems to have been ignorant of their private relationship.

Fact: Lorine refused alimony, and asked only that her maiden name, Niedecker, be legally restored.

10

New Goose

1942–1946

the poems called Goose / separated by stars / to save the sun—
"To a Maryland editor, 1943"

Lorine moved back in with her parents, she and Daisy upstairs, Henry down so he could freely come and go. After buying War Bonds, she'd saved a bit from WPA, but could find no suitable work on her return. Henry gave her an allowance of eighty dollars a month. She compared herself to the always struggling Zukofsky: "Of course his economic problem was much worse than mine, at least I had a parental home I *could* stay in, gratis, if I wanted to pass so much of *life* by."

Progress had not ignored Blackhawk Island. Lorine had seen it deteriorate from a rural paradise to a blue-collar tourist destination, with trailers, shacky cabins, and "BAR BAIT BOATS" resorts.

Ray and Myrtle Prisk owned a house, grocery store, gas pumps, and cottages on the river. Ray also made himself indispensible by excavating, hauling fill, and installing septic systems on the island. Prisk, shrewd Myrtle, and their four sons dominated the island.

Harriet, a former Chicago stripper, co-owned Mimmack's Resort. Mimmack's had white cabins with blue trim.

Alex and Stella Kohlman owned the Last Resort, popular with residents and tourists for its sixty-five-cent Friday fish-fry with creamy slaw and American fries. People called Mrs. Kohlman "Stella by Starlight" and liked the Kohlmans. Sometimes Lorine and Henry ate there.

Al Billet ran the resort at the point of Blackhawk Island.

Two resorts catered exclusively to African Americans. Frenchy's had a luncheonette with six stools, sold tackle and bait, and rented boats. Upscale Burns's Resort, always full, sat on a rise overlooking a lagoon. Patrons could paddle the lagoon or go down to the river to fish in rented boats. If an African American ventured into other resorts, however, he might be asked at gunpoint to leave.

The Rock River was changing too, with private motor boats replacing the pleasure launches that since the 1880s had chugged leisurely upstream from Fort Atkinson to the Fountain House and hotels on Lake Koshkonong, carrying people in their Sunday best. The pace would only accelerate after the war.

"Sunday's motor-cars / jar the house," wrote Lorine, who now often found herself turning to the printed word for poetic inspiration rather than to her deteriorating natural surroundings. Reading about the broad-leaved arrowhead plant, for instance, she marked the page instead of going out to search for the real thing. "I suppose / if I sat down beside a frost / and had no printed sign / I'd be lost."

In 1943 Lorine disappears from view. Only Zukofsky's encouraging letters prove that she is writing more "geese." He thinks her poem about the marsh rail quite perfect:

> Don't shoot the rail!
> Let your grandfather rest!
> Tho he sees your wild eyes
> he's falling asleep,
> his long-billed pipe
> on his red-brown vest.

In this undocumented year, an event occurred that would force Lorine to sublimate her feelings for Zukofsky more than ever: the birth to Louis and Celia, on October 22, of a son, Paul. Though no letters from Lorine survive the occasion, she would adopt the stance of worshiper at the manger, writing in 1945: "Oh me, the pictures of Diddy—lovely, Zu! . . . You two togedder—I wear it on my heart— reminds a person of an early religious painting [ ], a child so calm (with a pencil instead of a halo) and that look in his eyes like both yours and Celia's—so mild and clear, a kind of inner integrity, an intellectual listening look. . . . My three pictures—my three children, I hug 'em." An Objectivist scholar would refer to Louis, Celia, and Paul as "the holy trinity." Lorine was before him.

Still, Lorine was more intent on getting *New Goose* into print than on the Zukofskys. She and Louis, whose *Anew* Lorine had typed ("Louis never typed *any-thing*," according to Celia), sent their manuscripts to that extraordinary venture, the

Press of James A. Decker. "Our woiks are sealed in a big envelope ready to be mailed off tomorrow. The Decker-Niedecker deal should soon take place."

In the unlikely outpost of Prairie City, Illinois, the young and visionary James Decker had decided to publish poets. *Compass*, his quarterly venture, featured Marianne Moore, Wallace Stevens, William Carlos Williams, and Weldon Kees. Operating on a shoestring (unlike Laughlin), assisted by his dark-browed, unhappy sister Dorothy, Decker had contracted in 1939 that money from two hundred copies went to the author after the author's investment of two hundred dollars was realized—a common practice in those times.

By 1939 Decker had published sixteen books by nationally known writers. Overwhelmed by manuscripts, he went into the anthology business, publishing E. E. Cummings, Marianne Moore, Kenneth Patchen, Archibald MacLeish, and Langston Hughes. With the publication of *Illinois Poems* and *Along the Illinois* by Edgar Lee Masters, author of the great *Spoon River Anthology*, the Press of James A. Decker won national attention, giving him the courage to take on Zukofsky's playfully learned-obscure *Mantis*.

"Although Decker never chose to be a critic, a poet, or a scholar," wrote James Ballowe, "he was by the age of 23 a discerning publisher who was willing to accept the enormous task of type-setting one of the most demanding of contemporary poets. Dealing with Zukofsky must have been a lonely task. With whom in Prairie City would he have shared the poet's idiosyncrasies?"

Still, Decker accepted *Anew* and *New Goose*. Or perhaps his brooding sister Dorothy had, since Decker had joined the army. Lorine and Louis had no idea their "woiks" wouldn't be published until 1946: Decker had a backlog of writers waiting for books they'd already subsidized. Returning from action in the South Pacific in 1945, he "desperately tried to honor his old contracts." *New Goose* and *Anew* were among thirty titles published in 1946 and 1947 in an inexpensive "Pocket Poetry" format instead of Decker's formerly elegant productions. To achieve even this, he was forced to sell his press to a Prairie City lumberman, Harry Denman.

Lorine had been out of work since June 1942, isolated on the island. "Woman with Umbrella" reflects her frustrated solitude:

> Lonely woman, not prompted
> by freshness from the sky
> to run with friends and laugh it off,
> arrives unsparkling but dry—

she's felt the prongs of her own advance
thru the crowded street,
knows that lonely
she is dangerous to meet.

In 1944, Fort Atkinson, a thriving city of six thousand, boasted three commercial superstars: the Jones Dairy Farm, producer of nationally famous pork products; Jamesway, manufacturers of "Labor Saving Equipment for the Dairy Barn"; and Hoard's. In May 1944 Lorine was hired by W. D. Hoard's, publisher of the nationally distributed *Hoard's Dairyman*. Stenography and proofreading were the last work she should have been doing with her poor eyes. Better to clerk in a shop. But Lorine was a writer and reader.

Among people again, Lorine still felt isolated. She kept to herself: these coworkers were not her WPA group. Lorine usually ducked controversy. Unfortunately at Hoard's she met another Alice Foster head on. Her name was Cora Lohmaier, and though she bossed everybody, she persecuted Lorine.

"Past few days been fearfully low," Lorine told Zukofsky, "almost walked out on the proof reader—she has high blood pressure. Nobody has been able to work with her. She treats everyone as something inferior."

Cora Lohmaier dressed up for her low-paying job: nylons, heels, dresses from Westphals. Arriving frozen from her too-frequent four-mile walk into town, Lorine would sit huddled at her desk bundled in hat, scarf, and boots—"*not* proper attire for one working in the stenographic department."

Lorine was a better proofreader than Cora, but because of poor eyesight she was slow, peering at proofs through a magnifying glass, pushing back her chair to rest her eyes. Cora seized on Lorine's slowness. A battle raged between them. Lorine refused to kowtow to her. In turn, Cora would use all her clout to get Lorine fired.

Lorine's smart and practical school friend, Florence Dollase, had started work at Hoard's in 1925 and was now the secretary of the boss, William Hoard, working in his office, far from lowly typesetters and proofreaders but hardly better paid. She knew about Cora's feud with Lorine, but could do nothing. She didn't quite approve of the hat, scarf, and boots herself.

On April 12, 1945, Franklin Delano Roosevelt died suddenly from a cerebral hemorrhage. Though Lorine would write poems about Churchill and John F. Kennedy, no word of hers survives about FDR. But then he held office during her leftist, proletarian years when even many workers employed by his relief programs had their heads buried in the Communist ideological sands.

In Madison on a terrifically cold and windy Saturday, April 21, Lorine

> ran into a girl I used to know who was on the edge of being on the
> liberal fence about politics, and not very serious about anything,
> yet closer to me than any girl there—seeing each other we threw
> our arms around each other on the street and she looked so tired
> and worn and the first thing she said: "I'm feeling so low—
> Roosevelt—Lorine, what's Truman going to be like??" The sun
> came out a little while later and I was tempted to go with her to the
> Union and walk on the Terrace and look at Mendota—but—I
> keeps to myself, better so.

Lorine had read about Truman's early life, admired the way he'd told the anti-Catholic Purity League that he'd give jobs to any Catholic boys who wanted 'em. Truman was tough and down to earth, more sympathetic to Lorine than the aristocratic FDR. Then Truman dropped the atomic bomb on Hiroshima and Nagasaki.

"Reason explodes," she wrote. "Now hide / who can bombarded particles / of international / pride." The game had drastically changed, the ante upped. Now civilization could be destroyed by a single weapon. "Will man obsolesce / when he sends the rays against himself?" The Bomb became a theme of her work, most terribly when school children sing "atomic bomb" for "Oh, Tannenbaum."

Sometime after meeting her WPA friend, she had a nightmare. She was in Madison, "and all the streets were empty and nobody in sight and I went everywhere looking for *some* human and only I was there—and one other: the old hag of a proof reader that caused my throat to tighten and harden and night before last I woke up with that fearful thing that makes me call out in fear of fainting. I called very loud to Henry because I knew BP would never hear and because he's two flights down. . . . The closest I have ever come to going under, I'm sure."

Working under Cora Lohmaier was punishing. Lorine deliberately concludes her letter to Zukofsky on a lighter note: Decker has published August Derleth and Ruth Lechlitner—"both tripe, especially the former." But the *Saturday Review of Literature* and *New Masses* reviewed both books, so "maybe they'll send ours to both, too."

A French classic came to her mental rescue that April: the philosopher Denis Diderot's *Interpreter of Nature: Selected Writings*. Lorine reported:

> This is what I could have used long ago, alongside Engels and
> while I was wondering what Emerson was getting at. . . . I really

> begin to believe that there is another life for us after we die, one
> not like ours, at least not for a long, long time. Elements for awhile
> before we again become, if we ever do, another mass. Time is nuttin
> in the universe. . . . "Fontenelle's rose saying that within the memory
> of a rose no gardener had been known to die." (This is the loveliest
> and most important thing I've read in a long time.) If we knew
> more chemistry and physics I'd have more faith. Only thing about
> death—loneliness for those that are left, but that's present anyhow.

Niedecker the materialist can be cheered by the idea that human matter may in time be rearranged and energized, if not in human form.

Lorine occasionally made light of "philarsophy," believed no one philosophy could guide a person's life. Marcus Aurelius was her steadiest companion: "Nowhere can man find a quieter or more untroubled retreat than in his own soul; above all, he who possesses resources in himself, which he need only contemplate to secure immediate ease of mind—the ease that is but another word for a well-ordered spirit." This was stuff she could feed upon. Zukofsky would send her Aristotle and Lucretius in 1950. No references survive to the former, but Lucretius—who taught that human life lay crushed beneath religion until Epicurus countered with reason and the laws of nature—spoke her language. Plotinus's distrust of property and possessions was also her own. But it was to Marcus Aurelius's *Mediations* she turned most often.

On August 14, 1945, Japan announced its surrender: the costliest war in history was over. War recurs again and again in *New Goose* and later poems. Russia's and Britain's hand-to-hand struggles against the Nazis haunt Lorine most: the siege of Stalingrad, bombs incinerating London's Somerset House "where records go down / to Shakespeare who never ceased," and the number of Britons killed by German bombs equaling "the number of lakes in Wisconsin." In her high school years, she'd known young men who'd died in World War I: legalized murder (as Bernard Shaw called war) had been a major factor in her life and art. But "[w]ar is more than a theme or subject for modern writers," says critic M. L. Rosenthal. "It is a condition of consciousness, a destructive fact that explodes within the literature as without it. Just because the fact is so grossly obvious, we are in danger of overlooking its omnipresence."

Lorine and Zukofsky had been waiting impatiently for Decker to fulfill his side of the bargain. In March 1946 she found a packet in her father's mailbox. Opening it, she held in her hands a small volume of fifty pages bound in chestnut-colored boards and stamped in gilt: *New Goose by Lorine Niedecker*.

Eighteen years after the publication of her poem "Transitions," here was her first book.

Most of the forty-one poems deal with poverty: threadbare coats, impoverished farmers and sharecroppers, charming destitute woman, cheated farmers and cheating stockbrokers, Audubon jailed for debt, Van Gogh faint with hunger. Written largely during Depression years, *New Goose*—though Niedecker is never an obviously angry poet—sticks it to the rich.

She is a radical, a Prol, a Marxist (though in her *Handbook* she writes that left-wing communism is an "infantile disorder"): a carp-seiner's daughter. Yet her mother's family owned property, could be counted among the Haves. And Niedecker herself never considered herself "down among the people." Why her intense sympathy for the down and out?

She'd seen Henry dissipate Kunz money and property. She'd watched Daisy break her back for no reward at all. As a girl she'd worn for seven years one dress for town, one faded blue-striped for home. In high school she'd been rejected by the clique whose fathers were doctors, dentists, merchants. She had been influenced by Zukofsky and his leftist friends. Most of all she was an artist plying a trade that paid nothing. She felt one with poets in garrets, Mozart dancing in his rooms to keep warm, Van Gogh faint with hunger in the dunes.

Zukofsky excused himself from reviewing *New Goose*. He did, however, suggest that she send Decker the following jacket copy: "She speaks and sings against all that's predatory in 'Mother Goose.' Whatever in it is still to be touched or felt she recreates for people today, to feel and touch in her—their—own way." Or "I read only two modern women poets Moore and Niedecker. One feels closer to Niedecker." He also advised her to give copies of *New Goose* to the New York Public Library and to Columbia, Harvard, and Yale universities since they probably wouldn't buy it. He praised her work as being in the finest realistic tradition and named twenty-four of forty-one poems favorites. The musicality of the poems particularly delighted him. But what he said didn't sell Lorine's poetry.

Although dismayed by Decker's careless mixing of light and bold face type, Lorine still sent *New Goose* to Charles Reznikoff. "I picked it up when I was tired and dispirited," he replied, "and put it down quite refreshed by the words and music. Decker has done a handsome job. And I hope the book gets many good notices—and sells." Reznikoff had inserted the *quite*: "good, quiet, cautious Rez."

William Carlos Williams did not qualify: "The book's a good one in the way I want books of poems to be good. It is good *poetry*. It is difficult and warm. It has a life to it." Lorine took the letter in stride. "Ten years ago such a letter would have sent me higher than the great blue heron. Guess now I've got my feet on bombed ground." Unfortunately, Williams did not review *New Goose* as he did *Anew* in the *New Quarterly of Poetry*: "This poetry is lyric in a way that we have hardly sensed at all for a century." Zukofsky's love poems "make love."

Poetry, however, liked Lorine better than Zukofsky. The reviewer attacks Zukofsky's "I walked out, before / 'Break of day,'" as a copy of Edna St. Vincent Millay's "I turned and looked another way." Though he calls Niedecker "of geographic interest," the reviewer admits more:

> Lorine Niedecker of Wisconsin in *New Goose* writes with comic strip precision of many objects both familiar and strange: wall-thermometers, paring knives, plaster of Paris deer heads, and spit-boxes. If you think of "little Jumping Joan" of original *Goose*, do not be deceived. Here is a poet with scope:
>
> > The brown muskrat, noiseless,
> > swims the white stream,
> > stretched out as if already
> > a woman's neck-piece.
> >
> > In Red Russia the Russians
> > at a mile a minute
> > pitch back Nazi wildmen
> > wearing women.
>
> Miss Niedecker composes ordinarily in rhymed quatrains, but she also makes good use of what, I suppose, is free if not blank verse.

Lorine wanted to send a copy of *New Goose* to Daisy Lieberman, but nobody knew where she'd gone. She did mail three copies to friends, writing to Florence Dollase: "A little book herewith. Since you are one of three to receive it in Fort I don't know if you should be puffed up or suspicious about something. I have to ask that it be kept mum—folks might put up a wall if they knew ('she writes poetry, queer bird etc. . . .') and I have to be among 'em to hear 'em talk so I can write some more! Believin as I do that poetry comes from the folk if it's to be vital and original."

New Goose did not sell as Reznikoff (who knew better) hoped it might, but it placed Niedecker within the contemporary poetry scene. (Later the hard-to-find poems would be mimeographed by admirers, read aloud, passed hand to hand.) But *New Goose* changed Lorine's domestic circumstances.

At Decker's acceptance of *New Goose*, Lorine went to her father. Though Daisy had been diagnosed in 1943 with chronic heart disease, she told him she could not be her nurse/companion any longer. She must live alone. She had been the fourth player in an embittered marriage too long. Her poetry came first.

Grandfather Charles Niedecker
and wife Emelia Schneider, 1870s
(courtesy of Dwight Foster Public
Library)

Theresa "Daisy" Kunz Niedecker,
ca. 1900 (courtesy of Hoard His-
torical Museum, Fort Atkinson,
Wis.)

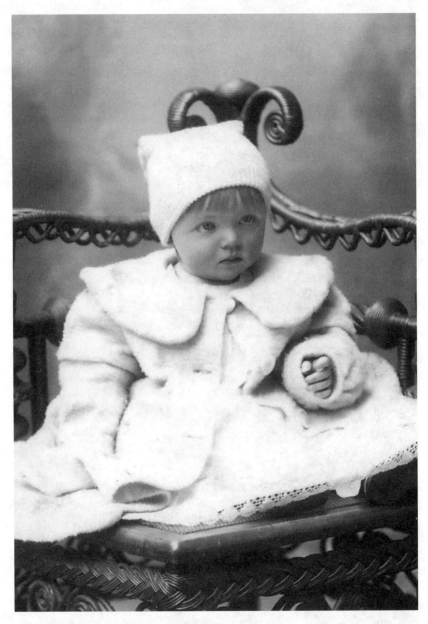

Lorine Faith Niedecker, 1904 (courtesy of Hoard Historical Museum, Fort Atkinson, Wis.)

Lorine Faith Niedecker, ca. 1909 (courtesy of Hoard Historical Museum, Fort Atkinson, Wis.)

Top: Florence Dollase and Lorine, schoolmates (courtesy of Hoard Historical Museum, Fort Atkinson, Wis.)

Bottom: Theresa Niedecker (*head of line*), ca. 1912: "My she was tall!" (courtesy of Hoard Historical Museum, Fort Atkinson, Wis.)

Top: Lorine and Henry Niedecker, 1912 (courtesy of Dwight Foster Public Library)

Bottom: Lorine at ten (courtesy of Hoard Historical Museum, Fort Atkinson, Wis.)

Lorine and her mother, ca. 1912 (courtesy of Hoard Historical Museum, Fort Atkinson, Wis.)

Henry Niedecker in his boat *The Idler* (courtesy of Dwight Foster Public Library)

Lorine on the banks of the Rock River, ca. 1917 (courtesy of Dwight Foster Public Library)

Top: Lorine as a teenager (courtesy of Hoard Historical Museum, Fort Atkinson, Wis.)

Right: Ernest Hartwig, admirer of Lorine and brother of her husband Frank (courtesy of Dwight Foster Public Library)

Lorine as high school graduate, 1922 (courtesy of Dwight Foster Public Library)

Lorine as Beloit College student, 1923 (courtesy of Dwight Foster Public Library)

Facing top: Lorine at Beloit, first row, second from right (courtesy of Beloit College Archives)

Facing bottom: Lorine back on Blackhawk Island, ca. 1925 (courtesy of Dwight Foster Public Library)

THE FORUM CLUB

OFFICERS

LILLIAN SPALLA	*President*
DORA KELLEY	*Vice-President*
LORINE NIEDECKER	*Secretary-Treasurer*

Frank Hartwig (*back row right*) and Lorine (*middle row center*) at Anna Ramsey's wedding, June 29, 1929 (courtesy of Hoard Historical Museum, Fort Atkinson, Wis.)

II

Changes

1946~1951

I'm not young / and I'm not free / but I've a house of my own / by
a willow tree.

"In moonlight lies"

Henry ordered a do-it-yourself log cabin from a catalogue and built
a home for Lorine on an acre lot with 180 feet of river frontage,
fire address W7309 Blackhawk Island Road. As a guard against flooding, he set the
one-room dwelling toward the road on fill and a cement base, seventy feet from
the river. At Lorine's request he painted the cabin a spring green. The cabin door
faced east. Four cement steps led up to a sturdy door sheltered by a small roof on
wood supports. Entering, one almost stumbled into a brick chimney to which a
space heater was attached. A miniscule kitchen to the right was equipped with a
double hotplate, a small sink with pump, and inadequate cupboards. Bookshelves
stood on either side of the north window and beneath the picture window that
looked west at trees and lake. A daybed with no headboard was jammed into the
northwest corner. A desk, Windsor chair, drop leaf table, and the mandatory cedar
hope chest completed the furnishings. Rare guests found it a charming, rustic,
interesting room. The bookcases under the west window contained the cherished
works: H.D.'s *Heliodora and Other Poems*, Marcus Aurelius, Francis Bacon's *Essays*
and the *New Atlantis*, Robert Burns, Henri Bergson, the complete poems of Blake,
Herrick and Donne, Mark Twain, D. H. Lawrence, T. S. Eliot. Lorine sewed
pillows and a tablecloth with uneven stitches in unmatching thread. She loved
sitting by her picture window as afternoon turned to dusk, a book in her hand,
and by moonlight. She often chanted her poems as music.

But comforts were minimal. Though she'd planned "in the air" for a pump, pipes, and "indoor terlut," she wound up with an outhouse. No telephone, of course. Still, she was elated to be a homeowner. She wrote Zukofsky: "Found three tiny shoots of red dogwood and transplanted them to my estate. Suzz. And they are staying alive despite the hot sun. Got a notion to put all the lower side of lawn into shrubs and trees so's not to have to mow it." Later Henry would put up a mailbox for her, a real sign of independence since she'd always used his. Lorine described the mailbox: "A huge one, big enough for a rabbit hutch. I'm thinking of living in it (aluminum) and putting my house out as a mail box. The name plate glows in the dark."

Though Zukofsky congratulated her on her new home and freedom, the urbanite must have been appalled: no plumbing, no running water, no phone. Coincidently, in late 1945 he and Celia had bought their first home, a four-story row house at 30 Willow Street in Brooklyn, made possible by Zuk's job writing technical manuals for Jordanoff Aviation. The Zukofskys may not have owned a car but they lived in civilization.

Henry's collaboration in Lorine's escape deepened an already tight bond. She made him noodle soup when he had all his teeth out and admired his care for the islanders during the March flood as he went from neighbor to neighbor helping them lay planks. Daisy tartly explained: "He's out soothing everybody today—an old soothe-see-er. I suppose they'll all decide to live on a little just because he's been to see 'em." Lorine herself got a lift to town and "bought a pair of hip boots—water here is 8 inches on the driveway. . . . With boots I can go to work every day."

Zukofsky knew how that delighted her. Hoard's had an active social program for its employees, but Lorine avoided picnics, the annual Most Beautiful Cow judging, Christmas parties, and after-work excursions to Club 26 south of town where older women taught the novices how to drink. She had made, however, a few friends.

"There were no regular coffee breaks, no lounge, you took a break when you went to the bathroom," said Nathalie Kaufman. "Nine or ten women would meet for fifteen-minute breaks morning and afternoon," remembers Charlotte Wendorf, "in a small room connected with the restroom. We might bring cookies or apples. Lorine never ate anything." During those furtive gatherings, the three got to know each other.

Nathalie wrote jokey poetry for Hoard parties. "I dabble in poetry," Lorine evaded. Nathalie suspected Lorine of more than dabbling: "She was very deep within herself." Charlotte knew Lorine wrote poetry, but "it was never mentioned."

"I loved her," said Charlotte. "She giggled and there was a sparkle in her eyes. She didn't initiate talk but if the women asked her anything she was quick to respond. She was a sweet, dear person—a butterfly or a bird. . . . She was never angry, never annoyed, never catty like some of the others."

Nathalie learned that Lorine could be annoyed and angry. Her ride into Fort Atkinson dropped her at Hoard's an hour before starting time, so she sat in the Blackhawk Hotel lobby reading the newspaper, "my spirit as dark and unshaven as the hotel night clerk looks." She hated reading audits (names and addresses of *Hoard's* subscribers) to Caroline Schuhlenecht, because it punished her eyes and because Caroline tapped out every word with her pencil. She hated carrying "my bundles of hog feeder price lists" to the print shop, where they mocked her as "Blondie"—even though friendly Cal Langholff from high school worked there as typesetter-in-chief. And she hated Cora Lohmaier. Nathalie would defend her friend against her persecutor: "Lorine *is* doing her job, Cora!" Despite Nathalie, Cal, and Caroline, work could be hell. "Disastrous week," she wrote Zukofsky, "—I can't oblige you to listen."

Sometimes it was all she could do to center herself after a day with Cora. She wrote Zukofsky:

> [A] great many things about her I can't tell—just wouldn't be believed. . . . [S]ocially unacceptable, taking a laxative and then f—ting all afternoon. . . . In the midst of that ordeal two weeks ago (proof room) I said to myself when I came home and saw a picture of the sora rail, "Only two or three things make the world": the bird, Robert Burns's poetry, silence and the child Paul. I wish now that suddenly my job would be taken away and I had to write prose for a living, that somebody would say, here, write on this subject.

Unsurprisingly, Lorine wrote little poetry between 1945 and 1948. Yes, the publication of *New Goose* and creating a new home occupied her; but the stress of working at Hoard's muted inspiration as well as stole time. Though in dreams she was still a poet: "I have a story, too, that unfolds & grows only in my dreams. . . . It never happens in waking life, only in dreams & while I'm adding to it in sleep I realize that I'm composing & think of myself as quite a genius. What a life!!" Awake she could be more certain: "My own mind is like a star that got to be one through no great effort of its own, just part of world stuff, and the light from it hasn't fallen on *me* yet. But I feel sumpn—oh yes, they can't take *that* away from me!"

One Hoard-related event did inspire a poem. Nathalie Kaufman invited Lorine to her wedding on June 19, 1948. Lorine had spent days before working on "a little marshy, soggy piece west of the house," cutting grass and planting willows, "my eyes to the green ground so much that I can almost feel sea-water in my veins." Reluctantly she pulled off her boots and put on her best dress to attend Nathalie's wedding at the First Methodist Church in Fort Atkinson. The church glowed with candles, the organist played "At Dawning" and "I Love You Truly," launching into the "Wedding March" as the bride appeared on her father's arm in a "fingertip veil of sheerest illusion" carrying a bouquet of white gladioli and stephanotis. Lorine watched as Nathalie—slender, glowing—pledged herself to amiable, good-looking Donald Yackels, who worked for the telephone company and had arranged a honeymoon in northern Wisconsin.

From marsh and Nathalie's wedding came a poem that years later Niedecker still considered one of her best:

> I rose from marsh mud,
> algae, equisetum, willows,
> sweet green, noisy
> birds and frogs
>
> to see her wed in the rich
> rich silence of the church,
> the little white slave-girl
> in her diamond fronds.
>
> In aisle and arch
> the satin secret collects.
> United for life to serve
> silver. Possessed.

Lorine amplified the experience for Zukofsky: "Saturday I arose from my primordial mud with bits of algae, equisetum, etc. . . . to attend an expensive church wedding. Whole of history went thru my head, a big step from algae to CHURCH (for some people there can be no procreation without the Church!), from cell division to the male sweating it out while the other collects International Sterling Silver and dons and takes off satins and [he] continues to sweat to pay for 'em. The little slave girl bride and the worse slave, her husband."

The text of "I rose from marsh mud" may be Lorine's evolutionary survey of sexual procreation from plant life to Church-sanctified human copulation, but its subtext is more explosive: the wedding that Lorine and Frank didn't have, the official union Zukofsky never proposed, her mother's drudging marriage, and, above all, the acquisitiveness of women—always personified by Gertrude Runke. Her 1953 poem "So you're married, young man, / to a woman's rich fads" again excoriates the wife who must have washers, dryers, deep-well cookers and bodice uplift while her husband works two jobs to support her. Niedecker lived without amenities as she lived without a husband's love. "I rose from marsh mud" coruscates with scorn for convention as well as pride in her own integrity.

Obviously, Lorine did not show the poem to Nathalie, who cherished Lorine's friendship as well as the scarf Lorine gave her as a wedding gift. Besides, Lorine *liked* Nathalie Kaufman. Jealousy may in part have motivated "I rose from marsh mud," created by the stark difference between their circumstances; yet the poem conveys Niedecker's antimaterialism rather than attacking Nathalie as an individual.

Though writing little, Lorine had the satisfaction of finding herself, along with Marianne Moore, in Zukofsky's 1948 *A Test of Poetry*—two women in a volume weighted by Homer, Virgil, Ovid, Catullus, Lucretius, Shakespeare, Chaucer, Burns, and William Carlos Williams. (Zukofsky intended to include Emily Dickinson but dropped her when her estate demanded a twenty-five-dollar fee.)

The test of poetry, says Zukofsky, "is the range of pleasure it affords as sight, sound, and intellection. . . . Writing presents the finished matter, *it does not comment*. . . . Condensation is more than half of composition. The rest is proper breathing, space, ease, grace. . . . A simple order of speech is an asset. . . . The emotional quality of good poetry is founded on exact observation which is often a combination of humor *plus* sense." Using these basic criteria, he tests a fascinating range of poetry, pinpointing repetition, empty rhetorical flourish, and lack of truthful emotion as acutely as he does a genuine poetic voice. Marianne Moore admired the poem he chose of Niedecker's:

> There's a better shine
> on the pendulum
> than is on my hair
> and many times
>
> .. ..
>
> I've seen it there.

Here in six memorable lines is sight, sound, intellection, exact observation, condensation, proper breathing, space, humor, and sense. A brass pendulum is more beautiful and enduring than her flesh, yet the poet avoids bathos. Though the crucial dots in line five count pendulum strokes as well as her life inexorably ticking away, the poet's spare, exact observation conveys stoicism, not self-pity.

Who, one might ask, was Zukofsky to put greats from Homer to William Carlos Williams under his microscope? In fact, his judgments are mostly dead-on. If some conclusions aren't new—everyone knows Robert Burns's English couplets don't compare to his Scots dialect poems—they are usually enlightening, and the range of poetry he tests resurrects many authentic masterpieces.

Lorine accompanied him every stage of the journey from writing to publishing the book she was sure he had written for her. When she finally had the volume in her hands, she responded: "Isn't it a beautiful little book????? Ah me, my dear little Test. [ ]." Her appreciative review appeared in Madison's *Capital Times*: "Zukofsky's arrangement is as clean in form as its criticism and the good examples of poetry it offers." She was undisturbed by Zukofsky's placing "There's a better shine" with three other poems of "recurrence" by Keats, Lord Herbert of Cherbury, and Shakespeare; her pre-feminist sensibility did not imagine that by doing so Zukofsky transformed it "into a poem which seems to confirm, from the mouth of a woman poet, that women are rightly depicted as dangerously seductive creatures of passion by the male poetic tradition."

Zukofsky's letters to Lorine were always about their poetry, often about real or imagined health problems, often about financial problems. But since October 22, 1943, he'd had an irresistible new topic.

Called Diddle, Dinty, or Diddy, Paul Zukofsky dominated his parents' lives from birth. Celia was the stricter parent, capable, when Diddle disobeyed, of bundling him in coat and hat and shoving him out into the dark street: "Go!" Zuk supported Celia when she told him about the incident but privately was appalled. He considered his day spoiled when he got home too late to tuck Diddle into bed. He was teaching Diddle to say *Lorine* instead of *Maurine*, the name of his nursery school teacher. He fretted about Diddle's colds and coughs, reported fondly his plaintive, "I'm tired, where can I sit?" He wrote a poem "To my baby Paul" and an essay, "Poetry, / For My Son When He Can Read." Little Paul had inherited Celia's gift and Louis's passion for music, and at three was enrolled in music classes. He might be a prodigy.

Lorine responded with such enthusiasm to Diddle, or the idea of Diddle, that it became clear she must come east to visit, particularly since they now had a house. They would also celebrate the publication of *New Goose* and *Anew*.

Only words after the fact survive about her visit to the Zukofskys in June 1947, as when Zuk tells her that at four and a half Diddle still has the same serious baby face as when she saw him, or when Lorine remembers how Paul "stood before his big map" asking her "what kind of boats" she had on Blackhawk Island. From subsequent letters, we know that Lorine took a plane to New York ("now that I've flown"), discovered how much of Zuk's poetry Celia was setting to music and how thoroughly they were a pair in promoting his work. She also learned about Zuk's break with his old friend Jerry Reisman in January that year, Celia saying only that Jerry and Louis had developed different interests.

Reisman had his own version of the split. Granted, he hadn't lived up to Zukofsky's expectations as a writer, but as founder of Techlit Consultants, he'd hired him in 1946 when Jordanoff Aviation folded. According to Reisman, Zukofsky was not grateful: "If you were *really* my friend, you'd use your money to publish my works"; "If you were *really* my friend, you'd give me half-interest in your company."

When business fell off sharply, Reisman had to let go both his brother Carl and Louis. Zukofsky didn't thank him for a bonus, warning, "If you ever sell the scenario [Reisman's *Ulysses*], I want half the money." According to Reisman, sexual quarrelling marked his last visit to Louis and Celia. Louis was scornful that Reisman was marrying his secretary, Josephine DeFrancisci. Celia was bitter he'd told Josephine he loved her: Louis had never said the words to *her*. (He had, in many poems.) "Louis lifted his head and stared at me. 'Don't you know Celia's in love with you?'" Reisman left, "sick at heart."

Reisman's future bitterness against Zukofsky questions his version of the break. Yet Zukofsky had a penchant for quarreling with friends. George Oppen was discussing the manuscript of his *Discrete Series* when Louis "turned with a quizzical expression" and asked, "Do you prefer your poetry to mine?" "Yes," said Oppen, and "the friendship was at a breaking point." (Oddly, Zukofsky did not quarrel with the fascist, anti-Semitic Pound.) According to both Oppen and Reisman, Zukofsky had to control everything within his reach.

It is possible that during this visit Lorine and Zukofsky went through her letters written between 1931 and 1941 and destroyed all but three fragments. Given his drive for control (and Celia), Zukofsky probably initiated the purge.

By 1948 poetry had returned to Lorine. She wrote Zukofsky: "I don't know how the old time poets did it—the poetic vein was the soft-spoken, hushed, sweet-worded kind of thing, almost artificial, but maybe in their time it was earthy enough for poetry . . . now I find when one hasn't been writing for awhile, you start off in something like that soft vein, but as soon as you get used to writing again, you pick up everything for poetry, get into everyday speech etc."

In "Regards to Mr. Glover" Lorine has recovered her genius for distilling poetry from plain speech, in this case that of her editor at Hoard's:

> Yes, I've lived a good life—cows, the soil—
> but what do we know for sure? Light from stars
> dead a billion years still pricks . . . see! . . .
> I can't conceive . . . let the cost of war out
> of it. You say each birthday you know more,
> better. Well. I don't. And I'm not stuck
> in that old stuff: cosmos versus puny
> man, God, no. What is life? (not always
> does one feel this intimate) My only
> fear: I'll go blind before I give
> the soil my phosphorus. And you, my friend,
> happy anniversary.

Zukofsky provided the title when he sent his "Regards to Mr. Glover." She also borrowed his use of "These are not my sentiments, / Only sometimes does one feel that intimate. / God, L.L.D." Lorine snatched at it: "Zu, could I use it and quote it? Maybe I should re-write the same idea, tho, because if yours becomes famous, there'll be the feeling of the joke about it??" Both Niedecker and Zukofsky could jealously guard lines, but Zuk did not object.

Lorine wrote, "Was shoveling snow the other morning at 5:30 when big round moon was almost setting—just like night, bright moonlight, lovely [ ]." The experience became a poem:

> Swept snow, Li Po,
> by dawn's 40-watt moon
> to the road that hies to office
> away from home.
>
> Tended my little oil-burning
> stove as one would a cow—
> She gave heat—till spring.
> River-marsh-frog-clatter—
> peace breaks out—

no fact is isolate—
grasses, heron, China,
days of light:
Saturday,
Sunday.

Four drafts later she deleted the last stanza and tightened stanza two:

Tended my brown little stove
as one would a cow—she gives heat.
Spring—marsh frog-clatter peace
    breaks out.

Though the "no fact is isolate" stanza is a poem in itself, she didn't keep it. Niedecker wanted no overt philosophy but an objective account of how snow gives way inevitably to spring and, after winter labor, peace—the eighth-century Chinese poet Li Po's style, in fact. The first two lines—"Swept snow, Li Po / by dawn's 40-watt moon" are among her loveliest. Lorine knew Li Po's "Drinking Alone by Moonlight," translated by Arthur Waley, her reason for invoking his name:

The moon, alas, is no drinker of wine;
Listless, my shadow creeps about at my side.
Yet with the moon as friend and the shadow as slave
I must make merry before Spring is spent.

The winter of 1949–50 was a hard one, lasting into early March. B. P. would come to the cabin "with a handkerchief tied over her face like she was going to commit a hold-up." One night Lorine "arrived home against a 50 mile icy west wind with a scarf tied over my face to find my oil barrel almost dry . . . and my cistern pump in the kitchen frozen. I looked in my drinking water pail and hardly a drop there so I turned around and went to the folks. . . . My house was 46 and I turned up the heat. . . . Supper was partaken with boots and scarf on."

Lorine was suffering not only the cold but the conditions at Hoard's, where she'd worked since May 1944. One day she'd "reared up" and "told them that either they give me a better place to sit afternoons when I type or I'll look for work somewhere else." She was seriously thinking of applying at the National Agricultural

Supply Company (NASCO): "Hoards has become a sweat shop with bad physical working conditions, each girl doing the work of two and no thanks and no raise in pay for over a year and a half."

But it was her eyes, not the sweatshop, that forced her to hand her resignation to A. J. Glover on June 14, 1950: "Good-bye to proof reading. Good-bye to a living." Six years of scanning fine print had caused nystagmus, a disease that involves rapid involuntary eye movement from side to side. In Lorine's case, nystagmus was combined with 80 percent vision. She applied for and began to receive disability payments drawn from President Truman's $41.9 billion budget for the fiscal year 1950; she went back to living on Henry's allowance of eighty dollars a month, and her small savings. From time to time Zukofsky sent five-dollar checks. "No, *don't* send me money," Lorine protested. "I'm eating off the folks and staying alive."

Hoard's inspired more poems than can be documented because the disenfranchised are a major theme of her poetry, and at Hoard's Lorine considered herself on the bottom rung:

> I'd never get anywhere
> because I'd never had suction,
> pull, you know, favor, drag,
> well-oiled protection.

"In the great snowfall before the bomb," "Regards to Mr. Glover" and "The elegant office girl" directly reflect her experience, which, had it not been for Cora Lohmaier, could have been positive. At least her job paid for her cabin.

Short of money, Lorine got a job at the Fort Atkinson library mending and shelving books. Phyllis Walsh, a coworker, remembers her well:

> Under the draconian head-librarian, Irene Metke, we were tense. I knew how much Lorine wished to avoid her, so I'd signal Metke's whereabouts when Lorine came in. She was a good worker, but with little training, had to perform menial jobs. I knew Lorine wrote poetry, but her friend Juanita Schreiner, also employed at the library, warned me that Lorine tolerated no discussion of her work. Once during a political campaign, I created a billboard saying, "VOTE—AFTER YOU THINK AND READ." Lorine approved. She was very up on world events, very pleasant with library patrons. Pity that lack of experience limited her job opportunities.

Irene Metke: here was another female dragon—like Alice Foster, like Cora Lohmaier—who made Lorine's work a torment. In the 1940s, women in positions of (relative) power often adopted the crudest male models of domination. Yet other women employees got along with Foster, Lohmaier, and Metke, while Lorine seethed. She did not take to female domination easily.

According to Lorine, Daisy had definitely "gone off her rocker." Henry had built a two-story house at W7265 Blackhawk Island Road. "Gert Runke helped the folks move—the whole thing a frightful nightmare to BP and she hasn't struck anywhere near normal since." This was in 1947, though deafness and her husband's infidelity might well have unhinged her mind a decade earlier. Now she was physically deteriorating as well. Since 1943 she had been treated by Dr. Notbohm for heart disease; in the last months of 1950 she was very unwell and, as Lorine saw, more than a little crazy. Sensing death and profit, Gertrude Runke played nice, sending over roast duck with dressing and gravy for Christmas dinner and presenting Daisy with a handmade quilt. By July 1951 mitral valve decomposition had become so advanced that she had difficulty breathing and was confined to bed. Heavily dosed with morphine and digitalis, she raved. Henry feared he'd have to commit her to the County Home for the old and insane. Instead, Jefferson Hospital admitted her.

Lorine described those last days to Zukofsky: "It was always amazing how clear she was, at that! You'd think she'd be sleeping and when Henry would pull out his watch to see if visiting hours were almost over, she'd say, 'Now don't sneak out.' One day she said in a frantic moment, 'Don't omit these visits up here.'" On July 25, at the end of visiting hours, Lorine and Henry rose to go. "Wash the floors," BP admonished, "wash the clothes and pull weeds." They were her last words to her daughter. She sat up, ate her supper, and fell back dead at 5:30 p.m.

Daisy's words sound harsh, but they came from a dying, mentally ill woman. Lorine caught her crazed panic in "Old Mother turns blue and from us":

> "It's a long day since last night.
>   Give me space. I need
> floors. Wash the floors, Lorine!—
>   wash clothes! Weed!"

They chose a "burnished brown metal casket for $646" (embalming included). Why, Lorine asked Nitardy's Funeral official, did they need a casket when they had a cement vault? "Well, people seem to want em—look at your automobiles." Henry told Lorine she was to get her mother's $3,000, after probate. She wildly considered splurging on a fur coat, yet was still job hunting through a Madison bureau (Zukofsky supplied a letter of recommendation) and babysitting for pin money.

The funeral was held on Saturday, July 28. Lorine told Louie: "[I]t wasn't hard for me to go through it because I kept thinking how music and church meant nothing to BP, she couldn't hear and never went out. She'd have got some satisfaction out of her name in the paper—obituary—and from watching the people who came to the funeral and how wonderful the flowers would have looked to her. As it was, she lay there looking not too much like herself, far from it all, noble at last, as unique as she was when she lived. Christian burial for a barbaric genius."

The barbaric genius, seventy-three, was buried in the new section of Union Cemetery, a quiet green slope not far from the country church where she had married Henry fifty years before. Though Henry spelled his name *Niedecker*, the stone carver engraved *Neidecker*. Henry didn't bother to have the stone changed.

The tone of Lorine's letter to Zukofsky about her mother's death is matter of fact, ironic, even cheerful. Yet the poems Theresa Niedecker inspired are uniformly tragic, depicting the fate of her frustrated, humiliated mother who "spent [her] life in nothing." Resentment, pity, sorrow, regret, wry admiration—these are the emotions Daisy inspired in her daughter. In the most moving poem, the image of a leaping deer mourns a Daisy who once was young, strong, graceful, and free:

> Dead
> she now lay deaf to death
>
> She could have grown a good rutabaga
> in the burial ground
>   and how she'd have loved these woods
>
> One of her pallbearers said I
>   like a dumfool followed a deer
> wanted to see her jump a fence—
>   never'd seen a deer jump a fence
>
> pretty thing
>   the way she runs

12

For Paul

1951–1953

made a Vivaldi sequence his, / better than I could have done with
poetry

                    "Understand me, dead is nothing"

Seeking a job less visually intensive, Lorine applied at Moe Light as a
switchboard operator. She turned the negative experience into a
poem and a short story, "Switchboard Girl." In the sleek office, interviewed
perfunctorily by the telephone girl as she plugs connections, Lorine casts herself
as a "September dandelion—forty, female—seeking a place among the young
fluorescent petunias." "I lost," says the narrator flatly. "'No natural aptitude.'"

Lorine was inexperienced; her high voice, too, may have counted against her.
Her rejection solidified a lively resentment against sexually attractive young
women. "The elegant office girl / is power-rigged," Lorine wrote. "She carries her
nylon hard-pointed / breast uplift / like parachutes / half-pulled." In other poems
she criticizes "the street's bare-legged young girls with their bottoms out," girls in
shorts on bicycles, the "little peet-tweet-pert girls" of summer—stark contrasts to
women like herself in threadbare coats armed with sharp umbrellas.

In her love story "The Evening's Automobiles," Lorine adopts the persona of a
man returning to his beloved island after twenty years of newspaper publishing. In
male guise, Lorine crucifies Cora Lohmaier's "desperate" singlehood, her "bitter,
obscene purity." Though the narrator is supposed to marry Norma ("Why is
it that women about to be married need a mineralogical fulfillment—silver,
diamond?"), he's enchanted by a woman with burning red hair who knocks at his

door carrying a basket of chicken and salad. After agreeing that they need never be familiar no matter how close they become, the young man says, "Let's sit here in the long afternoon and last." Summary simplifies a story that pits greed and waste against spontaneous love and solitude.

A former scriptwriter for WHA-Madison, Lorine also wrote a radio adaptation of William Faulkner's *As I Lay Dying* and a two-act play about William, Henry, and Alice James, who never ceased to fascinate her. *As I Lay Dying* is the more complete script; only a fragment remains of *Taste and Tenderness*, which she sent to Zukofsky in 1952 as a Valentine. He was tough on the play, advising a stick of dynamite to blow up the situation.

Did Henry mourn Daisy? Perhaps, if he remembered his old pal who helped tar nets and row boats; yet they'd parted long before. If possible, he became more sociable after his wife's death. Every day Lorine gave thanks for "a house of my own / by a willow tree": "Henry had another one of his big spreads—dinner for 10—baked ham with pineapple and cherries on it, cooked salt pork, baked beans, mince pie the filling cooked in wine . . . and every ten minutes all during the time from 5 o'clock to 2 am—drinks, highballs and beer. . . . Awful night, everybody looked so haggard as time wore on, as time poured away, Henry most of all but— oh well, it's over."

Withdrawing, Lorine stopped walking to the Point because "all the neighbors would tear their lace curtains trying to find out what I was up to." Henry's rentals confronted her with human nature at its worst. "We've been washing walls + floors in one of the cabins—some pigs lived there . . . and Circe never got around to changing 'em." In one house she'd found the bathroom in perfect condition but only because the family had been urinating in the kitchen sink.

Poetry and Zukofsky were her escape. "Ah that A-12! . . . This whole first part that you sent is another one of those deep things, organ sound etc. your good vein—it reads as though you bled for it which in fact you did. [ ]." But she was about to become enthralled by another Zukofsky.

Louis continued to report his son's endearing and remarkable feats, Lorine to marvel: "Paul with scarlet fever! Ye, gods, that child is sick often!" (like father, like son) . . . "I can always see Diddy at the piano, big eyes, lips out pronouncing, fingers" . . . "Diddy 47 inches tall . . . almost 4 feet. Thin as a rail! [ ]" . . . "does he write his name all by himself?—such a child, playing Mozart! I think of him all the time."

At five and a half, Paul had chosen the violin as his instrument. Zukofsky sent his homemade recordings of Bach's *Anna Magdalina Büchlein.* "Play those little records again, no sweeter music than the violin," Henry would say. Enchanted, Lorine tried to interest Paul in birds and wildflowers: "I mailed him wild flower books for your vacation [ ]. Wish I could talk with him. I'd tell him about the jewel weed that grows here and Joe Pye way up over your head by a little creek and we cut it in the fall and take it in the house for winter bouquet. And bindweed (morning glory) that I have to pull off the little trees and plants to keep them from being choked out and in a week's time they grow right back there again."

Paul as subject fired Lorine. Like all writers she was thinking of the next book. Why not poems "For Paul"?

Dissatisfied with her first attempt, "You have power politics, Paul," she reworked that poem into "Lugubre for a child," which ends with Paul's violin as a force against humanity's destructiveness:

> Dear fiddler: you'll carry
> a counter that sings
> when man sprays
>   rays
> on small whirring things.

Between 1949 and 1953, Lorine wrote and rewrote approximately fifty poems about and for Paul, deciding to group them chronologically and finishing groups VII and VIII in late 1953. Considering that she was writing other poems as well, these were intensely creative, driven years. Indeed, Paul Zukofsky became an obsession, on the deepest level perhaps a substitute for her aborted twins and motherhood. Much of his attraction was that he was musically gifted. If Zu's child had been a chess or math prodigy, she probably wouldn't have felt such a bond. After all, the original Greek *mousai* were goddesses of music and poetry.

But Paul was also a member of an exclusive ("holy trinity") family she needed to be part of. She and "the Zookies" exchanged family news. Louis was fond of Henry, amused by accounts of BP, inquired about her parents often, and wrote Lorine tenderly when Daisy died. Henry followed Paul's doings, "beaming with pride" when the six-year-old played on the radio. Lorine, Paul, and Celia exchanged letters. "When I get a letter from you I wait for a good moment in the big chair when I am composed (I *prepare* for youse)," Lorine wrote Zuk, "but when it's one from Celia I know it's MOMENTOUS and full of surprises and I tear it open immejiate."

Under parental supervision, Paul printed letter after letter thanking Lorine for presents; she would still be sending him "birthday bucks" in 1964. (When Mary

Oppen learned that Lorine regularly sent the Zukofskys money, which they accepted, she was appalled.) They exchanged Valentines, Christmas cards, and gifts—money, nylons, bits of jewelry, phonograph records, gifts of cloth for Lorine to sew, books until Zuk cried "No more!" Lorine sent fruitcake, branches of orange-berried bittersweet, handmade quilts or pillows. (Louis once wrote of coming home exhausted from teaching at the Brooklyn Polytechnic until—shown a pillow Lorine had made for them—he felt all his cares fall away.) Lorine actually dared to call Paul "that little mainspring of our lives." *Our* lives, not just the Zukofskys'.

The private Zukofsky could hardly object to Lorine writing about Paul since he was feeding her material regularly—inviting her, really, to use it, since they both incorporated letters into their work.

He paid, however, strict attention to the *For Paul* poems. After all, Paul was *his* subject: he was currently working on a Paul-inspired novel, *The Adventures of Little Baron Snork*, and had used Paul and violin themes in "A"-12. Besides, both he and Lorine were highly possessive of their words. He speculated how future scholars would sweat over who had first owned an idea or a line; both wrote "copyright" in margins of letters. "Yes, we take things from each other [ ]," agreed Lorine, "if it's from anything you've written in poetry I'm apt to do it unconsciously." However, Lorine was very aware of Zukofsky's watchfulness and sent him draft after draft of *For Paul* poems for suggestions, ignoring them less than usual.

In earlier *For Paul* poems she avoids her folk-tone, using a more elevated style appropriate for addressing an icon:

> Child at your mountain-height—
> your cello and bow in Easter's
> high, lovely, light,
> climb this one, tone feaster.

Other poems address "Paul / now six years old," "the child with bigger stiller eyes than sora's," Paul "at six and a half," Paul "now old enough to read," Paul who's "reading Twelfth Night / all Viola said," "Dear Paul," and "Master Paul." Zukofsky approved this style. But Paul was also a kid who liked jokes and nonsense. What to say when Lorine explained that his last letter had prompted her "to descend practically to doggerel. . . . Dare I use it FOR PAUL?":

> The slip of a girl-announcer:
> Now we hear

Baxtacota in D Minor
played by a boy who's terrific.

This saxy Age.
Bach, you see, is in Dakota
but don't belittle her,
she'll take you where you want to go ta.

In fact, both Louis and Celia were hyper-serious with Paul, who wanted to play baseball, swear, hang out with peers. Celia was the more repressive; at one point Louis felt ready to let Paul give up the violin and just *live*. But even Louis complained how they struggled to get him to practice, how he'd rather play games than read the *Iliad*. How exhausted they both were after a day with the often difficult prodigy (once, expecting reverent silence, Paul exploded at classmates who sang along to his playing of "Home on the Range"), how much Paul cost them in lessons, violins, and good suits for performances.

Here was another reason to resent Lorine's Paul poems: *they* were the pelican parents dipping beaks into their own breast-blood to feed genius. Louis went without lunch; Celia sold her Persian lamb coat for eighty dollars. What right to their child had Lorine? Difficult to share their son to the extent that Lorine craved.

Lorine was writing about other subjects—her mother's death, for example (five poems in 1951), and a tribute to favorite poets:

If I were a bird
I'd be a dainty contained cool
Greek figurette
on a morning shore—
H.D.

I'd flitter and feed and delouse myself
close to Williams' house
and his kind eyes

I'd be a never-museumed tinted glass
breakable from the shelves of Marianne Moore.

On Stevens' fictive sibilant hibiscus flower
I'd poise myself, a cuckoo, flamingo-pink.

I'd plunge the depths with Zukofsky
and all that means—stirred earth,
cut sky, organ-sounding, resounding
anew, anew.

I'd prick the sand in cunning, lean,
Cummings irony, a little drunk dead sober.
Man, that walk down the beach!

I'd sit on a quiet fence
and sing a quiet thing: sincere, sincere.
And that would be Reznikoff.

If Lorine had not been a southern Wisconsin marsh bird, she might have flown into the spheres of these poets and become part of the flock, although "I can't imagine myself in the same room with M[arianne] M[oore]! But I feel she's much warmer than her poetry."

As always, the island asserted itself. It was a deadly thirty-eight below zero one winter night. Lorine whipped up Henry's favorite buckwheat cakes for breakfast the next morning and stored the bowl "on top shelf of my bookshelves—on the floor it would turn to ice. The other day when it was terribly windy I took a book down and through the space where it was came the cold wind! And it's all settled in my hip."

Floods came in spring 1952. Her cabin became an island. Lorine's sheepskin coat registered the high-water mark as she waded to Henry's to help him bail out his first floor. As the flood receded, she could hear carp thrashing their tails as they chewed her banks. By November that year, after ten weeks of drought, "I wake up at night and go from window to window looking for signs of fire. You'd think the wind rubbing two things together would do it or birds' wings wd. ignite the straw weeds. I've put a few treasures in a drawer next my head so I can run out with 'em if necessary—yr. books of poetry and mine and the Jameses, deed to my house, insurance policy, etc. The only other things wd. be my typewriter and my fur coat [ ]. Suzz . . . it *must* snow or rain pretty soon."

She was looking for work, any kind of work. A couple offered her sixty dollars a month to sit two girls, four and eight, "excitable children, both cross-eyed [ ], tom boyish, hair hanging in unwashed strings, seldom wear anything but overalls. . . . The thing is sleeping there all night." No, she was too squeamish. She did try sitting an infant for thirty-five cents an hour. Fifteen minutes before the parents returned, the baby woke up—"he wouldn't take the bottle lying flat and I suppose in time it would have dawned on me to pick him up!—she burped him, that wouldn't have occurred to me. I was afraid to pin the diaper close and he kicked off his boot all the time and I was afraid to tie it on *tight*. . . . They gave me $2.00 and I only took $1. because I was just learning . . . and besides one hates to take money from neighbors as I ride with all of them at various times."

Despite babysitting, *For Paul*, the prose pieces, battling the island, and trying to find work in Madison, she managed intensive reading: Einstein (one day her radio announced that Einstein had discovered *relatives*), Henry James, biographies of the Jameses and Jane Carlyle, Boris Pasternak, Logan Pearsall Smith, Santayana, Spengler's *Decline of the West*, Goethe. "I don't think I've read anything that ever got to me more," she wrote Zuk, citing Goethe's "Against the great superiority of another, there is no remedy but love." Love, then, was her remedy against Zukofsky.

She also followed current events during these nightmare cold war years when Senator Joe McCarthy of the five-o'clock shadow was persecuting "Communist sympathizers" across the country: "I see they're trying to smear our Robert Oppenheimer.—I've never felt the times to be so dark, so ignorant as these."

Though he critiqued Lorine's *For Paul* poems rigorously, Zukofsky generally repressed criticism of her project; and Lorine, innocent at first, dutifully informed him of plans and progress: "Have decided I must do something folky for the next section of For Paul. Only it's getting so you go almost anywhere for it but to the people—in their barbarity—no wonder I keep going to the birds and the animals." She reports that group III is about three and a half pages so far.

She sought an intimate relationship with Paul, sending him money, Audubon's *Birds of America*, the *Iliad*, courting him as a pal. She wrote: "Let me see what stories I can tell you from way out here in Wisconsin. The other morning when I went over to my father's house to do the sweeping, I cd see from the ash trays & the spitoon & the chairs huddled together that Henry—H. is my father— had had company the night before. It turned out that a salesman for tombstones had come after supper & stayed till 11 o'clock!"

Unfortunately, Lorine didn't know how to communicate with this child. She was hyper-folksy ("Hi, thar, fiddler-genius!"), apologetic, straining for laughs. Paul answered her politely (more politely than he addressed his parents), but he could be scornful. He teased his father about the Wisconsin hick until Louis suggested that she write Paul as she wrote him. He was right. Reading her letters to Paul, one feels uncomfortable for Lorine, who is trying too hard.

Gradually she began to sense in Zukofsky a reluctance, a possessiveness. She wasn't waiting to finish *For Paul* before submitting individual poems to journals. Her Madison WPA friend Edwin Honig, now editor of the *New Mexico Quarterly*, accepted *For Paul* (group I), and the often dilatory James Laughlin *For Paul: Group Two*. She was typing groups III, IV and V, hoping Mentor Books would take them.

Zukofsky was tracking. "Of course, Zu, I wouldn't send Group III out before you saw it—what do you think????" Lorine propitiated. "In my next letter I may send it to youz. It's the folk group, the American group, even! I'd like to end this group with one more very quiet piece (peas) and that'll be anudder Peaszee, 10 poems in it including the one not yet written." Tugging her forelock: "Remember the cooked pea pods in the Chinese restaurant the last time I was in NY? Ummmmmm."

Zukofsky was not "appeased." Lorine wrote him: "Well, Group III my god, what a time we're having—I've taken out whole stanzas now . . . doing a new poem either to end this group with or become the second one. . . . I have the feeling you don't quite get me these days [ ] I'm writing you too much and you are too busy."

Lorine grew more restive with Zukofsky's strictures as he grew more dubious about her use of Paul. "*Don't* look at my poems this week and maybe not next," she wrote him in September 1951. "You're on the run—so run carefully and wait for my stuff till your breath comes easily." His criticism of group V "[t]ook my breath away, your further corrections on poems, but I seize the light or mostly. [ ]."

Yet she never stops appreciating him. She forgets what poetry is like until she reads "A"-12, the *Canterbury Tales* of our time "only it's more than that." A letter is "TERRIFIC—enchanting, impossible, impassable, incomparable—I've read it three times." Tenderness, so often masked by goofy humor, leaps out: "Oh Zu, you wonderful Zu [ ] If you're laughing now then we're laughing together!"

On April 19, 1952, after years of heavy menstruation, deluging hot flashes, and hormone treatments, Lorine had a hysterectomy at the Fort Atkinson Hospital. She hadn't enough money to visit the Zukofskys in November at their invitation, but before going into hospital she typed a short note "To be opened in case of my death": "My personal belongings such as clothes and books and papers to Celia Zukofsky and her husband Louis Zukofsky. Also to them $3000 from the sale of my house and land, to be held by them for Paul Zukofsky or for all three in some educational or travel or publishing project. Notify Louis Zukofsky 30 Willow Street, Brooklyn, NY." She could not spell out more clearly how much she wanted to believe that the Zukofskys loved her.

13

Æneas

1953–1955

I saw young Aeneas / on the shore
"As I shook the dust"

Aware of Lorine's poverty—not enough money to visit Willow Street, only two thousand dollars in savings—Zukofsky appealed to the poet, critic, and Columbia University professor Mark Van Doren to recommend her for a National Institute Award. With Marianne Moore's backing, the institute awarded Lorine a "Writers' and Artists' Relief Fund" check for the two hundred dollars she'd asked for. The money reimbursed the two hundred dollars she'd paid the Press of James A. Decker for *New Goose*. The little she'd earned from *Poetry* she had spent mailing out poems. To date her earnings from poetry totaled zero.

A better thing happened to Lorine in 1953: Æneas McAllister. And to Æneas McAllister, Lorine.

In June 1953 Mona McAllister and her grown children Æneas, Mary, Jack, and James fled their increasingly dangerous south-side Chicago neighborhood to move into a house at W7263 Blackhawk Island Road that Henry Niedecker had built. He'd shown them the place in May. Wading through weeds shoulder high, they'd still liked his "nice, amiable smile" and the rural feel of the island, and bought the place on land contract. It wasn't long before Mona and Henry "were sort of keeping company" behind Gert's back.

Æneas (McAllister's pronunciation: *Eenus*) would be twenty-eight that July 19, twenty-two years younger than Lorine, who'd turned fifty in May. He'd joined the Army in 1943, served three years in the Pacific, suffered malaria, and was discharged in 1946. Æneas was tough and sensitive, with dark head and chest hair and sexy dark eyes. Though only high school educated, he was intelligent, an autodidact. His manner was breezy, confident; he talked well.

At first shy Lorine took little note of the new neighbors. Anyhow, her mind was on joining the Zukofskys on their thrifty summer holiday in Elizabethtown, Pennsylvania:

> People tell me it costs at least $10 to stay overnight in a hotel? My god. Wish I could omit hotel for at least one way of my trip. I believe, tho (I'll check all schedules in another week or two) that would mean I'd get to E. town about midnight and I'd hate to ask you to meet me or stay up to that hour. No! If I can take a bus out of Fort at midnight in order to take 8 something plane from Chicago I could get to E town around 7 at night, but don't know if I can manage midnight to town here—we'll see.

By August she was willing to postpone her trip until Christmas. A neighbor had introduced her to the McAllister clan.

The next day, Saturday, Æneas had Beethoven's *C Minor Piano Concerto* on the phonograph. Passing by on her daily walk to the point, Lorine heard the music. She paused, then hurried to the door and gave her rat-tat-tat that seemed to say "I don't want to bother you."

"Oh, do you like that kind of music?" She sat down without being invited, hands clasped to her chest.

"I can play it," Æneas said.

"'You can play it? Let me hear you play!"

Æneas turned off the phonograph. Self-taught, he sat down at his upright piano, flexed his fingers, and began the adagio: solemn chords developing into rolling cadences like rain meeting water, then subsiding into yearning harmonies.

At this moment the knot of "isolation thick unto impenetrability" in Lorine's chest began to dissolve.

"Oh, my, you're talented. Why aren't you on the concert stage?"

Besides the house piano, Æneas kept three uprights and a nickelodeon in the garage. He loved music the way Lorine loved music—not the way that Celia, a musician, and Paul, a violin prodigy, knew music. With the Zukofskys Lorine constantly stumbled, wondering how contrapuntal Bach could be played on the violin; wanting to buy Paul a silk handkerchief for his playing (*cotton*, Zuk informed her: didn't she know silk affected the tone?); offering to send Henry's old Stainer, to which Zukofsky replied that Paul had no use for a cheap violin. But after Æneas, Lorine only pretended remorse at falling for a pop classic like Beethoven's *C Minor Piano Concerto*:

> I'm ashamed to say it before you [ ]: but I've taken a sudden liking to Beethoven—give me a Beethoven piano concerto and I'll drop everything and all systems of thought for its duration. I want A. to hear Vivaldi's Four Seasons in Madison, too. He is partial to the harp. And then we want—he wants to buy a good boogie-woogie! Aren't we a mess?? Just so it's piano, you see. If Pauly is reading this, I'll get down on my knees and lay my face to the floor and salaam up and down with my arms and beg O Master, Master, forgive this low, low taste in me.

She loved being part of the McAllister mess.

Though the Zukofskys still commanded her attention, Little Diddle with his fiddle was no more. On February 23, 1953, nine-year-old Paul Zukofsky had made his public debut playing the first movement of Mozart's *Violin Concerto No. 3* at a New Haven Symphony youth concert. Lorine wrote the *New Haven Register* for copies of its three-page picture spread of the triumphant child prodigy; for that was now officially Paul's status.

She had also begun an essay called "The Poetry of Louis Zukofsky." Focusing on "A" (currently at two hundred pages in twelve movements), Lorine also addresses *55 Poems* and *Anew*: "A great deal of modern art and literature is tissue wrapping paper, not stuff that is tough. Zukofsky's stuff is tough. . . . Poets who reach out ahead of readers necessarily find themselves called obscure. A current of reality always exists in Zukofsky even if involved."

Niedecker's praise contains a complaint. Zukofsky's willful obscurity had always been the sticking point that kept her from completely admiring his work. Writing him, she'd say simply, "I don't get youse" or "'A' has never lived with me like your small poems." Considering Zukofsky's large output, her private list of favorites is short, including "Not the branches," "Anew, sun, to fire summer," "Catullus viii," the Paul parts of "A"-12, and three favorites she cited in her essay: "Celia's Birthday Poem," "And so till we have died," and "Hello, little leaves." Reflecting her own poetics, she calls these poems "at once objective and intimate, written, many of them, for members of the family and for friends," all of them "more or less subject to the order of Mozart's 'poetry must be the obedient daughter of music.'"

Meanwhile Zuk was weeding out her letters from 1944 to 1949, a stack more than two inches thick, along with remnants from their first decimation. At least she wouldn't have to face that job when she visited them, he told her. This time Zukofsky's weeding concerned a volume of collected letters, a project he was forced to drop when Pound and Basil Bunting refused inclusion.

In November Lorine was still making plans for visiting the Zukofskys: "Yes, a cab to Willow St. I have 3 hrs to spend in Chicago so will to go to Art Institute." But travel plans don't sound as important as her latest McAllister fling: "Friday night we played Chopin records at McAllisters and when it came to Chopin waltzes we danced! Families are wonderful! [ ]."

The McAllisters were fun, the Zukofskys serious. Well, Louis had been fun before Celia; after his marriage there was "a closing out of others, a bitterness, an un-generous spirit" incompatible with the Zukofsky who had liberated creativity in others. Louis himself complained that people dropped by only when they needed a touch of culture: nobody asked them over for *fun*. When the Zukofskys and the Oppens (reconciled) went to Mexico in 1959, George and Mary had the same complaint: Louie was engaging, Celia a wet blanket. When Lorine was thinking of a visit during Christmas 1952, Louis had warned her that they wouldn't be "fun." One poem survives from Lorine's 1953 Christmas visit, which, fun or not, was meat and drink to her. Paul, down with yet another heavy cold, recited his poem, "'Oh ivy green'":

> "Oh ivy green
> oh ivy green — "
> you spoke your poem
> as we walked a city terrace
> and said if you could hear — sneeze
> sneeze on the corner —
> Handel clean
> Christmas would be green
> Christmas would be cherished.

"She was stagnant when we found her," said Æneas, "like a sleeping beauty; we woke her up; we brought her into the present time."

Prince Æneas thought Lorine a pretty woman and, now that she was awake, "dynamic." He persuaded her to buy a Webcor hi-fi with twin speakers, for which she put down twenty-five dollars on installment; they split the cost of two LPs of Wilhelm Backhaus's Carnegie Hall concert that included Beethoven's *Les Adieux* and *Pathétique* sonatas. Mary McAllister drove them to Madison on weekends when Æneas was off work from James Manufacturing, dropping off the aesthetes to scour Patti's Music and used-book stores on State Street. At Lorine's suggestion, they both set her favorite Shakespeare sonnet, "When to the sessions of sweet silent thought," to music, Lorine in the key of C major, Æneas in D flat major. "I've had two revolutions in my life," she told Zukofsky, "—one when I first laid eyes on your writing and two when I read Shakespeare! Sonnets. Notice the evolution—first you, then 23 years later, Shakespeare!" Now it was Æneas, rather than Zukofsky, who made Sonnet 30 resonate: "But if the while I think on thee, dear friend, / All losses are restored and sorrows end."

Æneas had built his own telescope. He couldn't stargaze in summer because of mosquitoes (nor under full moon), so he scoped a lot in winter: "Cold! Fifteen degrees below zero and I'm out there shaking like a leaf." Lorine joined him a couple of times after midnight. "How can you look at stars after you've worked all day?" she'd complain, stamping small cold feet in boots. "Oh, I'm going in, I can't take it anymore!" More congenially, they danced to the McAllister phonograph, played Æneas's piano in the garage with gloves on in winter. Her cabin "was so pretty and cosy," said Æneas. "I loved to come there." They sat together evenings, Lorine "scribbling," Æneas listening to music. They read biographies of Beethoven and Chopin, discussed their lives. The Chopin inspired a neatly clever poem:

> To Aeneas who closed his piano
> to dig a well thru hard clay
> Chopin left notes like drops of water.
> Aeneas could play
>
> the Majorcan sickness, the boat on which pigs
> were kept awake by whips
> the woman Aurore
> the narrow sand-strips.
>
> "O Frederic, think of me digging below
> the surface—we are of one pitch and flow."

Æneas did indeed dig: the McAllisters had swiftly exhausted the well on their property. Lorine is fascinated by the contrast of the delicate, ailing Polish genius, composing notes like drops of water, and Æneas digging for water at the sand level (pun on George, Chopin's lover) with hands that are strong yet able to play. The miserable Majorca winter turned out to be one of Chopin's most productive periods; Æneas's well-digging a productive act. Comparing Æneas to Chopin, she romanticizes the self-taught amateur, hardly a crime. When she handed him the poem, Æneas was outraged.

"Lorine, you goddamn spelled my name wrong. The E is capitalized!"

"But what do you think of the *poem*?"

"I got nothin' to say about the poem."

Like Jerry Reisman, Æneas found Lorine passionate, witty, and surprisingly uninhibited. One night at the McAllisters, "snookered up on wine," she tried smoking. And, though she didn't really like TV, "Oh, how she would shriek and laugh" Saturday nights at Cid Caesar and *The Honeymooners*. (She censored the news: "I don't understand why we have to watch a *man* talk.") More fun were joy rides. Æneas would pull up the floorboards of his 1928 Chevy, pile everybody in, and tear up and down the Island. "Ænie, Ænie, don't drive so fast!" Lorine would scream, but "[s]he *liked* it."

Lorine didn't cook meals, she nibbled. Considering her bone-thin, Mona McAllister invited her on Sundays when she fixed big roasts with trimmings. The family also picked her up Friday nights for the Kohlman fish fry. In the restaurant Æneas would plunk down on a chair in his billed cap. "When you going to take off your hat?" "After I get my beer." Lorine would grab his hat and sit on it.

One winter evening Æneas went to Lorine's cabin to find her huddled in bed in scarf, jacket, and three pairs of socks. "I don't have any money to fill the oil tank," Lorine chattered. He repaired and filled her tank, not just once but, at Mona's insistence, whenever it was empty. "I've never felt so warm in my life!" Lorine would say. "I can't understand that oil! Sometimes it seems to last all winter." He was not only appalled at her poverty, he was courting her.

Æneas revealed, "I was a half-assed lover of hers, but that didn't last long. . . . What happened was she sat on my lap one evening, while listening to music and we hugged and kissed and one thing led to another. But next day we both felt embarrassed and only kissed and hugged from then on. . . . I guess our age difference hobbled us."

Equally conscious of the years that separated them, Lorine controlled her feelings for Æneas, yet she wanted to love and be loved. In 1951 she'd written, "How I wish / I had someone to give / this pretty thing to / who'd keep it—/ something of me / would shape." Now she wrote of sexual time relentlessly passing:

> Woman in middle life
> raises hot fears—
>
> a few cool years after these
> then who'll remember

flash to black
I gleamed?

Yet because of Æneas, turning fifty-one was not the bleak event it might have been. After a birthday supper, the McAllisters presented her "with a box of candy tied with a sprig of real flowers (almond, I think) and all of them so lovely and we played Beethoven on A's phonograph . . . after all this and talking to Brooklyn I walked in the moonlight twice past my place before going in and stood in my back yard—shadows of trees almost all leafed out, lazy frog-sounds and not a sweet scent but a nice smell in the air (might be from orchard across the river). I'm happy tho 51."

In the spring of 1954 Henry, seventy-five, was suffering from heart problems. By June 26 he'd put himself under the care of Dr. Peter Majerus, founder of the first Fort Atkinson medical center. He moved to the second floor of his green and tan house on the river, and Æneas came over to chat while he smoked his pipe, to drink ErinBrew, and to spend the night. Æneas also protected him from the Runkes: "Trash, terrible people, bloodsuckers. My brother Jackie and I threatened to beat the Runkes into the ground if they didn't leave Henry alone."

Henry died at six a.m. on Wednesday, June 30. Æneas found him before he went to work. He notified Mona first, then Lorine, "who couldn't believe it. She came over, stood wringing her hands, looking at Henry, just saying 'Oh my, oh my' in a low voice." Seeing that Lorine couldn't cope, Mona took over but not before the Runkes tried to plunder.

"I found Henry in bed this morning dead," Lorine wrote Zukofsky the same day. "He has been sick for a week. McA's are wonderful in helping all they can. I'll try to sell the house he's been in but don't let this upset yr plan to come here."

Not the letter of a stricken daughter, though Lorine had loved her father. Neighbors Mr. and Mrs. Carl Hausz "recalled that Niedecker entered a period of withdrawal following her father's death." Æneas disagreed. She was "ticked off somewhat to have to be bothered about burial arrangements & selling the house & lawyers. . . . After things quieted down she was her old self again." Lorine's poetry is testimony that Henry's death did not haunt her like Daisy's. Henry had lived an outgoing life with no regrets. In "The graves" Niedecker likens Daisy to an armed thorn apple bush, her father to a serene catalpa tree, "his mind in the air." That airy mind burdened her with his business:

The death of my poor father
leaves debts
and two small houses.

To settle this estate
a thousand fees arise—
I enrich the law.

Before my own death is certified,
recorded, final judgement
judged

taxes taxed
I shall own a book
of old Chinese poems

and binoculars
to probe the river
trees.

She hated handling Henry's unfinished business because she felt inadequate to deal with despised property. She sold his house, worth much more, for $8,800. Æneas tried to talk her out of selling short, but "she was headstrong as all get out. Once she made up her mind, that was it."

Sublimating much of her anger over her father's betrayal of her mother, she focused her hatred on Gertrude Runke. Her poetry is charged with scorn for women like Gertrude, "hotly caring" for Henry's "purse petals falling." Henry the duped was forgivable.

Henry's death did not put off the Zukofskys, who were headed cross country, beginning with a visit to Ezra Pound, now in St. Elizabeths insane asylum in Washington. They came to Blackhawk Island in July that summer, staying for more than a week in Henry's house, which Lorine had scoured top to bottom. She'd asked Æneas to help her entertain the Zukofskys, and he tuned his best upright for Celia to use for accompanying Paul. In 1950 Paul had been admitted to the Julliard School of Music to study under the legendary Ivan Galamian. He practiced daily, enchanting Æneas as the notes poured forth, though clearly also wanting to be a kid and run free in this wild place. Æneas observed how much Lorine adored Paul; she couldn't help showing it. He didn't think Lorine "gave a hoot for Celia."

Æneas and the Zukofskys were immediately wary of each other. He found Zukofsky "a strange person," skeletal, bent forward, always in a suit and tie. Celia, "typical artist, hair drawn back in a bun," was also "very distant." In his opinion they were intellectual snobs who unforgivably snubbed Lorine, who appeared "down in the mouth" during their visit as "the holy trinity" made their exclusiveness felt. But then Æneas was hyper-conscious of his high school education.

Vulnerable after her father's death, Lorine was fine-tuned to the underlying tension. She felt loyalty to both Æneas and the Zukofskys, but her ties to Louis went far deeper, and he was her guest. She could not help contrasting this visit with the time he'd come to the island, with Jerry Reisman, and they had been lovers. And of course, Louis saw how close Lorine and Æneas had become.

Tension exploded the day Æneas took Paul ripping up the Rock in his boat, then cut the motor while they explored the far wild shore. They got into muck, had to scramble through bushes to shore: "I showed him small streams & creeks & climbed some easy trees & he howled with delight; you know what I mean—like a kid really enjoying himself. Then we heard Celia & Louis calling . . . COME BACK! COME BACK! HIS HANDS! HIS HANDS! . . . they were furious with me & kept us apart from then on. Paul was never out of their sight . . . and oh, boy, you'd thought I'd committed a sin, that was sacrilegious, for me to take that boy across that river."

"HIS HANDS, HIS HANDS!" could only widen the chasm between the Zukofskys and Lorine and Æneas, who'd been brought up on physical labor as the rule. Henry had once played the violin, but had to give it up because his hands, winter after winter, were glazed to the carp seines.

The Zukofskys' visit apparently bonded Lorine and Æneas. Shortly after they left, Æneas proposed marriage. At least Zukofsky, writing on July 19, indicates a proposal: "Don't know what to say about you and Ae—you know best." After the Paul episode, she could hardly expect either Zuk or Celia to endorse Æneas, yet she must have wished for a positive answer. Æneas gave her so much.

Yet there were drawbacks. The McAllisters were too gregarious for Lorine's taste and she often excused herself from their gatherings, preferring to eat her own scraps and pore over Bergson, Walter Savage Landor, or Zukofsky's major new project, *Bottom: On Shakespeare*, which she offered to type. They were flashy, Mary dressing like a movie star—all her culture in her pearls; too much smoking, drinking, lavish spreads of food. Socially promiscuous—Æneas zooming up and down the river that summer pulling squealing girls on water skis. She was jealous, taunted him with "Eenie," which he hated. Then there were those times when they were together but she was intent on the poem shaping in her head. She would look up with unseeing eyes, lips moving, breathe "Aah!" write again. After a time, Æneas would nudge her arm: "Lorine?" Re-entering, she would shake herself. At times like these, she knew, he considered her strange. And there was his love for children, which she shared. But she could not have children.

He cared for her, but how durably? A single stanza, unpublished in her lifetime, expresses doubt that Æneas had the stamina for the long haul with a divorced woman twenty-two years his senior, not only in age but in the art of hard living:

> I don't know what wave he's on
> if he'll be slowed.
> Once was one extended his hand.
> I've lived on a bigger river—
> I present a load.

14

Blows

1955~1959

and now I must rake leaves / with nothing blowing / between your
house / and mine

"I've been away from poetry"

Lorine was knowledgeable and persistent about submitting her work for publication. In 1955 the *Quarterly Review of Literature* accepted her article on Zukofsky's poetry, as well as "For Paul: Child Violinist." Robert Creeley, the prolific young poet currently commuting between the Spanish island of Majorca and a teaching–editing post at Black Mountain College, accepted four poems for the *Black Mountain Review*: "She now lay deaf to death," "He built four houses," "In Europe they grow a new bean," and "As I shook the dust." Zukofsky thought it one of her best sequences. And she was corresponding with the novelist Edward Dahlberg, who had requested her work for a planned anthology: "I'm almost overcome, this would make my 6th publication in 10 years!" (Dahlberg's anthology fell through.)

But good little magazines didn't pay. Lorine worried about finances, her eyes, her indecision about Æneas. Henry's two rental houses burdened her, even when renters were congenial like Chuck and Doris Perkin and their son Butchie. Lorine "had a good heart," said Doris, a nurse at Fort Atkinson Hospital who shared a dread with her landlady. "She *hated* mice and when she caught one in a trap she would put on gloves and throw mouse and trap out the window." Other renters were nothing but trouble: a pregnant woman who didn't pay her rent, slobs after whom she had to clean up, people with barking dogs. Mary McAllister confronted her: "You don't get those dogs shut up and *bang* goes your ride to Fort Atkinson!"

Fearing another Depression, she wanted to sell until an islander advised her to keep her property for income: she could always give her cabin to the county when the time came. Social Security from years at Hoard's amounted to a hill of beans. A woman from the Madison disability office set up an eye exam, then said her eyes would have to be much worse to file for permanent disability. She desperately needed another job; income from the rental properties didn't pay her taxes let alone daily essentials, and there were Henry's debts.

Lorine wrote Zukofsky: "I'm all right [ ]. I take down not my Bible but Marcus Aurelius and follow up with Lucretius and Thoreau's Journal. . . . Was going to copy a page or two from Letters of Yeats for you but got started on a poem about my mother ['The Element Mother']—this is her birthday and the snow and Marcus Aurelius and my overloaded loneliness [ ] and it's a temptation to write like Yeats, a kind of mellifluous, lush overloading . . . but I must not."

But she did type pages of Yeats's letters for Zukofsky (the "Oirishman" repelled him), as she'd typed pages and pages of notes from books that her irrepressibly curious mind found fascinating. Yes, they were mostly for herself, but making carbons was tedious and costly to mail, and she often typed things like information about Yehudi Menuhin she thought he'd like. She had also typed his manuscripts and now was urging him to let her type his *Bottom: On Shakespeare*. And she kept sending the Zukofskys money, which, Zuk said, they used for an occasional movie and dinner.

The more he became unwilling to endorse her *For Paul* poems, the more restive Zukofsky became. Why *should* she type fifteen and a half pages of notes, then tell him her eyes are too bad to watch Kabuki on TV! And though she loves sending money that Paul loves to get, *she should not*. Presumably he did not tear up her checks, even the ones she sent to him and Celia, because he thought she'd be hurt.

Æneas was still in the picture: "He brought over last night some new records—Chopin's Etudes (o exquisite—there need not be anything else in the world for me—just let me have a phonograph before I turn over my body and soul to the county!) and a Mozart piano concerto—also Beethoven's Kreutzer sonata but I must someday get a better violinist for that—I'll wait for PZ. on record."

It had been almost a decade since the publication of *New Goose* in 1946. "[W]hat the hell is the correct name of that woman living in Wisconsin, I think, 'Loreen Nedicker,' or something like that?" William Carlos Williams wrote Zukofsky. "She used to write some damned good Objectivist poems, had a small book of them published. Her name, please—you are the only one who will remember it." Lorine knew that publishing *For Paul* was crucial but she was still battling Zukofsky.

"Now Zu, the last poem in this group you may frown on but I was only trying to be honest. Remember that when you read it."

"They live a cool distance" praises the Zukofskys, with their "concise art," "intelligence in beauty," their lack of the surfeiting American comforts. Difficult to see what Zukofsky could object to in the poem, unless it was being written about at all. "At any rate," begged Lorine, "*don't* set it up between us."

She had abandoned the original eight groups of Paul poems and added twenty-five others (twelve about her parents) to the manuscript she sent Zukofsky in December 1956, requesting "No red penciling—indicate by letter what's wrong if anything is." She mused:

> Question in my mind as to order—don't like the ballads mixed up with the serious—might make headings of groups e.g. Ballads—(whatever to call the more personal-original ones)—(and the 5-liners with 2 words rhyming [did I create a new form or cremate?—influence of Haiku I suppose] which form I'll be using often from now on if you like it)
>
> *Should* the title be FOR PAUL?? Yes, I guess so. Nice if whenever it's printed, Paul's handwriting: AND I ACCEPT—PAUL. Suzz? If he does accept! !

In a "nice, nice letter," Zukofsky suggested cuts, omissions, and dividing the manuscript. Obeying this time, she mailed forty-one poems on December 12, 1956, to Jonathan Williams, Zukofsky's contact at the Black Mountain Press:

> Louie and Celia tell me you've been so kind as to glance at some of the poems enclosed: . . . I've tried to make a selection, thereby removing 18 or 20 from the collection Louie had. If necessary I could remove still more poems. The title *For Poem* [she means *Paul*] may not be best. Perhaps dedicate the book to Paul and use as title: *Forms* or even *Forms for Paul* or *Fellow Matter*. . . . I presume I could manage not too big a sum of money to help in the printing if subscription in my case seems unfeasable tho to spend more than $200 or $300 would be too difficult. . . . Testimonial from LZ—yes!

Twenty-seven-year-old Jonathan Williams, poet, publisher, photographer, aesthete, and founder of the Jargon Society Press, was a sympathetic reader for Niedecker. No lover of urban culture, he celebrated "what I could unearth and respect in the tall grass." Like Niedecker, his mission was "raising the common to grace" while paying "close attention to the earthy." He was a contradiction: perfect grooming and refined speech jarring with an irascible nature and a louche tongue. Long before Gay Pride, he proudly said he was gay.

Though Williams insisted on elegant bindings and quality type and paper, he had more taste than cash. He told Lorine he considered a foreword by Zukofsky essential to selling the book.

Zukofsky refused to write one. He explained that, in view of her article about him in the *Quarterly Review of Literature*, people would consider a testimonial to her poems "logrolling."

"I feel that I shouldn't go ahead with printing," Lorine wrote Williams. She gave reasons: Williams was going abroad, his Zukofsky book still wasn't published, she was short of money, and she hated to trouble Edward Dahlberg and William Carlos Williams for a testimonial. They could talk about publishing her another time: she was developing in the direction of "short Japanese-derived poems like *July, the waxwings* and *Old man who seined*." Perhaps in a year or two . . .

But Zuk's refusal was a blow. Nothing shows Niedecker's generous spirit more than her pleasure when Williams finally published Zukofsky's *Some Time* in 1957 after he had made her *For Paul* unpublishable: "Beautiful book, isn't it. . . . Let the world take heed." Jonathan had seen a great deal of the Zukofskys in these years and become especially important to Paul; but eventually Zukofsky would chill and the relationship became a disaster.

Williams tried to change Lorine's mind about her book, but she refused, hurt evident in her reply: "I'm involved in hot water heaters for my cottages, in drilling for a flowing well and in job hunting, the last named the greatest nightmare of all even when I find the job." She had no funds. She lamented: "Poetry is the most important thing in my life but if sometime someone would print it without asking me for any money I'd feel it would be important to someone else also. . . . You'll return my ms soon, please?—it would save my eyes to not copy it again. I enclosed 30 c stamps with it."

On November 30, 1956, at thirteen, Paul Zukofsky made his debut at Carnegie Hall. It was something like being published by the Press of James A. Decker: you joined excellent company but paid for the privilege—except this was New York privilege. Louis and Celia paid $1,800 for the hall; $100 for a Bachrach photograph; $120 for a suit, shoes, tie, and a Chesterfield winter coat for Paul. Zuk thought they might have to sell the house and take out a loan. Lorine, of course, sent money. James Laughlin sent more; the *steel* heart, said Zuk, forever bitter about not being published by *New Directions*, evidently could melt. He donned his old charcoal suit for the event, Celia wore hand-me-downs. After staying away from the Brooklyn Poly Tech all week, he was shaking backstage with the grippe when Paul went on. Bill and Floss Williams and the Reznikoffs were in the audience. (Ill, Marianne Moore canceled.) If Lorine hadn't sent so much money, she might have been there as well. She sent a wire that Louis received backstage.

Unlike his father, who wept when he played, Paul Zukofsky showed no emotion. Zuk sent Lorine reviews; she should ignore idiot critics who disliked Paul's deadpan manner; his son had been superb. Riding a wave of triumph, Paul wrote Lorine, quoting Kipling's *Just So*, which she'd given him: she'd better smile with "a smile that goes twice round your face."

Paradoxically, Paul's Carnegie Hall debut marked the end of Lorine's intense connection with him; intense, at least, on her part. She wrote him one last poem, "Violin Debut," with a provocative closing image of young Paul as something potentially lethal:

> Carnegie Hall, the great musicbox—
> lift the lid on the hard-working parts
> of the boy whose smooth power
> is saved—
>
> his tone and more: what he's done with his life
> —those two who sent the flow thru him have done—
> he's been true to himself, a knife
> behaved.

For Paul and Other Poems was essentially finished. Though her interest in him would continue during her lifetime, he had fulfilled the dazzling promise she'd imagined in her poetry, when she had thought of him as a fellow artist and surrogate son. Louis and Celia would half-heartedly invite her to future concerts, but she never saw Paul again.

Not only did he not endorse *For Paul* as she'd dared to hope, but Paul eventually repudiated the poems and turned against her. The *For Paul* poems, he said, "make me feel creepy." After Louis's death, he refused to let his father's letters to her be published, to allow Zukofsky's biographer to include her as more than a passing reference, or to allow her to be mentioned in a proposed volume of Zukofsky's selected letters. One hopes Lorine was spared the knowledge of Paul's total rejection; yet, uncannily, she had predicted it:

Paul, hello
        what do you know
Goodbye
        why

Lorine been looking for a job. Eyework being out of the question, on February 1, 1957, she reported to the red brick Fort Atkinson Hospital on Sherman Avenue as a cleaning lady in the Dietary Unit. (Daisy would have been grimly satisfied.) Mornings she rose at 5, left home at 6:15, returned at 5. She had to rely on neighbors for rides, or walk to town and back:

> I should draw a picture of myself covered with dust mops, pails, kitchen cleanser, cloths, broom etc. wondering where I am down those long halls past all those doors. Not really hard—the floor is, most important thing is to wear spongy soles. Arms and feet feel it. Noon hour not a working time but paid for it and given the meal so really 7 hrs. on time sheet. I take care of the dining room so far as cleaning but someone is always coming in to sit there and talk and I have to watch and wait till I can get back in to finish up before the next meal. Hospital convention bids me sit at table at coffee break in morning (15 min.) and at noon with other cleaning ladies—elderly cripples already drawing social security checks. . . . [E]veryone trembles a bit before and behind Miss Gobel, the Superintendent (and on Tuesday mornings I have to make her bed and dust her apartment—somethings observed as senseless as the stiff white caps on the nurses' heads. Pretty democratic system, tho, at that—office girls on easy terms with cleaning women, at least with me, but I dunt keer—what happens to me after I get home and a little rested and Sat. and Sun. is all that matters to me.

A few poets have been independently wealthy (Byron, Shelley) or supported by family (Christina Rossetti, Elizabeth Barrett Browning, Emily Dickinson—too "sheltered" to work). Most have been forced to earn a living as clerks and clerics, bank employees, doctors, critics, teachers, insurance company executives. Yet being a blue-collar cleaning woman did not shame Lorine. She wielded broom, mop, and rags with no sense of debasing herself. Work was work. A secret sustained her through the long weeks of physical labor and forced-friendly coffee breaks: "I think they know they have a cleaning woman who is a little different from the usual, but it wouldn't do the slightest good to show them how different."

As Lorine found a job, Æneas was laid off from James Manufacturing, which had closed its plants temporarily because "James are out to break the union." For Lorine (selfless again), the Zukofskys' plan to spend the summer in Europe was "the one bright spot in this dark cold spring and lost year anyhow." Lost, because her hospital job cut radically into poetry time.

There were still special moments with Æneas, such as the soft April night she saw shooting stars stain the sky and, through his telescope, Jupiter with "its three moons with a fourth peeking around from behind . . . frogs chirping as tho they were a part of the stars. Rails and gallinules all up and down the river, their funny little pealing noises." Still, it was now clear that they would only be friends. After the McAllisters' 1954 celebration of her birthday, she'd walked twice past her house before going in, savoring the night, happiness, potential. For her 1957 celebration, after fish-fry takeouts from Kohlmans', they "planted before me a tall cardboard box with Steinbach, Germany, written all over it . . . just a tall, highly decorated pink and blue and yellow thing the top of which goes round as the music plays Brahms' Lullaby. Nice little tinkly tune." A blow, having her passion for music reduced to a mechanical toy.

While the Zukofskys traveled in Europe, Lorine got as far as Madison, where she bought a volume of Chinese poetry, Gerard Manley Hopkins and Heinrich Heine—"so I get around." She also saw *Island in the Sun*, the 1957 movie based on Alec Waugh's novel about a West Indies island torn by racial strife. The plot was too familiar to be entertaining. Native Americans had been driven from her island long before, no question of a native uprising. But as a property owner, she dreaded selling to blacks because they put off other buyers, lowering value. She was aware of the hypocrisy of paying lip service to racial equality until confronted with financial reality, and "how dark" her capitulation must be:

> When brown folk lived a distance
> from my cottages my hand full of lilies
> went out to them
> from potted progressive principles.
>
> Now no one of my own hue will rent.
> I'll lose my horticultural bent.
>
> I'll lose more—how dark
> if to fight to keep my livelihood
> is to bleach brotherhood.

She was also reconsidering other "potted progressive principles." After reading the British poet and critic Herbert Read's declaration in the *Black Mountain Review* that "[t]he proletariat *is* the wall of ignorance, the army, that bears down upon us—their indifference," she decided that, in the 1930s and early 1940s, "I must have known this when I was wasting myself on action for the working people."

Lorine knew Marx's theory of class struggle. The proletariat fear the slave, the middle classes the proletariat. Caught between, the educated poor, like Niedecker, fear both middle and lower classes. She had never been comfortable with the bourgeoisie, nor with "the folk from whom all poetry flows, / and dreadfully much else"—though when she was a young dissenter her poetry had relied heavily on the latter. Yet she had always distinguished between folk with dignity and "white trash." People who park trailers, toss their garbage out the window, drive off. People who let their property run down. Casual weekend car drivers:

> Don't tell me property is sacred!
> Things that move, yes!—
> cars out rolling thru the country
> how they like to rest
>
> on me—beer cans and cellophane
> on my clean-mowed grounds.
> Whereas I'm quiet . . . I was born
> with eyes and a house.

Or

> People, people—
> ten dead ducks' feathers
> on beer can litter . . .
>   Winter
> will change all that.

Not really class issues here. Niedecker—nature lover, environmentalist, Daisy's clean daughter, no bearer of multiple children—resents an encroaching population that pollutes the land. Blackhawk Island had become touristy, trashy, trailer-ized. Now she fears "people, people"—mobs who invade her island to drink, speed on the river, murder wild birds and muskrats.

And she fears water:

There is always in the back of a buyer's mind: does water come over this land? With my new buyer from Chicago it's not negroes but floods. . . . I went to our Savings and Loan in Fort to ask what per cent the buyer had to have before that company would lend them the balance. The head man said: We no longer grant loans to anybody in that section. Because of the floods. I pointed out that the section was growing nevertheless, that in the last six years not a drop of water has come over the land. I think bankers and this very man turned down my father also and I understand now why he catered to them to get anything he could out of them—loans, notes. That's why we had banquets at our house and liquor when you could hardly find bread for the three of us. You live with the knowledge that this land where your life and your money are completely tied up is a lost cause and it must be kept secret otherwise you're totally sunk.

Compounding the problem, the Sportsmens Club of Mud Lake proposed erecting a dam, adding to the flood threat. Lorine went to a July 1958 meeting, complete with state biologist, engineer, and surveyor. "The Bible they thumb on Sundays in their pews is not open on Fridays," she wrote of hunters who mouthed the word *conservation*. "Conservation!—the killing of thousands of ducks each year by conservationists! The mud of civilization."

In six years, Lorine assured prospective buyers, not a drop of water had come over her land. She spoke too soon. "For pure orneriness this old winter of 1958–59 certainly takes the prize," announced the *Daily Jefferson County Union*. Heavy snows, freezing rain, nighttime temperatures plunging to thirty-two-below battered the area. While the McAllisters dragged kids on tires behind their Ford on the river, Lorine huddled next to her stove. Æneas came daily to coax her oil tank to flow.

In February, river-savvy folk saw that key ingredients for the Perfect Flood were locked in place. Record snows, thick ice on the Rock River, deep ground frost, and up to thirty inches of ice on Lake Koshkonong, blocking excess water from flowing out its exit channel. Wise ones murmured about the flood of '29.

On March 5, twenty additional inches of snow hit the area, on March 15 twelve more, drifting to six feet, the "Cruelest Blow of Long Winter." Marie Gobel, Fort Hospital Superintendant, thanked staff, police, and highway crews for keeping the hospital running. On March 20 there was another heavy snowstorm, yet the March 26 *DJCU* reported "No Real Flood Threat Seen."

By April 1, everyone knew they were in trouble. Rising nine more inches in hours, the Rock washed over its north bank retaining wall. "Hardest hit were residents of Black Hawk island south of the city . . . All but a few of the 560 residents reportedly left their homes Tuesday night to take refuge in Red Cross shelters."

Lorine refused to leave until, on April 3, the Rock rose another eight inches. Æneas and his brother Jackie motored over in their boat. Water lipped her doorsill; inside, water stood two inches deep. They raised her furniture on cement blocks and boards; let the rug go, she decided, since she couldn't take up the linoleum. While the motorboat churned at her door, she yelled, "Don't rip up my bushes!" as they tumbled her boxes into the boat:

> I was evacuated! . . . Water up to top of hip boots as I walked out of my yard. . . . Wind very high, grey high waves, I was glad to get out. . . . Disorder and leaving home—but I was thinking too with no time to write it down. Intense emotion generates thought like a coiled spring. And my thought: some day I'll leave this place for good.

She stayed in town with Roland and Maude Hartel at 210 McMillan Street. They were the kind of people "that have chicken almost every day and popcorn for snacks and take you car riding," though their bleating television assaulted her nerves. The Rock River crested on April 9, a disappointing (to some) three inches below the 1929 record. "If we don't get any high winds coming this way (east) for awhile," Alex Kohlman reported in the *Daily Union*, "we'll be all right here." Yet with water four feet deep, Lorine couldn't check on her cabin until Saturday, April 18. When she and Æneas opened the door she was horrified to find the cabin writhing with fish and worms. Next time she went back she "[t]ook a man along to get the tacked carpet and mat up—soaked and gooey and weighing a ton. . . . I have no other 'loss' except portable clothes closet . . . For awhile I'll use just wood floor with scatter rugs. Still have to get linoleum up off kitchen and bathroom floors. Left windows open (screens in) and stove burning on low. I'll get along! Next weekend if I can get this man again we'll have it ready to live in again. . . . O well, the place still stands!"

But the flood of 1959 was a blow she faced without Henry, "who bailed boats, houses," and Daisy, "who knew how to clean" out muddy houses with a hose. It washed away her soil, her plants, the runway to her shed, and her confidence that 1929 couldn't happen again. The flood persuaded her to sell the two small houses Henry had left her; it was trouble enough to maintain her own.

She was fortunate in the lawyer she chose to negotiate the sales. Frederick Hobe was intelligent and congenial, a member of the Toastmasters Club, and a singer who performed in local opera productions. Lorine impressed him as someone "very precise about what she wanted" yet at the same time "rather eccentric" and "a little bit flighty"; yet, as he got to know her, "Really, just a delightful person." He also drew up a new will, and again she left everything to the Zukofskys.

But selling houses on land contract wasn't the answer, because when buyers defaulted, she had to foreclose, further entangling her in legal business. With reason, she admitted that after the flood she never felt quite the same way about Blackhawk Island again.

There was another, personal blow. Æneas had become involved with his neighbor, Dorraine Regina Henze, a divorcée with children. Lorine had felt first in Æneas's life since 1953; no longer. When he and Dorraine married on September 17, 1960, she did not attend the wedding. Like the McAllisters, she considered Dorraine low-life, a waste of Æneas's gifts.

Yet, when Æneas visited in years to come, she would beam as she threw her arms around all three of his sons at once.

15

Lorine in Love

1959~1961

You are my friend—/ you bring me peaches / and the high bush
cranberry

"You are my friend—"

I
n touch with Jargon Press, Lorine sent money for its books:
Zukofsky's *Some Time*, Robert Duncan's letters, Denise Levertov's
Overland to the Islands, Charles Olson's *The Maximus Poems 11–22*, Robert
Creeley's *A Form of Women*. With *For Paul* on hold, it was small comfort that
Penny Poems contacted her on the recommendation of Gilbert Sorentino, editor
and publisher of *Neon* and future book editor for *Kulchur*: "I dunno, short poems
on letter paper with the letterhead Penny Poems. No pay, College towns." The
Chelsea Review also solicited: "Am I becoming fam*e*ous? Trouble is I haven't much
on hand—I'll have to *write* one of these days!"

Compared to her (for Niedecker) prolific output during the *For Paul* years,
only fifteen poems survive from 1957 to 1959. The joy of writing about Paul and
the close contact with Louie it brought had subsided. She *was* writing, but brief,
exceptionally disciplined work, as though in emotional rebound from the personal
intensity of *For Paul*. Influenced by Japanese *tanka*—five lines but without a
5-7-5-7-7 stress pattern—these are five-line poems punctuated by two rhymed or
near-rhymed words in lines three and four. "Linnaeus in Lapland" expands this
form into two stanzas:

Nothing worth noting
except an Andromeda

with quadrangular shoots—
        the boots
of the people

wet inside: they must swim
to church thru the floods
or be taxed—the blossoms
        from the bosoms
of the leaves

Neon published "Linnaeus" with four others in 1959. Her most famous poem in this form is "My friend tree," inspired by her decision to cut down five trees on her property. She sent Paul (who'd played again at Carnegie Hall in February 1959) a drawing of a treeman high in a big ash, straddling branches, working ropes and a gasoline saw: "I hail the sun and the moon. . . . But you do have a feeling about destroying a tree." That feeling informs a poem perfect of its kind, with the low vowel of *sun* asserting weight and longevity over the high front vowel of *tree* after the strategic pause created by *attend, friend*:

My friend tree
I sawed you down
but I must attend
an older friend
the sun

Lorine did not admire Japanese poetry unreservedly. She found *The Lacquer Box* by Shoson Yasuda "mostly dull—dull as Rexroth's Englished Jap verse, and a sameness ad infinitum. The cherry blossoms and ocean-waves and autumn forever and forever. Yasuda writes as tho he is unaware of Pound and recent movements. The Japanese should to go Pound for Jap. poetry!! (The translators should.)."

In 1959 Zukofsky's *"A"1-12* was published by Cid Corman, an American poet soon to move permanently to Kyoto, Japan, and the visionary editor of the poetry magazine *Origin*. Lorine had called *"A"1-12* "without any doubt the most important book of poetry in our time." Rereading now, however, she was struck by its opacity. "You are so difficult. [ ] But the glimmers I get will do it." (She was hardly alone in finding Zukofsky opaque. "Rather than fall in with the usual dead poetic patterns," Williams wrote him, "you prefer to be utterly unintelligible. In THAT you succeed admirably!") In contrast, she'd spent "a lovely day" reading Reznikoff's *Inscriptions: 1944–1956*: "I have always felt he was writing my poems for me only better."

The hospital increased Lorine's wages by twenty dollars per month, but now charged her for meals. Her income tax had soared from the sale of the two houses, though her flood loss claim from 1959 offset one payment. She lived with utmost frugality: Malt-o-Meal and a banana for supper, the purchase of snow boots in Madison a major event, any extra money going for books, LPs, and to the Zukofskys.

She and Nathalie Yackels were still friends, and Lorine sometimes stopped at her house after work to talk. Nathalie would give her a ride out to the island. Several times Lorine invited Nathalie to lunch with her two children, Claudia and Kim. Nathalie thought the cabin "cute and cozy—it looked like Lorine: small." Her kids were enchanted by Lorine's outhouse, and Lorine the kid-lover had games and cookies for them. Nathalie thought Lorine was "pretty happy" at the hospital.

There were good moments. One day Dennis O'Connor, a hospital equipment salesman and poetry lover, struck up a conversation in the hall with a small cleaning woman toting mop and pails. Sensing that she was special but needed drawing out, he expanded on poetry he'd loved in high school—Coleridge, Whitman, Wordsworth—and "the damn shame poets were paid so little for their work." The cleaning woman warmed, smiled. He never forgot her.

Dr. James Nora in obstetrics worked on his novel during a long labor, poetry during a short. "We nodded and talked only a little / —not wanting to intrude," he wrote of the "gray-haired woman / with the mop and pail" who smiled approval when he admitted he wrote poetry. He too did not forget her. "What I could have learned from you," he wrote in 1993, " —if only I had known: You are my ideal of a writer."

Betty Griffiths, a hospital gift shop volunteer, remembered how she willingly moved stock to facilitate Lorine's cleaning. Lorine's appreciation led to conversation; Betty asked Lorine to join her for lunch at the K & F Tea Room on North Main. Lorine was remarkably knowledgeable about Betty's alma mater, Rockford College: "the flood gates were opened!"

But those who thought they knew Lorine during her cleaning woman years did not. Lorine wrote Zukofsky, "The business of loneliness—the mind has to be sharp to keep one from getting uselessly involved just for the sake of a moment of less loneliness."

In 1960 Lorine met an old acquaintance who remembered "a small, thin girl" of fourteen with light hair and weak eyes. His name was Harold Hein. In his teens he'd come to Blackhawk Island summers to stay with his uncle Fred Bowen while his father worked on a degree at Madison. Lorine had lived with the Bowens. Harold had lost his wife Florence to cancer in 1954. He was now in Fort Atkinson to fish and research his family tree. He re-met Lorine, they shared memories, she offered to help with his research. He was a Milwaukee dentist, an educated man two years younger than she, born, coincidentally, on her birthday, May 12. They were immediately drawn to each other.

On Sunday, June 19, he called for her at her cabin and they drove south to Lake Koshkonong's mounds. Explained Harold:

> We climbed the hill, scaled a fence and found the Indians old camping ground. From the turtle mound we looked down into the distance as their sentinels did, seeing the lake spread before us, grand and silent. Sensing Lorine was anxious [sic] for this place, I let her lead, to perch upon a picnic table where we talked of many things. It was a magic place. We had the world to ourselves. And she was devilishly delighted to see the speed boats waving about the lake and none of their noise reaching us. After supper she said a secret thing, "a little dog's leg was warm with life." . . . After forty years we had another sunny day.

"I never laughed just previous to the time Harold came," Lorine wrote Zukofsky. "Just about the time you're rotting with seriousness or serious boredom, something happens or else you'd die. I laughed of course at some of your remarks in yr. letters but I mean with someone in the flesh!" In the months to come, as she wrote about Harold, Lorine's letters to Zukofsky changed, "becoming warmer, gentler, fuller— less tart, less staccato, less abbreviated." Like a flower exposed to unaccustomed light, she opened. She wrote the "Zukies":

> Well, I think it's going to be all right! [ ] He's very gentle, soul shines out of his eyes etc. He ate my dinner well, placing my chair for me at table and hovering while I momentarily dashed to the kitchen for something I'd forgotten. And *no church*—isn't it marvellous? Had been Episcopalian and too strict an upbringing. 1955 Buick car but won't buy a new one for "prestige value." We went to a big woody hill, beautiful sky, walked and walked and looked thru his powerful binocs. His birthday is same day as mine. Brought me roses. He'd been to Milw. library to read New Goose.

She discovered he'd been born in Horicon, Wisconsin, moving to Milwaukee when his father became a school principal there. They lived in South Milwaukee, then in Bay View, where he and his two brothers went to high school before going on to Marquette University. He graduated from the School of Dentistry in the late 1920s, set up an office at the corner of South Kinnickinnic and East Potter Avenues. He seldom mentioned his high-school sweetheart wife, Florence, except to say that after he'd almost gone broke paying for her illness, their circle of affluent friends had dropped him, killing forever his desire to mingle in "society." He didn't talk much about his love of landscape painting or his membership, since 1937, in the Milwaukee Men's Sketch Club. She did know he belonged to the Sons of the American Revolution and was intensely interested in genealogy.

Zukofsky welcomed her news of Harold—if *she* was content. Celia urged her to marry him. Lorine responded:

> Your letter—so nice. Yes, he's nice. At supper last Sun. we were talking about Milwaukee—things to see there, what it's noted for and I asked how far Whitnall Park is from the center of things. He mentioned the number of miles, not many. When his letter came it said he had phoned the two art galleries to get their hours open to the public and he said "Whitnall Park is always open." He remembers what I like and want and what he can do about it. He says "I'm a loafer at heart and should be able to fit some time into your vacation" (July 15–Aug 1). Insists on meeting me in Milw. to take me to the galleries and Whitnall Park. . . .
>
> A simple person with innate goodness. Sensitive, warm, warm-hearted, terribly lonely since his wife died 6 years ago. She was dying for 3 years—cancer. He spent a great deal of money on her and worked long hours to earn money and his new wealthy friends weren't the ones who came to the funeral or gave sympathy, it was the older friends, some from high school days. So he moved his office into the working class district and now has friends there.
>
> Seems to *know* painting. I haven't seen anything he's done.
> I'm so happy [ ].
> He's coming next Sun. . . .
> What can I count on? He's so genuine. I'll just take the hills, the present, for now.
> Celia is right—marry him—wonder when he'll ask me—

Zuk encouraged with restraint. If she was happy, he was happy. Lorine sent them a photo of Harold. Both Celia and Paul agreed he had something of Lorine's expression, and Zuk too could see a resemblance; perhaps it explained why their outings were so *sympathique*. Lorine challenged them to bet when he would propose. Louis demurred; he was not a betting man. She should relax, live in the moment. Yes, of course, marry him—if *she* liked. She confided that she was talking silently to Henry and Daisy about Harold. Zuk understood.

Harold came for three days the next weekend, staying overnight at the Black Hawk Hotel in Fort Atkinson. He brought her one of his abstract paintings. She was underwhelmed by "3 fishes, bright blue with chartreuse fins and some black and something like a tree with a fish in it that looks like a bird, all this on a bright reddish background and framed with a blonde-oak wood." But she hung it above her walnut drop-leaf table. He also brought her rich dirt for her flowers ("These things touch me so"), filled bad cracks in her poplars. It stormed Saturday, so Lorine took an art book from her shelves. Harold said things like "Look, those little objects—one brush touch—like Van Dyke's buttons—he always did them whitt, whitt!" For supper she made pancakes and sausages. Sunday morning he fished; Sunday noon "we went to a beautiful quiet place to eat called the Green Shutters in Whitewater"; that afternoon they stopped at an antique shop where he surreptitiously bought her a piece of chartreuse pottery she admired, then "we drove all around the lake, ending up in a pioneer cemetery where some of his ancestors lie, the stones being almost too worn to read the inscriptions." That evening the McAllisters gave them a ride on their new pontoon: "It's like going on water on a porch." Afterward, Mary whispered, "Say, I like that guy!"

She was so happy—and yet:

> He said he wants to come here—forever, probably, to see me, but has no definite plans to change his life, i.e. marriage not really in the picture. I in my weak indigestion stage, went to pieces, but he said his wife was sick six years and he feels used up and he wants friendship + has found it with me such as he never hoped to find. So what can I do but continue to see him and just accept it as my luck, my bad luck, no my good luck. As I recover my balance I find I look forward to seeing him again which will be in Milw. July 20 + he's the soul of generosity and goodness + will meet the bus and in all likelihood drive me home—and stay the rest of the week out here.

Planet-gazing at midnight Saturday, Lorine had had a severe attack of indigestion that forced her home to bed. Although she periodically had gall bladder problems, the indigestion she reported so often when with Harold may have reflected her frustration with their different agendas. She wanted commitment, marriage; thus far, he was content with friendship. Sexual frustration was tormenting: Harold lingering until after midnight, then retreating to a hotel. "But I'm resolved to be happy," she concluded a long letter to Zukofsky, "altho I feel at times close to a nervous breakdown. [ ]."

Lorine "never wore anything important," but for the excursion to Milwaukee on July 20 she trimmed a hat with a rose band and made herself a rose-colored cape for a sheer navy dress lined with a cerise slip that glowed beneath. Her message was hardly subliminal. Though it was chilly with a brisk wind off the lake, she called it "o lovely day." They visited the Layton Art Gallery and the Milwaukee Art Museum with panoramic views of Lake Michigan. Harold expanded on a painting of an old man playing a cello that Lorine thought unrealistically lurid: "Well, skies aren't always blue, the water is colorless unless reflecting colors, a face can have green in it." After exploring the woods and flowers of five-hundred-acre Whitnall Park and passing a statue of the poet Robert Burns ("his face black from the weather—like a negro's but a man's a man for a' that!"), Harold drove her to his home at 340 Leanore Lane in the west suburb of Brookfield:

> His yard wonderful for a city lot—several young fruit trees bearing apples, pears, peaches etc. Raspberry and currant bushes, flowers blooming here and there. Small simple house with not much furnishing, early American, several corner cupboards throughout the house. Fireplace with antique cooking utensils, bellows etc. and running through the center of living room an old board from a table top on which he paints. Not too dirty considering he lives alone. No dust at all on the floors but after supper I washed dishes and worked awhile cleaning up his electric stove. He made package mix pancakes and fried bacon. . . . [F]rom now on . . . life is serene and I'm not worried, in fact quite happy, come what may.

Harold came the next weekend, again booking a hotel room. On Saturday they went to Madison so he could do research at the State Historical Society. After that they explored the museum, lunched, saw the short documentary *Goya, tiempo y recuerdo de una époch*, then walked through the Arboretum. On Sunday they fished, Lorine rowing or letting the boat drift.

The weekend of August 5 they drove to Kingston, fifty miles north of Madison on Clear Lake, where Harold's only child, Susan, and her husband, Gerard Fisher, were staying at his parents' cottage. "He said he told Susan he has a friend he'd like to take along and she said all right. Ah me, here it comes—wants me to belong to the family? So she can meet me. And pass judgment? She is pregnant, 26 years old. The young. But after all, she's Harold's daughter so must be O.K."

On August 20 they fished under the bridge at Indianford, a historic portage where the Rock River pours over a dam and splits around a willow island before merging again. It "sprinkled a little rain and we clambered over rocks to get under that bridge. I couldn't seem to negotiate the stones so he had to come back and lead me over 'em. After we got all set and I was holding a pole I realized I had forgotten my fishing license so he had to hold mine and his. No nibbles." Afterward he took her to dinner at Tibbie's, a popular, "knotty-piney" restaurant overlooking the river. On a wall he discovered a painting of an Indian battle scene done by the father of his wife's sister-in-law [the genealogist in action]; she discovered he liked the pop poet Edgar Guest. "Zukofsky's Test of Poetry for *you*, Harold Hein!" said Lorine.

"Come what may," poetry came.

Harold brought her his notes on Leonardo da Vinci; she read them eagerly and spilled her enthusiasm into a letter to Zukofsky. Leonardo had written, "Nothing can be loved or hated unless first we have knowledge of it. True and great love springs out of great knowledge and where you know little you can love but little or not at all." In capitals, Leonardo wrote "THE SUN DOES NOT LOVE." He said, "May it please the Lord, Light of all things, to lighten me so that I speak worthily of the light." Lorine discovered, delighted, that while painting "The Last Supper," Leonardo invented a sausage-grinding machine. "I was so fascinated I wrote a poem. . . . Closest to a love poem I ever writ":

> In Leonardo's light
> we questioned
>
> the sun does not love
> My hat
>
> attained
> the weight falls
>
> I am at rest
> You too
>
> hold a doctorate
> in Warmth

The poem expands in the context of the Leonardo notes. Light is enlightenment, and in that light, Lorine questions the truth of Leonardo's dictum that one cannot love without knowledge. She loves Harold, but how well, how deeply does she know him? They debate Leonardo's claim that the sun does not love. "My hat / attained / the weight falls" is cryptic; the poem's force comes from her admission that in Harold's sunny warmth her loneliness falls away and she knows rest. Significantly, she structures the poem in pairs of lines.

"You are my friend—" employs the five-line stanza form she began using in 1957:

> You are my friend—
> you bring me peaches
> and the high bush cranberry
> you carry
> my fishpole
>
> you water my worms
> you patch my boot
> with your mending kit
> nothing in it
> but my hand

Surely he was more than a friend? Though he lingered weekends at her cabin until after midnight, he chastely retreated to the Black Hawk Hotel to sleep. He was courtly, considerate, and warm, yet had not uttered the word *love.* He thoroughly enjoyed her company, yet talked about moving to California after he retired in five years. "He told me that right away at first," Lorine wrote Zukofsky, "but I counted on this coming winter when he can't get here too often to become lonely enough to revoke that decision or take me with him. And five years is a long time anyhow. I suppose I no longer count on his marrying me. All the doors have never been opened to me in my life but closing some of them has let more of something else into a few or into one or two and there'll be poetry and that's that."

Lorine wanted marital companionship, stability, and financial support that would give her time to write. And though she may not have been able to *count* on a proposal, she certainly didn't give up hope. How could she, when he came faithfully every weekend? They took a boat far out on Lake Koshkonong, then ate dinner at a tiny restaurant with miles of piers and sleek motor boats. He took her to a genealogical meeting in Madison, browsed in a bookshop while she shopped for paperbacks: D. H. Lawrence's *Etruscan Places, Selected Letters of Henry James,* Rilke's *Letters.* They drove through the countryside, "lovely soft fall day, and we stopped at the cemetery where my folks are buried. I said a few words silently to them—that I sold the places they left me at the best price I could, that I'm working, that I went thru a major flood but still like Blackhawk Island tho not quite so well as I used to, and that now Harold Hein comes to see me."

For Thanksgiving he took her to his elder brother's home in Glen Ellyn, a suburb of Chicago, where Frederick Hein was Director of Health for the American Medical Association. (Another test?): "Nice house in a section of ranch type and colonial houses." The family greeted them warmly at the door. Though they drove expensive cars, "show is not the usual thing with the Heins of Glen Ellyn. It's all education, science, teaching, family life. Quiet, well brought up family of three kids, the youngest just entering college. Even the big, beautiful Shepherd-collie dog barks quietly." Vera Hein, Fred's wife, brought out a bowl of punch "with not a drop of liquor in it"; she discovered that none of the Heins drank. They opened Japanese fortune sticks; they told her—she squinting at the small text—that she was to have a lovers' quarrel. Vera bustled in the kitchen, helped by Harold's daughter, Susan. Conversing in the living room, Lorine felt particularly drawn to the youngest boy, Owen, "who hears Callas and paints and has the face of an angel." A happy day.

After the holiday excitement she spent a contented Sunday alone washing clothes, cleaning house, ironing, and typing quotes on religion to add to the folder she'd made Harold of Dickinson and Zukofsky. That evening she wrote in her journal and to Zuk: "At 57 I have two people ED and LZ, after a lifetime, almost, of reading, and a handful of words by Santayana, Marcus Aurelius, Thoreau, Emerson, Leibniz, Plato. . . . I felt so well today. My name is Dinah-mo."

By December 18 Harold was in Florida: "A queer week end without Harold but I need the rest." She gave him his Christmas presents before he left: Zukofsky's *A Test of Poetry* and *Dear Theo*, Vincent Van Gogh's letters to his brother. She was alone on Christmas day when she wrote the poem "Come In":

> Education, kindness
> live here
> whose dog does not impose
>   her long nose
> and barks quietly.
>
> Serious wags its tail
> —they see us—
> from curtain tie-backs
>   no knick-knacks
> between us.

The poem would trouble her in form and content more than any of her *For Paul* poems. She wrestled with different versions. Should she send it out for publication? She thought not. Perhaps she might let Owen Hein see it? Her doubts reflected her doubts about Harold. He took her to meet his family. He came every weekend. He delighted in her company. Perverse that a relationship so rich and pleasurable to two lonely people should not lead to marriage.

16

My Friend Tree

1961~1962

Strangest thing happened . . . Ian Hamilton Finlay
Niedecker to Zukofsky

Harold returned from Florida laden with mineolas, tangelos, oranges, pecans, seashells, coral, jellies, cookies from his hosts, and "a large loosely organized Australian pine cone." He might as well have taken her with him. Lorine was most interested in the cone, wondering whether its architecture mirrored the shape of the conifer. She began to daydream:

> I'd like to go to Florida and take the bus trip there circling from Jacksonville south thru the lakes region—Bird Island on Orange Lake, Cypress Gardens, Lake Wales . . . because it is situated in a bird sanctuary—I've never seen the roseate spoonbill or the ibis . . . then Tarpon Springs, Tampa and down to Sarasota on the Gulf to the Art Museum in lovely surroundings, then across thru the Everglades to Miami (not that I especially want Miami) then up the coast on the ocean side to Palm Beach and Lake Worth and to St. Augustine, then back over to Jacksonville. . . . If Harold would take me with him when he drives down (next Xmas) and back I'd save money but he wouldn't do that, has seldom wavered from the conventional, not to the extent of 800 miles. No, I'll never take the trip anyhow. I'm surrounded by luscious Eastman colored folders of Florida and I'm reading books on it and Henry James and imagining and I'll have had it that way. . . . After all, my old

refrigerator might give out, need replacing, my oil heater likewise, or whatever, and I shouldn't spend the money traveling in a bus all over the state when what I'd want better would be to sit down somewhere there beside a sea and Harold to come and take me nearby.

She translated her longing into "Florida," a poem that begins

> Always north of him
> I see
>
> he's close
> to orange, flower
>
> roseate bird
> soft air
>
> the state
> I'm in

The new year, 1961, brought other offerings. In January she received a copy of *The Dancers Inherit the Party*, the Scots writer Ian Hamilton Finlay's first book of poetry. "*I* review it???" she backed off. "*No* but it will liberate poems in me, a half dozen of his will. Folk, wild, witty things. A few of his a trifle too weird for me." Still, she said, "Nothing in a long while has reached my particular kind of home like they have. Certainly one-third of them have simply set me free."

She shared Finlay's poetry with Harold, who liked only the Scotsman's fishing shack poems: "He was so disgusted with the four-line Christmas one called Bi-Lingual, he got what the umbrellas meant and by the time [we] got to the 'peedie Mary' poems we were in a gay mood." Harold had no ear for music, nor could he read a poem other than literally. Lorine was indulgent, gentling him along.

The new year also established a correspondence with Cid Corman. In 1960 Zukofsky had suggested she send "In Leonardo's light" and "Why do I press it: are you my friend?" to Corman for *Origin*, a magazine he'd founded as a forum for young and likely to be unheard poets. Though Corman had objections—"slight" and "too much written"—he accepted Niedecker's poems. "It gives me pleasure to appear with or 'against' the young," she wrote back. "I wondered if you would be interested in knowing which ones of all the poems I've written I consider my best." She enclosed "Old man who seined," "Paul," "I rose from marsh mud,"

"There's a better shine," and "The clothesline post is set." Three of these, she added pointedly, were from a manuscript ready for publication. Corman did not publish *For Paul*, but wrote Lorine "your quiet . . . your small things warm me."

She had found a friend who would become second only to Zukofsky; someone, moreover, who could publish her. "Cid *is* poetry," she wrote to Zuk; and to Corman after receiving a copy of his *for instance*: "You now inhabit a corner of my immortal cupboard with LZ (especially the short poems), Emily Dickinson, Thoreau, Lucretius, Marcus Aurelius, John Muir, bits from Santayana, D. H. Lawrence, Dahlberg, William Carlos Williams, and haiku."

Her correspondence with Corman would differ markedly from hers with Zukofsky. With Corman she was frank and friendly, with none of the teasing fondness, language play, goofy humor, or intimacies she shared with Zu. Unlike Zukofsky, Corman was always appreciative, accepting her poetry fait accompli. He allowed her to vent her frustrations with Zukofsky. And she could praise other poets to Corman.

Both Zukofsky and Corman claim to have brought Niedecker to Finlay's attention. Lorine sent Finlay more than twenty poems—"the first time I've written a fellow poet on my own initiative since that long ago time when I first wrote Louie Zukofsky." Finlay was "fair bowled over," as Lorine told Zukofsky: "Read the enclosed blue letter and fall over. Who is Jessie McGuffie? A name right out of the folk. What have I got to lose? But—one must be careful with whom one associates. Has she established a reputation, a good one or what kind of one—I don't suppose it's a band of outlaws. I've already typed 22, half of them from New Goose. A wee profit or a wee nothing, just I don't have to *pay*."

Much about the Scots connection puzzled her. Why must her poems be translated into Gaelic and broad Scots dialect—"Don't they read English over there?" What about copyright and permissions, since most poems had been published before? Would the press actually pay her? She proposed three titles: *Great Grass! Don't Shoot the Rail*, or *My Friend Tree*.

Most baffling of all was Finlay himself. Jessie McGuffie turned out to be an able manager and editor at Finlay's Wild Hawthorn Press in Edinburgh, but the thirty-six-year-old Finlay was a free spirit who had worked as a shepherd, wrote short stories, plays, and poetry, painted, drew, and crafted boats. (He would become famous for Little Sparta, the five-acre garden he created with other artists in the Pentland Hills south of Edinburgh.) Ruggedly handsome, with black hair and tufted eyebrows, he was given to quarreling violently with people, then throwing himself into their arms; writing high voltage, barely legible letters; committing himself to hospital because of agoraphobia. Though once admired by the reigning

Scots poet Hugh MacDiarmid, by 1965 MacDiarmid would refuse to be published in anthologies containing Finlay's Glaswegian poems, which he considered terrorist acts against traditional literary Scots.

Lorine pored over Finlay's communications with a magnifying glass. "I smiled when you said that a poet should have 'a pregnant intuition,'" wrote the Scot. "Yours and [Zukofsky's] poems are like gold to me. . . . You wouldn't be my sister or something would you—your poems are a delight." Finlay was currently developing a "concrete poetry," chiseling away syntax until only blocks of meaning remained. (Eventually he literally engraved his poetry into stone.) Small wonder he appreciated what Niedecker sent him from her condensery, though she admitted that for her "the sentence lies in wait—all those prepositions and connectives—like an early spring flood." She copied Finlay's letters for Zukofsky, begging him to return them "because I cdn't bear to try reading his writing again!"

On Finlay's request, she asked Zukofsky to write an introduction to her new book. She should have known better: Zukofsky had refused introductions for both *New Goose* and *For Paul.* He replied that he'd sworn off writing about other poets' work, refused a dozen requests, no longer wanted introductions to his own books, and was not thinking about poetry these days. Besides, Lorine's work could stand by itself. Still, it was a hurtful letter from a friend of thirty years who'd been helped enormously by the patronage of Pound and Williams and had written introductions for other poets. And to whom, in a new will made in 1960, Lorine still left all she possessed.

But then Zukofsky was still displeased by the *For Paul* poems, currently by "Now go to the party" published in *Origin* 2, a poem that describes "Master Paul Kung" dressed as Confucius in Celia's black silk dress with a "whisk brush for a beard." Poems based on such incidents, Zukofsky wrote to Corman testily, cannot survive *qua* poems because they are based on "sentiment of the affections." The real issue, however, was that his "A"-13, part 2, slated for *Origin* 3, also described Paul dressed as Confucius for a party. Lorine had anticipated him with material taken from *his* letter.

Lorine's response to Zukofsky's refusal was brief: "Dear Louie: No intro. and I have removed biog. note from the two For Paul poems to Jessie Mcg.—one said: For Paul, 5-year-old violinist, and the other: For Paul, musician, when he was five. But *removed* altho without these the poems can't very well stand."

In the past, Zukofsky had generously helped Lorine, connecting her with August Derleth, James Laughlin, Harriet Monroe, and Cid Corman; writing letters of recommendation; praising her to his colleagues. His support ended with *For Paul.*

Jessie McGuffie chose the title *My Friend Tree*. "[T]heir words and tone are 'fair smashing' and dashing," Lorine told Zuk, burying her hurt at his refusal, "tho both Jessie and Ian can be very serious I'm sure. . . . Where do they get the money??? . . . They let me make the selection for my book and it seems whatever I say goes."

Although Lorine was happy with the Wild Hawthorn Press, Harold Hein still tormented her. Five days before her fifty-eighth birthday, they had shared a spring afternoon:

> On the hill Sunday, wide view of the lake because foliage not yet thick. May flowers (little white things, not too attractive to my notion), buttercups—yellow, you know, glistening, freshest, coolest, cleanest sweet smell—and field sparrows, song that starts slow, then a rush and then ending with an empty dry seed-rattle. . . .
>
> He brought me a little round barometer for a birthday present. Gold and black center and polished brown-red wood on outside. . . . It doesn't want to leave *fair*!
>
> I have nerved myself to talk next time I see him. If I'm not to be his wife I have to turn back to my own kind of life with time in it (tho never enough) for reading, writing, sollytood. Hurts to know the truth but better so.

Before she gathered courage to have it out with him, they spent the beautiful spring together, Harold showing her where moist white trillium hid. They also vacationed in June, their companions Harold's fishing pal, William Koepke, a Milwaukee school principal, and his wife, Ome. The Koepkes owned a cottage on Little Star Lake near Manitowish Waters. Lorine's first taste of Wisconsin's north woods made Blackhawk Island seem almost urban:

> Yes, Manitowish Waters—o what glorious country! . . . Air is clear and clean up there, a chain of lakes one of them named Scattering Rice Lake. Birch woods, pines everlastingly, wild blackberries— and bears (Vilas County) and I saw a deer, beautiful thing, not too afraid of our car as we slowed almost to a halt, saw a porcupine, heard a loon etc. . . . Of course we froze at times—the second night I slept with my clothes on. Too windy and cold for Harold to go fishing so we drove miles and miles on those newly built hard-top roads thru endless woods, meeting maybe one car in three miles. We stopped in one place and our men rushed out to pick Calla of

the Swamp or Water Arum for us—greenish-white lilies with heart-shaped leaves.

The postponed talk finally took place Sunday evening, June 25, in Lorine's cabin, as Harold was ready to leave. No, he told her: he would never marry again. Yes, he still planned to retire to California to live with his brother. But they must not lose each other as friends. Miserable, Lorine agreed. However, she "told him I must have more time to myself, writing and just to build up something within myself as against the time when I'll be entirely alone again—he has a future . . . and I don't even know what I'll call home by that time. He said all right, less often, said I need have no fear, there'll be no other woman."

She rationalized Harold's refusal. He hadn't as much money as people thought, felt driven during the week, stayed up late reading or doing genealogy, was perpetually busy caring for other people. But she must have known the truth. Unless he'd promised his wife never to marry again, Harold Hein was too cautious, too conventional (and perhaps too undersexed) to commit himself permanently to a loving and gifted woman. The failure was not hers.

That week he wrote to say he wouldn't come next Sunday. "Dear Louie and Celia: Are you lonesome?" she wrote on the day. "I was yesterday when I got H's letter saying not coming out this week end." Now she felt foolish for speaking her mind frankly, yet she had had to *know* once and for all.

She missed him terribly: "Queer about time having to pass—if only I could *turn on a switch* this week of vacation, alone, interests that might as well shut out—but nerves don't quiet down so fast." Incoherence was followed by blunt fact: "Lonesome is such a physical thing."

To steady her nerves she talked to Zukofsky about books. She'd been reading Edward Dahlberg's and Herbert Read's *Truth Is More Sacred: A Critical Exchange on Modern Literature*. "Dahlberg at his best here—I think, tho rarely speaking well of anyone. But he knows words—earthy, wonderful, rich words—'cormorant' words!!'" Despite Dahlberg's black view of modern literature—"Poetry today has been sacked by pleasure and novelty just as Troy was by Helen"—she took comfort from his "There is no hurt that man or the earth can do to us that is not some advantage provided the words employed in telling it are not feeble." True, she wrote Zukofsky, and Henry James too had said, "*Use it*, the misery, set-backs."

She used her setback, comparing Harold to a "a large pine-spread"—upright, strong, fragrant, inviting yet impenetrable. Herself, she was "swamp"—floating, feminine, uninviting, yet "sworn to." The poem's last word, with its beat before utterance, has a terrible finality:

The men leave the car
to bring us green-white lilies
    by woods
These men are our woods
yet I grieve

I'm swamp
as against a large pine-spread—
his clear No marriage
    no marriage
friend

Lorine did not get her way, either, with *My Friend Tree*. The Scots "have a way of wanting to do what *they* want," she discovered. Coming fifteen years after *New Goose*, the book *must* contain enough new poems to qualify as a "Selected"; but Finlay and McGuffie whittled the total number to fourteen, omitting two she considered among her best. Lorine wrote Zukofsky:

> I must inform you of my disappointment—they are leaving out Ash woods and I rose from marsh mud and three tiny ones. I told them they can't do this as I wanted to think of this book as a Selected. . . . It seems the artist failed to draw for these and besides it brings expense down to omit. I said I'd send $25 if they'd include Ash woods—after all, if this poem doesn't belong with folk, where does it? Or $50 if they'd put both in—and do it without pictures! They answer the book is too near ready to do any of this and that it is enchanting and they know I'll like it and what they want is to go easy on this one, introduce me to Scotland in little poems first. O Lordy, I know this that nobody is going to get me in on art work again, certainly not in *this* country. What do poems need an artist for?

McGuffie returned Lorine's fifty dollars. Lorine was "terribly disappointed," felt the poems "spurned." Then the Gaelic translator fell through. Lorine didn't care, though she hated what Finlay's Scots did to her "little granite pail":

> Remember my little granite pail?
> The handle of it was blue.
> Think what's got away in my life—
> Was enough to carry me thru.

Finlay's version:

> D'ye mine on wee bit paillie?
> The haunnle wis blue when new.
> Och, think on aas gane bust ii ma life.
> Weel aye, but we've warselled thru.

"Ah, think of all that's gone bust in my life. / Well, yes, but we've wrestled through" is effective. But, as Lorine protested, "The wee bit of wit that mine had: *carry* pail or in pail, and *carry* me thru life—is lost!"

The poet Edward Dorn wrote an introduction that was interleaved in *My Friend Tree*. Raised in rural Depression poverty, Dorn had appreciated Niedecker in *Black Mountain Review*. "I don't 'understand' the poems very well," Dorn admitted. "The 'meanings' are always a little mysterious, to me." But he liked them. Compared to the high-decibel "calculated poem," Niedecker's poems had "an undistractable clarity" of word welded to a "freely sought, beautifully random instance—that instance being the only thing place and its content can be: the catch in the seine."

"I greatly appreciate that someone has stopped to express concern," Lorine wrote Dorn politely. To Zukofsky, she wrote: "Suzz. If he doesn't 'understand' me poems, there are spots of intro. *I* don't understand." She was not happy about *My Friend Tree*.

That fall of 1961 Jonathan Williams asked if he might call on Lorine during his pilgrimage to visit August Derleth. Lorine replied, "Your visit to Wis.—I have no telephone and no car (I'm three miles from Fort at Black Hawk Island) and work in the Fort hospital. I'd be glad to see you if you think you could find me in this limbo."

Williams charted the limbo, arriving Saturday, October 28, just after Lorine had finished lunch. He found her copying D. H. Lawrence's letters for Zukofsky, as she'd copied pages for him for thirty years because she longed to engage him in her passions. Williams was hungry, but she held back the chicken she'd stewed for Harold. Lorine later told Louie: "I would have made biscuits but I told him I couldn't talk and make them at the same time and couldn't cook anyhow. He said he was 'hung over' having been up till 4 a.m. Asked for aspirin. So with coke, cottage cheese and cookies he had to make a meal."

Williams would commemorate the occasion formally in a review of *My Friend Tree* in *Kulchur*. The 1960s had arrived with a vengeance:

She has never fled to pre-beat or de-beat San Francisco. She's not on LSD or a Wisconsin Pen-Woman either. Nor is she a snarling caitiff, feeling despised by Gross Middle America. I know because I've been there to see. Miss Niedecker, I guess in her fifties by now, lives in a tiny, green house out at Black Hawk island, three miles from town. Right out in back is the sparkling Rock River, on its way to Lake Koshkonong. No phone, almost no neighbors. . . . The river is a major fact in her life—lying there sparkling and running, often flooding and worrying the people. It's in the poems. The October day I stopped for lunch I found her reading some of Lawrence's letters, which she compares with Keats'. Letters are doubly important to us poets.

"He talks so well," Lorine told Zukofsky. "Didn't smile too much—we smiled over August Derleth's number of books (by himself)—his 94th has just come out. . . . Jonathan said I should send him a ms to print when I get one together again! Suzz We spoke of Louis Zukofsky, of course, with the utmost pleasure and respect! Did your ears burn?"

Williams left a copy of his book *Amen, Huzza, Selah* with Lorine. To Zukofsky, who had refused her a preface but written one for Williams, Lorine wrote: "Oh and your preface—nice, in form of letter. With that lovely, lovely bit from Barely and Widely." Lorine's "nice" reflected a hurt that hadn't gone away.

My Friend Tree, an elegant book printed on tan paper in brown ink, was in her hands by January 1962. It contained fourteen poems: "My Friend Tree," "You are my friend," "The young ones go away to school," "There's a better shine," "Black Hawk held," "I'm a sharecropper," "Remember my little granite pail?" "Along the river," "Old man who seined," "Don't shoot the rail!" "He built four houses," "Not feeling well, my wood uncut," "Well, spring overflows the land," and "The clothesline post is set." Only "Along the river" had not been previously published; five were newly collected. Lorine disliked Walter Miller's bold Celtic-type linocuts that "don't vibrate on my frequencies." It wasn't the book she'd imagined, the book that would reveal how far she'd developed as a poet since *New Goose*.

What was she griping about? Zukofsky shot back. She had a book, hadn't she?

17

Alone Again

1962–1963

If only my friend / would return / and remove the leaves / from my
eaves / troughs

"If only my friend"

Lorine had lived through World War I, the Great Depression, the rise
and fall of Fascism and Communism, World War II, the Atomic
Bomb, and McCarthyism, and she was currently enduring a nearly forgotten reign
of terror. The Cuban Missile Crisis was triggered by John F. Kennedy's Bay of Pigs
action, the foiled invasion of Fidel Castro's Cuba on April 17, 1961, by CIA-trained
Cuban exiles. She explained to Zukofsky, "I can't get over Cuba invasion and J.F.K.
with the Republicans—that it turned out unsuccessful seems beside the point." In
"J. F. Kennedy after the Bay of Pigs," she marvels that the "black-marked" president
can still "walk / the South Lawn" unscathed "by the storm."

In response to the Bay of Pigs, Russia built missile sites in Cuba; nuclear war
seemed imminent. Americans built bomb shelters: dread hung in the air. Lorine
remarked to Louie: "Any sense to think of going to another country to live?—
South America, Israel, Australia? World War, yes, but actually in just US and
Russia."

In October 1962 Kennedy sent warships speeding toward Cuba. Lorine
commented: "Each person silently suffering out a delayed action fuse as to Cuba.
Each of us manoeuvered into a spiritual position? What does the Bible say, I keep
thinking. Remember Confucius, Stoics—*and Bertrand Russell.*" But the potentially
catastrophic threat backed the Soviets down.

Not that Americans could relax. Kennedy was sending troops to Vietnam, where the French had been mired since 1954. Black Americans were rising to agitate for civil rights. The sex and drug revolutions were in full swing. In 1963 the feminist women's liberation movement would be spurred by Betty Friedan's *The Feminist Mystique*.

Like her family, Niedecker had been a pacifist since her teens during World War I. As for African Americans, she was instinctively anti-racist until vital income was jeopardized by renting to black people. It disturbed her to "bleach brotherhood" for gain. She was interested in drugs (though not in taking them) because the subconscious fascinated her; she paid attention to Aldous Huxley's claim in *The Doors of Perception* that mescaline and lysergic acid vaulted the mind to visionary heights.

The feminist groundswell would not be widely felt until the 1970s. Had Lorine caught an early beat, she would have endorsed some but not all of its tenets. For instance, she would not, like some feminists, see men as the enemy. She had adored her father and Grandfather Gottlieb. Her ever-curious mind explored traditionally "male" subjects: politics, botany, history, geology, ornithology, geography, music, philosophy. Though Abigail Adams, Mary Shelley, and Margaret Fuller are subjects of hers, far more often she writes about John Adams, Johnny Appleseed, Audubon, Black Hawk, Churchill, Darwin, Jefferson, Linnaeus, William Morris, Ruskin, and Swedenborg. And, although Harriet Monroe had taken poems and Marianne Moore nodded in her direction, far more important to Niedecker were Zukofsky, Williams, Finlay, and Corman. As Edwin Honig said of Lorine in the 1930s, her strongest feelings were for human beings, not ideological argument. She took the side of exploited people—men or women.

She also was not part of a poetic revolution. Though the 1960s is often called the decade of Robert Lowell, and though English departments still used the standard anthologies, the 1960 publication of Donald Allen's *The New American Poetry: 1945–1960* "caused shock waves of outrage and horror throughout the American poetic establishment" when it revealed the presence of a wide range of poets working under the establishment radar. The Objectivists, of course, had worked under the radar since the 1930s; Zukofsky would not be published by a major press until 1965. But the Objectivists never felt the sense of community that Allen's anthology established.

Why was Niedecker excluded? Primarily because of age. Most of the antholo-gized poets were born in the late 1920s or 1930s; Allen excluded the Objectivists who were no longer "new," though Niedecker's first book was published in 1946. One aspect of Allen's publication was not new, however. Of forty-four poets anthologized, four are women: in an anthology of 210 poems, Helen Adam, Madeline Gleason, Barbara Guest, and Denise Levertov account for 16.

Niedecker's work was known and admired by many of the anthologized poets—Edward Dorn, Robert Creeley, Denise Levertov, Charles Olson, Gary Snyder, Gilbert Sorrentino, Jonathan Williams, and Allen Ginsberg—as she admired much of theirs. Still, she was destined to remain "one by herself"—not quite an Objectivist, not a third generation modernist either.

Cid Corman would publish seventy-five Niedecker poems. *New Directions* and *Poetry Magazine* had been important to Lorine's early career; *Origin* was as significant because it printed her often and because Corman became such a firm friend. At times Lorine almost seemed to imagine herself as coeditor: "The poetry of Robert Kelly interests me very much. Let's watch him." Or "I'd like to see a book of short poems, just the essence of poetry, you know. Let your 'The Offerings' be the touchstone. Maybe two to four poems per poet."

She praised Corman's poetry, calling him the essence of poetry, though she could criticize—his book *All in All*, for example. "Too perfect for this civilization, too large a book, too much space left vacant around the little poems, too many exquisite abstraction-x-ray-moon pictures," she wrote Jonathan Williams, "but there it is." Still, it was Corman, more than the now bitter and disaffected Zukofsky, who made her feel *joined* to contemporary poetry.

Personally, though, Lorine was lonely. Nothing could be the same since Harold's final "No marriage / friend." Still, she couldn't help expecting him. One warm Sunday in February she'd been so sure he'd come she prepared chicken, biscuits, cauliflower, Jell-O, and cake—which, at 1:30 when he hadn't arrived—she had to eat herself, "much let down." Her loneliness did not allow her to give him up. "Not much ahead for me where H. is concerned but at least nothing taken away," she wrote Zukofsky. Nothing? Only her hopes of the permanent companionship of marriage. Those flooded June nights—river lapping her third front step, barred owl hooting, muskrats grinding their mice and frogs outside her door—she completed a poem the more poignant because it contained a warning Harold didn't need:

> My life is hung up
> in the flood
>   a wave-blurred
>   portrait

Don't fall in love
with this face—
　　it no longer exists
　　　in water
　　　　we cannot fish

　　　Blackhawk residents remember Lorine Niedecker as a solitary, walking along the road with quick, neat steps past the former Fountain House to the end of the island, where the exclusive Hunt Club once flourished, property now owned by the four Prisk sons who, with their parents, bossed the island. In winter she wore stadium boots and her ancient sheepskin coat, in summer Keds with ankle socks. They observed that she often had a book in her hand and stopped to peer at wild-flowers or gaze into pools of water. She also could be seen crossing to Prisks' store, returning home with a small bag of groceries. She was quiet, unobtrusive, impeccably pleasant when stopped, but never initiating contacts. To Blackhawk Island residents she was just a hospital cleaning lady, though a "different" one.

　　　Kids like Terry Ganser, Butchie Perkin, and Linda Kreger liked to play fort on wooden pallets lodged between trees next to her drive, and Terry and his friends chose Lorine's place to play cowboys and Indians, because her lot had the most bushes. She was kind to children, passing out candy on Halloween and occasionally inviting Terry to walk with her. "She always pointed out things I'd never notice, like plants and butterflies. But she intimidated me because she was quiet and lived by herself. Women didn't usually do that."

　　　Lorine did have one good friend on the island. Mae Ward and her husband, George Ernest (Ernie), a Fort Atkinson banker, lived further toward Lake Kosh-konong, and Lorine would sometimes stop at their house on her walks to the point. Mae took Lorine further afield to explore pinewoods and spring thickets, and one cold spring day the Wards, Lorine, and Harold watched herons and migrating whistling swans. The Wards also invited Lorine to go to the Kohlman fish fry together Friday nights.

　　　Roland and Maude Hartel also occasionally befriended her, introducing her to Club 26 on the outskirts of Fort Atkinson. Lorine gazed about her in awe:

> [S]till daylight with sun shining through large gleaming windows
> and reflected in huge mirrors on sides of walls. Dark red carpet.
> Quiet. Air conditioning (too cool almost). Men in suits and keep
> their jackets on. A shining bar in next room. White, very clean

walls and tables. Unbelievable. Prices high!, unbelievable that way, too. . . . I had a whiskey and sour before dinner and a creme de menthe after it. . . . I thought of old Greece while I was there, Plato's symposium, until I remembered very few of these people open books, then as I found I couldn't eat anywhere near all the plate of chicken and wondered how Roland could eat that immense plate of lobster tail, I thought of Nero . . . I got over it with milk of magnesia and metamucil.

The event inspired "Club 26," a surrealistic blend of nature and artifice, water lily morphing into red-carpeted, white-walled restaurant, roots into the stems of cocktail glasses, the guests' pollinating talk agitating the lily stamens:

> Our talk, our books
> riled the shore like bullheads
> at the roots of the luscious
> large water lily
>
> Then we entered the lily
> built white on a red carpet
>
> the circular quiet
> cool bar
>
> glass stems to caress
> We stayed til the stamens trembled

Though "wunnering" how Zukofsky would like it, Lorine knew "Club 26" was good. "In a way it's a mongrel—has both sentence—melodic line, and fragment of a sentence. But something got achieved there—ecstasy, why go any further."

Needing help—Harold no longer raked out her eave troughs—she called on Darrell Prisk. Darrell explained: "She wouldn't change a light bulb, though she kept a spic and span house. She couldn't talk to people easily but I was so full of bullshit I got her to loosen up. My dad Ray did jobs for everybody on the island, including her, like plowing and hauling fill—half of Blackhawk Island is fill from our quarry on County J. Islanders always help each other. Often my dad took a pie or donuts for payment. Hell, Harriet Mimmack would give him a kiss and say 'There's your pay.' Lorine always paid right away in cash."

In 1946, with the publication of her first book, she had moved into her own house, in which she'd lived without plumbing while her two rental places were fully equipped. After the publication of *My Friend Tree*, she asked Ray and Darrell Prisk to turn a closet into a bathroom. She described the experience to Zukofsky:

> I've got plumbing! A horrible two days with two men tramping through my house with mud on their feet (feet of clay). . . . [My things] piled up around me in the living room, a couple of square feet allowed me to read in. The only thing that sustained me was Mary Shelley's and Percy's troubles seemed larger than mine. . . .
>
> But my little pressure pump is a darling, jet, hums like a fan. The toilet tinkles a bit after the flushing. The faucet shines—I have no tub or shower or water heater, no rooms, heavens it was a trick to get my clothes and dresser and hip boots and vacuum sweeper back into the bathroom as it was. As it is I sit in solitude with my nose pressed into a plastic bag with clothes hanging from the ceiling. What Harold will do in that spot I've no idea. The length from his hips to his knees is considerable.
>
> In the midst of my depression the second day when everything they touched turned out wrong . . . suddenly Aen[eas] appears with hi-fi records to exchange and when he left he said, "Now don't be depressical" . . . and from then on I revived a bit . . . The inconvenience of the conveniences. . . . Well, no more carrying pails of water a half a block.

Only half-playfully, she linked her long-delayed indoor plumbing to the tears she'd shed for poetry and for the long-delayed second book, a "trickle" which had taken a lifetime's weeping to create:

> Now in one year
>   a book published
>   and plumbing—
>
> took a lifetime
>   to weep
>   a deep
>   trickle

Though averse to any local knowing she wrote poetry, she had chosen a literate lawyer. Picking up the June issue of the California magazine *Contact*, Fred Hobe came across an article by Jonathan Williams that mentioned Lorine Niedecker's poetry. Hobe leaned across his desk: "I have discovered you are a poetess. Really we ought to let the *Daily Union* know we have a poet in our midst."

"If you do I'll never speak to you again!"

She also rejected Finlay's plea to record *New Goose* poems to guitar—"they are lovely, oh dear, how good you are!—and I was thinking, it seems ESSENTIAL to get these on disc or at least on tape. I mean they are like talking Blues and I have been thinking every day that I must persuade you how important it is that we do something with these poems. For the sake of the world."

"*I write*," Lorine replied. "I don't do all these other things." (Finlay did tape her poems to guitar accompaniment and sent the tape to Lorine.)

Weekends too often free, she jotted more frequently in the journal she'd begun in 1950. Most importantly, she was immersed in poetry again, rededicating herself in "Poet's work" to "no layoff from this condensery." *Poetry Magazine* accepted "River-marsh-drowse," "Property is poverty," and "Now in one year," paying an astonishing $17.50. *Midwest* accepted "Club 26." As always, she saved what she considered her best for Cid. "I've had a good summer as to writing," she could tell Zukofsky in September. Yet it came at a cost. "Nerves, that's it. . . . I think that's why I sleep so much—I never lose a chance to—it's an escape, a relief from every-thing, that's why at times I eat too much! It's a form of common mescalin[e]—beyond visions into the Void. Voiding, i.e. writing, is an ecstatic strain."

She was also slowly rebuilding a carapace against loneliness. Harold had not come to the Island since June.

The first edition of *My Friend Tree* sold out in Scotland, went into a second edition. Jonathan Williams and Gilbert Sorrentino reviewed it for *Kulchur* and *Midwest*, Williams writing chiefly about his visit to Lorine "because the poems are so damn good there's not much else to say about them. They say it, it's there." Though Lorine insisted on anonymity in Fort Atkinson and Blackhawk Island, peer reviews were crucial to her.

Gilbert Sorrentino wrote:

> These poems are brief records of failure in the overall world which surrounds them, and in which they exist as brilliant markers. They are clear, hard and without sentimentality, they take a classical shape, they exist in "the light of ordinary day." . . . Miss Niedecker has the genuine poetic genius and expertise to speak quietly and truly of absolute, real things and to make the words of that speech glitter with a quality which I can only call irrevocable; once she has said something there is no more room to add a postscript. *What*

she speaks of touches any human heart deeply. . . . These are such effortless, *true* registrations. Records of failure without self-pity.

It is one of the hardest things in the world for a writer to speak clearly of his own failures without either weeping over these phenomena or making them into something "heroic" or romantic. On the other hand there is the danger of speaking so bluntly, so simply that the pathos and poignancy of these failures refuse to communicate themselves to the reader. When the balance is achieved, we are given remarkable poetry, as in Catullus and Emily Dickinson. In our own time we have Zukofsky and Edward Dorn, among others. The quality seems to be an ability to simply *say* something straight out, and then to leave it alone—Williams, of course, has done it for years. Miss Niedecker does it constantly. It is beautiful poetry.

"Tonight I read [the reviews] for the third time," Lorine wrote Zukofsky, "and I still laugh and blush a bit—but with some pride, of course! . . . And you, my mentor and champion, he says—true, but I was very careful this shdn't come from *me* so's not to embarrass you—maybe it might, I don't know. It still seems too good to me to be mentioned in the same breath with Bill Williams and you—and Emily Dickinson! . . . Sorrentino has always been an admirer of me pomes."

The end of 1962 and beginning of 1963, however, came with domestic problems. On October 13, water jetting from a bathroom pipe flooded her living room: "I told the plumber to take all the piping etc. out, it is no convenience to me." The plumber soothed her: "Anything mechanical, you never know." The plumbing stayed, though it took two days to dry out the cabin; then both electric and pressure pumps defaulted. To her amusement, a man from Montgomery Ward drove up in a Cadillac to fix a "sensitive pump," in Lorine's fancy, that required "a proper balance of water, air and poetry."

More time-consuming, she had to foreclose on a house she'd sold on land contract. Consultations with Fred Hobe and battles with the buyer frayed her. Thoreau and Plotinus were right: "[T]o retain property is a greater loss than to forfeit it." She, who wanted to throw *things* to the flood, found herself owning again. "Just wrote poem on foreclosing," she wrote Zuk in January 1963. "Venom against property."

Early in 1963 a Milwaukee man came looking for a fishing cabin on the island. At the former Fountain House bar, he asked if anyone knew of a property for sale. "See Lorine Niedecker," someone advised him. "She's got a house for sale."

18

Little Lorie,
Happy at Last?

1963

Ah your face / but it's whether / you can keep me warm
"Ah your face"

In February 1963 Lorine wrote Zukofsky that she hadn't heard from Harold since before Christmas. Shortly afterward, Albert Millen knocked at Lorine Niedecker's door. It was opened by a petite woman with swept back blonde-gray hair who looked up at him through blue-rimmed harlequin glasses. She offered a hand that was red and coarsened by scrubbing. He shook with his left: she discovered his right hand was missing. He was handsome and straight, six-feet tall, with graying black hair combed straight back from his forehead and a "sudden melting look in black eyes." (The eyes were hazel.)

He said he was an industrial painter at Ladish Drop Forge in south Milwaukee, looking for a place to retire. She found his manner rough yet charming, his grammar "slipshod." His mutilation did not repulse her; after all, she wore disfiguring glasses. He must have told her he was divorced because immediately she thought: "[I]f this relationship grows it would be something like Lady Chatterley's lover." Clearly, she was sexually attracted to him.

Through Fred Hobe, she sold Millen on land contract the river cottage behind Henry's two-story house that fronted Black Hawk Road. The basic dwelling had a small kitchen and living room, bedroom, and bathroom.

On April 7 Al Millen took Lorine to dinner when, over drinks, he told her more about himself.

Sixteen months younger than she, born September 14, 1904, in Swan River, Minnesota, little more than a railroad lumber depot. Brought up in the woods in a log cabin with a root cellar; left the one-room schoolhouse after eighth grade. Lost the right hand in a printing press accident in Oshkosh when he was twenty-two, but managed damn well: drove, painted three-story houses, hunted, fished, tied his own shoes by grabbing the shoelaces in his teeth. Married and divorced, four grown kids. Jobs scarce for a man with one hand. Fuller Brush man, shipyard; renting, moving, sometimes on the county. Former Wobbly (International Workers of the World), still a strong union man at Ladish. Science fiction fan, lots of books in the house. Always had a garden even on Kinnikineck Avenue in Milwaukee. Raised tomatoes big as cantaloupes.

An astonishing three days later she'd made up her mind. To Zukofsky she wrote:

> I see there's more and more actually in common between us—he really reads, knows who I mean by Voltaire, Bertrand Russell, likes H. G. Wells' fiction, knows who Robert Frost was (when I tried to tell him what meant so much to me, poetry). But all this is nothing—he is even more gentle and tender than Harold—seems near to tears at times, like my father often seemed. And he has a lovely, lovely humor. *I know this is it.* What an adjustment for me—too bad for me to become used to daily companionship, to deep affection, to human (!) happiness. I fear it, upsetting to the other thing I've built up in me that, give me another couple of years, would withstand the world, would never need any other life but itself and things like money, peoples' follies and hatreds and all the silly coming and going wouldn't even be there.
>
> What—what—what? I'll marry him. Somehow I'll work it out, time and space for poetry

Was she *sure*? countered Zukofsky, currently battered by depression, real and imagined physical ailments, the cost of Paul's concerts, endless papers to correct, another move, and, on March 4, the death of his mentor and friend, William Carlos Williams. And his doctor was ordering him to quit smoking.

"No, not *sure*," Lorine shot back, "—is anyone ever?"

She also informed Cid Corman of her decision. The lack of floods that spring was as unnatural as her "immanent marriage. At sixty one does foolish things. Hope I'm happy! He's my connection with life."

For her sixtieth birthday, Al gave her a white teapot with "a couple of glinting decorations," saying, "These are your engagement diamonds." Applying for the license, Lorine discovered his middle name was Omar ("the tent guy," said Al). "[A] queer mixture of knowing and poor grammar is he, but what a *dear* thing he is."

They had planned to wed on Sunday, May 26, in the parsonage of St. John's Community Church, but at the last moment the minister, Dr. Alban J. Tippins, urged them into the church to be married at the foot of the altar steps. The change of venue rather annoyed Lorine: had she known, she'd have invited more people; a third of the hospital would have turned out.

Al discovered he'd forgotten the ring. He and his tall, blond son, George, raced back to his place on the river while Tippins murmured, "Not important, one can get married without a ring." When the groom finally took his place, he broke down in tears during the brief ceremony and failed to give his response until George, his best man, prodded him while offering a handkerchief. It was definitely a Christian wedding—"not quite all the folderol but almost." According to Lorine's second cousins, Arvella and Adeline, their father and mother, Roland and Maude Hartel, "stood up for the marriage and paid for the drinks."

After the ceremony, in relief and gratitude, Al put two ten-dollar bills into an envelope for Rev. Tippins; thinking better of his largesse, he removed one of the tens on his way out. But he was impressed enough by Tippins to think he wanted to join St. John's. ("I shall skirt that abyss," said Lorine.)

The couple was photographed outside the church. Lorine wore a neat light-blue suit with a short jacket, small hat, gloves, low black pumps, and a corsage. Millen wore his good gray suit, a narrow tie, and a carnation in his buttonhole. Lorine clasped her hands against her chest in the gesture people remembered from childhood. Bride and groom looked determined to succeed.

The wedding party went on to a tavern where the McAllisters threw a celebration. John McAllister persuaded Lorine to learn the Twist and threw his back out. They flowed on to Club 26 for drinks and dinner. Among the guests were George Millen and his wife, Alice; Al's daughter Alice with her husband, Gordon Fabian; Mary McAllister; Nathalie Yackels; and Ernest Hartwig, Lorine's former brother-in-law. Æneas did not attend. Also boycotting was Al's youngest daughter, Julie Millen Schoessow. Her mother's favorite, she felt her loyalty was to her.

Bride and groom were "lucky enough to get away *quick* toward Madison," Lorine wrote Zukofsky, and "stayed at a motel luxurious & clean. As BP might have said, 'I eyed it with wonder.' An electric meter connected to an apparatus that vibrated the bed springs in order to relax the occupants!"

Lorine hardly relaxed. Al Millen was pass-out drunk. His explanation of his belated response at the church—"Those words from the Bible are so beautiful and so full of meaning as my life from now on"—accompanied waves of remorse, tears, and confession. He admitted drinking had destroyed his first marriage.

According to Julie Millen Schoessow: "My father spent Friday nights in the southside Milwaukee tavern, where he cashed his paycheck. Wives met their husbands at the bar, that was their socializing, they closed the place down. On Sunday morning there'd be a Union meeting and Dad wouldn't come home all day. My mother would send me to the tavern to bring him home. The drinking ate up all the money. We never owned a house, never had a car, we pulled a wagon to Kleen-Kut for groceries. My mother divorced him because she couldn't take the drinking." Al Millen, said his daughter bluntly, "was a functioning alcoholic."

Next morning Al offered to have the marriage annulled.

Lorine knew heavy drinking. Her father drank, Frank Hartwig drank. In her "lovely man," however, she sensed a protectiveness like her father's. Though she still wasn't *sure* about their union, Al's humor, vulnerability, and warmth suggested a man she could deal and even be happy with. She brushed off his not-quite-serious offer.

Instead they drove on to the Wisconsin Dells, planning their future as they inspected a dream house on Mirror Lake that they might build on Blackhawk Island—"3 bedrooms but we'd use 1 of them as my room with my books & small writing table & 1 of them as utility room. Three immense picture windows in living room. Lovely bathroom tiled clear to the ceiling . . . Shower and bath. Spacious clothes closets. All this for only $6000."

She'd announced her wedding to Louie and Celia on a postcard; Zuk replied on same. Back on the island, Lorine packed up wedding gifts: glassware, a chrome sugar and cream set, huge pottery ashtray, waffle iron, sheets, pillow cases, and forty-five dollars in cash. "I have a box of wedding presents never used," she would write Cid, "no value to me whatever unless the blue Delft dish as something to look at sometime again." Though she'd asked the Zukofskys for an egg poacher, they sent tiny teaspoons and fruit knives they had no use for, claiming her request arrived too late. Lorine sent them photos; Celia thought Al had a nice face.

Safely married, Lorine whispered to Al that she was a poet.

"A . . . *what?*"

They were living chaotically between her cabin and the gray house. Anticipating building, Al insisted on laying down tons of fill for a new, high-bed driveway. Lorine paid a thousand dollars: it was her property. Al also wanted a new Buick, which he bought. Caught in the magic of "we," Lorine estimated that "if we manage, we can probably have that and a house both. Have. Have. And I had got along without *have*. O well, one lives but once—and that between 60 and 75!"

Controlling her "venom against property," Lorine explained to Zukofsky:

> We talked about our new house last night. Al has been advised by an old friend, a lawyer, to let me pay for the house since I have money that can be had without Al's having to borrow at a high rate of interest etc. And since the land is already mine. It would then remain in my name. When the place that Al bought of me this past spring is sold (this summer) that money comes to me and of course I sell the cottage I live in. I'll be compensated immediately thru these sales. But Al insists he is paying me $65 a month as long as he lives to kind of make up for my using my money which left where it is could accumulate compound interest. And of course he insists on buying our groceries already for the weekends.

Lorine's optimism reflected her happiness. Houses she'd sold on land contract in the past had only been trouble—buyers defaulting, deteriorating properties reverting to her; but, "I'm sure it's all going to be all right."

Zukofsky had been addressing her as "Lorine Miller." She corrected him: "Last letter in our name is n. Miller would be the German, Al's is Millen, English. . . . [B]ut why not continue Lorine Niedecker as no doubt Cid will and all mag. editors as I'll always use it as poet. I have both names on my mailbox."

Al went back to his job at Ladish Drop Forge on Packer Avenue. He would retire in five years; during that time they would build their dream house on the river. If she couldn't catch a ride with Æneas, who was employed at the Fort Hospital as a mechanic on her recommendation, she still walked nearly four miles to the hospital to scrub. She'd planned to retire "on the stroke of age 62"; now, if she joined Al in Milwaukee, retirement would come sooner. Only one poem survives from all her years at the hospital: five lines that express every cleaning woman's fury at the instant undoing of her work: "Return / the night women's / gravy / to the cleaned / stove."

Lorine allowed one last celebration. She and Al invited islanders to the Black Hawk Club: "We had our hoe-down for Black Hawk Island on the spacious porch of a large old building with a watch tower . . . and a bar in an inner room. They gave us money. I danced from 11:00 to 12:00, old-time things, waltzes, two step etc. Al & I furnished beer and buns & ham, the others—about 25 couples, brought a dish to pass." Some would criticize Lorine's choice of husband. Fred Hobe thought that "Lorine no longer had her fresh, ebullient outlook on life after she married Al Millen." According to Darryl Prisk, "Al Millen was no great one, didn't treat Lorine with a lot of respect. Had to be dominant, told Lorine what to do. I hate to see a man boss a woman. Hell, if *I* can't get away with it, why should any man?" Nathalie Yackels agreed. She felt Al Millen was highly controlling of Lorine. Æneas said, "I boycotted the wedding. He was rough with her, macho—I don't mean he ever hit her. But he was the opposite of us: we was classics."

Lorine would write eleven poems directly referring to Al, though never by name. She was as clear-sighted about the marriage as she was about life itself. One poem, at least, awards Al Millen the trophy over the "clean man," Harold Hein. Drunk, Al had fallen into the Rock:

> I knew a clean man
> but he was not for me.
> Now I sew green aprons
> over covered seats. He
>
> wades the muddy water fishing,
> falls in, dries his last pay-check
> in the sun, smooths it out
> in *Leaves of Grass*. He's the one
> for me.

Still, though she'd made a new will in August 1963 leaving everything to Al Millen, she was not sure she would stay married to him.

Carp fishing on the Rock River, ca. 1920 (courtesy of Hoard Historical Museum, Fort Atkinson, Wis.)

Louis Zukofsky (*left*) and Jerry Reisman visit Lorine, September 1936 (courtesy of Reisman Family Trust)

Downtown Fort Atkinson in 1942, with bridge over the Rock River in foreground (courtesy of Hoard Historical Museum, Fort Atkinson, Wis., and Fort Atkinson Historical Society)

Æneas McAllister, ca. 1954 (courtesy of Dwight Foster Public Library)

The June 19, 1948, wedding of her friend Nathalie Kaufman to Donald Yackels, which inspired Lorine's poem "I rose from marsh mud" (courtesy of Claudia Church)

Harold Hein, 1950s (courtesy of Milwaukee
Public Library)

Lorine's cabin, ca. 1959 (courtesy of Dwight Foster Public Library)

Albert Miller escorts his daughter Julie down the aisle at her marriage to Eugene Schoessow, June 20, 1959 (courtesy of Julie Schoessow)

Cid Corman in Japan, 1958 (courtesy of Shizumi Corman)

Basil Bunting, British poet and admirer of Niedecker's poetry, 1972 (photo by Jonathan Williams, courtesy of the Yale Collection of American Literature, Beinecke Rare Book and Manuscript Collection)

Jonathan Williams, 1960 (courtesy of the Poetry Collection at SUNY–Buffalo)

William Carlos Williams, 1961 (photo by Jonathan Williams, courtesy of the Yale Collection of American Literature, Beinecke Rare Book and Manuscript Collection)

Blackhawk Island after the flood of 1959 (courtesy of Dwight Foster Public Library)

Frederick Hobe, Lorine's sym-
pathetic lawyer, 1960s (courtesy
of Dwight Foster Public Library)

Gail Roub, 1967 (courtesy of
Hoard Historical Museum, Fort
Atkinson, Wis.)

Lorine's painting of the apartment house at 2042 South Sixth Street, Milwaukee, ca. 1964 (courtesy of Hoard Historical Museum, Fort Atkinson, Wis.)

Lorine in front of 2042 South Sixth Street, Milwaukee, 1966 (photo by Jonathan Williams, courtesy of the Yale Collection of American Literature, Beinecke Rare Book and Manuscript Collection)

Lorine and Al Miller at the Schoessows' for Christmas, 1964 (courtesy of Julie Schoessow)

19

Milwaukee

1963~1964

Consider at the outset: / to be thin for thought / or thick cream blossomy

"Consider at the outset"

For his vacation Al proposed to show Lorine his own turf. Leaving July 21, they drove across Wisconsin to where the Mississippi and Wisconsin rivers converge at Wyalusing State Park. Its 2,628 acres offered forests, wetlands, waterfalls, backwaters, deer, fox, beaver, and more than ninety species of birds. Al had a pair of good binoculars. They drove through the park in his big Buick, Lorine elevated on pillows so she could see.

Then Al headed north to Swan River to show Lorine where he had been born a stone's throw from the vanished depot and general store with its pot-bellied stove and checkerboard. According to Lorine, "We stood and looked at the spot where the Millen place was supposed to be. No sign of habitation. A small clump of pines. Gone back to nature." Al reminisced:

> We had a deer that would cry to come in out of the flies. Ma would then pull aside the mosquito netting from her bed to let the deer come in and lie down. . . . I fell in love with [my teacher Esther Morris], of course, as many boys do with favorite women teachers. . . . At thirteen I started work—on railroad ties at the village. I was tall and strong and the work did not hurt me. . . . Following that, I worked in a gravel pit at road construction. I walked two miles to get to it, worked ten hours a day there, and on

returning home at night helped with the chores. And on Sundays Pa would say, "Take the gun and see what you can bring home to eat."

Lorine's reveling in her "grand man" is apparent in a post-trip letter to Zukofsky:

> Have I written you since we got back from Duluth and Millelacs in Minn. and been north again to Dells (to see about our new house)? If so I add how nice about PZ at Tanglewood and you and Celia can go there etc.
>
> Am writing up the trip. You'll see when completed. Will give each of his children a copy in a notebook with copies of the pictures we took, as Christmas present. His former home, Swan River, near Grand Rapids, Minn., all the old customs. . . . Al is modern but his speech has a flavor—e.g. "Leonard Palmer introduced me to how much pleasure there is in reading" or "We kids picked wild roses for Ma—we ate the buds at other times, they have a mild flavor" or walking across a busy street, "I'm safer in a car than I am on foot." He's a grand man—I'm so happy I married him.

Never before had she tossed off Zukofsky with "Have I written you?" At the same time, Zuk's poetry still meant more to her than almost anything in the world, and now he was asking her to return his gifts to her, *55 Poems* and *Le Style Apollinaire*, so he could send them to the University of Texas–Austin, which was collecting his work. Lorine responded: "I wish you'd ask me to return some hair or flesh. This really hurts. . . . I don't think it's an exaggeration to say: I can hardly live without one kind of possession: books, and chief among books, those of Louis Zukofsky. Knowing this, you can still ask me for '55'??" Eventually she copied twelve short poems from *55 Poems* and sent the books. At last, Zukofsky was getting solid attention: in May 1964 Denise Levertov, W. W. Norton's new poetry editor, approached him about publication. He had waited more than thirty years to be noticed by a major publisher. "Respectable at last!" exclaimed Lorine, though his proposed title *All* reminded her that "We use *All* soap detergent when we go to the laundromat when we don't have *Family Flakes*!!"

Yet Lorine continued her Zukofsky letter project. Hang on to my letters, he'd told her in 1961; Texas will be interested eventually.

She hadn't needed his advice: she had dreamed of a book of LZ–LN letters, though she gave up the idea when he intimated he'd destroyed most of hers and weeded out personal bits in those he'd kept. (Actually more than two hundred, though often fragments, survive.)

He did not discourage, however, a book of *his* letters, though he insisted that she eliminate all personal references except for safe literary jabs like "Yeats is an ass." She tackled each letter with magnifying glass and scissors, excising anything she guessed the ultra-private—or paranoid—Louie would object to. Some letters survived only as scraps, which she pasted separately onto sheets of typing paper. She believed she was distilling immortal literature: "As to your letters, they have been clipped and everything except *good* LZ with LZ flavor thrown away. Nothing personal kept. Having done all this I might as well destroy what's left but somehow I don't know why I should—they are letters written to me. Why shouldn't I keep them? I have no plans for getting them printed, if I did I'd consult you first."

"Nothing personal kept." Lorine's credo was "throw *things* to the flood"; yet words were living things that she cherished. But then, as she told Corman, "I've always abided by what he's asked."

Lorine retired as a cleaning woman November 29, 1963—officially, at least. Al's Milwaukee apartment needed serious elbow grease.

He installed her at 2042 South Sixth Street on the then-unfashionable south side, where thrifty Poles had built "Polish flats": three-story apartment buildings set one behind the other on long narrow lots. Al's first-floor apartment was in the back of a house fronting Sixth Street, accessed on the side by a narrow sidewalk. The space included a kitchen, bathroom, and bedroom divided from a tiny sitting area by a curtain. Al considered the apartment more civilized than Lorine's cabin with its cold-water taps and wind-leaking walls, but his daughter Julie found it "dark and depressing." Lorine agreed, pouring out her complaints in a long letter to Zukofsky. Yet, as usual, she's equal to this challenge:

> [T]he cleaning of the first four days—such filth you could not possibly experience even in New York in the old days—this apartment reminds me a little of the dark, always dusty, noise-thru-the-walls-apartment, where was it—47th St.? . . . We live not in a cultured section of Milwaukee but in the Pol(e)ish Sausage section. *Old* Milwaukee is here with a vengeance, shabby, grimed over brick houses—this house we have the first floor apt in, *leans.* . . . But Al pays only $40 a month and needs this only 3 years more, so we can afford to hang on—sideways.

Al worked the third shift at Ladish, eleven p.m. to seven a.m. ("I do think third shift can't make for a normal life.") He came home for breakfast, went to bed shortly after. When he woke in the afternoon they ran errands. They loved prowling the Goodwill store and took two shopping bags of wash to the Laundromat once a week:

Casual, sudsy
social love
at the tubs

After all, ecstasy
can't be constant

Al often cooked dinner, singing as he boiled rutabagas, fried bacon, and braised pork shanks. Like many heavy drinkers he didn't eat dessert, Lorine's weakness, which (she claimed) she now gave up. They ate on a card table in front of the TV, Lorine enjoying the Flintstones, the Danny Thomas Show, and Benny Goodman; not much else. Or they read.

Lorine: "What are you reading?"

"*The Fallen Sparrow*—one of those books that has meaning and all that."

With morning and early afternoon hours to herself, Lorine explored. She fancied the small, lagooned Kosciusko Park a "bit of Black Hawk Island on a hill," swore that "[t]he park saves my life—a statue in it of Kosciusko on his horse as he fought in our Revolution." Department stores like Goldman's, Schuster's, and the Grand lined Mitchell Street nearby. Lorine would take the Sixth Street bus to Mitchell and buy sale items at Goldman's with its wooden floors and out-of-date stock. More often she hiked to shops ten blocks away, or down to the Kinnickinnick River to lean her arms along the railing and watch the ducks and the "huge red ore boats with that terribly *white* superstructure." Boats of all kinds began to fascinate her. If she got lost, she needed only to search the horizon for the blue dome of the Romanesque Basilica of St. Josephat, a church rivaling European cathedrals in splendor if not antiquity and "[t]he only way I'd ever look up to Catholicism, I'm afraid."

Al showed her how to explore the city. She'd catch the Sixth Street bus, which took her north across a bridge over a valley and deposited her at Wisconsin Avenue. Nearby stood the magnificent Milwaukee Public Library with its broad flight of steps leading to a vestibule of marble columns and soaring rotunda, a dome she could look up to. She could walk two blocks north to the new Milwaukee Museum, with its re-creations of European village streets and American Indian dioramas. Or, transfer in hand, she might board the bus that nosed east down Wisconsin Avenue, Milwaukee's main shopping street, and get off at the end near the abandoned, clock-towered Northwestern railroad depot. Before her stood Eero Saarinen's art museum, where she'd disagreed with Harold Hein over a portrait's vibrant colors. A series of parks high above the lake led her north to Robert Burns

Park, triangled between Prospect and Franklin. She gazed up at the comely figure of one of her favorite poets; pity he'd turned green with age.

On these outings she often carried a sketchbook: for years, with a simple Prange box and brush, she'd painted watercolors of the Fountain House, the Rock River, boats, trees. The *silence* of painting profoundly attracted her; she took pleasure in creating something wordless: "[E]veryone uses words. If I had started / painting / earlier that would have / been it."

She jotted notes about her painting:

> 1. It's my trip to the moon! A silence in this art. It's so quiet it's dumb. What If I forget words??

> 2. The line attracts me, the simple line, but painting is not really line, it's color. Color absorbs line. At first I drew with pencil and then filled in with color. Good enough if all you want is to faithfully reproduce buildings. I now paint boats without drawing.

> 3. First, original, painting has more life than truth. The second is better work but worse as picture.

> 4. You paint what you love—what you've seen well or deeply and what you've loved, same thing, and it's in your hand before you sit down to it.

> 5. It's a compulsion that won't let you rest but easier work than writing.

In a postscript, she addressed a temporal difference: "Writing is toning down the ecstasy that 'came.' Painting (for me) is creating ecstasy in the act of the painting."

She painted the derelict depot and the Art Museum, a "huge glass mushroom transported from some Walt Disney desert." She painted her South Side's pointy turrets and cupolas, the basilica's blue dome, their apartment house listing to the left. She painted an evergreen tree on a hill.

"I don't know, Al. It looks like a tall weed."

"Just write *tree* under it."

She also painted the Red Top Tavern across the street from their apartment, with its neon sign that looked like a cross: "Here the taverns point to heaven. The wife's cross is the tavern and they all go reeling to church."

That Christmas 1963 Margaret Millan, Al's ex-wife, invited Lorine and Al to her apartment at Twenty-Sixth and Mitchell to celebrate with their family. It was an awkward situation for Lorine. Margaret was feminine and lovely, a good cook, a professional milliner and seamstress though also, according to her daughter Julie, "a domineering type." Traditionally she made aprons for her daughters Virginia, Alice, and Julie; so perhaps when she handed Lorine her gift apron she wasn't saying, "*You* clean up after him now"; again, perhaps she was. What Lorine would have absorbed was the affectionate camaraderie between Al and Margaret. She cannot have had a comfortable time, and Christmas at Margaret's was never repeated.

During those holidays Al came home drunk several times ("tipsy," Lorine called it), "said things with an edge, forgetting, I'm sure, when he woke up sober. O me. But normally he is my good, good, sensitive, *loving* person." The drinking didn't stop with the holidays. On paydays Al banked his check, then headed for a tavern where he and his Ladish "hoodlums" (Lorine's term) drank the morning away. By February 1964 Lorine had had enough. "We have made a pact—two hours less of drinking on pay days, Fridays, so he shd. be home by 11:00. He goes to the bank at 9:00 when it opens: this gives him about 3 hrs. of leisurely drinking—beyond that I can't take it."

Al's drinking figures directly in four of Lorine's poems, one written during the cold winter months of 1964:

> Alcoholic dream
> that ran him
>   out from home
>   to return
> leaning
>
> like the old house
> in this old part
>   of town leaves him
>   grieving:
> why
>
> do I hurt you
> whom I love?
>   Your ear
>   is cold!—here,
> drink

"Why do I hurt you whom I love?" is every heavy drinker's question: Jekyll loathing his Hyde. Yet, touching Al's cold face, Lorine comforts him with another drink.

Yet there was the other Al, the comfortable, joking, emotional, loving husband and, at times, the distinguished man. "My lovely husband dressed all up beautifully in a grey suit, grey overcoat and hat and white shirt and took me down to the Art Center," Lorine told Zukofsky, frankly appreciating Al's good looks. She responded, making Al blush when she said that before him she "never wore beads" and sewing a new dress so she could "move before" him "smooth-draped and color-elated."

Whether Al lived up to the pact or not, Lorine proved as tensile as wire cable. She faced her marriage squarely, the good and the bad; the good weighed heavily: "You know Al doesn't know literature like I do . . . but at least I can talk to him about it, my correspondence with writin' people etc. That is an advance, you see, over anything, anybody I've ever known outside of yourself. He's folk and I enjoy it. His grammar is often off but that doesn't bother me."

That first married winter in Milwaukee, inspired by Al's love of cooking and her own inadequacies in that line, she collected a book of some 115 recipes. They belong to pre-gourmet USA, when tuna casseroles glued together with Campbell's cream of mushroom soup, cheese, and crushed cornflakes were deluxe, and molded Jell-O salads fashionable. (Lorine's favorite: lemon Jell-O with vinegar, cabbage, tart apples, stuffed olives, and "a shake of cayenne.") Despite her recipes, Lorine was delighted to turn over the pots and pans to Al, who cared about food.

"It says in Ben Franklin's *Almanac*: 'Eat few suppers and you'll need few medicines.' See! If he were here, I'd shake his hand."

"Yuh, but he didn't work third shift."

Still, for a Christmas gift to Maude and Roland Hartel, Lorine compiled *A Cooking Book*: "The fact that I don't know much about cooking should entitle me to write a book about it." She is bemused by Al's dicta: "Pork shanks and cabbage, these are the finer things in life; liquor in food—sure, pour wine over cabbage and over almost anything; seldom empty a fry-pan of its bacon grease, let it stand to be used again." Al, she notes, reads at the table whereas, "[a]way from the table: I eat books."

Embroiled in unfamiliar yet welcome domesticity, her dialogues with Zukofsky and Corman were the more vital. Sitting at Al's Royal typewriter on the card table, she wrote Louie, full of the fall 1963 issue of *Poetry*, a publication they'd both dismissed as moribund for years: "[A]ctually some things there aren't too bad, Louie, e.g. 2nd and 3rd stanzas of John Berryman . . . parts of Hayden Carruth, Ronald Johnson . . . even [Denise] Levertov is better, getting a bit more concentrated, and I like Henry Rago. . . . Charles Olson here, *no*. I still like Duncan's prose better than his poetry."

Lorine comments a great deal on poets published in *Origin*: Clayton Eshleman, Theodore Enslin, André du Bouchet, Daphne Marlatt, and Jean Daive—above all on Cid's poetry and Japanese translations.

Yet one longs to know more. Which were favorite poems of Dickinson, D. H. Lawrence, Moore, Stevens, Reznikoff, and Williams? Did she read Muriel Rukeyser, Elizabeth Bishop, Weldon Kees, or Pablo Neruda? One gets glimpses; for example, when she replies to Corman's suggestion that she reread Wallace Stevens's poems for "song": "I had the impression that's *all* some of them were!" This is the sort of thing she recorded in her journals, which do not survive.

Now, freed from hospital work, emotionally grounded, stimulated by a new environment, she was writing more. The new magazine *Joglars* accepted "To foreclose," "To my small electric pump," and "I visit the graves" for its spring 1964 issue, a group she'd titled "Three Poems in One Year, Jonathan" to tease Williams, who claimed "[a]bout one poem, like the frailest of peony blossoms, drops from Lorine Niedecker's typewriter every year." And during the winter she'd written thirteen poems for *Origin*. She was brimmingly alive: "There is sumpn in moving to a new place and now when I go back home this summer maybe it will seem new to me. I'm trembling on the verge of something, a form of poetic thinking that depends maybe too much on readers' imagination but we'll see. I don't know if it's called metaphysical or not, not necessarily, I guess, but anyhow this has been in me from the beginning and somehow it's got to come out."

Lorine hesitates at "metaphysical," a dirty Objectivist word with its meanings of beyond the material, abstract, supernatural, transcendental. Receiving a copy of Cid Corman's *in no time*, she also thought he was going toward "conversational— metaphysical?? (You won't like that word metaphysical anymore than I do) but you know what I mean—and going into it faster than I am. All our lives we steer away from it but when we do attain it we know there's nothing like it." She read "over and over" this poem by Corman:

> The shiver
> which is death.
> And the last red
> leaf, last of
> sun warm wind
> stuck to my
> sole—

Certainly it is a poem that spiritually transcends objects like leaf, sun, wind, boot sole. Yet Corman strenuously rejected "metaphysical" as applied to his poems. Lorine apologized: "Please don't mind my 'metaphysical' in my last letter. I meant it but evidently didn't use the right word. Your work and Louie's, there's no use—for me—to look farther."

What was the "nothing like it" that Lorine had steered away from and now almost attained? In surviving letters and documents, she never defines precisely what she means by a "form of poetic thinking that depends maybe too much on readers' imagination": she had always depended on readers' imaginations to fill gaps in her terse lines. Perhaps she had in mind a poem like "In the transcendence," in which little is explained and the star is less important as an object than a stimulus to a state of mind:

> In the transcendence
> of convalescence
> the translation
> of Bashō
>
> . . .
>
> I lay down
>   with brilliance
> I saw a star whistle
>   across the sky
> before dropping off

She had also backed away from political and economic content. The young Niedecker, so militant in *New Goose* about privilege and poverty, has gone underground. This is the more striking considering America's chaos: John F. Kennedy assassinated on November 22, 1963; escalating protests against the Vietnam war; sit-ins, love-ins, flag-burnings; draft-age men fleeing to Canada; Martin Luther King Jr.'s nonviolent civil rights policy increasingly challenged by militant blacks. Her surviving comment about Kennedy's assassination is after the fact: "We are reading newspaper pages of Warren Report—we feel with Bertrand Russell (ahem) that something is hidden." She did write a poem about Winston Churchill, who died January 24, 1965. She'd watched his funeral on TV: "the Thames, St. Paul's, the solemn faces, Handel on the organ—I found it very moving." Yet this was nostalgia. Obviously, her new marriage dominated her poetry at this time.

She was hand-copying poems onto small pads of paper that she bound in cardboard and covered with patterned wrapping paper. She titled these creations *Homemade* and *Handmade Poems*, and would give the books to Louis, Cid, and Jonathan for Christmas 1964. But she always thought of publication, asking Cid the cost of getting out a book in Japan: "I'm afraid to ask, but would $100 go anywhere at all toward such an LN book? I'd send it along about Sept. 1st [1965]. A Selected (I'd be adamant on a few I'd want included) or if you insist an entirely New."

Many *Homemade* and *Handmade* poems are personal. "Consider at the outset" poses a question Lorine hadn't faced since Æneas had woken "the sleeping beauty"— whether to give in to life's pleasures or stint oneself for a life of the mind:

> Consider at the outset:
> to be thin for thought
> or thick cream blossomy
>
> Many things are better
> flavored with bacon
>
> Sweet Life, My love:
> didn't you ever try
> this delicacy—the marrow
> in the bone?
>
> And don't be afraid
> to pour wine over cabbage

Here Al is tempting "thin for thought" Lorine to suck the good things from life's bones. According to Al's daughter Julie, she never fully responded to his invitation: "My father and mother were spontaneous, fun-loving people. Dad would pull over to buy a watermelon from a stand and we'd spread a blanket and picnic by the roadside. They enjoyed the big Ladish picnics, my father in charge of the games. There were boxes of chocolates on Valentine's Day and Christmas, and warm hugs. My mother never hesitated to ask my father for money and he liked giving. Lorine was so used to living with little she didn't know how to *accept* from my father."

But with her high threshold for pleasure and equally low expectations—not to mention her marrying Al Millen—Lorine was accepting as much as she could.

That March they drove to Blackhawk Island for the first time since moving to Milwaukee:

I cooked, washed dishes without plumbing, a bit too early to turn on (drained for the winter). But oh those views from my windows—ice out of river, swamp dogwood so *red* and bits of green in the grass.

Al and I were saying on the way back to Milwaukee that we would stay in our new house to the last moment of our lives, he waiting on me and I waiting on him. Lugubrious thought but we're really happy.

As spring advanced, they fled Milwaukee for the island every weekend—living in the gray house on the river, Lorine's since Al stopped making payments. They'd made trips to western Wisconsin to look at river villages; Al wanted to live on a Mississippi houseboat. Lorine told Zukofsky: "We aren't building—I can't see giving out $7000 or more in a place being taken over by negroes and my white neighbors aren't even as good as negroes." But she could not give up the island.

She managed to sell her cabin and Henry's two-story, but always on land contract and often to deadbeats. She was forever consulting Fred Hobe about foreclosing. One man, Marvin Heise, was a drinker. The other foreclosed himself: trying to collect payment, they found him days-old dead on the toilet seat.

Without cash from the sale of Lorine's property, the dream house they'd planned—three bedrooms, bath tiled to the ceiling, living room with picture windows—shrank. She paid for the very modest cottage they built. On May 3 men started laying the foundation near the river for a house of roughly five hundred square feet: tiny kitchen and bathroom, eating area, one bedroom, living room. At least Lorine got two picture windows fronting the river. She insisted on three things: that the house be painted white and grasshopper green, that it be elevated on eight cement foundation blocks, and that the windows be high to give her privacy from river traffic. Al scoffed at the foundation; when floods came in the fall of 1965, he wished they'd hoisted it more.

Al made her special shelves she named "The Immortal Cupboard." The nine-by-fifteen living room also held Lorine's one-drawered writing table overlooking the Rock, Al's desk, and two chairs facing a television. The bedroom had a double bed, Lorine's cedar chest, and Al's guns, including a prized Luger pistol. The six-by-eight kitchen was too small for the refrigerator, which stood opposite the table in a tiny dining area where they ate with a river view.

Lorine wrote Zukofsky that fall:

> [O]h how we work when we're out there, winter coming on. I carried 21 pails of water Sat pm from the river to plants I brought over from the old home, while Al slept (worked Fri. night, you

see). Then yesterday I painted storm windows while Al did other painting. . . .

Odd to think next May I'll collect social security. My year and a half of marriage made me look older but I'm really no worse for it. . . . You see . . . expenses still go on because one goes on and on, altho I swear next year spending must stop. This place remains in my name for simple reason that I haven't been sure that I could stay married. Even tho I go right on with that too and probably always will! But I refuse to spend any more of my money on us both.

The spending hardly stopped the next year. In March, June, and July 1964, Lorine wrote checks totaling $5,664 to North Crest Homes for the building of their cottage. Water pipes, paint, gravel, and fill cost another $1,616, surpassing the price of the Dells dream house. Yet building solidified her commitment: "I gave my binoculars to Al's son [George] today—Al has a pair even better. As I did so I thought: this must mean I intend to stay with Al. Objects carry such profound implications! I who needed no one—I might as well admit it, though, am happy with him very often."

20

Husband to a Poet

1964~1965

A husband and wife had a difference, but now everything's all right. He conceded. The man always concedes

"Kooky Conversations"

D on't ever marry anybody famous," Al Millen would tell his daughter Julie. Surely he had little to complain of? Lorine Niedecker did not mingle with other poets, steadfastly refused invitations to read her poetry, never played the artist, remained virtually unknown to the American public.

Yet mail for Lorine arrived steadily. Magazine editors requested poems. Admirers wrote to ask where they could find copies of *New Goose* or *My Friend Tree*. ("I get half a dozen letters a year asking for copies of NG.") Brown University told her they would take any of her papers "even before I die!" Cid Corman and Jonathan Williams corresponded with her regularly. And Lorine had vowed that she would carve out "time and space for poetry." She did, writing more than a dozen poems during the first year and a half of their marriage. Al hadn't anticipated the depth of her commitment. He found himself—blue-collar worker with an eighth-grade education and uncertain grammar—married to a dedicated artist. He could be humorous about it. Lorine had been typing from 6:30 p.m. until bedtime for days; now the British periodical *Agenda* wanted poems. "Send 'em the typewriter," said Al.

The distance between them on this level, and his acceptance of it, saved the marriage. Because he couldn't enter her creative mind, he showed his other attributes: love, warmth, generosity, spontaneity, humor. Al Millen was Lorine's lifeline to normalcy. In turn, she deferred to him by calling the poetry she wrote these years "homemade" or "handmade," not wishing her professionalism to intimidate him. It's hard to imagine Lorine sharing her poems with Al. What would he make of

> How impossible it is
> to be alone
> the one thing humanity
>   has never really
> moved towards

but a rejection of marriage, though Lorine titled the poem "T. E. Lawrence," who fascinated her because he lived, as she wished to, "in the center of his own silence no matter how much action went on around him." Al's daughter Julie remarked: "I really don't think they talked about her poetry—at least not about the serious stuff."

Lorine was stunned to learn that Cid Corman was suspending publication of *Origin* in July 1964. "I somehow feel compelled to send you the product of the last year, just to keep in touch," she wrote that October, enclosing thirty *Homemade Poems*, prefaced by a watercolor of her Blackhawk Island cottage. That December she sent Corman money, as she always had: "I cd. do better if I weren't once again somewhat caught up in *things*. Your life, I think is comparatively free of things— as mine was tending before my marriage. . . . I had been quite free of Christmas or I had Christmas, let's say, in a free kind of way. Now my husband's daughter tells me she's already bought my present and will get it to me early because I need it. I need something?—that Julie wd. be buying??"

With *Origin* suspended, she looked for new outlets, turning again to *Poetry*, which accepted a group of five poems for its August 1965 issue, and to *Granta*, the *Paris Review*, *Arts in Society*, and Ian Hamilton Finlay's *Poor.Old.Tired.Horse.* To Finlay, she sent the kind of short folk poems he preferred:

> Popcorn-can cover
> screwed to the wall
> over a hole
>   so the cold
> can't mouse in

Reluctant to give up her connection to Corman, however, Lorine proposed he publish an anthology:

> [I] was thinking last night I'd like to see a book of short poems, just
> the essence of poetry, you know. Let your "The Offerings" be the

touchstone. Maybe two to four poems per poet. . . . LZ's "A"-16, "Celia's birthday poem" . . ."And so till we have died" or "Strange / To reach that age" or "Hello, little leaves" or "O sleep, the sky goes down behind the populars" or "Being driven after the hearse thru suburbs." Reznikoff's subway rails or fields or rocking chair on the porch. Louise Bogan perhaps—"Morning" was in an Origin? Pound—"Sing Goddam" for one. Robert Kelly . . . Surely I'd want Mary Barnard's Sappho. . . . Might include Ian Finlay, [Theodore] Enslin and the two of [Clayton] Eshleman in Origin. William Carlos Williams' "The Red Wheelbarrow." (For this anthology Marianne Moore comes as an afterthought though she should never be that) If anyone wants LN might use "Old man who seined" and "I rose from marsh mud."

Her enthusiasm grew as she typed. The anthology could "go way back" to perfect short things like "O western wind, when wilt thou blow"; to haiku and Mother Goose and Herrick, Keats, Thomas Fuller, Dickinson, Blake, Donne, Dante, Hopkins, Burns. "We might let Shakespeare in!" Applying the brakes: "It shouldn't be mentioned to Louie that I spoke of all this—as you no doubt know, Louie is so very sensitive about just everything."

She would regret her proposal. Reasonably, Corman thought she would coedit the book; but as always Lorine shied from commitments that threatened her writing. "I couldn't say that I'd refuse to help altho there is something in me these free days—free from working for a living—so filled with the life I've always wanted. I'm afraid of feeling *busy*. . . . [Y]ou may count on me as a most absorbed listener. Perhaps we shouldn't plan on my being an active editor?" The most she could do was send him a few poems she thought worthy of inclusion. At her age she needed "silence" in which to create.

Next morning, she wrote a postscript: "Couldn't sleep last night thinking I've let you down altho all I meant when I spoke of a book of short poems was: I'd like to see such a book in print. . . . I shdn't like any difference to come up in our very fine relations. As you know, I'd be happy if a book of my own poems could come out by some publisher somewhere before I die—so I've been frank, and let's speak no more of it."

She not only needed silence for poetry, but she was also trying to finish editing thirty years of Zukofsky's letters: "As I go thru this mountain of small penmanship I'm amazed that so much of his time got taken in correspondence. He has been generous. O very generous." She had distilled his words to "just the essences, tincture . . . a drop to a page, that constant, deep-in spot in his being. . . . [L]ong

ago I destroyed the parts of the letters that he wouldn't want the public to see—
oh things that were sharp and brought out the full flavor of LZ, however. . . . I
said 'book'—it might take a long time before Louie can get to reading it after
the long time it'll take me to choose and type—years maybe before any publisher
would get around to it when Louie finally releases it for publication. Well, we
are the long range people." She called the work "a chore tho I wouldn't want him
to know that"; at the same time, she enjoyed *reducing* Zukofsky, having him
under her control. Again, she warned Cid not to tell Louie that she wrote about
him.

Al proposed a two-week vacation in July 1965, the Black Hills their destination.
"Why Black Hills?" Lorine answered Corman: "I dunno. Al likes the history
behind it. Maybe I'll like the color in the fantastic rocks? I have to take my eyes
from the minute for two weeks—to the spacial [*sic*]."

Al had bought a like-new 1962 deluxe tan Buick with push-button windows.
("I regard it with wonder," BP would have said.) The crawl across Wisconsin,
Minnesota, and South Dakota to its western border was deadly. Lorine sat
propped on pillows, usually jotting in a notebook and looking up too late to see
what Al pointed at through the window. They overnighted in cabins (six dollars)
or motels, "always very luxurious and clean" (ten or twelve). Lorine noted: "The
trip was worth it for me when we drove thru the Black Hills, four hours of deep
forest. . . . All those evergreens—smell of cedar etc. very strong—densely covered
enormously high hills . . . miles up to a little blue sky."

Though they avoided "Old West" saloons and stores, Al made sure Lorine saw
Deadwood, Needles Drive, and the Needle's Eye in Custer State Park, where they
enjoyed waiting for buffalo to cross the road and "a cowboy on a horse [who] came
along right next to the highway—his large hat, high heeled boots and beautiful
shining brown horse. Having color film I asked if he'd mind his picture taken. He
smiled and said no." It's one of two photographs Lorine took of a person: she
photographed scenery, not people posing in front of it. She bought postcards,
sketched a Golden Eagle in a museum. They admired Mount Rushmore and
Korczak Ziółkowski's magnificent memorial-in-progress to the Oglala chief Crazy
Horse at Thunderhead Mountain in the Black Hills. "The face wd. be $87\frac{1}{2}$ feet
long," Lorine noted in wonder. "The pointed finger itself wd. be $37\frac{1}{2}$ ft. long. . . .
It will take . . . 5 million dollars to see the job thru."

Lorine also remarked: "What maddens me on all automobile trips: you're
traveling that way because it's easier to stop whenever you want to, but you can't
stop, not just anywhere, you're in *traffic* or even without traffic it just isn't done

anymore, you have to keep going, actually it's one of the rules of the road. I see a flower I've never seen or rocks . . . or a glimpse of a blue lake, but you whiz by—you'd have to walk—someday—after you're dead."

A common complaint, but a crucial one for Lorine. With her poor eyesight she had to *pore* over things. Scenery flying by—"Acres covered with bright sweet clover"—were more frustration than joy. And the rocks: she wanted to stop, climb out of the car, touch them, pick over them—but they sped past.

In the Badlands—"150,000 acres of Hell with the fires out"—Lorine found the starkly eroded, pink- and red-striated rocks "rather delicate—in the afternoon. I'd like to be there, not alone, of course, in moonlight, the ruined ruins of Athens maybe. [Frank Lloyd] Wright called it ethereal, 'a distant architecture.'" Then at a rest stop she noticed a flag at half-staff and asked who had died: "I was very tired and when the man said Adlai Stevenson I almost lost consciousness." In the 1950s Adlai Stevenson, an unsuccessful Democratic presidential candidate, had been the hope of liberals, intellectuals, and anyone who perceived that international relationships must be the future of the United States. Stevenson's death inspired the only poem from the vacation:

> The Badlands
>   Adlai Steven-
>   son's death
>
> We'd have danced
> to sandstone spooks
> in a beige land
>
> but for stratified
>   vacancy

Lorine wrote at length to Corman about the trip, weighing its pleasures against its *longueurs*, ending with her return to work on Zukofsky's letters, a challenge more spatially congenial than blurred scenery. Though before leaving for the Black Hills she'd been crushed by "a letter from New York that smashed the retaining wall," obviously Zukofsky hadn't axed the project, because at the end of July she was typing the penultimate manuscript draft "before the final one that LZ approves or—discards."

Plagued by delinquent buyers and renters, Lorine kept in frequent touch with her lawyer, Fred Hobe. During a production of *Carmen* at the Black Hawk Hotel in

March 1963, in which he sang José, Hobe had met an accompanying musician. Thirty-seven-year-old Gail Roub (pronounced Rahb) was an inspiring history teacher at Fort Atkinson High School who had remodeled his father's Rock River cabin about three-quarters of a mile upstream from Lorine and moved to the island in 1959.

"Do you know," Hobe had asked opening night, "that you have a very fine poet living nearby?"

Roub was so incredulous that Hobe arranged a meeting at Lorine's cabin. She received them shyly, but responded to Gail's sympathetic talk. The first record of their friendship is her letter to Hobe of May 4, 1965: "I had no idea Gail was quite that knowing in all the arts. I talked too much that day." She sent Gail her Adlai Stevenson poem, would give him many of her poems, dropping them in his mailbox as she walked by. Sometimes she would drop in on Roub to talk about art, music, literature, politics, and his European travels. Though saying little about her own poetry, she talked enthusiastically about Zukofsky, Jonathan Williams, and Cid Corman. Finally, Gail confronted her:

"Lorine: *who are you?*"

"William Carlos Williams calls me the Emily Dickinson of this century."

Roub's friend Phoebe Sorenson says he was "half in love with her."

Their friendship was cemented one day when Lorine found Gail painting, in vivid green and yellow acrylics, a golden prothonotary warbler who, on its migration, pauses in wooded swamps. Lorine had often heard its one-pitched call in fall and spring: *zweet, zweet, zweet, zweet, zweet.* The vivacity of Roub's painting inspired a poem that went through at least three variations that do much to elucidate her poetic method.

In Version I she is concerned with everything but the objective reality of the bird, calling it "Clerk of May Court" because *prothonotary* means a chief law court clerk. The warbler is perched on Roub's statue of St. Francis, which alienates her; therefore "why judge" the warbler's choice of perch. Version III is an improvement except that she's still focused on St. Francis: "St. Francis' image / —no grimace— / looks down."

Discarding scholarship and St. Francis, Lorine then wrote the poem that was sleeping under Versions I and III:

> Bird singing
> ringing yellow
> green

My friend made green
     ring
          —his painting—
     grass
          the sweet bird
flew in

Al grew increasingly jealous of Lorine and Gail's rapport. He was also aware that both Roub and Hobe felt uncomfortable in his presence and thought Lorine shouldn't have married him. Al, the manly man, fell back upon his only resource and accused Gail of being homosexual. That should have calmed his jealousy, but it didn't.

One evening Gail invited Lorine and his friend Al Haller to his house to see his European travel slides.

"I don't know if I can."

"And certainly invite Al."

"I don't think he'll want to."

Lorine arrived, sat down tentatively, was conspicuously nervous, and soon said she had to leave. Roub and Haller walked her home. As they approached, Al blustered out of the house.

"Oh, darling, it's all right. Don't be like that!"

But Al had been drinking. He went to the bedroom, got the Luger. Lorine telephoned Gail: "He's left here and he's coming to you and I think he's got a gun! Lock the door and turn off all the lights."

Roub speedily obeyed. Al pounded on the door. Getting no response, he staggered home.

Soon after the episode, Gail went to Fred Hobe: "Is Lorine safe with Al Millen?" Hobe advised him not to put himself in the middle of the marriage. When Gail next talked to Lorine, she reassured him:

"Oh, well, Gail, it isn't *so bad*."

"Why did you ever marry him?"

"He's the only man who ever told me he loved me."

Al's behavior depended on how much he drank. As for the gun, he was proud of it: the Luger was a substitute for his missing right hand. Lorine understood this. Though Hobe and Roub felt Lorine's marriage was a disaster and sometimes feared for her safety, Lorine assessed how far her husband would go. True, he was possessive and temperamental. Yet her marriage wasn't *so bad*; it was what she had wanted and settled for:

I married

in the world's black night
for warmth
                    if not repose.
                    At the close—
someone.

"Very often" she was happy with Al. He was in for the long haul.

And there were limits to Gail's friendship. Not understanding her poems, he avoided talking about them, something he later regretted. He was not Zukofsky, Corman, or Jonathan Williams. He was a charming, vital, civilized friend, an escape from Al's TV shows, possessiveness, and, above all, drinking.

21

An End, an Experiment

1965~1966

Time means nothing here
LN about the Lake Superior region

Two uncertainties now dominated Lorine's professional life. Would Zukofsky permit publication of her version of his letters? More crucially, who would publish a "Collected Poems"? "I'm so optimistic about being printed—o me," she'd written Zukofsky in August 1963. The retrospective *My Friend Tree* had never satisfied her. Gail Roub, who may not have understood the poems, understood Lorine's drive. "Some people think she was self-effacing. No. She had a strong sense of who she was. She was afraid of being buried."

In 1965 Jonathan Williams wrote her "in a rapid, off-hand way" requesting all her poems for a collected volume they'd been discussing for years. He still had to find a patron, but "fret not"—she wouldn't have to pay. Yet Williams was so vague that she appealed to Corman: "I've typed for a Collected—61 pages, on the average two poems to a page. Maybe this can help you decide size of book, cost etc. I hate to sound so money-mad, so brash, but—it seems the time has come to make a decision. My heart is in Japan but my social security checks are committed to everything under the sun. However, something like $10 or $20 a month could be managed."

But Cid needed three hundred dollars to publish. Frustrated at having to pay (she who always supported little presses), Lorine sent her manuscript on Cid's recommendation to James Weill at the Elizabeth Press in New Rochelle, New York. Weill replied that he would take 15 of the 122 poems she sent him. Weill was "not easy to please—and that's all right!" Lorine told Corman. It was far from all right.

She turned again to Williams: "Wonder what to call the book. How do you like Tenderness and Gristle—something Lawrence Durrell was talking about one time—I'd like it called *T&G* with explanation or title in full inside and I suppose acknowledgment. However, maybe you can think of something better." She wanted the book published within a year and a half. "If sooner than that," she bribed, "I'll meet your bill somehow." She had *no need* of a deluxe edition.

She wrote in a P.S.: "I'm editing the letters to me of LZ . . . no idea in this world what will happen to it or even if the now very solitarily retired man will approve of all of it (I have his permission, of course, but please do not mention any of this to him, on pain of certain banishment from that far-off, intensely sensitive, cubicle-citadel)."

On September 19, 1965, she mailed the edited letters to Zukofsky. "[V]ery heavy," she told Corman, "cost $10.26. I should have disguised it as second class! 370 pp. You haven't said anything to Louie? I think best not till I get his final say on it—might take him a month now to look it over. . . . God! help me!"

But Zukofsky replied with speed. He approved very little of the manuscript and had little time to spend on it; Catullus and "A" came first. He demanded Lorine's carbon copy. Lorine wrote to Cid:

> [T]he fact that he wants my carbon in no uncertain terms means either that he doesn't trust me—or ANYBODY—or he's thinking of going over enough pages to send you for Origin. Which?
>
> He's afraid of gossip—I swear to you then [French statesman] Poincaré's essays were gossip, Schweitzer's etc . . . altho I'm not above a word or two that brings in the *human*. He thinks of it as biography, I think of it as chunks of beautiful literature, something he wrote not just for me but the world. And while we live.

Lorine could still believe in Zukofsky's good will. In December 1965 she actually urged Williams to ask him to write a foreword to *T&G*. "A bit of a shock," said Lorine (incredibly) when Zukofsky flatly refused. Petitioning again, she asked Zukofsky to allow quotes from his *New Goose* blurb or his supportive letter for her 1951 Guggenheim application. (After all, he had blurbed Mina Loy's *Lunar Baedecker and Time Tables* published by Williams.) Lorine informed Williams: "No go with Louie on using direct quotes from him. It has been difficult for thirty years, Jonathan, yet I suppose he has been—the association thru literature—the most valuable part of my life. I can do nothing but respect him now, black as tho things seem."

Things would get blacker. It's uncertain when Zukofsky finally axed the letter project. Only a few words survive of her side of the correspondence between her mailing the manuscript in September 1965 and a letter of August 8, 1967. She didn't stop communicating; after reading "A"-15 in October 1966, for instance, she wrote "WHAT???—is that Yiddish-gibberish-horse-ish beginning?" Zukofsky must have destroyed letters that, if they mentioned her continued hope for publishing his letters, would have been as unpalatable as their 1930s correspondence.

Lorine had worked hard and long. She was "bitterly crushed," said Corman. In his opinion, Zukofsky was "somewhat disingenuous in pushing against letters, etc. I find it hard to believe he never read Keats' letters or Paige's volume of EP's [Ezra Pound's] or those of the great composers. And wd he have disdained reading Shakespeare's or Homer's—if such existed? He feared being caught with his pants down. Preferred keeping his risks to his honed work. I can understand this—but it won't satisfy." When one considers the inestimable value of the letters of a Keats, Millay, or Wallace Stevens, it decidedly does not satisfy. Yet his refusal is a testimony to the spontaneous intimacy with which he wrote Lorine. Even excised, he could not allow that intimacy to become public.

Rebuked, Lorine stopped sending copies of her poetry to Zukofsky. She wouldn't know that, when he endowed the University of Texas–Austin with his papers, he would include drafts of her poetry. She defied him by preserving enough of his letters from the 1930s to establish once and for all their intellectual and emotional intimacy. Had Lorine kept Zukofsky's letters whole, she would have left posterity one of the richest surviving records of friendship between a male and female poet. But then, she always did what Zukofsky asked.

She had an unexpected encounter with the man. Darning Al's socks one August evening in 1966, Lorine looked up to see Louie in cap and overcoat loping across the black-and-white TV screen. She threw down her mending, ran to wake Al: "Come quick, LZ is on the TV!" She hadn't seen him for twelve years.

The half-hour Public Television program riveted her. Louie looked older, of course—white hair, emaciated (in 1960 he weighed 106 pounds)—"but *there*, the same as when I saw him last in '54. Looked the same—does not feel the same, I know. During the half hour it all came out—Shakespeare, Catullus, Celia, Creeley and Duncan mentioned as admirers, and Cid Corman mentioned, Spinoza, philosophy of history, valentines."

Filmed in his Brooklyn Heights apartment, Zukofsky reads, among other works, "An impulse to action sings," "Little Wrists," "A marriage song for Florence and Henry," and two valentine poems whose effect, he says, "is like prayer." Between poems he talks about Shakespeare, valentines ("I've gathered quite a number of them in my life"), and Catullus, reminding viewers that his translations attempt to "render the noise of the original." Celia can be seen in the background working in the kitchen; he mentions her music for *Pericles* and jokes drily that she once thought Hollywood should film *Bottom: On Shakespeare.* Paul does not appear.

The voice that thrilled Lorine is a compelling mix of New York City, Columbia University, Jewish cantor, and sinuses. His delivery can be eccentric: sometimes he drops the final *r* in a word, sometimes not; pronounces "Little Wrists" "little riss." Sometimes he reads energetically, others languorously, but always intoning the lines. His technique is the opposite that Niedecker's poems—which he called "as atonal as Honegger"—invites; but then the logorrheic Zukofsky's bent is to proliferate while Niedecker's is to condense.

Lorine reported to Cid:

> And the talking between readings was lovely and he does it so easily and naturally and with that soft hint of sighing humor. Altogether it had *vitality*, something I felt was missing from the Robert Lowell and Richard Wilbur films I'd seen. . . . The long, skeleton-supple hand reaching for a book or pointing to a couch cover (afghan, I guess) beside him [that Celia had made from old wool] and his saying "I don't think my poetry is any better than this." . . . And "my publisher (of Bottom) asked me to explain the book after it was printed."—and a change in the sound of his breath to indicate a hint of amusement. He did not look sick but I was conscious of knowing he was. . . . This came on between 9:00 and 10:00 pm and of course sleep for two or three hours impossible."

Good things were happening, nonetheless. Corman wanted to relaunch *Origin*, featuring Lorine. She agreed to have thirty-eight old and new poems ready for the July 1966 issue, though "you know a deadline bothers me even if it's set for landings behind the moon a century from now."

Then Stella Leonardos, a Brazilian poet, requested poems for an anthology. Heady, being translated into Portuguese. Eventually the anthology arrived in the mail: "A book larger than our apartment in Milwaukee and addressed to Sweet Lady Lorine from Stella Leonardos. All I have to do now is find a translator. And add a room to the house."

Another new connection was Morgan Gibson, poet and professor at the University of Wisconsin–Milwaukee who'd written her wanting a copy of *My Friend Tree.* Gibson edited *Arts in Society*, a university publication he was trying to leaven with poetry; he asked Lorine for poems. (She was delighted to receive five dollars for "Churchill's Death.") With her usual generosity she recommended Gibson to Corman: "I can honestly say I believe you will be satisfied. I've never met him and I'll probably never feel he's my 'friend' . . . tho we live within what—four miles of each other." They might have met: Gibson invited her to readings and to read at the university, "but I fight shy of that kind of thing."

Gibson asked Lorine to review nine books of Corman's poetry for *Arts in Society*. For the silence-loving Lorine, Corman was the poet of quiet: "Each man an empire when he enters / a silence." She quotes favorite poems, some, like the following, that she might have written herself:

> rain stops
> night knows when
> to listen
>
> what falls
> glistens now
> in the ear

She'd reviewed Zukofsky and Corman, she told Cid: it was enough. When her piece finally appeared: "how tiny my comments on you in that heavy, pedantic periodical!"

One evening as Lorine was watching TV, Gibson suddenly appeared on the screen—"good, young face with dark-rimmed glasses, lovely head of hair." She felt, she told him, "both happy and terrified"—happy to "meet" him, terrified that his political activism would not only endanger his career but distract him from poetry. Politely she refused to contribute to an anti-Vietnam collection he was publishing: "I share your views for the most part as to Vietnam but for me to get involved in the controversy would be for me to forget poetry. I speak from past experience."

In their "callow youth," Lorine and Zu had jeered at the "hollowdays." Lorine was mellowing. For Christmas 1965, she and Al bought Al's granddaughter, Bonnie, a huge red dog from the chain store Copps. (They loved Copps.) Lorine toasted the holiday in wine with the family, giggled, and smiled. To Julie and Gene they gave "Kooky Conversations," a booklet of spousal exchanges recorded by the still-bemused bride:

> Al, one stormy morning: "Well, I'm going to sleep. Watch the weather."
>
> Lorine: "We voted, both going into the one booth . . . must have thought it was a hunting blind."

Al: "I must become acquainted with the caretaker of a cemetery so
I can have access to his compost heap."

Lorine used his dark humor in "Tradition" to equate gardening/writing with
the compost-making of death:

> Time to garden
>   before I
>   die—
>
> to meet
>   my compost maker
>   the caretaker
> of the cemetery

For some reason, Æneas McAllister was on Lorine's mind; she wrote two
nostalgias. In "Autumn Night" the "lisp and wisp / of dry leaves" remind her of
their walks with his sons and "those glimmering talks." The second poem recalls a
lonely summer and Æneas's return, bright as Orion, with his dog:

> I lost you to water, summer
> when the young girls swim,
> to the hot shore
> to little peet-tweet-
>   pert girls.
>
> Now it's cold your bright knock
> —Orion's, with his dog after him—
> at my door, boy
> on a winter
>   wave ride.

The Æneas poems appeared with thirty-six others in *Origin* for July 1966.
Lorine wrote Cid: "The issue received—mother and child doing fine I almost
want to say! . . . At first I worried a great deal—letters you said were included—
Lordy, what had I said? But turns out OK. Got the mail in yesterday along with
some groceries. I read Origin standing up, every line, before putting the meat and
milk in the refrigerator. I sweetened while the milk soured."

Considering passages of Lorine's letters poetry, Corman included six, among
them "Niedecker Weather": "Well—Milwaukee had eleven and one half inches of

snow but no rain. The piles at street corners are turning black. Ruskin would have perished here, but then, poor man, he perished anyhow." The issue was a solid tribute to the poet Corman admired.

And then Jonathan Williams announced that *T&G* was imminent. Lorine responded, delighted: "T&G coming out—cheers. A moment of raising glasses to each other (and Pound heard the clink as they touched)—I wonder how many will swallow it." But Williams was optimistic.

Lorine was taking notes for Al's weeklong vacation beginning July 26, when they would make a circle tour of the north shore of Lake Superior. She clipped *Milwaukee Journal* travel articles, took the bus to the Milwaukee library to read about Great Lakes geology, read Harlan Henthorne Hatcher's *The Great Lakes* at the Fort Atkinson library. She read the memoirs of Henry Rowe Schoolcraft, who discovered the source of the Mississippi River and wrote books that Longfellow relied on for *The Song of Hiawatha*. She read Loren Eisely's *Darwin's Century*; took notes on Azoic Time, Pre-Cambrian Time, and the Paleozoic Era; on place names and French explorers; on how to identify tourmaline, hornblende, granite, gneiss. She jotted down evocative names: Scalp Lake, Fish-line Lake, Winnibigoshish Lake; Pigeon, Knife, Chocolate, Laughing Fish, and Leaf rivers. She noted points of interest: Pictured Rocks National Park, the Sault Ste. Marie International Bridge, Split-Rock Lighthouse, "Eagle Harbor—slow down for it—old store with railing operated since 1859." She notes where agates, jasper, and carnelians can be found, where to see "knobs of Archaen rock, oldest rock known, some rounded by glacial action."

She bound four half-sheets of brief notes between construction paper and fastened them with brass pins. "Green Bay," "Remember Rocks," "Schoolcraft," and "Minnesota Alphabetized" would go along in the Buick for reference. She charted their route north along Lake Michigan: Oshkosh, Shawano, Oconto, Menominee, Marinette.

Such effort for a seven-day vacation seems excessive. Yet her reading of Trelawny's *Reminiscences of Shelley and Byron* had yielded only the eighteen-line "Who was Mary Shelley?" and a biography of Margaret Fuller a poem of four lines. Lorine was planning to get a long poem out of this "Traverse des Millens"— hence she required "[a] millennium of notes for my *magma* opus!"

At any rate, her curious mind made not researching for the trip unthinkable, poem or no. She was interested in everything—history, ethnicity, land-mass, flora, fauna, fossils, Indian carvings, shipping, languages, place names, lighthouses, Indian tribes, the Hiawatha territory, fur trading. Language: how *bonjour* was corrupted to *bosho*, *Groselliers* to *gooseberry*. But she was overwhelmingly interested in rocks; they would become "the heroes" of her poem. It fascinated her that *impurities* in rocks made them beautiful.

There were other reasons for extensive note-taking. Lorine could not count on the spontaneous visual discovery most travelers take for granted. She had to *know* points of interest beforehand so she could tell Al—hell-bent on making good time since he'd already made the Lake Superior trip with Margaret—what to look and stop for. As point of pride, she also wanted to know more geography and geology than her knowledgeable husband, who'd driven the north central states extensively. Finally, time was short, with little opportunity for spontaneous exploration.

On July 26 they drove north, left Wisconsin at Marinette, and took Highway 35 into Michigan's Upper Peninsula. Swaths of wild sweet pea edging birch and evergreens spun by. Told at Pictured Rocks National Lakeside Park that the best view was from water, they bought postcards instead. The Indian Agency House built by Henry Schoolcraft was boarded up. They stayed the first night in Manistique on Lake Michigan, then crossed into Canada via the Intercontinental Bridge connecting the twin cities of Sault Ste. Marie, where they heard Brit-English and "French spoken like a brook over pebbles." They began circling "the shining big sea-water":

> What I didn't foresee was that the highway doesn't always run right next the lake . . . and that you can travel almost entirely around [the north shore of] Superior . . . without finding more than a couple of accessible beaches. Where you can with some difficulty walk over that terrain to the shore you suddenly find you're on a high bluff and how are you going to get way down to the water. And you're whizzing along the highway with a glimpse of beach but there's traffic behind and you simply continue to whizz. Or the shore when you do get down is sand, not pebbles. . . . [T]he only animals we saw on the trip were dead porcupines on the road. . . . [T]he stones that had a shine turned out to be bottle-caps.

Lorine's notes paint a more cheerful picture of the vacation.

> Lorine: "One could say that impurities in the language make the beauty just as impurities in the rock cause the beauty of color there. And speaking of language, how does Sault ever become *Soo*?"
>
> Al: "Yes, well, help me read the road signs, they're so small in Canada—and greenish, they melt into the forest."
>
> Lorine: "What signs?"

Lorine: "In every part of every living thing is stuff that once was rock that turned to soil. In blood the minerals of the rock."
Al: "What's that?"
Lorine: "The beginning of a poem I'll send to *Arts in Society.*"

Al: "Ah, Agate Shop, north of Soo, Canada. Touch it: polished ruby out of corundum, lapis lazuli from changing limestone, apricot-glow red-brown carnelian-sard and silica-sand agate Greek-named, Exodus-antique, kicked up in America's Northwest, how do you do, Agate."
Lorine: "I'm off!"
Al: "Yes!"

Al: "There's a Moose Crossing sign!"
Lorine, expecting a moose: "WHERE??"

The comedians dropped south into the "land of the sky-tinted water" and found Lake Itasca, "a sweet little swampy place where the great river rises." "Is it really *the* source of the Mississippi?" asked Al.

Lorine: "Schoolcraft called it the primary source. You feel a roll— a journeying of rocks, soil, water, in all this. The pebble was once leaf and the leaf becomes pebble. And the silence. Where is mind in all this? Shakespeare's 'nature's blemish is the mind.'"
Al: "He didn't read his science fiction or he'd know everything is mind."

They also found what Lorine craved: a public beach for stones. She was "happy for a time"—until the Buick got stuck in loose sand. The last night of the trip they stayed in Little Falls, Minnesota, crossed into Wisconsin, and took the "everything looks the same" expressway to arrive at Blackhawk Island on Monday, August 1.

Along with postcards and brochures, thrifty Lorine brought home only a Lake Superior agate, Uruguayan carnelian, and Canadian sodilite. Yet the trip was "a great delight if I can make the poem. . . . I'm going into a kind of retreat so far as time (going to be geologic time from now on!) is concerned."

Sending for geological survey maps from the U.S. government, she continued to research and write. In September she sent "Circle Tour" to Morgan Gibson for *Arts in Society*, explaining that it "shows a working out of (thru) trouble into a kind of rest or free feeling." Re-reading the poem a few weeks later, she was horrified. "Between typographical errors and weak spots in the poem itself I'm actually embarrassed," she wrote him. "Oh, the terrors of the long poem (altho I maintain a long poem is made up of short ones). May I trouble you to return it?" She revised, then retitled it "TRAVELERS / Lake Superior Region"; Gibson accepted it for the 1967 fall/winter issue.

Wallace Stevens believed that "a short poem is more difficult to write than a long one because a long poem acquires an impetus of its own." Niedecker did not agree. She hadn't written a long poem since *For Paul*—and the Paul poems (336 lines) were written individually over five years, during which she wrote many others. Though she intended "TRAVELERS / Lake Superior Region" as a long poem, she eventually chiseled it into some of the purest Objectivist work she'd ever done: "short, sharp (we hope) nuggets of that rocky tour—why would anyone ever want to write a *long* poem?!" Niedecker was having her cake and eating it too. The unity of "TRAVELERS / Lake Superior Region," therefore, derives chiefly from its subject—a journey—and from Lorine's cosmic, materialist philosophy. It is also the philosophy of Herman and Nina Schneider in *Rocks, Rivers and the Changing Earth*, which she read for the trip:

> The leaf was once the stone, the cloud was once the sea. The earth tells its story over and over again—the leaf will become a stone, the cloud will become the sea again. . . . You are part of the earth's story. In your blood is iron from plants that drew it out of the soil. Your teeth and bones were once coral of the sea. . . . Every bit of you is a bit of the earth, and has been on many strange and wonderful journeys over countless millions of years.

Niedecker believed in a universe in which what dies is re-created, long before she told Al on the trip, "You can see how we return to our source. And there is never any death. After 'death' there are life cycles, even tho inanimate." Her favorite philosopher, Marcus Aurelius, had taught her to "wait with a good grace for death, as no more than a simple dissolving of the elements. . . . If those elements themselves take no harm from their ceaseless forming and re-forming, why look with mistrust upon the change and dissolution of the whole?" Thus her ending question:

> The smooth black stone
> I picked up in true source park
>   the leaf beside it
> once was stone
>
> Why should we hurry
> Home

The "hurry / Home" segment is one of only three in which Lorine appears—and she mentions the Great Lake proper not at all; "you have been in my mind / between my toes / agate," she writes in section eight and ends the poem, in defiance of weighty research, lightly:

> I'm sorry to have missed
> Sand Lake
> My dear one tells me
> we did not
> We watched a gopher there

"LAKE SUPERIOR" adheres closely to her notes as it balances the temporary influence of humans—Native American tribes, Radisson, Marquette, Joliet, Schoolcraft—against the longevity of "peaks of volcanic thrust," "wave-cut Cambrian rock," and "Sea-roaring caverns." "Strange," she'd written Corman before the trip, "—we are always inhabiting more than one realm of existence—but they all fit in if the art is right."

Was the art of "LAKE SUPERIOR" right? In *Origin* Lorine had read Bashō's account of his travels when, in the spring of 1689, he set out on foot with his friend and disciple Sora on a dangerous nine-month journey from which they might not return. Bashō's pilgrimage poems are "cries of their occasions, of someone intently passing through a world, often arrested by the momentary nature of things within an unfathomable 'order.'" His journey is as much about the heart and spirit's geography as about the land he passes through as he encounters people to whom he reacts. Thus Bashō is always emotionally present in the poems: "I, wordless, tried sleeping but couldn't"; "We found our hearts beating faster"; "The pain of one who goes, the emptiness of the one left behind."

The Lake Superior trip was a delight, she'd told Corman, if she could *make* the poem—strange word for a poet who believed that "[w]riting is toning down the ecstasy that 'came.'" "LAKE SUPERIOR" did not come in ecstasy; nor, since it is made of distinct poems, does it acquire a long poem's impetus. The segments are hardly "cries of their occasions," nor does emotion bind them. "LAKE SUPERIOR" is a poem artfully wrought by intellect, skill, and a passion for knowing. Her taut forms are elegant, as always.

Yet Lorine knew Bashō's poem intimately. Her frustration at the difference between Bashō's poetic pilgrimage and her pre-charted, researched, air-conditioned vacation charges her account of the "Traverse des Millens." She knew it must produce a very different kind of poem, and "by the way," she admitted to Corman, "it's *not* the best I've ever done."

Yet she was unapologetic about her passion for natural science—"Geology has done so much for me!"—and hardly through with her north central subject, which she would continue to explore in "TRACES OF LIVING THINGS" and "WINTERGREEN RIDGE."

22

North Central

1966~1967

a way of writing poetry which is not Imagist nor Objectivist
fundamentally nor Surrealism alone . . . reflective, maybe
Niedecker to Gail Roub

B̲ob Nero, an English major at the University of Wisconsin–Milwaukee, had struck up a correspondence with Cid Corman as well as read the July 1966 Niedecker *Origin*. Nero remembered: "Cid had written me that Lorine was the only poet in my part of the country (Milwaukee) who could offer me any sense of what the world of poetry was all about. . . . The poets and writers I was hanging around with all knew of Lorine and she had taken on an aura of somewhat mythic proportions, enhanced by the fact that no one had actually ever seen her."

Determined to unravel the mystery, Nero wrote her. Lorine replied. They discussed writers: Wallace Stevens's *Letters* and the Scots poet Hugh MacDiarmid, whom Nero couldn't stand, though Lorine defended a poet who used difficult geological terms. They discussed the 1964 *City Lights Journal* Ezra Pound interview. "I can't get it out of my mind," wrote Lorine of Pound's denunciation of his past. "I mistrust something—it's not probably all on the up and up. *If* he means his fascist mistakes, why doesn't he say so? But I feel the pity of his 'pain,' his lonely old age."

Nero suggested they meet at her apartment. Lorine put him off: her husband slept during the day, she couldn't accommodate visitors. He proposed meeting downtown. "I'm closeted (closed up) just now with a longish poem," Lorine replied on August 12. A month later she phoned Nero, "sounding on the telephone . . . like a twelve-year-old girl, a small bird-like voice, maybe a sparrow." She could meet him the next day at the Milwaukee Public Museum on Wells Street. He should look for someone with blonde hair wearing blue glasses. Nero described their first meeting:

> She was a slight person, modestly dressed, looking like a retired schoolteacher; walking down the street, she would be invisible. I almost didn't recognize her because the blonde hair was mostly grey. We sat on a leather couch near the museum book and gift shop and talked—about what exactly I forget, poetry probably, literary gossip, likes and dislikes. It was the strangest meeting I have ever had with anyone: a strictly formal meeting in a public place. Lorine had come to the museum to research geology for her Lake Superior poem.

Encouraged, Nero invited her to dinner, but Lorine fought shy. "I did meet Bob Nero for an hour or so at the new museum here in Milwaukee," she wrote Cid. "Nice boy, very much interested in poetry but I could form no idea as to his abilities. . . . I gave him an extra copy I had of *Test* [Zukofsky's *Test of Poetry*]. I can't enter into social meetings with him and his wife . . . since I housekeep— plural: houses—and write and read and walk and sew and sing at the top of my voice when folky records are being played on the phonograph." To Nero she wrote: "Fate usually intervenes to keep me from being socially active—nicely social I mean. . . . But fate has worked hand in hand too with my writing life—I don't mourn the lone-ness of it for poetry. In fact, I couldn't do it any other way and I have the presumption to feel that others writing should retire into themselves deeper than they do."

On February 7 Jonathan Williams came to Milwaukee on the condition that the university give him two days of readings and several parties. "I am not so socially inclined," Lorine wrote Cid, "but I feel if he is not presenting me with a bill for the book in whole or in part, I can afford to be nice when he comes." She planned to attend only his evening reading, meet Morgan Gibson and others: "[I]t's commendable in a poet to live secluded but no use to make them feel I'm hiding away." But Nero persuaded her to go to both Williams's afternoon and evening sessions, with dinner at the Neros' apartment between.

Nero remarked: "Lorine was noticeably edgy about the whole thing. I think she was mainly afraid of running out of energy (she was then 63), and the thought of that much sudden social stimulation and contact, for a recluse like herself, must have been disconcerting. . . . When we went to pick her up, I was struck by her very, very poor circumstances—a two room flat with gas space heater, dark." Lorine sensed Nero's shock, took him by the hand, and explained: "Here, Bob, this is where I write." He barely made out a shadowy board or desk with a small typewriter perched on top.

In the hall on campus, "several young poets and students began introducing themselves to Lorine. A local literary critic, Rich Mangelsdorff, came up and told her that in time her work would come to take its rightful place in the body of world literature. Lorine was clearly overjoyed and embarrassed by all the attention."

Lorine wrote to Gail Roub:

> Jonathan Williams dug his car out of Chicago—all that snow there, you know, and got here just a few minutes before his scheduled reading Tues. afternoon. . . . Merrill Hall . . . frightfully cold and when the radiators did come on they made a noise hard to hear thru. He read with a cigar going, maybe to help keep him warm! . . . poetry out of an incense burner. . . . No, no sign of my book [*T&G*] but large mention of it, introductions to everyone, heads of departments being very nice.

The dreaded socializing with the Neros lay ahead. Bob tried to put her at ease by playing a tape of Wallace Stevens, whose "elegant sonority" seemed to impress her, though she'd told Nero that what "one hears as he reads to himself is the best, probably. LZ—only he should read his poems—a kind of continuous chant." During dinner she talked of how she anticipated Jonathan's evening reading and mustn't overexert herself. Her fear was purely nervous; she was in tolerable health. With blankets to cover their knees, they returned to campus.

A more typical picture of non-mainstream Poetry America would be hard to find: Niedecker trapped in a dark apartment, Jonathan shunted into an "old, almost abandoned hall" for two sessions attended by a handful of English majors and a few heads of departments. According to Morgan Gibson, the English Department responded only to big names like Auden, Lowell, and Dickey. The West Coast Beat poet Allen Ginsberg, denied access to Catholic Marquette University, attracted an audience of a thousand when Gibson invited him to the UW–Milwaukee campus. Though Ginsberg was hardly as distinguished as Auden or Lowell, dissent was popular and his obscenities and trashing of convention pleasurably shocking.

Lorine was aware of the West Coast ferment—"buzzing" with it, in fact. Ginsberg's "Kaddish" moved her, "but why must the show of vitality come by way of misery, dirt, sexiness. No better poetry than the quiet." Yet she thought Ginsberg eminently preferable to the mediocrity found in most poetry magazines. "Funny, I can't get the roaring, ranting, filthy, spiritual *Kaddish* out of my mind."

Next day Jonathan came to lunch. Al and Lorine had painted walls, washed windows and curtains in anticipation, but "Al slept right thru—he was just in the next room with a thin curtain between." Jonathan promised proofs of *T&G* when he returned to North Carolina after this reading tour. He brought his tape recorder, but the former debater and singer refused: "I've thought so much about poems read aloud and poems printed. . . . Poems are for one person to another, spoken thus, or read silently." She feared that if she wrote poems to be read, she would feel the need to heighten the drama, thus losing "a tight, perfect kind of poetry." She also feared nervous interaction with a potentially restive audience: "If the silence could be governed among the people, if your voice came from somewhere not seen, i.e. radio, or out of suffused light—perhaps OK."

Yet why did she object to a very private recording? Memories of being called "Squeaky" in school; self-comparison to Zukofsky, whose voice she so admired; the fact that she had to use a magnifying glass; stubbornness? Perhaps all of the above.

After lunch, in front of the bleak apartment building, Jonathan photographed Lorine looking trim and self-contained in a dark coat, blue turban hat, and the blue-rimmed glasses. Then the excitement was over. "Thought you might like to know," Lorine wrote Gail Roub, "—now after being Queen for a Day—two days—my riches have turned to rags and I'm back in my chimney corner again."

The previous year, after sending Corman poems for the Niedecker *Origin*, she had "felt something like subliminals coming on—dream, mind at rest, automatic writing etc. . . . reverting to my youth (my interest in the 1930s) so I let it come! I loved it but the spring is not quite so fresh and jet-fast as it was back then . . . funny thing, tho, when you get used to it, it does seem to be enough." Lorine did not send out the five-part sequence "SUBLIMINAL," though these poems were not nearly as impenetrable as the experiments Harriet Monroe had rejected in 1934:

> Sleep's dream
> the nerve-flash in the blood

> The sense
> of what's seen

> "I took cold
> on my nerves"—my mother
>
> tall, tormented
> darkinfested

Lorine had hoped that exile from Blackhawk Island might reinvent it for her. "SUBLIMINALS" turned out to be preparation for an "ecstasy" that came as she was still working on her north central poems:

> My life
> > by water—
> > > Hear
>
> spring's
> > first frog
> > > or board
>
> out on the cold
> > ground
> > > giving
>
> Muskrats
> > gnawing
> > > doors
>
> to wild green
> > arts and letters
> > > Rabbits
>
> raided
> > my lettuce
> > > One boat
> two—
> > pointed toward
> > > my shore
>
> thru birdstart
> > wingdrip
> > > weed-drift

                              of the soft
                           and serious—
                              Water

This is Niedecker in top form. Ecstasy disciplined; sensuous, finely tuned
music; flowing enjambments controlled by chiseled words. The poem's energy
springs from the conflict between danger and beauty, nature and art. One can
float with birdstart, wingdrip, soft water; yet rabbits raid lettuce and the gnawing
wet muskrat threatens the poet's "wild green arts and letters." Henry had kept two
boats tied to his dock; Lorine disliked boats, so while they seem to symbolize
escape, yet pointed toward her shore, they suggest a possible threat. The pivotal
word in the poem, however, is "serious," a felicitous example of "Niedecker's knife
buried to the hilt before you know it's drawn." That is, just when the reader is
lulled by drip and drift, the water turns deadly. The poet's art celebrates wild
green, but wild green is equally the adversary.

She was to have taped the poem for Jonathan. Corman accepted it with ten
others for *Origin* 7—these poems, Zukofsky would write her, were among her
very best. Lorine informed Corman: "Wild, wild praise from the 'neglected' (!)
and neglecting one." Meanwhile, England was extending its hand "like a brother"
due to the efforts of Jonathan Williams, who had praised Niedecker to Stuart
Montgomery, founder of Fulcrum Press in London. Fulcrum published Basil
Bunting, Ed Dorn, Robert Duncan, Roy Fisher, Ian Hamilton Finlay, Tom Pickard,
and Gary Snyder. Montgomery offered to publish *T&G* simultaneously in England
with Williams's Jargon Press edition. "Overwhelming whatever he means, very
nice," Lorine told Jonathan.

Lorine was known in England. Montgomery sent her a review by Kenneth
Cox that half-pleased her with statements like "Lorine Niedecker's poems are few
and short but their character is not easy to define" and "The poems of Lorine
Niedecker leave the reader in peace." Her poems were not few—319, to date—nor
do the cited "Remember my little granite pail?" "There's a better shine," "Now in
one year," and the wrenching "I've been away from poetry" leave a reader in peace.
Yet Cox is often perceptive. Niedecker's poems are "the speech of the American
people, whittled clean," and, though "simple in appearance and sparing in expres-
sion," convey a complexity "beyond the reach of analysis." After consideration,
Lorine commented to Jonathan: "well, I suppose on the whole it isn't a bad piece
of work and actually after he gets going he seems genuinely appreciative of me
poems."

More England arrived: Basil Bunting, friend of Pound and Zukofsky, visited the island in June. After poverty and neglect, Bunting was spending the academic year at the University of California–Santa Barbara following the successful Fulcrum Press edition of his autobiographical poem "Briggflats." He arrived with his two daughters, Roudaba and Bourtai. Lorine had no food in the house so took them to the tea room in Fort Atkinson. Basil wistfully said: "I don't suppose it would be possible to get a glass of beer here?"

Bunting had a Wisconsin connection, having married Marian Culver from Eau Claire and also having once considered going into the carp-seining business with Henry Niedecker. Bunting had long admired Lorine's work; the talk was animated. He told her he'd invited Zukofsky to his reading at the Guggenheim that spring, but fearing "drafts," Zukofsky refused to attend. Later they spent a "painful hour" together. Bunting was surprised to find his old friend "very bitter and, strangely, very jealous." Lorine was unsurprised; she'd long known that Louie had become "very selfish" in his later years.

Basil asked if Lorine ever wrote long poems. She explained *For Paul* and "LAKE SUPERIOR," told him she thought his poetry "tough and lovely." Bunting called her work "[v]ery delicate, many implications, none obvious." They had much in common as poets (and crucial differences). Lorine wrote Corman: "And of course the question came up of reading poems aloud. The world is mad, MAD on this subject." But Basil charmed her: "his manner is timid and tender. Withal so kindly. O lovely day for me." To Jonathan she wrote: "a high point in my later life. I think in my afterlife I'd like T. E. Lawrence to come. And the Jameses—Henry, Wm. & Alice." Basil invited her to come to Madison while he was there, but she declined, telling him they'd meet in *Poetry*. Only later did she regret not asking him what kinds of wild plants grew in his northeastern part of England—"how dark / how inconsiderate / of me." About Lorine to Williams, Bunting wrote: "nobody else has been buried quite so deep."

Island summer weekends were heaven. Lorine wrote mornings while Al fed birds, polished the car, hoed the garden. After lunch they mowed the lawn and weeded her flowers, "a glorious time" though she still had problems with renters and ghastly cleaning jobs when they left, and she still loathed owning property.

Another thing disturbed her. She was sincerely fond of Al's daughter Julie, her husband Gene, and their children Bonnie and Steven, though, said Julie, "she was not a grandmother. She would blush and giggle like a girl when my kids hugged her." Julie knew they had to leave Sundays before Al and Lorine's favorite TV program *60 Minutes*; she didn't realize that Lorine could not be dropped in on. "Gene and the kids and I drove out to Blackhawk Island on a whim. Lorine was very upset—we'd interrupted her writing. 'Why didn't you call!' We did not stay long." Lorine was upset enough to complain to Louie: "They don't wait to be asked, just 'we're coming.' . . . maybe they look on our place as a cottage by a river whereas to me it's home."

But even planned visits could distress Lorine. "Captive in my own house yesterday," she told Gail Roub, "—family gathering. Enough said." A snapshot from one family visit shows her on the cottage steps with pretty Julie and her children. Lorine sits on a lower step, wearing a short-sleeved green and black plaid cotton dress. Her slender arms and legs are pale; she is wearing white ankle-socks and tan sandals. She looks away, her pained expression not unlike her look in Anna Ramsay's wedding photograph. Yet the trouble could be Al as much as Al's family: "Why can't I be happy / in my sorrow / my drinking man / today / my quiet / tomorrow."

She was working hard: "sent out 16 poems last week. Production is good." One she sent Corman was "rather spontaneous from a folk conversation and I suppose some of my own dark forebodings." Forgetting her early belief that artists must talk to and about themselves, she apologized for "another *I* poem. My god, I must try to get away from that." Yet she continually debated her marriage:

> I married
>
> in the world's black night
> for warmth
> if not repose.
> At the close—
> someone.
>
> I hid with him
> from the long range guns.
> We lay leg
> in the cupboard, head
> in closet.
>
> A slit of light
> at no bird dawn—
> Untaught
> I thought
> he drank

too much.
I say
    I married
    and lived unburied.
I thought—

Lorine also, as she explained to Gail Roub that summer of 1967, continued to ponder how to

> define a way of writing poetry which is not Imagist nor Objectivist fundamentally nor Surrealism alone . . . reflective, maybe. The basis is direct and clear—what has been seen or heard—but something gets in, overlays all that to make a state of consciousness. . . . The visual form is there in the background and the words convey what the visual form gives off after it's felt in the mind. A heat that is generated and takes in the whole world of the poem. A light, a motion, inherent in the whole. Not surprising since modern poetry and old poetry if it's good, proceeds not from one point to the next linearly but in a circle. The *tone* of the thing. And awareness of everything influencing everything. Early in life I looked back of our buildings to the lake and said, "I am what I am because of all this—I am what is around me—those woods have made me." . . . I used to feel that I was goofing off unless I held only to the hard, clear image, the thing you could put your hand on but now I dare do this reflection.

On July 24, Lorine and Al drove north again for a two-week vacation, first to Copper Harbor, Michigan's northernmost point, then along Lake Superior's south shore. Lorine recorded little of this excursion or their next in early September to Door County. A few notes, photographs, and postcards, and a brief mention to Corman of Door County: "you know—that thumb-peninsula out into L. Michigan—limestone, autumn leaves, fishing villages. The whole north country, I'm completely absorbed in it, I'm buried and rise again." She had been working on "TRACES OF LIVING THINGS," the second part of the poem series to be called *North Central.* Door County would give her the third, "WINTERGREEN RIDGE."

They returned to a Milwaukee in racial turmoil. An activist Catholic priest, Father James Groppi, was leading north-side blacks on regular "Freedom Marches" to Milwaukee's south side to protest segregated schools and housing. One of the marchers' routes was the 16th Street viaduct spanning the Menomonee River Valley, considered a symbolic divide; the other was the 6th Street bridge, Lorine's bridge. Groppi was arrested frequently; in September the National Guard was called in.

Al was "extremely prejudiced against blacks" and neither he nor Lorine were sure that Groppi was the right leader, since his being a priest inflamed the Polish Catholic south side. Lorine wrote to Jonathan Williams: "Tense situation in Milwaukee. . . . Each week end going out to the river I take a box of books and extra clothes in case the roads get blocked and we can't get back into Milwaukee. My Polish neighbors are to blame for some of the worst disturbances." The protests apparently inspired no poetry, though "*Shelter*"—"Holed damp / cellar-black beyond / the main atrocities"—speaks of besiegement.

Every letter now to the peripatetic Jonathan pointedly asked about *T&G*. A flood of sustained creativity made her increasingly frustrated with the delay. Stuart Montgomery in England was ready to publish *T&G* and asking for other poems ("I'm hungry to help"), other editors wanted her, *Arts and Society* was paying her sixty dollars for "LAKE SUPERIOR," she had finished "TRACES OF LIVING THINGS." Frustrated, she sent "LAKE SUPERIOR," "*My Life by Water*," and "TRACES" to Montgomery for Fulcrum Press, apologizing to Cid: "I hope I haven't done the wrong thing. . . . Probably all it means is another long stretch of geologic time before anything really gets printed. The only time the lava flows is those moments while the poems are being written. I should remind them tho, that they don't see time as I do who haven't too much more of it."

Though eclectic, "TRACES OF LIVING THINGS," said Stuart Montgomery, has a "strange feeling of sequence." That sequence derives from Niedecker's constant merging of human with nature. Man is "leafing towards you." A man "bends to inspect / a shell / Himself / part coral / and mud / clam." Wave lines on sand are repeated on the human forehead. Humans are as contact-hard as stone. A leaf's eye and spine morph into "neverending / head / to see." The poet wishes to move before her husband "in a favorable wind." John F. Kennedy is a "black-marked tulip / not snapped by the storm." Thoughts unfold like fans on mergansers' heads. Few poets have so hauntingly expressed the commonality that binds human animal to animal, earth, and its atmosphere.

That fall she wrenched her back from sawing down two small trees. "Can't get to the long poem I spoke to you about tho any moment it might happen. Could we make Christmas the dead line? If not, we'll forget it, Cid."

But illness "knocked out" of her the "something wild" she longed to do: "I feel it won't be done unless as a coda for the marsh ["*My Life by Water*"] and my life long poem ["PAEAN TO PLACE"] to be done next year sometime. . . . it's wintering in a grub stage, only hope it transmutes into something as nice looking as the dragonfly next summer—the kind of thing I mean is in the air, Cid, it will be done by somebody else if I don't—then again maybe I'm all wrong or I can't do it: would have to be painted or put into music notation." Finally, she couldn't do it. This "other song"—a wild letting go—was beyond her power because it went against her poetic grain.

She had some studio portraits taken for the jackets of *T&G* and *North Central.* Gail Roub so hated them that he offered to photograph her himself. "Mebbe I offended you after working for me all day Sunday—I said no to almost all the photos." On second thought, she'd decided that the glossy one, blown up a little, "would not show the aging, the fissures in the rock—not so much. . . . you see: at least until I get *well* known, a non-candid might be best. Also, let's suppose Willa Cather & Emily Dickinson's photos were anything other than those we know of them, perfectly calm & beautiful—they belong with Time, you might say."

As it turns out, Jonathan's and Gail's photos are the only ones to capture the essence of the mature Niedecker. "She had the figure of a girl even in her sixties," says Julie, "a few wrinkles, but pale, unfreckled skin. Always that light step. Gray-blonde hair. Never 'old.'" Roub's photographs of Lorine do show some fissures in the rock; they also show mental and spiritual toughness in the strong nose and chin and unflinching gaze; and, in the stoic, parenthetical lines about the mouth, pain.

23

Full Flood

1967–1969

Nobody, nothing / ever gave me / greater thing / than time / unless
light / and silence / which if intense / makes sound
"WINTERGREEN RIDGE"

In late November 1967 Lorine completed the 282-line poem
"WINTERGREEN RIDGE," inspired by her visit to the Ridges
Sanctuary on the Lake Michigan side of Door County Peninsula that September.
The Ridges is a uniquely preserved succession of curved swells and hollows,
remnants of original beaches laid down by wind and sand and thatched with
boreal plants that create a living museum of change and succession from the Ice Age
to the present. Like Wordsworth in "Lines Composed a Few Miles above Tintern
Abbey" or Robert Lowell in "The Quaker Graveyard in Nantucket," Niedecker
used the Ridges as a catalyst to reflect upon life, death, history, creation, and art as
she begins a journey "Where the arrows / of the road signs / lead us."

Lorine used William Carlos Williams's triadic stanza to shape the longest poem
she had written; it mitigated her "terror" of writing at length. Opposite to the intent
and method in "LAKE SUPERIOR," her aim was a circular poem written in clean,
hard words overlaid "with the mystery of poetry" that must somehow "connect with
each other and into the next line," sense deriving from sound. "WINTERGREEN
RIDGE" must flow thematically and musically back, forth, and around.

Besides pamphlets available at the Sanctuary (telling, for instance, how
Bailey's Harbor women fought to preserve the Ridges), her chief sources were
Charles Darwin and natural history books. She also certainly read Virginia Eifert's

Journeys in Green Places: The Shores and Woods of Wisconsin's Door Peninsula. Eifert wrote:

> The lady's-slippers, *Cypripedium*, evidently are built to attract and fit small bees, and the whole mechanism of the flower is thus geared to just this one kind of insect. . . . There must be something to attract the bee—color. And there must be a place to land—the curving lip . . . of the pouch. Something must serve to draw its attention into the pouch—hence the nectar on fine, downy hairs in the bottom. Then the insect must be led to an exit which is different from the door by which it entered. It is and must be different because the bee on its way out must contact the pollinia and carry them away, and at the same time leave on the waiting stigma some pollen from a flower previously visited.

Lorine's distillation:

> Lady's slipper's glue
>   and electric threads
>   smack the sweets-seeker
>
> on the head
>   with pollinia
>   The bee
>
> befuddled
>   the door behind him
>   closed he must
>
> go out at the rear
>   the load on him
>   for the next
>
> flower

Niedecker wryly dramatizes the event: the befuddled bee with a load on bumbling to the next flower, obeying nature's law just as (though she doesn't urge the comparison) women and men stumble into sex.

Eifert studied the Ridges for years. Although Niedecker draws on some of her elegant descriptions, the poem is hers. As the narrator climbs the second ridge from the lighthouse, the contrast between the artist who "imagines durable works" and the durable limestone cliffs nurturing horsetails and mosses that have survived the dinosaurs is striking; yet artists' work survives too through "Evolution's wild ones" who "*saved* / continuous life / through change / from Time Began."

Explaining a poem, as Wallace Stevens said, can be both tedious and futile. The "what" of "WINTERGREEN RIDGE" is not hard to grasp. The "how" is crucial. Craftily and intuitively interlacing stanzas, lines, words, syllables, and sounds, Niedecker weaves a supple philosophic web that encompasses the trivial—her "skirt dragging an inch below the knee" as she climbs the ridge—to the cosmic evolution of matter. On her journey of pauses, abrupt stops, observations, memories, and digressions, the narrator juxtaposes the peace and beauty of the ridge against the bulldozers that tried to raze it, the hydrogen bomb, space rockets, mind-changing drugs and the Vietnam war that "cannot be stopped." The Ridges' peace is illusion, of course. At her feet carnivorous plants devour insects, while acidic lichens grind granite to sand. Yet these natural processes do not dismay the dispassionately curious narrator as do human need and greed: "Great God—/ what men desire!" Niedecker consistently sees life steadily and sees it whole, placing herself as an atom in the cosmos without self-pity.

Personal experience plays a greater part in "WINTERGREEN RIDGE" than in the Objectivist "LAKE SUPERIOR." Near a dark wood (death), for example, Niedecker suddenly hears her mother's cry. A friend—Zukofsky—wields a stabbing pen "close to the heart." Like a tree, the aging poet finds relief in shedding her most colorful leaves. And the great gift—time and silence to write in—comes from her (unnamed) husband, Al Millen.

Underlying the poem is her feeling, too, of identification with the flora of the Ridges. Many of the plants are "have-nots": in Eifert's term, plants "which manage to live with too little water or with too much water, in too much sun or in too much shade, in too much acidity or with too little nitrogen, in too much heat and too much cold . . . in too much wind or in too little air." This vegetation has survived as Niedecker has survived.

On their way home she responds to current atrocities: the ugliness of a modern church ("Murder in the Cathedral's / proportions") in Valders, a hacked-up body wrapped in newspaper found at a Milwaukee church (Al quoting from his ever-handy *Milwaukee Journal*), the suicide of a Milwaukee steamfitter. The poem's journey ends back at Blackhawk Island. As the Ridges' wintergreen—grass of Mount Parnassus, sacred to the Muses—symbolizes poetic inspiration, a sunflower in her yard that bows to no one but "Great Storm / of Equinox" stands for the resilient poet bowing only to a natural force she understands and accepts.

Before the poem was finished, Lorine sent a prompting letter to Clayton Eshleman, poet, translator, and founder of the 1960s journal *Caterpillar*. When he duly asked for a poem, she mailed "WINTERGREEN RIDGE." Immediately feeling guilty, she wrote Corman:

> I should have sent you Wintergreen Ridge. . . . [Eshleman] asked for something and I'm weak. It suits Origin so much better and really is I think the best thing I've ever done. . . . I think that is what got me off the track of sending it to you: I expected Montgomery would have [*North Central*] out before Origin could use the poem. I've now had time to ponder the fact that there is very likely a long wait in store. Well, what's done is done. . . . *Please* don't feel I deliberately wanted to avoid you.

Once Lorine waited patiently for publication. No more. She would be sixty-five and still there was no sign of *North Central* or *T&G*. She was terrified of going to earth with little left behind.

In stringent January, she appealed to Jonathan Williams: "I've had an offer to be published this spring. Would you release T&G—ms—to me? . . . I've no wish to have the book done by anyone but you, but it's becoming a little embarrassing so far as date of publishing is concerned. Yours in friendship as always." At the same time she asked Corman to take over publication "if I can manage $500 by Sept. . . . It's not too ethical for me to withdraw the ms from—[Williams] but if not printed by next fall I'd be tempted to tell him FORGET IT." Corman agreed to publish *T&G*.

Then Jonathan telephoned assuring her his *T&G* would happen. She fought back. Stuart Montgomery wanted to publish the book immediately in London; Cid Corman in Kyoto. She wrote: "[N]ow even more—wish to be released from any agreement we may have had. . . . I don't want to disturb the good relations that have always existed between us, Jonathan. You were almost the only one over these years who has believed in me and I count you friend. However, I'm 65 (this coming May) and I'm weaker than Emily Dickinson. I want to be printed by Stuart Montgomery and to tell him so immediately, and this with your blessings."

Williams played his trump card. With *T&G* proofs in hand, Lorine resigned herself to him. Now eager, she stipulated printing preferences. A "tiny design, a leaf or two" between the poems, italicized headings of some poems set right to the text. But her closing words—"have good traveling"—were ominous, for Jonathan was off again and she still believed more in Montgomery. The elusiveness of a collected volume maddened her: "I think I'll go home to the marsh and pull the waters over me."

With no word from Williams, she signed with Montgomery for *T&G*. Even with Fulcrum Press, however, the complications seemed endless: debatable contract clauses, copyright limits and duration, book distribution, payment— royalties? Then, after flurries of British correspondence, dead silence until Jonathan finally called "across many states. Sure, talked me into waiting a half dozen months more. . . . I said September, I'll wait no longer."

In her sixties Lorine was troubled by the Sixties. In the 1930s she'd revolted against basing poetry on political ideology. Now she denied that poets could commit themselves both to politics and poetry.

Meanwhile, she was corresponding with Clayton Eshleman, thirty-two years younger. In his visceral poem "Walks," Eshleman told her, he had let "sound and word patterns seethe and drive out into their own configurations and overcome all [his] resistance to a fear of incoherency; it is a kind of being bathed in the sea of the poem." This, he felt, was what Niedecker had not done in "WINTERGREEN RIDGE." Getting into the flow, he argued, was getting rid of weak attitudes like her lines about LSD, hippies, and beats:

> We are still, all of us controlled, and I think the sooner we get free of all traditional measured writing the better. In your own WINTERGREEN RIDGE your reactive comments on LSD and talking cool etc., are no more incisive than small-town hear-say and they are brought into the poem I would say not by your feeling toward young and/or experimental people but because you are traveling in the belly of a form of writing that was engendered as an upshot of a generation still reactive to what is now, to many of us, ways out, or the ways, simply, curious people, young people, our brothers, are doing things. I have eaten acid a half dozen times and do not think of myself as an acid-head or not, but more of having the experience of that drug and being able to use it now in my relation with the world and others.
>
> Zukofsky is pertinent here; I don't know of any poet writing today who strikes me as more experimental on one hand and more up tight and critical, full of self-pity, on the other. . . . Zukofsky feels he should be crowned or something, receive some sort of great reward for the years he has put in as a poet, and this is a very

sad attitude for someone as talented as Zukofsky is; it cuts into his poetry and comes as a kind of belated self-acknowledgement.

Lorine disliked writing about poetry. "I can talk in a kind of note-taking language—grocery list kind of thing," she explained. Attitudes, she argued, seem weak because they're "tied to coherence in the traditional sense." More important to her in "WINTERGREEN RIDGE" than coherence had been

> movement, gist, vibrations, a sense of floating. . . . I was afraid probably of losing myself—you know we want to lose ourselves and we don't want to. You were correct on Wintergreen Ridge, yet there I think I begin to show this "something else" I feel is now in the air—among the best poets—I'd reach it, I told myself if I told myself anything, in Wintergreen, through my own feeling of the music. . . . [A]ctually the poem had its way and I figured after 40 years of more or less precise writing, I cd. afford to let go. I only hope I may never regret this. . . . I know that my cry all these years has been: into—into—and under—close your eyes and let the music carry you.
>
> And what have I done?—cut—cut—too many words—wit is not to be ruled out (wit as we know it, perhaps there's another kind?)—say it in five words what you've spent a page on—touch your fingers to an emerald.
>
> O I don't know!!

Eshleman shot back a two-page, single-spaced reply on Self, Creation, and losing Self. "I believe that our Soul Force," he concluded, "has its own Control that is only tapped when we let 'er rip and that in that Control is the Plummage and Core of the experience we call Art." He considered his "Moistinsplendour" an advance in letting 'er rip.

Lorine kept up with trends. "I'm reading The Electric Kool Ade Acid Test," she wrote Fred Hobe. "Gord! We've come a long way from such small single fascinations as sex deviation and alcoholism." In younger poets, she searched for a new poetry she felt was in her. Side-tracking, she seized upon the French poet Jean Daive's elegant abstractionism; she read Larry Eigner, Theodore Enslin, and Eshleman for clues, thoroughly disliking Eshleman's orgasmic "Moistinsplendour"— "this time he has gone too far." Even his tamer "Walks" caused her physical discomfort: "I'm caught up in a fiery nebula, Clayton. . . . Give me instead just one of your short poems. . . . I mean: why set fire to page after page—why not stand still more often, stand within a frame—we are composing art, art we not?? . . . But I respect you for whatever you feel you have to do." "Art," she wrote Corman, "is cooler than he thinks."

But contemporary poetry gripped Lorine because she debated where her poetry was going: "It's true I'd like to resolve this daring and not daring that has haunted me for almost a year. Usually I get the start in my mind: reverie-memory-out of sleep-delirium kind of thing and before you know it I'm making a short and sharp whole i.e. frame. Wintergreen Ridge was in parts my first let-it-go. I don't connect this with sex, I'm sure. But here I go again, talking as tho making a poem is at any time too conscious. However, one is concerned with the business of *making a poem*."

"Silly, but I've become lately very—*painfully*—interested in poetry!" she confessed to Corman. She'd been reading the naturalist W. H. Hudson, author of *Green Mansions*:

> W. H. Hudson says birds feel something akin to pain (and fear) just before migration and nothing alleviates this feeling except flight (rapid motion of wings). I must be going to migrate. If I don't get over into the strange and new thing I feel I'll bust! . . . It's a feeling of the vertical more than the simple straight line. . . . It's probably only that old *dream* thing that threatens to mess things up but never really does—still, this time when it comes, it might. Someone here said my verse takes flight but if only he knew it I've not yet got off the ground.

On reflection, however, it was Eshleman's "Walks" (and his recommendation she take twenty-five micrograms of LSD) that finally persuaded her that controlled ecstasy was her forte. They were pitted against each other, not only generationally but in the timeless debate over art as emotion disciplined and art as unleashed Self. Robert Duncan's words came back to her: "I like rigor and even clarity . . . as I like muddle and floaty vagaries. It is the intensity of the conception that moves me." Forming in Lorine's mind was a poem of intense conception: a migration.

In December 1967 Gail Roub had given Lorine a sheaf of poems written by Michael Vandre, a 1965 Fort Atkinson High School graduate currently serving in Vietnam. Lorine "was amazed" at his work, felt that he had a gift for "picking out of the air" the feeling of much current poetry. "She thinks it is remarkable in one so young," Roub wrote Vandre, "and wants to see more of your work, and I think she would like to hear from you and write to you."

Lorine did like Vandre's poems, particularly the spare, condensed:

Lack of love
my brothers
I
in understanding
the oak leaf
falls
a fine garden
remains
existing unit shown
not alone
yet
without believer

In a small but decisive way, she had become known as a consummate poet. Out of the blue Keith Owen sent her four Japanese-influenced poems from London; she immediately recommended him to Cid and Morgan Gibson. A young professor at the University of Wisconsin–Whitewater, working on his PhD dissertation and burning to write poetry, wrote her.

"Oh, you found me out," said Lorine, greeting him with a smile. Ron Ellis noted the shelves of books around the room, the tone of austerity. He found her cordial and "inordinately impressed" that he was a professor. They talked about *New Goose* and *My Friend Tree*; Lorine read him a few of her poems—well, he thought. But Ellis's gods were Frost, Lowell, Williams, and Stevens. He appreciated the haiku-like economy of Niedecker's work without conversion.

They exchanged letters. "We are nothing compared with Gerard Manley Hopkins & Emily Dickinson," wrote Lorine. "We don't dare like they did." She sent Ellis some poetry, warning him not to publicize her: "I live among folk who couldn't understand and it's where I want to live. If I appear a freak to you I won't mind so much—might even be a compliment!" She complimented him on a poem published in *Commonweal*: "I'm no critic, but I feel I know what's alive." When Ellis observed that she was "emancipated from the clutches of our society," she corrected him:

Well, wasn't ever thus, not entirely free yet! Now it's property but I'm slowly working my way out of it. In the thirties when I was in *my* thirties it was jobhunting, depression, you know. And then, if you felt the influence of any poetry it was Proletarian (God forbid) poetry. In NY it seemed too absolutely difficult to even *try* for a job. Then WPA—Writers Project in Madison which led to a program of my own at WHA. Then a short vacation at home (Blackhawk Island) and then everyday grind no matter what the job would have been. . . . My only joy was the little house you and Herbert [Ellis's brother] saw. Too tired at that time to write. The present which should be nothing except writing was the passion of senseless activity, the job, keeping one's health etc. I could write maybe 6 poems a year. . . . Well, I don't want to become a nuisance with my letters—perhaps now I've caught up for a long time to come.

"We were acquaintances," says Ellis. "She could have been a great teacher, she had patience, empathy, willingness to share. The few times we met I felt expanded and awakened."

Like her mentors and colleagues, the hopeful poets who came to Lorine were male. Though she had women friends (Nathalie Kaufman Yackels, Maude Hartel, Mae Ward), they remained in her emotional and mental background. Not only had her culture taught her that intellect and influence resided with men, men were almost invariably the ones who could get her published. Yet she may not have attracted female disciples because of the cryptic, ironic, secular-scientific nature of much of her poetry. Men might assume they understood it.

Now she was taken with Michael Vandre and his poetry, sending him an *Origin* inscribed "To Michael Who Hears and Sees also, from Lorine." Jonathan had forwarded a letter from Thomas Merton, the famous Trappist monk and writer, soliciting poems for an anthology. With eleven of her own, she submitted Vandre's, four of which Merton accepted for *Monk's Pond*. Merton told Lorine, "I think he has the right kind of poetic luck and finds good words." Lorine wrote Michael the good news in Vietnam. He roused not only professional but maternal feelings. She referred to him constantly as "the boy."

The winter of 1967–68 was strange and difficult. Though she'd finished *North Central*, Lorine closeted herself in the dark apartment reading Gilbert White's *Natural History and Antiquities of Selbourne*, Fabre's *The Insect World of Jean Henri Fabre*, and Edward Dolan's biography of Alexander von Humboldt. She denied herself walks and fresh air, as though book learning were imperative in her life. If she was planning another "magma opus," she would not write it. Cloistered, she imagined opening her island door some spring night and hearing the sora rail "running down the scale—the spoon-tapped water glass." But when she did venture out, "your senior citizen poet missed a step coming out of a store and the sidewalk reminded me rather forcibly. Nose and face bleeding, glasses had to be sent in to be replaced." Lorine was so tense that Al suggested asking the doctor for tranquilizers.

In early March she revived. "This strange winter of mine is passing away," she wrote Cid, "—my correspondence with Clayton Eshleman, my walled-up intensive natural history reading, the battle with myself as to the new form I feel but don't quite dare use, the Vietnam boy, my trying to 'help' him. And now Stuart Montgomery's offer to print T&G alone, over there. . . . The new 'form' may materialize all unconsciously sometime but I've made a turnabout again toward the short poem, don't feel I shd. leave what's been a part of me all these years."

Apartment changing interrupted poetry. For an undisclosed reason, they moved from South Sixth Street to 539 Maple Street, "three blocks up and around the corner in a row of old houses under the bells of St. Stanislas, cherry blossoms and dirt." While Al painted, Lorine scrubbed Venetian blinds from the new apartment "where the people wallowed in filth." The neighborhood was less cramped and dark, with a yard behind the building instead of a "Polish flat," and a view of the twin domes of St. Stanislaus Catholic Oratory on West Mitchell Street, gilded in twenty-three-carat gold leaf from the melted jewelry of its parishioners. Al's son George helped move the heavy pieces "like the ancient gas range which we call Custard's Last Stand." He loved Lorine: "A really sweet woman, small, pretty, gentle and kind." Lorine scoured and scrubbed, tackling, among other horrors, "alluvial deposits to be dug out of window sills." Still it was May. Weekends on the island awaited, with bird mating calls and green springing everywhere.

A meeting with the Zukofskys in Madison also awaited. L. S. Dembo, a professor specializing in contemporary poetry, had invited Zukofsky to read and be interviewed on May 15 for an article on the Objectivists. (He would also interview Rakosi, Oppen, and Reznikoff.) Unless Al drove her to Madison, Lorine took the bus and met Louie and Celia the day after his endeavors. She hadn't seen him for fourteen years:

> Lovely day in Madison. I found Louie not depressed that day, not so much that as weary from his previous day. I find letters don't do it. . . . [T]alking clears the air and brings out half a laugh here and there. A glance and a certain tone makes all the difference. We poor beings with what we think—life is made up of more and what strikes the feelings directly *that's* our best way—one person

facing another. . . . [Dembo] wanted very much to understand Objectivism. Don't know if he feels he *got* it—which I take as a compliment as I don't think Louie wants to be brought down to a pinpoint on this subject or any other. He hasn't gone back on those principles but by now it seems he might feel that it needs no one name.

Lovely day in Madison? "Knowing in a professorial way," Dembo focused on Zukofsky while Celia also focused on Zukofsky, leaving Lorine outside both the Zukofsky marriage and Dembo's projected work on the Objectivists, which would cut her dead. Besides Pound, few if any of the "Objectivist" poets had attained Objectivism except Niedecker in *New Goose* and "LAKE SUPERIOR"; ironically, Carl Rakosi had always believed Niedecker the ultimate Objectivist. Her exclusion by Dembo was a sexist act by a scholar who probably didn't know what sexism meant.

But Lorine the sublimator was hard at work. Louie's glance bridged their estrangement. Dembo might not understand Objectivism. She declared she had never been a true Objectivist. She was right: but then neither had any of the others. Her perspective on Objectivism would have been important. And after all, she lived just thirty miles down the road.

Before they left, Dembo drove them to the University Arboretum to see the lilacs. Celia bent to peer at the Latin names of the shrubs, Louis bared "his grey head to the sun." It was the last time they would meet. Shortly afterward, Corman confided to Lorine that Zukofsky was difficult. "Yes, well, I know," she replied. "[T]hink of me all these years."

That May Gertrude Runke died at sixty-seven. Though Henry had been dead fourteen years, she had herself buried a yard or so from his grave, nose-thumbing Daisy and Lorine.

In June Al dropped Lorine off at Blackhawk Island for a week while he went up north fishing. She wanted to get down to "PAEAN TO PLACE," "the marsh poem" that had been forming in her head since Kenneth Cox had asked her to give him some background facts for an essay. Yet the assassination of Robert Kennedy shortly after midnight on June 5 in Los Angeles, minutes after he delivered a speech urging withdrawal from Vietnam, made work impossible until after the funeral, which she watched, thinking that Kennedy might be the "best and maybe the last of the liberal individualists."

Still, the poem was uppermost. "I don't know why I must always be placed in the middle of '"theatre" of such painful intensity'—this thing about place," she complained to Corman. "PAEAN TO PLACE" was a poem that had to be written: "When you're over sixty, your whole past life rolls out before you!" The rock she celebrated in "LAKE SUPERIOR" seemed too solidly material to her now. Her 205-line song of praise celebrates lives lived by water—its seductive, amniotic, all-penetrating quality the antithesis of earth. Niedecker uses the word "water" eleven times, "flood" six; the poem swims in swamp, swale, marsh, streams, lake, river, sea, wave, pond, ocean, slough, and slime. She called the poem "a kind of In Memoriam of my father and mother and the place I've never seemed to really get away from." Significantly, she wrote the poem chiefly away from Blackhawk Island; distance intensified memory and nostalgia.

Using the five-line stanza, often with rhymed or assonant third and fourth lines, Niedecker divides the poem into twelve parts. Yet the narrator's voice carries the reader so irresistibly from segment to segment that "PAEAN" emerges as an integral whole. Though flowing, this remembrance of things past has fundamentally a vertical structure. As the poem considers all water, from slime-slick to ocean's depths, so the narrator takes us from the objective thing observed—a water lily, say—deeper and deeper into memory and consciousness as she plumbs the past. Her realization "I was the solitary plover / a pencil / for a wing-bone" bursts upon us as discovery and insight, as do realizations that her father "netted loneliness" or that "Effort lay" in her family "before religions."

"O my floating life," she cries, both of surrounding waters and of her sub-conscious where "impulse tests the unknown" and from whose depths poetry surfaces. Her urgent "Throw *things* / to the flood" expresses not only Stoic anti-materialism but her need as a poet to yield to the flood of memory that, in birth imagery, "maneuvers barges [poems] thru the mouth of the river."

Lorine acknowledged "WINTERGREEN RIDGE" as a good poem, perhaps her best, but said little about the great "PAEAN TO PLACE," calling it "lush, mush-music but like this place." Because it had not involved research and effort, she undervalued her accomplishment.

In August, Lorine and Al took another trip north: "Just home from driving through Minnesota and North Dakota (my god those empty stretches between towns), touched on Canada at International Falls, Minn., slept in air-conditioned motels which always lowers my vitality. . . . International Peace Gardens were nice between N.D. and Canada. . . . But between towns we very nearly committed murder on each other to let the bones bleach on the prairies."

Al had once traveled the territory as a Wobbly recruiting members for the International Workers of the World, so the trip offered him at least nostalgia—but poor Lorine, who had once dreamed of Florida's "orange, flower / roseate bird / soft air." Red quarries at Pipestone, Minnesota, from whose sacred rock the Sioux fashioned ceremonial pipes, did excite her. Cid had been urging her and Al to visit him in Japan, but, "I think we never will. We're just stick-in-the-muds and at our age home seems best. I don't suppose there's ever been much going away adventure in my blood except those half dozen times (less than that, I think) I went to NYC many years ago."

On return, she found an advance copy of Fulcrum Press's *North Central* in her mailbox. The book, pale gray paper between brown boards with a dust jacket of green and brown ferns, contained "LAKE SUPERIOR," "TRACES OF LIVING THINGS," and "WINTERGREEN RIDGE." The jacket featured praise including Basil Bunting's "She is the best living poetess." ("Sometime I must tell Basil about Marianne!") *North Central* was "not beautiful in the sense that your books are or Jonathan's," she wrote Cid, "but looks strong and durable as I like to think the writing is and at least one of the subjects: Lake Superior." Jonathan was still promising *T&G* in three weeks, "but this is as will (may not) be."

At Corman's request she'd written a poem about Zukofsky ("I can't see how it could be [offensive] tho one never knows. I could have delved into deeper things but one can't risk—") for an *Origin* honoring his sixty-fifth birthday:

> He walked—loped—the bridge
> Saluted Peck Slip
> —his friend shipped fish—
>   My dish
>
> *Test*
>
> and the short verse
> Now he stops for lilacs
> —in the *sun's* fame
>   he'd say—
> Stops?
>
> Even for death
>   Z
> after all that "A"
> would dip his wool beret
> to carp-fed roots

Henry Niedecker is the friend who shipped carp to Peck's Slip; the Madison arboretum was where Zukofsky stopped to smell the lilacs. Lorine knew the poem's possible offense: Zukofsky's family never having eaten carp, his roots were hardly "carp-fed." In November she was still worrying: "LZ doesn't even know about it—not from me. (I've gone forward and back and stood on my head in this poem and for the life of me I see nothing in it to offend LZ, at the same time I want to make this stipulation: destroy it or keep it well hidden if the anniversary number is not made up.)" "LZ" did appear in January 1969; LZ wrote that, since nothing personal, fine. "[Y]ou may know," Lorine wrote Cid, "how much freer I breathe." Lorine seems almost to be begging Zukofsky to object, to show some emotion.

It was the fourth poem Lorine had written specifically about Louis. He names her in his "On Valentine's Day to Friends." She is also present in "A"-12 as "a rich sitter"—Zukofsky commending her devotion to her craft. He quotes her on New York weather: "Like hell of flames / Shooting out of the tops of your heads / While your feet freeze / L.N. wrote me of our winter." He quotes his letter beginning, "Dear L.N. So your mother's dead." Perhaps she is also "a friend / Who's constant."

Lorine had considered placing "PAEAN TO PLACE" with Corman or *Poetry*, but in October Stuart Montgomery, with the poet Tom Pickard, came to Blackhawk Island. "And Stuart wormed out of me Paean to Place . . . to be the concluding poem in the next book which . . . will be named not T&G but My Life by Water. Nice?" Lorine told Cid with notably less guilt than she had about "WINTERGREEN RIDGE." A medical student from then-Rhodesia, the independent Montgomery was doing more than any other small British publisher to put the work of late British and American Modernist poets before the public during the three years of Fulcrum Press's existence.

Lorine found the slightly built Montgomery arresting, with a face like Edgar Allan Poe's or Robert Louis Stevenson's. He and Pickard arrived a day late for dinner, but "my day old potato salad and ham (their fault) and frozen peas and apple pie disappeared as I like food to do when I've cooked." Al was very much present, regaling the visitors with island stories and how his mower collided with carp on the river edge "with disastrous results to fish and mower." Both longed to fetch shears to clip Pickard's long hair. Montgomery was the fourth poet to have sought out Lorine.

That December Gail Roub married Bonita Sigl, an English and Latin teacher at Fort Atkinson High School. Gail had brought Bonnie to Lorine's house to meet her; Lorine had cupped her face in her hands, gazing deep into her eyes to "know her." Lorine braved the couple's wedding reception at Gail's house. Joan Jones remembers meeting a small woman who seemed to be hiding behind a door. Joan smiled and said, "Oh, are you Bonnie's mother?" "Bonnie's mother is dead," said the small woman and vanished.

At Christmas, Lorine suffered what she called "doloroso," and on her way to the doctor the next day "wondered if it were not death." The doctor prescribed digitalis for an erratic heartbeat and minor pills. "I don't feel it's serious tho I do feel slowed up considerably these days," she wrote Corman. "All will be well after remembering which pill and which liquid comes when and the sun shines once more on me in April and May."

Before the sun could shine, however, she was unwell enough to go into hospital for X-rays and tests. Though she feared a brain tumor, she was diagnosed with hardening of the arteries. "I fainted one midnight there and had to have 7 or 8 stitches taken to the back of the head," she wrote Corman. "And Al was sick at home. Also during that time somebody clobbered our car parked in front of the house—and January was fog and ice here almost all month—how has it been with *you*??" Al would retire September 14, his sixty-fifth birthday—"he from work, I from Milwaukee hovels." Meanwhile, "Out home the beautiful barn swallows darting from river to house, lettuce up, red tulips spindly in the wind, fuzzy white things from willows floating about, grass grass grass to mow into eternity"—these thoughts were enough to carry her through.

24

The Urgent Wave

1969~1970

If I could float my tentacles / through the deep . . . / pulsate an invisible glow

"Waded, watched, warbled"

O n February 25, 1969, page proofs of *T&G* arrived for Lorine's inspection: "o Lord, a beautiful book!" Yet there were spacing and punctuation errors; she typed a list of fifteen corrections. "Please answer questions above, only way I'll know we're progressing. And thank you, o thank you."

That early spring she was working on "His Carpets Flowered." Her subject was William Morris (1834–96), the British textile designer, poet, writer, Pre-Raphaelite painter, Arts and Crafter, socialist, and founder of the Kelmscott Press. "I maintain a long poem is made of up short ones," Niedecker had said; and though she wrote Kenneth Cox that "poetry should be much more mysterious and flowing than any style we more solid citizens have allowed," she stalled mystery and flow by dividing "His Carpets Flowered" into three sections of eight-, two-, and five-line stanzas.

"I know how to evaluate—Ruskin etc., their kind of socialism—paternalism— but the letters of Morris have thrown me," she wrote Cid. "I can't read his [medieval and Icelandic] poems, I'd probably weary of all those flowery designs in carpets, wall papers, chintzes . . . but as a man, as a poet speaking to his daughters and his wife—o lovely." Niedecker had always loved "the letters of big people" with their "delightful deshabille style, talking to someone, not just talking."

Her title alludes to Morris's floral textile designs (with a glance at the flower carpet of "WINTERGREEN RIDGE"). From his letters Lorine distills what she found fascinating: the hands-on workman, the visionary artist who on the same day designed a dogtooth-violet carpet and spoke socialism to a full hall, the voyager, and the tender husband and father. They had something in common. He wove carpets by the Thames at Hammersmith, she wove poetry by the Rock. They both knew nature intimately and used it in their art. They both knew how "society's / corruption stains throughout." Both were incorruptible.

Poetry rejected the poem. "Do you notice *Poetry* (Chicago) is deteriorating?" Lorine wrote Jonathan. "[M]y William Morris poem returned, first thing sent back to me in ten years . . . but it will be printed elsewhere." (It was, in *Origin* 3, no. 19 [October 1970].)

That summer Sergeant Michael Vandre, on leave from Vietnam, visited Lorine several times on the island. He remembers her gingham dress, the bright flowers planted around the house. She offered him tea, was "absolutely cordial. Lorine was about as even keel as you can be. I found her benevolent, honest, so genuine. I liked her poetry from first reading."

"You're a natural poet," she told him. "Don't make your poetry so difficult, don't flower it. What do you really mean? See and hear. Refine, refine. My purpose in writing is to give my perspective as clearly as possible." Vandre mentioned the popular Rod McKuen. "The most successful poets are in the archives," replied Lorine firmly, "not a penny earned." He left promising to write more poetry, return.

On July 20 the Millens left for a three-week trip north ("why I don't know, I'm cold enough right here"). The vast Lake of the Woods, over seventy miles long and wide, occupied parts of Ontario, Manitoba, and Minnesota, with more than 14,552 islands and 65,000 miles of shoreline. Only a few photos and jottings survive from this trip. They apparently stayed at Kenora, a small lake city originally called Rat Portage, a fact Lorine would have loved. Lorine notes: "bridge to Winnipeg on L of the Woods; Copper Country, from Copper Harbor to Ontanagon to Isle Royale." The vacation inspired no poetry. "Canada—too tiring," she wrote Cid, "—probably our last lengthy trip."

She headed the letter "only 8 days longer." Ladish had let Al go nine days before his official retirement day. There were only a few pieces of furniture to be transported from hovel to cottage; George Millen helped with the move. "[N]o room of my own but I have the bedroom pretty much any time of the day with small table and comfortable chair. North window there with a lot of sky. . . . Small color TV for UHF (educational network)—I can see color better than black and white." She sent out change-of-address notices: Lorine Niedecker (Mrs. Albert Millen), Route 3, Box 395, Fort Atkinson. She did not want to be addressed "c/o Albert Millen," she told Jonathan, because neighbors would think, "Oh, didn't she ever marry him???" In fact, mail should be sent "Millen care of Lorine. Well, that's another story."

When they arrived on September 13, *T & G* was in the mailbox after a five-year wait. "Well, my first feeling was one of slight disappointment, tho," she told Jonathan, "—I expected a white and black cover—how distinctive it was on page proofs. . . . But then, the book is with us. Hardly a single error. Spacing within the poems drives me crazy—they'll never get reprinted correctly if anyone wants them." Though criticizing the printer, Lorine seems ungracious, something she realized when she signed the letter "Not curtly but friendly." Yet she'd also recently inscribed *My Friend Tree* to Jonathan, calling it "my best book so far"—though she'd disliked it in 1961. Lorine was severe with Jonathan.

T & G is a beautiful book. Two black shafts of grass decorate a green cover below the title *T & G: The Collected Poems (1936–1966)*, "Lorine Niedecker" in dark red ink. Inside, on thick creamy paper, 125 poems are printed in matte red, separated by stylized red peony sigils, with eight plant prints by A. Doyle Moore. On the front flap, Jonathan's encomium reads:

> Lorine Niedecker is the most absolute poetess since Emily Dickinson. . . . We are in the presence of a poet whose peers are the Lady Ono Komachi and Sappho. Few others come to mind. . . . Miss Niedecker is as faithful and recurrent, as beautiful and homely as my favorite peony bush. Every year for over thirty years she has been putting out these blossoms. Perhaps other eyes are ripe for them now?

"Tenderness and Gristle" describes Niedecker's poetry better than peony blossoms. She was grateful to Jonathan, however, who had indeed only been waiting for a grant (the National Council for the Arts came through) to publish the poet he admired. The book earned her "$350, maybe even $500"; that brought her total earnings from poetry to something like eight hundred dollars, all of which and more she had spent supporting small presses.

Would *North Central* and *T & G* be noticed?

Charles Tomlinson had reviewed *North Central* in *Agenda*, to Lorine's bemusement: "The chief focus for her writing lay in Wisconsin, in that region of dangerous waters, and it was the pressure of vast provincial American space that brought the content of her highly individual style to bear." Lorine's British colleagues tended to be vague about American geography, confusing Lake Superior with Koshkonong, the Rock with the Mississippi River. Lorine joked that she should send Corman the review by sea. But Tomlinson had committed a more grievous error. "Tomlinson says I got my Wintergreen Ridge music from LZ!" she wrote Kenneth Cox. "It seems to me nothing could be further from the truth." Most dissatisfying, Tomlinson called her poetry minor, "but with the pulse of life in it." Niedecker did not consider her poetry minor.

Another bane was being classified as regional. "I sent University of Wisconsin Milwaukee a copy of T&G way back in Sept.," she complained. "A few days ago I wrote: Did you fail to receive? They answer they've placed it with regional materials. I should ask: What region—London, Wisconsin, New York?" The dust jacket of Fulcrum Press's *North Central* promoted the myth of regionalism: "Lorine Niedecker has lived most of her life on Rock River in Wisconsin, where it empties into Lake Koshkonong. . . . Now lives isolated in Fort Atkinson, Milwaukee with her husband." (More uncertain geography.) Niedecker's mystique as "the best and most subtle living American poetess," hiding from the public and appreciated only by the discerning, grew.

But Lorine dreamed of being published by Random House, Simon and Schuster, or (like Zukofsky) Norton, a chance, she admitted, slightly less certain than death. She also thought of the Pulitzer Prize. "I rise to that book of yours—An Ear in Bartram's Tree—at 5:AM," she wrote Jonathan. "I absolutely prize it." It was the second book she'd seen "that *should* get the Pulitzer—the other one is mine—T&G!" She then corrected immediately: "No, actually, compared with J. W. I feel without wit, without essential beauty, certainly without some of those perfect sources you've found to draw from. Sometime I feel so without access—your traveling about must get a bit tiresome but lord it opens up so much to you."

She would have to wait until Michael Heller's 1970 review of *T & G* in the *Nation* for real appreciation: "This book, along with Fulcrum of England's *North Central* (1969), a somewhat overlapping selection, should introduce her to the larger audience she deserves, for until recently her poems have been read and appreciated by only a handful of people (mostly other poets)." Heller calls Niedecker's poems "notations of isolation . . . natural and seemingly artless constructions . . . neither self-pitying nor mean, for there is in Miss Niedecker's work an obstinacy, an almost iron commitment to valuing her world, a moral concern for her art that is rare and important."

"I'm so afraid people won't know about the one rather big review I've had so far," Lorine wrote Cid. "By Michael Heller, teacher at New York Univ. He has a nice feeling for the poems. Sometimes a review doesn't mean more than that but without that one wouldn't want a review."

Still, Lorine had what she'd always wanted: published books, her island home, a husband/companion, and time to write. Everything but fame, to which she was not averse.

They established a schedule. She rose early to take her daily two-mile walk to the point, carrying a bag for collecting beer cans, looked for birds, and in season stopped to pick wild flowers to press in books. Sometimes Bonnie Roub walked with her. Like Lorine, Bonnie was quiet and Lorine opened to her, describing how autobiographical "PAEAN TO PLACE" was, or how her "humiliated" mother could only communicate with her by notes: "When I took care of my mother, I became the adult, my mother the child." Once, Bonnie remembers, Lorine threw back her head, exclaiming, "I feel like a goddess when I walk this island." Meanwhile, Al made tea, threw handfuls of seed out for the birds. After breakfast, she wrote at her table facing the river, binoculars at hand, until eleven "though a poet carries it all around in his head pretty much all the time, such a queer critter he is!"

Al headquartered in the garage, which he fixed up with a stove and rocking chair. "Al was the opposite of Lorine," said Æneas, "but she was so happy in their house. Al was a steady drinker, tippled wine by the jug, sitting in an old rocker in the garage. . . . That didn't bother Lorine. She laughed about that. 'You should come over and meet Al, you two could go out in the garage and talk, and don't mind that he has his little jug of wine underneath the workbench, that's just his little pick-me-upper." Lorine, who had read books on alcoholism after she married, had almost resigned herself.

In her short story "The Evening's Automobiles," Lorine says of her couple that they never need to be familiar no matter how close they get. In "Wilderness" that sentiment applies to Al Millen, who, no matter how necessary to her, is still foreign territory:

> You are the man
> You are my other country
> and I find it hard going
>
> You are the prickly pear
> You are the sudden violent storm
>
> the torrent to raise the river
> to float the wounded doe

They named the garage "University of Texas" because Lorine had finally sold Zukofsky's letter fragments to the Harry Ransom Research Center, repository of the largest manuscript collection of twentieth-century writers in the world. "How upset she was when Zu made waves about the letters," said Gail Roub, "and I seem to remember that she felt something irreparable had happened after she placed the letters at Austin. It bothered her grievously." Ironic that the Texas money bought Al his hideaway; or perhaps Lorine deliberately spent it that way: a gift to the man who stood by her from the man who, finally, didn't.

In the afternoon they did errands together in town. Running into Nathalie Yackels at Sentry, Al would hold forth while Lorine stood giggling. After Al dropped Lorine at the library, he retired to the tavern on the corner of Main and Sherman Avenue. Lorine might stop at Gruner's bookstore to pick up a book she'd ordered—Marion Gruner called Lorine "a honey, the best customer I ever had"—before continuing up Main Street to the bar and climbing onto a stool until Al finished his beer.

Though Al still cooked, Lorine was in the kitchen regularly, making soups, chicken, and Al's favorite New England dinner—all the while her "soup-conscious" active. After supper eaten at the small table looking out at the river, they sat in front of the TV, Lorine with a small table across her lap, a black and green plaid wool shawl around her shoulders, books, pens, pencils, and paper at the ready. TV's attraction was that it distracted the garrulous Al. Before retiring at night, Al would peer through the screen door hoping to catch reflected light from raccoon, possum, or fox eyes. In bed they'd listen to frogs: "In that dark nobody-here-but-frogs world I could easily believe they'll be the rulers of the world after we've gone."

In recoil from the intensely personal "PAEAN TO PLACE," Lorine's imagination turned to Thomas Jefferson, product of the Age of Enlightenment. "I'd very much like to go to Monticello, Thomas Jefferson's home, in Virginia," she wrote Kenneth Cox. "Reading almost everything on or about Jefferson," even though "[i]t may be John Adams is my man."

She had long been interested in America's third president, taking notes on the "so fascinating" Adams–Jefferson correspondence that she had discussed with Harold Hein. Like William Morris, Jefferson was a polymath: writer, horticulturist, architect, paleontologist, inventor. Unlike Morris, his statesmanship influenced the course of nations: "For austere education, the Stoics, for Tranquility of mind, the Epicureans and for love of fellow men and charity, Jesus." Lorine could agree.

She also approved of his distrust of cities and financiers, belief in the independent yeoman farmer, and insistence upon separation of church and state (all Niedecker and Kunz positions). But she was also drawn to the personal Jefferson: the lisp that made him prefer writing to speaking; his tenderness toward his daughters; his care for his strawberries, young chestnut trees, bantam hens; his interest in birds.

Jefferson was a rational mind with which she could communicate, the more so in an America that often seemed on the brink of irrational disintegration.

In the course of a year, she wrote five Jefferson poems: "Jefferson and Adams," "John Adams is our man" ("BULLETIN"), "Jefferson: I was confident," "Thomas Jefferson Inside," and "Thomas Jefferson." The 158-line "Thomas Jefferson" employs quotations for the immediate sound of the subject's voice. It had been Pound's strategy in the Cantos, Zukofsky's in "A." Beginning dramatically with Martha Jefferson dying and ending with Jefferson's own death, Niedecker distills her version of the man. The politician is there; but it's the private Jefferson that allures. The man who called political honors "splendid torments," who abandoned the dinner parties of the rich, who based his study of humanity on Latin and Greek; who built Monticello and sowed cabbages.

Some scholars claim that, with the exception of Abigail Adams, Jefferson could not abide learned women. They ignore the fact that, when his older sisters Mary and Martha married, he fell into a depression at the loss of their intellectual stimulation. The claim also contradicts his concern for his daughters' education:

> To daughter Patsy: Read—
> read Livy
>
> No person full of work
> was ever hysterical
>
> Know music, history
> dancing
>
> (I calculate 14 to 1
> in marriage
> she will draw
> a blockhead)
>
> Science also
> Patsy

"Thomas Jefferson" is as elegant and balanced as its subject. Lorine called it "deft," though comparing it to Pound on Adams and Jefferson, "I always feel kind of faded out—my way of writing—compared to some parts of the Cantos. I'm the piece of wash that has hung too long in the sun! . . . I'm a little bunch of marshland violets offered to the crooked lawyer—O no . . . how could I refer to Pound in that way???—I owe so much to him as most present-day poets do—and so much of the Cantos and the other poems of his is so beautiful." But Niedecker isn't faded compared to Pound, she's condensed. She is also concerned with the man, while finances and politics interest Pound. And, unlike the erudite Pound, caring less if his reader could translate his Latin, German, French, and Italian, she cares to be understood.

"BULLETIN" was inspired by a news story about a Miami reporter who, on the Fourth of July, asked passersby to sign a copy of the Declaration of Independence and was threatened with jail. "Would you believe it!!" she wrote the Roubs. By now, however, she was exhausted by her subject. "Who am I writing the poem for?? I give three packages of gum and cattails in tall grass for a title. But o my God what travail till this was completed." By February she'd finished the long Jefferson poem: "My Thomas Jefferson written and sent out. Up very early mornings—nearly killed myself—and all that reading beforehand (until I realized what am I doing?—writing a biography or history?? no, all I could do is fill the subconscious and let it lie and fish up later)."

That winter of 1969–70, Lorine felt "an undercurrent of hurry . . . never before a part of my life." She wrote Cid in March, "I look out and see winter goldfinches (wild canaries). Strange to see greenish yellow in winter. Red wing blackbirds here storming the trees, a noise-storm, and for three days geese going over with *their* glorious noise. It must mean early spring."

Currently a writer-in-residence at Madison, Carl Rakosi was interviewed by Vivien Hone from WPA days, who told him she knew Niedecker. Lorine invited them both to lunch.

"I had some misgivings about it," Rakosi recalled, "because I had heard in Madison that she was a recluse and something of a misanthrope, had had a tragic life and been a mental patient in a state hospital. But nobody in the English Department or in town had ever met her, and only two or three had heard the name."

The misanthropic mental patient greeted them warmly at the door. After lunch, Al drove Vivien about the area so the poets could talk. Rakosi remembered:

> She turned out to be as normal as apple pie. . . . A plain country woman, very plain . . . plain, broad face, plain gingham dress, everything about her cheerful and outgoing, as I knew it so well in the Middle West, optimistic, bouncy, and in her case, bright and

hard-edged alert. . . . tiny house that looked as if it had once been a fisherman's shack to which her handyman husband, Al, had built a couple of additional rooms with hammer and saw. The furniture was likewise plain and homey, probably hand-me-downs from her father. She was devoid of *any* affectation or literary manner, which was right down my alley, and I felt immediately comfortable and was all set for a memorable talk, but it didn't happen.

We started out all right, chatting about her correspondence with Zukofsky, his comments about the new work she used to send him. Were they complimentary? I asked. "Oh, no!" she cried, "they were cruel, mean-tempered, sometimes angry." There was no trace of any resentment or hurt in her voice, however. On the contrary, she laughed and looked fond, as if she were basking in a warm memory. As we talked on, I got an unmistakable sense of something very personal, even physical, in her commitment to Louie. . . . "Of course," she remarked, "you agree, don't you that Zukofsky is the greatest poet in America." The look she gave me was probing as well as pointed. . . ."Oh, no!" I replied, as if the idea were slightly amusing. Her face stopped and became serious for a moment, considering this unexpected response, then resumed being friendly, as if nothing had happened. We chatted for a while but this time only on safe, innocuous subjects. Finally I drifted away and spent the rest of the afternoon with Al. . . . I did not find him either ordinary or extraordinary, nor did I get any clue that would shed any light on this union of perfectionist poet and working man. When Lorine Niedecker and I parted, it was friendly enough but we both knew we had not become friends and that we would not be seeing each other again.

That is Rakosi in an interview published in 1993. In a 1971 letter to George Oppen, he gave a crucially different account:

> I met her for the first time last spring in her house on the edge of a creek, a house so small that if there had been one more person than the four of us there, it would have been impossible to sit down to table. She had been described as having some strange ailment and of refusing to see anyone, but she was delighted to see me and I found her as fresh and wide-awake as a daisy. I jolted her when I didn't go along with her adulation of Zukofsky. When she saw I was serious, she beamed and looked relieved. She said she found it refreshing. All in all, a very healthy person.

Did Lorine freeze—or beam with relief? The latter account, written to a friend less than a year after the meeting, is apt to be true. Pity, then, that public record has a fanatic Lorine shutting down when Rakosi disagrees that Zukofsky is supreme. Twenty years later, Rakosi had apparently bought into the Zukofsky myth.

On May 12 Lorine turned sixty-seven: "I guess I can no longer run a race with a child." In June she "dragged herself" to Madison to buy books about the French Enlightenment but found the university co-op's windows cemented over because of student rioting (which she did not support) and Diderot's *Letters to Sophia Volland* selling for a hundred dollars. Giving up Diderot, she began a poem about a man even more of her mind than Jefferson, who believed that Nature's Economy prohibited the extinction of species. That man was Charles Darwin.

The weather was warm and muggy, and she was not feeling well. "O too hot," she wrote the Roubs:

> How've you been?
> I'm a bit better. After the heat subsides I'll let you know the day
> I make noodles so if you wish, come up and observe the masterchef
> as she putters.
> At the moment this noodle drops a few lines of Darwin's
> Formation of Vegetable Mould, through the Action of Worms,
> with Observations of Their Habits into the soup-conscious.
>
> Stay cool—

Again, Lorine let works by and about Darwin simmer in her "soup-conscious" until key motifs condensed into poetry. Though "Darwin" is 124 lines, Niedecker achieves her "long poem made up of short ones" by dividing it into segments and paragraphs. But because content flows through segment and paragraph, "Darwin" is not created of nuggets like "LAKE SUPERIOR." Unlike Lake Superior, too, Darwin is very present in his poem. Quoting from his letters, alternating events he remembered with immediate experience, Niedecker brings both philosophic and private man to life.

Important to Lorine at sixty-seven is Darwin's conclusion that man is "in the same predicament / with other animals"—mutable. Not that this was a new thought. Her poems about her mother's death offer no comfort for loss. In another poem old age is simply "a high gabbling gathering / before goodbye / of all we know." "WINTERGREEN RIDGE" too deals with the mortality of all living things. "Darwin," however, conveys a new urgency as Lorine deals with Darwin's consciousness of his mortality. His words—"I am ill, he said / and books are slow work"—are hers.

In a key way, however, Darwin's and Niedecker's philosophies differ. The Victorian struggled to reconcile his discovery that species are mutable with the Christian certainty that the jewel in the crown of Creation is immortal. Niedecker had no such struggle: she calls Darwin's conclusions "holy." Yet she would concur with his ending words: "Let each man hope / and believe / what he can." She finished the poem by August 18, thought it "good," sent it to *Poetry* "with no great hopes."

In August Julie and Gene came to the island with their children. They photographed the event: Al hoeing his squash and beans (raccoons got the sweet corn). Gene launching Julie and the kids in Al's boat from shore. Julie, Al, and Lorine in a brown cotton dress holding her camera as Gene snaps their picture. Shots of Lorine and Julie talking under the trees and on the cottage steps. The Schoessows were making a career move to Australia. These casual photographs are the last photos of Lorine.

The Millens took a short trip that fall, driving into the beautiful wooded unglaciated hills of western Wisconsin. Lorine's notes of October 5, 1960, sketch the getaway that began with a return to the park visited on their honeymoon:

> Wyalusing State Park. 84 degrees. Very warm. Wyalusing "closed" for the season but went to Lookout Point and sat on a bench. All that wooded acreage—great silence. Yellow butterflies.
>
> Drive along Wisconsin R. beyond Spring Green. Colors— flaming sumac and yellow & red maples. That day it was 91 degrees at Aberdeen, N.D.
>
> Lovely motel—*Brisbois*.
>
> In from De Soto—Viroqua etc.—more windmills than we'd ever seen before in our lives.
>
> Baraboo—arrived too late to see the Circus Museum.

In October she finally received copies of *My Life by Water*, published in 1969 by Stuart Montgomery. "Me new book came out," she wrote Julie in Australia, "but actually it's a collection of all from 1936 to 1968 which means you've seen just about all of the poems." The book jacket depicted a map of lake and river area that she felt might be mistaken for "an organ of the body with ducts to and from."

In November she wrote Louis about his recently published *Little: For Careenagers*, a story about young Paul: "Halfway thru *Little*—o golly so much of it I remember from the letters! . . . A strange, funny satire and pictures all over again of that remarkable, beautiful child." She signed the letter warmly: "*Much love to both of you and PZ.*"

The anticipated event, however, was the long-postponed visit of Cid Corman and his Japanese wife, Shizumi, to Blackhawk Island in November:

> I'd like to have you and Shizumi for a meal—I can seat four people comfortably, or five. The important thing is that you and I have time to talk. We can put you in a hotel in Fort for a night (our expense). Driving *very far* i.e. Madison is not too good for us—Al's age and he's not used to doing it anymore. I could come to Madison during the day but I'd rather you'd come here. . . . Oak? surely the high moment of my life next to having met Louie in New York in 1934. . . . P.S. I want to hand you $25 while you're here to help with your expenses. No argument now!

Meanwhile, she was typing a manuscript she called "Harpsichord and Salt Fish" that included "Thomas Jefferson," "His Carpets Flowered," "Darwin," and nineteen short poems. At Cid's suggestion she sent it to James Laughlin at New Directions—the publisher she and Louie had dubbed in their "starred but not too often printed youth" James IV. "Reaching the age of 67, I feel I should clear the board though I suppose there'll be more poems. It would make me very happy to re-establish contact with NEW DIRECTIONS after all this time—since the latter 1930s."

"It was so good to hear from you again," Laughlin replied. "[Y]ou are writing as beautifully as ever." He turned down "Harpsichord," however, as not long enough for a book; besides, Jonathan Williams, just visiting, implied that he'd consider Laughlin publishing Niedecker "an intrusion." Lorine shuddered. "Jonathan Williams, yes, but a five-year wait for *T&G* (1968) convinces me I'd like to wait 35 pages more so long as life lasts, with New Directions as the goal." Laughlin replied: "Yes, I can well imagine that 'waiting for Jonathan' can be very trying, but he is a great man, in his wonderfully eccentric way, and we must all stand by him." He repeated his offer to publish any sequence of poems Lorine could send him.

Cid Corman, forty-six, and Shizumi, ten years younger, managed to find the Millens on November 14. Cid jotted in his notebook:

> In Fort Atkinson, arriving about 11:30. Both of us tired. Temp below freezing point. Called Lorine—who suggested the Black Hawk Hotel. . . . $10 a night. Nothing spectacular—but adequate— warm—comfortable—clean. As well as being centrally located. . . . 15th Nov (Sun): up about 8:30. Day partly cloudy/cool & bright. Expect to see Lorine & Al about 10:30 or so. . . .

Breakfast about 11 & as figured Al & Lorine came in while we were amidst it. OK. Al a Minnesota backwoodsman: a guy—with a satisfaction in the manly formula—gentle at heart, but clumsy. Lorine shy & gentle. Bright & true. Incapable of crudity. Lonely, eager for intellectual company but unable to foment it, fearful of the "larger" scene. Not quite as *bold* as Emily [Dickinson]—but a genuine voice & spirit.

Her preparations didn't altogether come off but *they* were *not* our "reason" for visiting. Al likes his football game etc. He likes the adventurous & vigorous: the quiet & meditative puts him at a disadvantage. . . . He's a fair storyteller & has good stories from childhood to tell. He lacks—however—"realization"—so that the stories can only have whatever depth someone else might draw from them. . . .

Supper was chicken, stuffing, stringbeans, orange cranberry, cottage cheese & plenty of everything. She will, no doubt, apologize for the meal in her next letter—needlessly. But their tiny place was cosy—good. They don't quite hit it off—but have both been thru enough to give way to each other—even when impatient. They cd *never* have mated at an earlier age. . . .

Stayed with them—at their riverside place till about 7:30 or so. (Given coat, jackets against cold.) Then back here for a drink at the bar: the "grasshopper" drink for L & S. . . . Al's play with S's name. To bed early—about 9.

Lorine wrote both the Roubs and the Schoessows about the visit: "a day o a day to be remembered. Shizumi is the *tiniest* thing—tiny, Cid said, even for Japanese women. . . . Al behaved quite well, overdoing his role as host only a little bit. Every time he wanted to address himself to Shizumi he pronounced it differently until it got to be something like Shoshone ('Oh,' I said, 'we have a Shoshone woman here?') and that little woman went into peals of laughter." To Julie she wrote, "Your father was funnier the more drinks he had."

Lorine claimed that, expecting her visitors Saturday, she'd cooked the entire meal that day and had to serve it day-old on Sunday. But her pre-preparation was deliberate. She never could talk and cook at the same time, and talking with Cid was top priority.

Lorine told the Schoessows: "When we took them back at night to town to the hotel Al asked if he could buy them some drinks. Cid said yes so before saying good night and good bye everyone was quite mellow. At the last good-bye moment Cid kissed me and Al kissed Shuzumi and he said afterwards it was something like kissing ten-year old Julie! But they are grand people."

Later Cid amplified his account of the meeting:

> She made it clear that, but for a younger teacher friend [Gail Roub] . . . she had no intellectual companionship in the area, and likely never did have any. Her library was well-stocked and ranging. She showed me photos of her father and herself on the river. Told me some of the history of Black Hawk. . . .
>
> Some children came to the door and Lorine instinctively, very gently, addressed them, went to the icebox and gave them some candybars, left over from Halloween, when they had gone, to her dismay, unclaimed. Al boasted of being frightening to [children] and was not averse to flashing a gun, if they got too noisy. Lorine naturally shied at his style, but didn't press the issue.

Corman produced a cassette recorder, said calmly, "Read from your poetry"— and Lorine "calmly read!! Amazing—not good reading, I think. . . . But what an experience." Corman, who noticed during the visit that Lorine shook visibly, reported: "She read poorly, but her eyesight was poor and she was using a magnifying glass to read by and she had never done it before. It was the music on the page that she explored."

With paper shuffling, minimal stumbling, and a delightful giggle, Lorine read ten poems from her manuscript "Harpsichord and Salt Fish," including "Jefferson," "Morris," and "Darwin." There is no Great Poet about her; she definitely does not explore the music of the poems. Her hyaline voice is matter-of-fact—objective, one might say. She was surprised to find it so easy: "Two things I did this fall for the first time: shot a can off a post thirty feet from me at the first shot, and read aloud."

Lorine had urged Al to finish the new bookcase before the Cormans' visit. "Do you think such a thing is made by *will-power*?" he'd demanded. At last it was installed, with her twenty-five-dollar Cutty Sark model ("I find myself getting further and further into England or things English-connected"), the Minnesota peace pipe, and Gottfried Kunz's model of his rowboat arranged on top. Above they hung a Moroccan scimitar, "the kind of gilded dagger T. E. Lawrence wears in that painting." After Morris, Jefferson, and Darwin, her heart had returned to the British Empire agent who'd shifted his loyalty to the Arabs.

She did not have long to admire the arrangement. On December 1 she was testing a Swiss steak in the Dutch oven when she said to Al, "Honey, I feel strange." Al carried her into the bedroom, set her on the bed. "I messed my blouse," she said. "Don't worry about it," said Al and called an ambulance.

By coincidence, the nurse on duty was Doris Perkin, Lorine's one-time renter.

"What I remember is how tiny she looked in that hospital bed. A little thing, lost. Of course we started an IV right away, took her temperature and blood pressure. When the doctor came he said she'd suffered a massive stroke." Technically, she'd suffered a cerebral hemorrhage. She was paralyzed on one side, could not speak.

Æneas McAllister was working as maintenance at the hospital. When he heard she'd been brought in, he rushed to her room and bent over her. When he said "Lorine!" she rolled her eyes and tried to speak but could not. Devastated, Æneas bolted from the room and never went back.

She lay in the hospital for thirty days. When Al visited he would talk to her and she would move. Occasionally she murmured something sounding like "koss" or "cuss"; he didn't understand.

On December 31 she was finally transported to Madison General Hospital. She died that afternoon on the X-ray table. Only after Al was told she was gone did he realize she had been trying to say "kiss, kiss."

Afterword

Al Millen was too broken by Lorine's death to take charge. George Millen's wife, Alice, broke the news to Julie in Australia:

Lorine died yesterday afternoon. They took her to Madison to have a neurologist see her & she died while they were doing an X-ray to see if she had a brain tumor. She didn't have a tumor or a clot & they did a post to see what was the cause of death.

It's hard for your Dad of course but he's really doing very well & will do well. He gets all shook & cries & shakes a lot when he's talking about her or when something special happens like a neighbor coming over etc. You know.

[George and I] went out today & with Lorine's cousin Maud[e] went to the funeral home. The funeral is Sunday at 2 p.m. The minister who married them will bury her. . . . I picked out her clothes today for her to wear. Also went thru some closets & got rid of all her clothes, purses, shoes, undies etc. I gave them to the Good Will. He wanted them out. He's going to give all her books to the library at Fort.

George and Alice paid $1,413.40 for a steel casket lined in crepe de chine and velvet, and $10.00 to dress Lorine's hair. Lorine's grave was dug on Saturday, January 2. The next day snow began to fall on top of eleven inches on the ground. The Royal F. Hayes Funeral Home asked to postpone the service, but George refused because of his father's emotional state. George greeted funeral home visitors: "I didn't know anybody but the Prisks, so it was hard. Of course my father was home drunk." Albert Tippins conducted a simple service; then the pallbearers—Alex Kohlman, Carl Hausz, Henry De Blain, Peter Ganser, Harold Sager, and Æneas McAllister—bore the casket to the hearse. Five cars edged through driving snow to Union Cemetery, where Lorine was buried beside Henry and Daisy. Al did not go to the cemetery. "She went hard to earth," muttered Mr. Draeger, one of the grave diggers. By Monday morning more than thirteen new inches of snow blanketed the Fort area.

In the *Daily Jefferson County Union* obituary, Lorine Niedecker died as "Mrs. Albert Millen." Basil Bunting, in Madison when Lorine died, communicated the news to Zukofsky. Lorine's last message to Louie had been a November 23 postcard closing, "Hope you carry yourselves with strength." Thriftily, Zukofsky wrote a brief condolence to Al Millen on the reverse of Lorine's postcard: "sad . . . how much she meant . . . you will miss . . . anything we can do."

The next weekend Al's daughter, Alice Zenisek, drove from Chicago to the cottage. Al had stopped crying, she noted, and was eating again and talking a lot about Lorine, which she thought healthy: "We went thru more of her stuff Sat. & burned a lot of things. She had notes in boxes & on her papers saying 'destroy upon my death' which we did & 'Give to the Univ of Wisc.' or 'Univ of Texas.' The lawyer will take care of that, also he will see if any of her journals etc are valuable. Also he will write letters to the people that need to know."

Al wrote two letters to Zukofsky. Acting on Lorine's request, he'd destroyed her notes and journal and now wanted to know what to do with remaining papers. Zukofsky referred him to the University of Texas at Austin, where he eventually sent Lorine's remaining Zukofsky papers, including photographs and letters from Celia and Paul.

Fred Hobe had transferred much of his practice to Milwaukee; Donald Smith was now Lorine's lawyer. Smith is dead; his wife recalls no Niedecker papers in his possession. Lorine had named Cid Corman as her literary executor; but no one contacted him about the disposal of her papers. There are no Niedecker papers at the University of Wisconsin–Madison, but according to Lorine's directions, Al sent typescripts of three collections of published poems to Boston University's Mugar Memorial Library.

Al eventually phoned Gail Roub, who, unaware of Lorine's illness, was shocked at her death. Gail and Bonnie rescued some books, scrapbooks, and papers that had not been burned. Al ceremoniously presented Lorine's personal library to the Fort Atkinson library. It is uncertain how much money Lorine left Al, in addition to her property.

Indignant at the lack of recognition upon her death, Jonathan Williams wrote a passionate (if statistically inaccurate) letter to the *New York Times*:

> Dear Sir, "Lorine Niedecker is the best living poetess. No one is so
> subtle with so few words." —Basil Bunting . . . "Lorine Niedecker is

the most absolute poetess in our language since Emily Dickinson."—
Peter Yates.

Miss Niedecker died in her home, Fort Atkinson, Wisconsin, on December 30th, 1970. She was 68. It strikes me as fairly dim on the part of the *New York Times* and what few other responsible journals there still are that not one of them has managed in the intervening weeks to inform the public of this loss.

During the four decades Lorine Niedecker wrote her savory, laconic, superbly crafted poems, she commanded the admiration of William Carlos Williams, Louis Zukofsky, Bunting, Edward Dahlberg, Kenneth Rexroth, Herbert Read, James Laughlin, Robert Duncan, Cid Corman, Robert Creeley, Edward Dorn, Guy Davenport, Ian Hamilton Finlay, Gilbert Sorrentino, Ronald Johnson and a small audience capable of telling real peony bushes from plastic hydrangea plants. Her work is in print on both sides of the Atlantic and we propose to keep it that way until journals, critics, and readers become re-cultivated.

His letter unpublished, Jonathan did not give up, but began collecting tributes from poets who had admired her. These he published in a small edition in 1973 as *Epitaphs for Lorine*, its primary purpose "to register a sense of what the poems— and her devotional life—have meant to a number of poets." Of the twenty-seven contributions (two from women), Denise Levertov's is the best:

> someone crossed this field last night:
> day reveals
> a perspective of lavender caves
> across the snow. someone
> entered the dark woods.

Lorine was not buried two weeks before Al wrote Margaret Millen suggesting they get back together. He told Julie: "Now this is something most of the family wont like, but I had about an hours talk with your mother this morning. She will retire in May and it seems we will be back fighting again. Out here of course where I can throw her into the river to cool hr. off. There are so many things happening. If you ever get married again dont marry a famous person. Lorine was famous."

Margaret moved to Fort Atkinson. Since she didn't drive, Al picked her up for grocery shopping, took her for country drives. They ate together sometimes, perhaps slept together. But Margaret refused to live with Al: "I won't be your housekeeper." For her he added a screen porch to the cottage facing the river. Al's daughter Julie reported: "My mother was demanding; she wanted a screen porch. If Lorine had wanted a screen porch my father would have built one, he was a soft touch. But Lorine didn't seem to want anything."

Al Millen lived on in the cottage, drinking more, which at this point didn't much matter. He gave up driving the big Buick, hiring a disabled veteran named Bill, who rented the cabin, as chauffeur. Eventually Al underwent surgery for glaucoma and prostate cancer. Then on July 28, 1981, while grocery shopping in Sentry, he said, "Bill, I don't feel well." He admitted himself to the Fort Atkinson Hospital shortly after and died that evening. (Next day Bill and Al's Buick were gone.) Al's obituary has him survived by Margaret Millen, one son, and three daughters—no mention of Lorine.

Yet in death this loving man was faithful. In 1974 he'd bought a plot next to Henry, Daisy, and Lorine and had "Millen" etched under Lorine's name on her stone. His gravestone reads "Albert Millen, Husband of Lorine Neidecker [*sic*]." Much as her calling may have at times bemused him, Albert Millen had given Lorine time and space to write. In that sense he was a patron of the arts.

Louis Zukofsky, having seen all his works to date published in 1969, continued the good fight, with more recognition, though never enough. The poet and man were "starkly the same," as Niedecker the poet and woman were not quite. Women necessarily let more everyday into their lives. He died of peritonitis followed by cardiac arrest on May 12, 1978, Lorine's birthday, which could not have pleased Celia, who, in 1979, wrote Cid Corman claiming that "Zukofsky had created Niedecker and that fully ninety percent of her poetry consisted of his revisions." The letters, the gifts had meant little: Celia had resented Lorine from the start.

Cid Corman continued to publish Lorine—in *Origin* in 1971; in a collection, *Blue Chicory*, in 1975; in a special 1981 *Origin* featuring her poetry, letters, and memoirs of colleagues and friends; and eighty-nine of her poems in *The Granite Pail* in 1985. Interestingly, Cid omits from *The Granite Pail* and *Blue Chicory* the early, populist poems that speak so strongly for the underdog. He omits too Lorine's searing poems about her mother, her frustrated loneliness, and Al's alcoholism. But Lorine never had a more loyal publisher than Corman.

"Lorine was very important to Jonathan Williams," says Tom Meyer, longtime companion of Williams. "He felt great affection for her." Jonathan proved his affection in 1985 by publishing *From This Condensery: The Complete Writings of Lorine Niedecker*, edited by Robert Bertholf, then manuscript curator at the State University of New York at Buffalo. Unfortunately, Bertholf was a careless editor. Jonathan hadn't realized that Bertholf was floundering, though "he agreed after publication that he had made a mess." In 2002 the University of California Press published Lorine's *Collected Works*, edited by Jenny Penberthy, the book Williams had hoped to achieve.

Meyer, however, argues that the Jargon Society "snapped things into place for Lorine." He refers not only to Niedecker winning the prestigious Banta Award in 1986 but also to her debut in the *New York Times Book Review*. Reviewing *From This Condensery* and *The Granite Pail*, Michael Heller calls the new availability of the poems "a distinctive literary event, for her poems, in their powerful yet nearly mathematical compounding of language and silence, are among the subtlest of our time."

Britain, too, was loyal. *The Full Note* is a book of essays and tributes that its editor Peter Dent hoped was part of a new appreciation for Niedecker: "The time is surely right for her singular, unaffected and subtle voice to be heard once again—heard and sustained." In 1991 Pig Press published her last manuscript, *Harpsichord and Salt Fish*, edited by Jenny Penberthy, with artwork by Walter and Garry Fabian Miller. Though Lorine fought shy of illustrated poems, she would have appreciated these subtle renderings of fish and leaves.

Determined that Lorine be recognized, Gail Roub proved an exceptionally loyal friend. He and Bonnie talked to groups about Lorine, urged teachers to use her poetry, and—crucial for biography—interviewed people who had known her. He was joined in this work by two Fort Atkinson librarians, Mary Gates and Marilla Fuge. Fuge became intensely interested in Lorine's ancestry and spent years researching Niedecker and Kunz genealogy. Fuge and Gates also interviewed important witnesses like Ernest Hartwig and Æneas McAllister. They were determined not to let Lorine Niedecker's life be lost.

Roub also chaired a local committee that in 1990 nominated Lorine's property for a State Historical Marker as "Poet of Place." Spurred by rejection because "her place in history does not yet appear to be firmly established," the Roubs solicited testimonials to Niedecker's status from professors, critics, librarians, and poets like Rakosi, Enslin, Williams, Sorrentino, and Levertov. The Historical Markers Council capitulated. On July 13, 1991, a group of loyalists assembled at a "once-in-a-lifetime literary event" to erect the marker. Beneath Lorine's name and dates are lines from "PAEAN TO PLACE":

> Fish
> fowl
>   flood
>   Water lily mud
> My life

in the leaves and on water
My mother and I
　　　born
in swale and swamp and sworn
to water

Present at the induction were Bob and DiAnn Ruh, owners of Lorine's property. After her death, Al had asked $40,000 for the place, a price the Ruhs thought inflated. After Al's death in 1981, Julie Schoessow became his power of attorney. Eventually, under pressure from siblings and tired of managing the property, she lowered the price; the Ruhs bought it for $28,500 in 1986. Though Bob made changes and the property is owned today by his daughter and her husband, Lorine's cabin, cottage, and riverbank property remain, a destination for all who admire her.

"My concern for and with LN will be as long as my life," Cid Corman wrote Gail Roub. Corman had important second thoughts about his visit to Lorine:

> Her style was neat, unaggressive without being timid or diffident. She knew what she felt and what she wanted, but she would not impose either feeling or desire on others.
>
> Her poems are often "literary"; that is, related to her reading— but they never are merely intellectual or abstract. You can feel her delight in the experiences of others and especially the language in which experiences have been couched and realized. She has an exquisite ear for detail. Every word is *lived*. You can feel her in them. She culls them. This is provender.
>
> She had ample cause to be selfpitying and bitter, but her letters to me show no trace of either qualification. Her complaints, when they occur, and only rarely do they occur, are clearly hard wrung and never in excess of provocation. She is unusually well-balanced in her judgments and perspicacious and particular. She is both unpredictable and characteristic. She has learned from others, but projects her own music and her own realizations. There is no sense of complacency.
>
> She is utterly without moralizing. She is never petty. Her warmth of relation to living and dead is pervasive. It is impossible not to love her. I never saw her handwriting—with its immaculate clear modest script—without at once feeling a twinge of pleasure— at whatever she was to say. I always anticipated some shared delight, or pain—which is never unalloyed. She didn't oversimplify, but she never merely decorated. Her haiku-like brief poems are as fine as any short poems of our or any time. . . .

She is never mystical and yet one feels a certain awe at times, a profound givenness to the mysteries. Most often she reverts to some natural relation, to water or work or plants or animals or acquaintances, books and news, the sense of locality.

It aches me yet—her absence. . . . Poetry was her life and her life remains for us as poetry—thanks to her magnanimous gift.

Corman testifies to Lorine Niedecker's personal and poetic power. Finally, however, it is only Lorine who speaks for herself. Appreciators though they were, Corman, Bunting, and Jonathan Williams tended to underestimate her poems as subtle, frail blossoms. Zukofsky and William Carlos Williams knew better. Actually Lorine Niedecker—from *New Goose*'s subversive folk tales to the searing "PAEAN TO PLACE" to the maturely complex "WINTERGREEN RIDGE"—is one of the mentally toughest, most strong-willed and appealing twentieth-century voices. She is both intricate and basic, acerbic and profoundly musical. As a 1997 *Times Literary Supplement* review of Andrew McAllister's *The Objectivists* says rightly, "She is a poet who demands attention."

Lorine received attention in 2003 when scholars converged from the United States, Canada, and abroad to celebrate the centenary of her birth with poetry readings, scholarly papers, reminiscences, and pilgrimages to Blackhawk Island. In 2004 the Friends of Lorine Niedecker was officially established; now it hosts an annual Lorine Niedecker Poetry Festival in Fort Atkinson. At the corner of Main Street and Sherman Avenue in Fort, drivers and pedestrians are treated to a colorful poetry wall with lines from "PAEAN TO PLACE." And thanks to Brian and Terrie Knox, the new Dwight Foster Public Library addition has a Lorine Niedecker room where appreciators now have access to treasures like Lorine's personal library.

And who could have guessed that in 2010 her inscribed copy of *My Friend Tree* to Jonathan Williams would be offered by a bookseller at $7,500?

Appendix
Niedecker or Neidecker, No Longer the Question

When even some people who admire Lorine Niedecker's poetry call her Loraine it's not surprising that she is often miscalled Neidecker. Lorine Neidecker, Loraine Niedecker—does it matter? Well, yes. Lorine herself would be concerned: only ignorance of her poetry could be worse than not knowing the spelling and pronunciation of her name.

It's true that sometimes Lorine's German last name appears as Neidecker (NIGHdecker) rather than Niedecker (NEEdecker). This fact has given rise to three myths: (1) That Lorine changed her name from NIGHdecker to NEEdecker in high school as a gesture of independence; (2) that Lorine changed her name from NIGHdecker to NEEdecker because she preferred the euphonious rhyming of NEE with LorEEN; and (3) that the spelling on her gravestone—NIGHdecker— was Lorine's finger flip at her NEEdecker parents.

A few facts:

- California records state that Lorine's paternal grandfather was Charles Niedecker
- Grandfather Charles's name on the marriage certificate to his second wife is Niedecker
- Grandfather Charles's name on the Wisconsin censuses of 1895 and 1905 is Niedecker
- Lorine's father's name on his birth certificate is Henry Niedecker
- Lorine's father's name on his marriage record is Henry Niedecker
- Lorine's name on her birth record is Niedecker
- Lorine's name on her baptismal certificate is Niedecker
- Lorine's father's name in the 1910 and 1930 censuses is Niedecker
- Lorine's name on her 1928 marriage certificate is Niedecker
- Lorine's mother's name on her death certificate is Niedecker
- Lorine's father's name on his death certificate is Niedecker

- Lorine's name on her 1963 marriage certificate is Niedecker
- LORINE'S NAME ON EVERY SCRAP OF HER PUBLISHED WORK IS NIEDECKER

So why the confusion?

One reason is that her father Henry's brother, George, changed his surname NEEdecker to NIGHdecker. Though George eventually lived in Janesville, he is buried in Fort Atkinson and evidently his spelling of his name had local influence. His granddaughter Mary Rockenfield declares (incorrectly), "It was never Niedecker, always Neidecker": But George was born Niedecker.

More important, in this southeastern Wisconsin region settled by Germans, NIGH names predominate: Hein, Heinz, Schneider, Heimstreet, Deinlein, Klein, Schmeiser, Stein, Gein, Feingold, Meintz, Steinmetz, Weiner, Zeigler, Zeitz. I realized this when, on three separate occasions, I asked for Lorine NEEdecker records at the Jefferson County Court House. Each time the clerk said, "Let's see, you're looking for Loraine NIGHdecker?"

In Fort Atkinson newspapers, therefore, Henry Niedecker's name gradually began to be misspelled as Neidecker, as it was on a plat map in 1950. When his wife, Theresa, died in 1951, he did not protest when the carver of the gravestone misspelled the name Neidecker. The *Jefferson County Union* obituary also spelled Theresa's name Neidecker. In a 1951 document about well rights, it's "Henry Neidecker," and in 1954 he too is Neidecker in a *Jefferson County Union* obituary. The misspelling could happen to Lorine too. In divorce proceedings against her first husband in 1942, the plaintiff is Lorine Neidecker Hartwig; and in a property document or two signed after Henry's death, Lorine is recorded as Niedecker, "also known as Neidecker."

These are, however, exceptions. Lorine was born Niedecker and wrote as Niedecker—though when she died in 1970 the *Jefferson County Union* neatly sidestepped the issue by calling her Mrs. Albert Millen.

Niedecker. Lorine. Maybe we need a movie titled *Lorine's Nie*.

Acknowledgments

I am deeply grateful to those persons, living and dead, who published and preserved Lorine Niedecker's writing and the facts of her life, making it possible for me to write a full-length biography of a remarkable modern American poet. Among the first Fort Atkinson appreciators were the late Gail Roub and Jane Shaw Knox. Roub, with his wife, Bonnie, talked about Niedecker, interviewed family and friends, and donated Niedecker materials to the Hoard Museum. Jane Knox wrote the first biography of Lorine: brief, but valuable because researched not long after her death. Marilla Fuge and Mary Gates volunteered as archivists for the Dwight Foster Public Library's Niedecker Collection, which began with Al Millen's donation of her personal library. Fuge and Gates also conducted interviews; Fuge researched Lorine's family genealogy for years. At the *Daily Jefferson County Union*, editor Bill Knox and reporter Chris Spangler have always given generous time and space to reporting Niedecker events.

Equally important to this biography have been Niedecker scholars. Jenny Penberthy's edition of Lorine's letters to Louis Zukofsky and Lisa Pater Faranda's of Lorine's to Cid Corman proved invaluable. *Lorine Niedecker: Woman and Poet*, also edited by Penberthy, contains key biographical and critical essays, while Elizabeth Willis's *Radical Vernacular: Lorine Niedecker and the Poetics of Place* provides close readings of the work. The Selected Bibliography confirms to how many other writers about Niedecker I'm indebted.

Special thanks to Professor Glenna Breslin for generously sharing her research from the 1980s and 1990s when she was working on a biography of Niedecker, not completed. Many thanks to Jenny Penberthy for corresponding with me at the project's start, and to people long interested in Lorine who brought me closer to her: Bob Arnold, Karl Gartung, Mary Gates, Paul Hayes, Faith Miracle, and Bonnie Roub.

In Kyoto, Japan, Professor Daniel Bratton connected me with Shizumi Corman. Many thanks also to Tom Montag, who recorded every note in every book in Lorine's library; the notes, and much other information, may be accessed at http://www.lorineniedecker.org.

For permission to quote from published and unpublished materials, I thank Bob Arnold, Robert Reisman, Clayton Eshleman, the Fales Collection of New York University's Bobst Library, the National Poetry Foundation, Thomas Meyer, Julie Millen Schoessow, and Michael Vandre. I am equally grateful to the Dwight Foster Public Library, Kori Oberle at the Hoard Museum, Shizumi Corman, Thomas Meyer, Robert Reisman, Pia Simig, and Julie Millen Schoessow for permission to reproduce images.

To those who assisted me with Niedecker library collections, many thanks: Lea Cline and Linda Briscoe Meyers, the Harry Ransom Humanities Research Center, University of Texas–Austin; Lisa Darms, the Fales Collection of the Bobst Library at NYU; James Maynard, The Poetry Collection, SUNY–Buffalo; R. I. Higgins, Basil Bunting Archives, Durham University; Fred Burwellf, Beloit College Library Archives; Iris Snyder, Morris Library, University of Delaware; Denison Beach, Houghton Library, Harvard University; Mark C. Meade, the Thomas Merton Center; staffs of the Wisconsin Historical Society and the Rare Book Room of the University of Wisconsin–Madison Memorial Library; Gail Sapiel, the National Poetry Foundation, University of Maine–Orono; and Isaac Gewirtz, Berg Collection, New York Public Library. Very special thanks to Kathleen Miskiewicz, who made copies for me of Niedecker's correspondence with James Laughlin at Houghton Library, Harvard.

In Fort Atkinson, Amy Lutzke, Dwight Foster Public Library research librarian extraordinaire, was always on deck; while at the Hoard Museum, Karen O'Connor brought out treasure after treasure from the Niedecker Archives. In Milwaukee, my thanks go to urban anthropologist Jill Lackey, who gave me an insider's tour of Lorine's south side neighborhood, and to Susan Ploetz, Research Librarian at the Milwaukee Public Library.

My gratitude goes to everyone who agreed to be interviewed about Lorine, first to Diane Dechar, who spoke out firmly on Lorine's much-disputed pregnancy and abortion, as well as to Barry Ahearn, Amy Arntson, Lois Bielefeldt, Daniel Billet, Daniel Bratton, Shizumi Corman, the late Florence Dollase, Ronald Ellis, Terry Ganser, Brook Hoglum, Joan Jones, Larry Ketterman, Brian and Terrie Knox, Clarence Langholff, Naomi Schwartz Marshall, Barbara Heath Martin, Thomas Meyer, George Millen, Dennis O'Connor, Doris Perkin, Darrell and Judy Prisk, Robert Reisman, Ruby Riemer, Trudy Thom, Mary Rockenfield, Bonnie

Roub, Robert Ruh, Linda Kreger Sawyer, Duane Scott, Carroll Trieloff, Michael Vandre, Phyllis Walsh, Kiki Ward, Charlotte Wendorf, and William Lux.

Julie Millen Schoessow merits special appreciation. Al Millen's youngest daughter not only knew Lorine but has donated Lorine's family writings and personal effects to the Hoard. With grace and humor, she has answered my questions by e-mail and in person. Thank you, Julie.

Very special thanks go to Jenny Penberthy, Ann Engelman, Faith Barrett, and my husband, Peter Jordan, for reading the biography in manuscript.

In June 2008, after attending a performance of Rae Brown's play about Lorine Niedecker at the Hoard Museum, I said casually to a woman staffing a desk, "I've always wanted to do a life of Lorine Niedecker." Sylvia Sippel took me seriously. You launched me on a great adventure, Sylvia, thank you. At the University of Wisconsin Press, Raphael Kadushin accepted my proposed Niedecker biography with an enthusiasm for which I am deeply grateful.

In 1985 I was talking to a friend over lunch about my biography of the Edwardian actress Mrs. Patrick Campbell. Suddenly a man rose from an adjacent booth. "Why are you writing about Mrs. Patrick Campbell when you should be writing about Lorine Niedecker!" Bonnie Roub recently reminded me of that encounter with Gail Roub, which must have registered, since that year I bought *The Granite Pail*. To Gail Roub, then, I owe an appreciation of Lorine's poetry jump-started twenty-five years ago.

Besides Peter Jordan, someone else has been in for the long haul. She is Ann Engelman, president of the Friends of Lorine Niedecker. To this biography she has unfailingly offered her support, appreciation, and knowledge. To her, I gratefully dedicate this book.

Notes

Abbreviations

ÆM	Æneas McAllister
AM	Albert Millen
BB	Basil Bunting
BC	*Blue Chickory*, by Lorine Niedecker
BP	Bean Pole, Lorine's name for her mother, Daisy
BYHM	*"Between Your House and Mine": The Letters of Lorine Niedecker and Cid Corman,* edited by Lisa Pater Faranda
CC	Cid Corman
CW	*Collected Works* of Lorine Niedecker, edited by Jenny Penberthy
CR	Charles Reznikoff
CSP	*Complete Short Poetry*, by Louis Zukofsky, edited by Robert Creeley
CZ	Celia Zukofsky
DFPL	Dwight Foster Public Library, Fort Atkinson, Wis.: Niedecker Archives
DJCU	*Daily Jefferson County Union* (successor to *Jefferson County Union*)
FTC	*From this Condensery*, by Lorine Niedecker
Fales	Fales Collection, Bobst Library, New York University
GB	Glenna Breslin's Niedecker notes
GR	Gail Roub
HN	Henry Niedecker
Hoard	Hoard Museum, Fort Atkinson, Wis.
HRHRC	Harry Ransom Humanities Research Center, University of Texas at Austin
H&SF	*Harpsichord & Salt Fish*, by Lorine Niedecker
IHF	Ian Hamilton Finlay
JCU	*Jefferson County Union*, later the *Daily Jefferson County Union*
JL	James Laughlin
JP	Jenny Penberthy
JS	Julie Millen Schoessow
JW	Jonathan Williams

KC	Kenneth Cox
LN	Lorine Niedecker
LNWP	*Lorine Niedecker: Woman and Poet*, edited by Jenny Penberthy
LZ	Louis Zukofsky
MFT	*My Friend Tree*, by Lorine Niedecker
MLBW	*My Life by Water*, by Lorine Niedecker
MP	Margot Peters
NC	*North Central*, by Lorine Niedecker
NCZ	*Niedecker and the Correspondence with Zukofsky, 1931–1970*, edited by Jenny Penberthy
ND	*New Directions in Prose and Poetry* (journal)
NG	*New Goose*, by Lorine Niedecker
PZ	Paul Zukofsky
RV	*Radical Vernacular: Lorine Niedecker and the Poetics of Place*, edited by Elizabeth Willis
T&G	*T & G: The Collected Poems (1936–1966)*, by Lorine Niedecker
TFN	*The Full Note: Lorine Niedecker*, edited by Peter Dent
TN	Theresa (Daisy) Niedecker
TPAL	*The Poem of a Life: A Biography of Louis Zukofsky*, by Mark Scroggins
WCW	William Carlos Williams
WHS	Wisconsin Historical Society, Madison

Introduction

3   "Out of the blurry": Tiffany, "The Rhetoric of Materiality," 000.

—   "really beating . . . We were": Heller, *Carl Rakosi*, 47.

—   "Not Ideas About": the title of a Wallace Stevens poem. Stevens, *The Collected Poems*, 534.

4   "With her the external": Evans and Kleinzahler, "An Interview with Carl Rakosi," 64.

—   "that has always": LN to KC, 10 December 1966, *TFN*, 36.

—   "in the company": *NCZ*, 4.

—   "one in the world": J. Williams, *Epitaphs for Lorine*, n.p.

—   "The United States": M. Oppen, *Meaning a Life*, 120.

5   "Wonder if there": LN to LZ, 28 April [LZ: 1949], *NCZ*, 138.

—   "And I'd have . . . *This I can't*": LN to CC, 27 August 1965, *BYHM*, 69.

—   "A tape of": LN to Bob Nero, "Remembering Lorine," 139.

—   "These moves to push": LN to CC, 21 February 1969, *BYHM*, 184.

—   "but I fight": LN to CC, 6 December 1965, *BYHM*, 77.

—   "I think I'm": LN to CC, 15 December 1966, *BYHM*, 108.

—   "a glorious shock . . . as so much": LN to CC, 21 November 1968, *BYHM*, 179.

—   "the 'Objectivist's' number": LZ, "'Recencies' in Poetry," 22.

5 "Eliot is still": WCW to LZ, 8 April 1946, in Ahearn, *Correspondence of William Carlos Williams and Louis Zukofsky*, 370.

6 "the best contemporary *poetess*" (my italics): J. Williams, *Epitaphs for Lorine*, n.p.

— "However much Niedecker": JP, introduction to *NCZ*, 3.

— "intense marginality": Rachel Blau DuPlessis, "Lorine Niedecker, the Anonymous," in *LNWP*, 114. DuPlessis argues that LN sought anonymity in the face of "materialism, bellicosity, bigness/bestness, and fame as it developed in the post-war period." I agree that LN rejected these, but not that she sought anonymity. On the contrary, she did everything she could to get herself published and recognized. "Could" is the operative word here: temperamentally she could not promote her works in public.

7 "*things* / to the flood": "PAEAN TO PLACE," *CW*, 268.

— "Scuttle up the workshop": "Scuttle up the workshop," *CW*, 87.

Chapter 1. Carp-Seiner's Daughter

9 "trees thick": LN's autobiographical short story "Uncle," written in 1937, *CW*, 308.

10 "She was tall!": HN's parents were Charles Niedecker (1840–1921) and Emelia Schneider (d. 1879–83?). HN's two brothers, George and Charles, and sister, Emma, were also born in California. HN's grandfather, LN wrote LZ 19 July 1959 (HRHRC), "had been born in Germany or, properly speaking, Alsace Lorraine, where his father, the Frenchman, had taken refuge with a family whose name he took, his own it seems was La Ventre or Le Vente or Le Venge. Doesn't Venge mean wind?? [*Venger, vengeance*, means "vengeance" or "avenging" in French; *vente* means "wind."] Great grandfather in France had stolen wood off an estate & other things badly need by the poor people and fled when it looked as tho he was going to be arrested." Obituaries state that the grandparents were born in Germany. In 1883 Charles Niedecker Sr., having lost his wife, Emelia, a child, and property near Sacramento, California, returned to Wisconsin, and later married Mary Brandel (1842–1927); HN names her as stepmother on his marriage certificate. George Neidecker's daughters Edna (m. Leon LeRoy Dodge) and Esther (m. Arthur Glover) were LN's cousins. George Neidecker (1869–1949) was married to Emma Ehlers (d. 1943). Charles Jr. married Minnie Ehlers (1872–1904), who died at thirty-two and was so mourned that the church could not hold the crowds; they had one son, Lawrence, who would own property on Blackhawk Island. Emma Niedecker married John Cormany and lived in Beloit. One of her daughters, Marie Cormany (Theron) Vickerman, cared enough about LN to attend her funeral.

LN's maternal grandparents were Gottfried Karl (Charles) Kunz (1837–1917) and Louise Amelia Schlosser Kunz (1840–?). Gottfried's parents, George Philip Kunz (1811–83) and Caroline Zeasar Kunz (1817–80), emigrated from Prussia; interestingly, it was Caroline who bought land in the Blackhawk Island area, from George Silverthorn in 1857 and August Stoppenbach in 1863. Gottfried and Louise Amelia had two children, Charles George Kunz (1870–?) and TN (1878–1951). Caroline Kunz's property went to

Gottfried and then to TN and Charles. Charles bought further property on Blackhawk Island, as well as on Long Lake in Washburn County, Wisconsin, where he established a resort, which he sold in 1950. John Allan Kunz (b. 1955), great-grandson of Charles, lives in Duluth, Minnesota. Marilla Fuge, volunteer LN archivist, did considerable genealogical work on the Kunz family, to which this account is indebted. Her notes are in the LN Archives, DFPL.

HN and TN were married at St. John's Community Church, Town of Oakland, 28 August 1901, with Walther and Mabel Kunz as witnesses. LN's birth certificate is in the Jefferson County Courthouse Register of Deeds office, vol. 8, p. 118. LN was baptized on 21 May 1904 at the same church; W. F. Ladwig and Frances Altpeter, from a prominent local family, sponsored. LN's birthplace, a modest two-story house close to the river surrounded by tall trees, became the Riverside Guest House before it was bought from Janice Brom by Jefferson County, then torn down in 1996.

10 "I see Lorine": Florence Dollase, interview by Marilla Fuge, 11 August 1999.
— "No one remembers": Knox, *Lorine Niedecker*, 7.
— "neat as a pin": Adeline Garthwaite and Arvella Humbach, daughters of LN's first cousin Roland Hartel and his wife Maude, interview by GR, 21 June 1991.
11 "a very lovely person": Adeline Garthwaite and Arvella Humbach, interview by Marilla Fuge, 3 January 1999.
— "Indian heritage": LN told this to her close friend ÆM, who moved to Blackhawk Island with his family in 1953.
— "descendent for sure . . . whole chunks": LN to KC, 10 December 1966, *TFN*, 36.
— "head thrown back": LN's short story "Uncle," *CW*, 305. LN disguises family characters: in the story Grandfather Gottfried Kunz, for example, is Great-Uncle Gottlieb and Grandmother Kunz is Aunt Riecky.
12 "Trees are the best . . . I always thought": "Uncle", *CW*, 307, 308.
— "[A] cute little girl": Ernest Hartwig, interview by Bonnie and GR, 6 January 1987.
— "My, she was tall! . . . Uncle Art *never*": Florence Dollase, interview by Marilla Fuge, 11 August 1999.
13 "Lorine and I . . . Our mutual": Edna Neidecker Dodge, "Down Memory Lane." In 1991 Mrs. Dodge sent two volumes of memorabilia to the LN Collection at DFPL.
— "A hummingbird": "PAEAN TO PLACE," *CW*, 264. HN was pictured in the *Jefferson County Democrat* (21 March 1912) at the wheel of his new automobile in an article satirizing his jaunty popularity.
— "redwinged blackbirds": LN to KC, 10 December 1966, *TFN*, 36.
— "took many honors": Juanita Schreiner's reminiscence of LN, [n.d.], DFPL. A "High-school Notes" article in the *JCU*, 12 March 1920, announced that the Opoponopokuk Campfire Girls "gave a program that was both interesting and novel . . . Reading: Lorine Niedecker."
14 "We had the sweetest . . . vague, ill-responsive . . . managed to succeed": Florence Dollase to Marilla Fuge, 11 August 1999, DFPL.

Chapter 2. High School

15 "She had a visual . . . but still": Juanita M. Schreiner's reminiscence, DFPL.

16 "cute little girl . . . She never went . . . I always spoke . . . Henry was never . . . Daisy, she was": Ernest Hartwig, interview by Bonnie and GR, 6 January 1987, DFPL.

— "I was not made": LN to CC, 7 December 1967, *BYHM*, 137.

17 "My father / thru marsh fog": "PAEAN TO PLACE," *CW*, 261.

— "put Gert up to": Arvella Humbach and Adeline Garthwaite, interview by GR, 21 June 1999.

18 "What a woman!": "What a woman!" *CW*, 108.

— "From the first sentence . . . the present congress": Robert La Follette, *Political Philosophy* (self-published, 1920), 257, 259. LN signed her copy "Lorine Niedecker Junior Year."

— "He was crazy": Arvella Humbach and Adeline Garthwaite, interview by GR, 21 June 1999.

19 "It is not . . . Well, Harriet": 1921 *Tchogeerrah*, DFPL. Harriet Westphal and LN were related by marriage. Louise Westphal was the mother of Minne A. Frederike Ehlers, who married Charles Jacob Niedecker Jr. on 13 May 1896 (Register of Deeds, Jefferson County Court House). Two other *Tchogeerrah*s survive with LN's inscriptions, both at DFPL. Elizabeth Hoard's 1919 copy reads: "English class—E. H. main speaker—Declamatory Contest—we did have a failure but never mind—Napoleon said Try, try again. Lorine Faith (Hope) Niedecker [added in pencil] and charity"; Marguerite Nettesheim's 1921 copy read: "Dear Margarite[,] English class was a snap, eh, but so interesting. French is hard but interresant. Il ait[fait?] chaud. Tres bien—Good luck—Lorine."

— "rowing a boat": LN to LZ, 2 September [LZ: 1957], *NCZ*, 238.

— "just doesn't . . . It took me": Ernest Hartwig, interview by Bonnie and GR, 6 January 1987, DFPL.

20 "A smart girl": Clarence Langholff to MP, 30 September 2008, interview at Wellington Meadows Retirement Facility, Fort Atkinson.

— "I have been . . . [W]e came up": 1922 *Tchogeerrah*, DFPL.

21 "My favorite studies": Beloit College Library Archives. I am indebted to Fred Burwellf, archivist, for what he has already written about LN in "The Poet's Years at Beloit College," *Beloit College Magazine* (January 1996), 7 (also at the Beloit College Archives website).

— "a very *unusual*": Evelyn Heiden, a Kunz relative, interview by Marilla Fuge, 20 September 1993.

Chapter 3. Beloit College

22 "If I were seeking . . . about forty per cent": Yale Bicentennial Volume, 308–9, quoted in Eaton, *Historical Sketches of Beloit College*, 151, 125.

22 "has affected a moderate": Eaton, *Historical Sketches of Beloit College*, 125.

— "[W]omen are in Beloit . . . It is a great desire": 1923 Codex, Beloit College Library Archives.

23 "intimately associated": Eaton, *Historical Sketches of Beloit College*, 126.

— "Niedecker was a model": "The Lorine Niedecker Celebration," *Beloit College Round Table*, 22 March 1991. The *JCU* also kept up with Beloit student activity, noting that Miss Lorine Niedecker and Miss Ione Altpeter of Beloit College were home Thanksgiving day, 1923.

24 "best read . . . akin to nothing": Beloit College annual *The Gold*, 1933, Beloit College Library Archives.

— "The Beloit team": *Beloit College Round Table*, 1 March 1924. LN was noticed in *JCU*, 23 February 1923: "Miss Lorine Niedecker of this city has been chosen a member of the Beloit college girls' debating team. She graduated from Fort Atkinson high school last year, being one of the twenty-four honor students" (7).

— "My dear": written in large, dashing handwriting in black ink. Ella Barton's 1924 *Codex*, Beloit College Library Archives.

25 "for the purpose . . . made the feast": *JCU*, 26 January 1923.

— "To bankers on high land": "To bankers on high land," *T&G, MLBW, CW*, 170. For six variations of this poem see *CW*, 411–14.

— "blunted female destiny": Heilbrun, *Writing a Woman's Life*, 51. A man's youth, says Heilbrun, is hopeful, a woman's uncertain if she does not choose a destiny of "flirtation, wedding, and motherhood."

Chapter 4. Searching

26 "There is no such place": *Mammonart* (self-published, 1924), 169, in LN's personal library, DFPL.

27 "The artist of the future": a clipping, "The Little Work of Art," n.d. or source, LN's personal library, DFPL.

— "tall, tormented": "Subliminal," *CW*, 287.

— "Well, spring overflows": "Well, spring overflows," *CW*, 107.

28 "She was *very* different": Arvella Humbach and Adeline Garthwaite to GR, 21 June 1991. Their mother, Maude Lezotte Hartel, was born in 1900, Arvella in 1916, Adeline in 1918.

— "incomparable preface": 13 July 1928, 7; "a brilliant history": 22 February 1929, 1; "Not enough can be said": 3 May 1929, 7; "supreme columnist": 8 November 1929, 7; "A book in the hand": 7 June 1929, 8; "It is said": 4 January 1929, 3; "It is reading": 30 November 1928, 1—all published in *JCU*. Some other books LN recommended are Stuart Chase, *Men and Machines*; E. F. Benson, *Paying Guests*; Sir James Jean, *The Universe around Us*; Sylvia Townsend Warner, *The True Heart*; Samuel McChord Crothers, *The Thought Broker*; Lytton Strachey, *Elizabeth and Essex*; Walter Lippman, *A Preface to Morals*; Virginia Woolf, *Orlando*; Edna Ferber, *So Big*; J. H. Randall, *The Making of the Modern Mind*; Van Leon, *Story of Mankind*; George Brandes, *Hellas*.

28 "like gorgeous quill-pens . . . dee round silence . . . Or it may be": "Transition," in *The Will-o-the-Wisp, a Magazine of Verse* 3 (1928): 12, and "Mourning Dove," in *Parnassus: A Wee Magazine of Verse* 2.2 (15 November 1928): 4, reprinted in *CW*, 23.

29 "killing pretty ducks": Ernest Hartwig, interview by Glenna Breslin, "Lorine Niedecker: The Poet in Her Homeplace," 191.

— "a doll": Ernest Hartwig, interview by Bonnie and GR, 6 January 1987.

— "What? You? . . . Frank never went": Breslin, "Lorine Niedecker: The Poet," 191.

— LN's marriage to Frank Hartwig is recorded in the Register of Deeds Office, Jefferson County Courthouse, vol. 9, 386.

— "It was odd": Breslin, "Lorine Niedecker: The Poet," 191.

30 "Lorine's marriage lasted": Nathalie Kaufman Yackels, interview by GR and Jeanine Strunk, 21 August 1991.

— "If that's all": Former Fort Atkinson resident Duane Scott, friend of Anna Ramsey and LN, in a telephone interview with MP of 28 October 2008, said these were LN's words to Anna Ramsey, who relayed them to Scott.

— "at night": Lois Bielefeldt, Frank Hartwig's niece, to MP, 8 October 2008.

— "*Why?* She wasn't": Florence Dollase, interview by Marilla Fuge, 10 January 1998, on the occasion of Dollase's presenting LN material to DFPL.

31 "Hatch, patch and scratch": "She grew where every spring," *CW*, 166–67.

— "Have you been married?": "Stage Directions," *CW*, 35–36.

— "Frank had drinking": Daniel Billet to MP in a telephone interview, 23 September 2008.

— "drank and was mean": ÆM, interview by Glenna Breslin, 2 August 1988, GB.

— "He's the only man": MP interview with Bonnie Roub, quoting GR, 14 July 2008.

— "Not many people . . . loose": Brian Knox, current editor of the *DJCU*, to MP, 17 July 2008. Another Fort Atkinson native, who called LN "loose," said that HN gave big parties after carp hauls, where he observed LN.

32 "Lake Koshkonong": LN Archives, Hoard.

— "Feign a great calm": "When Ecstasy is Inconvenient," *FTC* and *CW*, 25. The poem, says Jenny Penberthy in her valuable article "The Revolutionary Word," is "poised on the edge of breakdown" (78).

Chapter 5. Finding

34 "[d]esire for what": all Objectivist quotations are from LZ's special issue of *Poetry: A Magazine of Verse* 37, no. 5 (February 1931). LZ recommends works essential to the understanding of Objectivism: Ezra Pound's I–XXX Cantos, William Carlos Williams's *Spring and All*, Marianne Moore's *Observations*, T. S. Eliot's *The Waste Land* and *Marina*, E. E. Cummings's *Is 5*, Wallace Stevens's *Harmonium*, Robert McAlmon's *North America*, Charles Reznikoff's poetry, and issues 3 and 4 of the journal *The Exile*, edited by Pound.

35 "The emotional quality": LN to GR [n.d.], quoting from LZ's *A Test of Poetry*.

35 "the woolliness of what": Davie, "Lapidary Lucidity," 233.

— "[Objectivist] conveyed a meaning": Rakosi, *The Collected Prose*, 107.

— "Ezra Pound . . . and had cajoled . . . Zukofsky foiled . . . just wanted": Evans and Kleinzahler, "An Interview with Carl Rakosi," 61, 63.

— "[O]bjectivism—I never used": quoted in Mary Oppen, *Meaning a Life*, 91. Speaking on 19 August 1931 at the Gotham Book Mart, LZ denied he had tried to establish a poetic revolution; rather he tried to define issues perennially central to poetic art. For an excellent recent discussion of Objectivism, see Peter O'Leary's "The Energies of Words," online at Poetry Foundation, http://www.poetryfoundation.org/article/181672.

36 "clarity of image and word-tone": Zukofsky, "Sincerity and Objectification," 272.

— "*was the center*" (my italics): LN to KC, 11 June 1969, *TFN*, 37.

— "the 'Objectivist's' number": LZ's 19 August 1931 talk, "'Recencies' in Poetry," became the preface to An *"Objectivists" Anthology*, 22. Actually, there were responses to the February *Poetry* that Monroe printed in the April 1931 issue; evidently they were not enough for LZ.

— "beyond the reach": Terrell, *Louis Zukofsky*, 15.

— "Dear Miss Monroe" and following letters: LN, "Letters to *Poetry* Magazine," 175, 177.

Chapter 6. Zukofsky

39 "a very *unusual*": Evelyn Heiden, a Kunz relative, interview by Marilla Fuge, 20 September 1993.

40 "voluble, mercurial": Tomlinson, "Objectivists: Zukofsky and Oppen, a Memoir," 87.

— "sexually predatory": George Oppen's words, reported to MP by Naomi Schwartz Marshall in a telephone interview of 10 June 2009. Marshall was close to the Oppens between 1976 and Oppen's death in 1984; she says Oppen spoke often of Pound and LZ and LZ and LN.

— "[S]he and Louis . . . Later, when [Lorine]: Reisman, "Lorine: Some Memories of a Friend," 35.

— "relentless intellectual abstraction": *TPAL*, 125.

— "I don't think": Jerry Reisman to Glenna Breslin, taped interview, 3 May 1986, GB. Reisman's account contradicts that of Carl Rakosi, who believed LZ to be "terribly, terribly inhibited. . . . As a consequence he knew nothing about women—nothing. He was scared to death of them. . . . Very, very fearful of women" (Hatlen, "Interview," 99).

41 "Hope you don't . . . It takes six": WCW to LZ, 1 June 1932, HRHRC.

— "cavalierly": Mary Oppen's word in Glenna Breslin's unpublished interview with Jerry Reisman and Mary Oppen, 17 March 1986, GB; Oppen didn't think WCW took women's problems seriously.

— "a gel is only": Jerry Reisman to Glenna Breslin, taped interview, 3 May 1986, GB.

— "frightened me": LN to Ronald Ellis, 24 December 1966, a note added to an enclosed poem "To see the man who took care of our stock."

— "Rezy, yes . . . gentlest soul": LN to CC, 7 March 1970, *BYHM*, 219. "For a few years after my New York stay he sent me his books as they came out," LN added.

41 "A weekend visitor": Reisman, "Lorine," 35–36.

42 "honest, affectionate": Jerry Reisman to Glenna Breslin, interview of 17 March 1986, and phone call to Breslin of 23 April 1986, GB. I have rearranged his words slightly from Breslin's notes.

— "Will I! . . . Gay Gaunt Day": "Will You Write Me a Christmas Poem," *CW*, 37–40.

— "Written at Lorine's": LZ's ms. note at the end of "Will You Write Me a Christmas Poem," carbon typescript, n.d., Basil Bunting papers, Durham University Library.

43 "Canvass, For exhibition, Tea", *CW*, 33.

— "An experiment": LN to Harriet Monroe, 12 February 1934, "Letters to *Poetry* Magazine, 1931–1937," 182.

— "Would the enclosed": LN to Harriet Monroe, 7 April 1934, "Letters to *Poetry* Magazine, 1931–1937," 184–85.

— "Most dreams": Lawrence, *Fantasia of the Unconscious*, 194.

— "there are times": LN to CC, 30 January 1968, *BYHM*, 149.

44 "an acerbic . . . barely audible": G. Oppen, *The Selected Letters of George Oppen*, 294, 93.

— "They were wonderful company": Mary Oppen to Glenna Breslin, interview of 10 February 1986 and a joint interview with Jerry Reisman, 17 March 1986, GB.

— "and after waiting" and following quotations: M. Oppen, *Meaning a Life*, 145.

— "Too witty": LN, "Letters to *Poetry* Magazine," 185.

— "[M]y head might pour . . . experiment in planes": LN, 4 and 31 May 1934, "Letters to *Poetry* Magazine, 1931-1937," 185, 186.

45 "This is new": LZ to LN, 30 October 1934, quoting WCW, HRHRC. Of course they did have a press: the OP [Objectivist Press].

— "Glad you agreed . . . Surrealism . . . There's no use": LZ and Pound, letters of 17 February, 6 March, and 25 March 1935, quoted in Ahearn, *Pound/Zukofsky*, 161–65. Pound accepted "Canvass," "For exhibition," and "Tea" (LN: subconscious, wakeful, and full consciousness), and "Beyond What," "I Heard," and "Memorial Day" (LN: subconscious, toward monologue, and social-banal) for *Bozart-Westminster* (Spring/Summer 1935): 26–27.

— "Young man—She's unconscious": *Domestic and Unavoidable*, *CW*, 70.

46 "I am enclosing": LN to Harriet Monroe, 12 February 1934, "Letters to *Poetry* Magazine, 1931–1937," 181.

— "Proletarian (God forbid)": LN to Ronald Ellis, 24 December 1966, Ellis.

— "ideas I should . . . It is my belief . . . Is it logic? . . . he *would*": LN to Mary (Mrs. W. D.) Hoard, n.d., DFPL, and LN, "Local Letters," 87–88.

Chapter 7. Loss

48 "Her understanding" and following quotations: March–April, January, November, September–October, "NEXT YEAR OR I FLY MY ROUNDS, TEMPESTUOUS," *CW*, 47, 42, 64, 60, 41. LN pasted poems over each page of the 1935 edition of a

"Favorite" Sunlit Road Calendar. Naturally, there's a vast difference between her terseness and the saccharine sentiments pasted over.

48 "lived in a garret": Diane Dechar, in a telephone interview with MP, 19 March 2009.

— "I met Lorine": Diane Dechar to MP in a letter of 14 February 2009. Reisman confirms that some of his cousins were part of his and LZ's social life (see Reisman, "Lorine," 36).

49 "I want to keep": I have taken the liberty of turning Jerry Reisman's "Lorine wanted to keep the child, etc." into LN's direct speech (Reisman, "Lorine").

— "Now, as for the person": Diane Dechar to MP, letter of 4 March 2009. In the 1980s Professor Glenna Breslin, working on a (never completed) biography of LN, contacted Mary Oppen, who told her about LN's pregnancy and abortion. Breslin told Oppen she'd been in touch with Jerry Reisman. Oppen wished to see Reisman again, so Breslin drove her to Saratoga, California, where she interviewed both Reisman and Oppen extensively, taping much of their conversation. Both confirmed LN's pregnancy and, at LZ's demand, her abortion. Based on these interviews, Professor Breslin wrote: "Then she became pregnant. No one seems to know how she felt about the pregnancy, except that she wanted to keep the child. Zukofsky's distress was intense—his life at that time precluded such responsibility. Niedecker was willing to remain unmarried and return to her parents to have the child, but Zukofsky persuaded her against the plan and she borrowed money from her father to have an abortion" ("Lorine Niedecker and Louis Zukofsky"). See also Breslin, "Lorine Niedecker: Composing a Life," 145. Breslin also talked to the Oppens' daughter Linda: "She knew about the pregnancy and abortion; heard her parents talk about it." Furthermore, Naomi Schwartz Marshall, a close companion of the Oppens in San Francisco in their later years, told me, "George and Mary talked a lot about Lorine, mostly about her affair with Zuk, the abortion, etc." (telephone interview, 9 June 2009).

LZ died on May 12, 1978. The most recent biography is Mark Scroggins's *The Poem of a Life*. LN is scarcely present in Scroggins's book; instead, in an appendix he dismisses her and LZ's relationship as gossip driven by resentment, and "no proof of anything." He discredits Mary Oppen's testimony because in *Meaning a Life* she made the minor error of calling LN a student of LZ's at the University of Wisconsin.

Scroggins's exclusion of LN from a life of LZ seems inexplicable unless one knows that LZ's son Paul Zukofsky controls his literary estate and hence any biography. PZ is, by all accounts, an obsessively private person determined to eradicate anything that might discredit his father, particularly anything to do with his relationship with LN. According to the LZ scholar Barry Ahearn, PZ fired two biographers before permitting Scroggins to undertake a biography—under strict conditions. When I asked for permission to quote from LZ's letters to LN, PZ replied: "It is not my policy to permit quotations from my father's letters to Niedecker and your request is denied" (9 April 2009).

Fortunately, besides Reisman and Mary Oppen, there is another witness to the reality of LN's pregnancy and abortion: Diane Dechar, married to Jerry Reisman's first cousin, once part of Zukofsky's circle, and now living in Nyack, New York. Her report confirms Reisman's and the Oppens' and adds valuable information.

49   "One of my cousins . . . After the operation": Reisman, "Lorine," 36–38, also the source of the rest of Reisman's comments in this chapter. LN corresponded and exchanged gifts with Reisman's sister, Pauline Glenn, for a time after she left New York.

—   "was the most": Mary Oppen, interview with Glenna Breslin, 10 February 1986, GB.

—   "terribly, terribly inhibited": Hatlen, "Interview with Carl Rakosi," 99.

—   "[i]n NY it seemed": LN to Ronald Ellis in a letter of 24 December 1966.

—   "We all felt sad": Diane Dechar to MP, letter of 4 March 2009.

50   "To wit, the lover": "News," undated and unpublished until *CW*, 79–81.

—   "I'm no longer in depression": LN to LZ, 1936, HRHRC.

—   "Who was Mary Shelley?": "Who was Mary Shelley?" *Paris Review* 9, no. 36 (Winter 1966), revised for *Homemade/Handmade Poems*, *CW*, 212–13.

—   "I remember last year": LZ to LN, 6 February 1936, HRHRC.

—   "[Y]ou know how difficult": LZ to LN, undated fragment, HRHRC.

51   "[w]arm and friendly" and following quotations: Reisman, "Lorine," 37.

—   "domestic difficulties . . . I wish": WCW to LZ, 9 December 1936, HRHRC. Williams's wife, Florence, adds a note, "Bill ain't got no domestic difficulties," referring to LZ's complaint.

52   "She was not": Diane Dechar to MP, letter of 4 March 2009.

Chapter 8. Folk Magic

53   "No, STAGE DIRECTIONS": August Derleth to Frederick Larsson, 6 June 1936, WHS.

—   "I'd rather not": LN to Raymond Larsson, 12 June 1936, WHS.

—   "though I must confess": August Derleth to Raymond Larsson, 27 April 1936, WHS.

54   "'Now what do'": LZ quoting Evans to LN, 12 January 1936, HRHRC.

—   "Apples are high": "Their apples fall down," *NG* and *CW*, 120–21.

—   "Looking around": LN to Harriet Monroe, 25 February 1936, "Letters to *Poetry* Magazine, 1931–1937," 188. In a letter of 10 December 1966, LN set out her poetic development succinctly for KC: "I literally went to school to William Carlos Williams and Louis Zukofsky and have had the good fortune to call the latter friend and mentor. Well—there was an influence (from transition and from surrealistes that has always seemed to want to ride right along with the direct hard, objective kind of writing. The subconscious and the presence of the folk, always there. New Goose . . . based on the folk—and a desire to get down to direct speech (Williams influence and here was my mother, daughter of the rhyming, happy grandfather mentioned above)" (*TFN*, 36).

—   "Niedecker's knife buried": Karl Gartung, poet and Niedecker authority, in an interview with MP, 26 March 2009.

—   "O let's glee": "O let's glee glow as we go," *New Directions* 1 (1936) and *CW*, 85.

55 "poemness of the poem": LN's notes in her copy of Ciardi and Williams, *How Does a Poem Mean?*

— "She had tumult": "She had tumult of the brain," *NG*, *T&G*, *MLBW*, and *CW*, 94.

— "waking isolation": LN to Harriet Monroe, 12 February 1934, "Letters to *Poetry* Magazine, 1931–1937," 181.

— "yielded a legacy": Jonathan Alter, *The Defining Moment: FDR's Hundred Days and the Triumph of Hope* (New York: Simon & Schuster, 2006), 330.

— "O rock my baby": "Coming out of Sleep," unpublished in LN's lifetime, *CW*, 116–17.

56 "Time for BP": LN to LZ, 25 April 1949, *NCZ*, 159.

— "My mother was": LN to Ronald Ellis, 1966, Ellis.

— "The museum man!": "The museum man!" *NG*, *T&G*, *MLBW*, and *CW*, 101.

— "I'm a different character": LN to JW, 22 August 1965, SUNY–Buffalo.

— "Grandfather": "Poet's Work," *T&G*, *MLBW*, and *CW*, 194. Rachel Blau DuPlessis makes the interesting suggestion that LN's "'condensery' poetics may well be a bilingual pun on Pound's influential injunction in The ABC of Reading: that "Dichten= condensare (to make poetry is synonymous with the imperative infinitive to concentrate/ compress/condense)" (see DuPlessis, "Lorine Niedecker, the Anonymous," 123). Yet it's worth noting that the main business of Jefferson County was dairying, with many creameries and condenserys in the area.

— "Nay Nay": LN, "Letters to *Poetry* Magazine," 188.

57 "ruled them hopeless": JL, "A Brief History of New Directions," http://www.nd publishing.com.

— "a young god": Ezra Pound, quoted in *TPAL*, 133.

— "What an intense": JL, *The Way It Wasn't*, 336.

— "This is my story": LN to JL, 27 September 1937, Houghton, Harvard. The same day LN sent "New Goose": "as before no sequence, may use the ones you like best." The LN–JL papers at Harvard contain letters between them from 1937 to 1970. JL's last letter of 28 December 1970 arrived only a day before LN's death. The archive contains two letters from AM to JL, as well as correspondence from the 1990s when JL was considering publishing an LN collection.

— "I think your story": JL to LN, 11 October 1937, Houghton, Harvard. LN poems published in *New Directions* 1 (1936) were: "The President of the Holding Company," "Fancy Another Day Gone," "O let's glee glow," "Lady in the leopard coat," "Scuttle up the workshop," "Missus Dorra," "To war they kept," "Petrou his name was sorrow," "The eleventh progressional," "Young girl to marry," "I spent my money," "Trees over the roof," "The music, lady," "For sun and moon and radio," "She had tumult of the brain," "My coat threadbare," and "There's a better shine."

— "I'm sorry": JL, *The Way It Wasn't*, 202.

58 "Zuk was eager": JL, *The Way It Wasn't*, 336.

— "Ash woods," "Just before she died," "Grampa's got his old age pension," "Seven years a charming woman," *CW*, 93, 112, 100, 111, 97.

58 "poifick": LZ to LN, fragment, n.d., HRHRC.
— "My man says": "My man says the wind blows from the south," *NG, MFT, T&G, MLBW*, and *CW*, 97.
— "*speech must sing*" (my italics): LZ to LN, frag. [1938], HRHRC.
— "I hear the weather": in *CW*, 150. As Penberthy suggests, this poem is a later variant of a weather poem LZ wrote LN about, 9 March 1938, HRHRC.
59 "A monster owl": "A monster owl," *NG* and *CW*, 103. See *CW*, 375, for early version before LZ's suggested revisions.
— "The meaning the lines. . . . A derangement of the mind": LZ quoting LN in a letter of 6 April 1937, HRHRC.
— "2 small victrola": LN to LZ [LZ: 1937?]. The fragment is the only surviving LN letter to LZ from 1937.
— "Cold clear morning" LN to LZ [LZ: 15 July 1938], *NCZ*, 124.

Chapter 9. Federal Writers' Project

61 "What she omits": Reisman, "On Some Conversations with Celia Zukofsky," 143–44.
— "protect . . . Louis would never": Mary Oppen to Glenna Breslin, 10 February 1986, GB.
— "When we arrived in Brooklyn": Honig, "A Memory of Lorine Niedecker," 46. LZ's whereabouts on this occasion is confusing. Honig says they dropped LN at LZ's place in Brooklyn; Reisman ("On Some Conversations with Celia Zukofsky") says LZ was living in an apartment in Manhattan. Soon after the marriage the Zukofksys moved to an apartment in the Bronx, "overlooking the Bronx River and so near the zoo that they could hear the big cats roaring for their meals on weekend mornings" (*TPAL*, 172).
62 "In after years": LN to LZ, 12 January [LZ: 1947], *NCZ*, 142.
— "a large accumulation": Harold E. Miner, "General Preface" [to a history of Wausau, Wisconsin], unpublished, dated 30 July 1941, WHS. Subsequent Miner quotes are from this source.
— "distraught housewives" and following quotes: Honig, "A Memory of Lorine Niedecker," 43–47.
63 "Much of the official": Vivien Hone to Richard Caddel, senior library assistant, Science Library, University of Durham, England, n.d. Caddel had written Hone on 8 January 1978: "I am at present carrying out some research on the work of Lorine Niedecker, which has appealed to me since Basil Bunting first introduced me to it. I am told you were a long standing friend of hers, and had worked with her at some time, and I would, therefore, be very interested in any information you could give me about her." All further Vivien Hone quotes are from this source. I am grateful to Karl Gartung for providing me with a copy of Hone's three-page letter. Caddel also wrote AM for information about LN.
65 "If you had been . . . I used to think . . . who lost his women": LN to LZ, Sunday, 18 May 1941, *NCZ*, 125–29.

66 "always had to *see*": LN to LZ, 19 May [LZ: 1946], *NCZ*, 140.

— "I'm just a sandpiper": LN to Edward Dahlberg, 4 November 1955, HRHRC.

— "I was the solitary": "PAEAN TO PLACE" *CW*, 265; the pain and fear birds feel before migration: LN to CC, 30 January 1968, *BYHM*, 149.

— "Black Hawk held": "Black Hawk held: In reason," *NG, MFT, T&G, MLBW,* and *CW*, 99. LN took notes from Paterson's book on 28 May 1941, ten days after her letter to LZ.

67 "Asa Gray wrote": "Asa Gray wrote Increase Lapham," *NG, T&G, MLBW,* and *CW*, 105. LN either rewrote or checked the following biographies against sources: James Lloyd Breck (churchman and missionary), Azel Dow Cole (clergyman), Jason Downer (Wisconsin Supreme Court justice), Albert Gallatin Ellis (publisher), Stephan Faville (pioneer dairyman), Joel Foster (pioneer), Chester Hazen (pioneer farmer), Basil Giard (pioneer landowner), Jean Pierre Bugnion Gratiot (pioneer, lead miner, politician), Ansel N. Kellogg (newspaper man), Increase Lapham (naturalist), Peter Parkinson, Jr. (pioneer settler, soldier, historian), Pierre Pauquette (fur-trader with thighs as thick as most men's waists), Marcus Mills Pomeroy (newspaperman, La Crosse Democrat), Peter Rindisbacher (first resident artist in Wisconsin), William Harkness Sampson (Methodist minister, founder of Lawrence College), Hiram Smith (pioneer dairyman, University of Wisconsin regent), Daniel Whitney (pioneer merchant, lumberman, founded city of Green Bay), Eleazer Williams (half-Mohawk, self-declared "lost dauphin" of France). LN's initials also appear in a WPA survey of Trades and Occupations.

— "a positive genius": Marie to Harold Miner, Thursday [n.d.], WHS. I have been unable to discover the last names of Marie or her husband and partner, Jack, who was a project worker. LZ reacts to LN's grim tales of a "Miss Foster" in a letter of 30 October [1941]; presumably she is Alice Foster, the supervisor who replaced Miner.

68 "Lorine dropped in": Marie to Harold Miner, 3 June 1942, WHS.

— "When did you": Thirteen pages of LN's divorce records are courtesy of the Dodge–Jefferson County Genealogical Society. The documents misspell her name as Neidecker.

Chapter 10. *New Goose*

70 "Of course his": LN to Ronald Ellis, 24 December 1966, Ellis.

71 "Sunday's motor-cars": "Sunday's motor-cars," *New Directions* 11 (1949), and *CW*, 127.

— "I suppose": "The broad-leaved Arrow-head," *NG* and *CW*, 109.

— "Don't shoot": "Don't shoot the rail!" *NG, MFT, T&G, MLBW,* and *CW*, 92. This bird is the King Rail; the sora "of whom I speak sometimes a smaller rail and yellowish somewhere on breast": LN to LZ [LZ, 28 September 1949], *NCZ*, 161.

— "Oh me, the pictures": LN to LZ [LZ, 2 December 1945], HRHRC.

— "Louis never typed": Ahearn, "Two Conversations with Celia Zukofsky," 125.

72 "Our woiks are sealed": LN to LZ [LZ 1944], *NCZ*, 130.

— "Although Decker never": Ballowe, "Little Press on the Prairie," 16, 33, 35; subsequent quotes from this source. Both Decker and his sister Dorothy came to sticky ends. In

1948 a poet named Ervin Tax bought the press, eventually firing its founder. Working closely with Tax, Dorothy fell in love. Tax did not. One day Dorothy called for him in her maroon Frazer sedan, shot him with a .22 caliber automatic rifle, then shot herself. Thanks to Joan Hyer for bringing Ballowe's article to my attention.

72 "Lonely woman": "Woman with Umbrella," *Accent* 13, no. 2 (Spring 1953), and *CW*, 115.

73 "Past few days": LN to LZ [LZ, Oct 1944], *NCZ*, 131.

— "*not* proper attire": Florence Dollase, interview by Marilla Fuge, 10 January 1998. Dollase said that Lohmaier did not dislike LN, but all other evidence is to the contrary.

74 "I used to know . . . both tripe . . . maybe they'll send": LN to LZ [LZ: rec'd April 25, 1945], *NCZ*, 132–33.

— "Reason explodes": "New!" *CW*, 125.

— "Will man obsolesce": "Could You Be Right," *CW*, 129.

— "and all the streets": LN to LZ [LZ: rec'd April 24, 1945], HRHRC.

— "This is what": LN to LZ [LZ: April 29, 1945], *NCZ*, 134. Penberthy's text has "If we knew more chemistry"; the ms. in the LZ collection, HRHRC, reads "I." Penberthy (*NCZ*, 135) points out LN's "The only thing about death—loneliness" is LZ's philosophy in "A"-11 and "A"-18. Ralph Waldo Emerson is conspicuously missing from LN's surviving papers. See *BYHM*, 225–26, for Lisa Pater Faranda's discussion of LN and Emerson.

75 "Nowhere can man": Aurelius, *Meditations*, 63.

— "where records go down . . . the number of lakes": "Brought the enemy down" and "The number of Britons killed," *CW*, 112, 113.

— "[w]ar is more than a theme": Rosenthal, *New Poets*, 10.

76 "She speaks and sings . . . I read only two": LZ to LN, undated fragment [1946], HRHRC. LZ names the following poems as his favorites: "Don't shoot the rail!," "Bombings," "Ash woods," [p. 12 is incorrectly number 26 in the edition], "The music, lady," "For sun and moon," "She had tumult," "Mr. Van Ess," "Remember my little granite pail?," "My man says," "On Columbus Day," "The clothesline post is set," "I said to my head," "Granpa's got his old age pension," "There's a better shine," "The museum man!," "That woman!," "Hand Crocheted Rug," "I doubt I'll get silk stockings out," "To see the man," "Asa Gray," "Well, spring overflows the land," "Audubon," "Van Gogh," and "What a woman!"

— "I picked it": LN to LZ, April 28 [LZ, 1946], quoting CR, *NCZ*, 138–39.

— "The book's a good one": WCW to LN, quoted in LN to JW, 14 December 1965, SUNY–Buffalo. On 19 May [1946] LN wrote LZ: "Zu-Zu, look what Williams said enclosed! Air mail! It's really nice isn't it?—anyhow he can't say that about everybody's nowadays" (*NCZ*, 139).

— "Ten years ago": LN to LZ, 19 May [LZ: 1946], *NCZ*, 142.

— "Lorine Niedecker": Smith, "Patchen's Province and Other Landscapes," 111.

77 "The brown muskrat": "The brown muskrat, noiseless," *CW*, 109.

— "A little book herewith": LN to Florence Dollase, May 1946, DFPL.

Chapter 11. Changes

92 "in the air . . . indoor terlut": LN to LZ, 23 December 1945, HRHRC.

— "Found three tiny": LN to LZ [LZ: 2 June 1946], *NCZ*, 141.

— "A huge one": LN to LZ, 25 November 1952, HRHRC.

— "He's out soothing": LN to LZ [LZ: 26 February 1946], HRHRC.

— "bought a pair": LN to LZ, 10 March 1 [LZ: 1946], *NCZ*, 137.

— "There were . . . Nine or ten women": all Nathalie Kaufman Yackels quotes are from an interview of 21 August 1991 by GR and Jeanine Strunk; all Caroline Kutz Wendorf quotes are from MP's interview of 22 September 2008.

93 "my spirit": LN to LZ, Sunday [LZ: Christmas 1947], *NCZ*, 145.

— "my bundles": "In the great snowfall before the bomb", *CW*, 142–43.

— "Disastrous week": LZ quoting LN in a letter to her of 27 October 1946, HRHRC.

— "[A] great many things": LN to LZ [LZ: r'cd. 15 June 1951], HRHRC.

— "I have a story": LN to LZ [LZ: 16 March 1948], *NCZ*, 146.

— "My own mind": LN to LZ [LZ: 21? March 1953], *NCZ*, 213.

94 "a little marshy . . . my eyes": LN to LZ [LZ: 19 June 1948], *NCZ*, 149.

— "fingertip veil": *JCU*, 22 June 1948.

— "I rose from marsh mud": "I rose from marsh mud," *T&G*, *MLBW*, and *CW*, 170. See *CW*, 414, for LN's important letter of 20 December 1948 to Eugene Magner at SUNY–Buffalo on the poem. Whether Nathalie told LN that she was adopted by her parents as the illegitimate daughter of another member of the Kaufman family (which is why she and her sister Vergene were in the same grade in school) is unknown.

— "Saturday I arose": LN to LZ, 22 June [LZ: 1948], *NCZ*, 151.

95 "So you're married": "So you're married, young man," part of the *For Paul* group, *CW*, 165–66. See Penberthy's notes (*CW*, 408) for previous drafts and LN's "Of course St. Louis Blues streams through my head."

— "is the range" and following quotes: LZ, *A Test of Poetry*, xi, II-16, II-21.

— "There's a better shine": "There's a better shine," *NG* and *CW*, 101.

96 "Isn't it a beautiful": LN to LZ, Wednesday [LZ: 1948], *NCZ*, 155.

— "Zukofsky's arrangement is as clean": LN, "A Review of Louis Zukofsky's *A Test of Poetry*," in August Derleth's "Books of Today" column, *Capital Times*, 18 December 1946.

— "into a poem": Middleton, "Lorine Niedecker's 'Folk Base,'" 203–18. Referring to LZ's affair with LN, Middleton argues that Zukofsky's placement of the poems "makes the passage say things he perhaps cannot" about women.

97 "stood before his big map . . . what kind": LN to LZ [LZ: 25 April 1949], *NCZ*, 158–59.

— "now that I've flown": LN to LZ [LZ: 23 May 1946], *NCZ*, 147.

— "If you were *really*" and following quotations: Reisman, "On Some Conversations with Celia Zukofsky," 146–48.

— "turned with a quizzical" and following quotations: Mary Oppen, *Meaning a Life*, 144.

— "I don't know how": LN to LZ [LZ: 23 May 1948], *NCZ*, 147.

98   "Yes, I've lived": "Regards to Mr. Glover," ms. dated June 1948, *CW*, 126–27.

—   "These are not my sentiments": "Light-4" in LZ, *CSP*, 116.

—   "Zu, could I use it": LN to LZ [LZ: 28 May 1948], *NCZ*, 147.

—   "Was shoveling snow": LN to LZ, n.d. [probably November 1947].

—   "Swept snow, Li Po": "Swept snow, Li Po," *T&G*, *MLBW*, and *CW*, 126. See *CW*, 379–80, for three different versions. Pound translated Li Po in Cathay (1915), though not "Drinking Alone by Moonlight." LN was evidently familiar with Arthur Waley's translation.

99   "with a handkerchief": LN to LZ, fragment, [LZ: 18 January 1948], HRHRC.

—   "arrived home against": LN to LZ [LZ: 6 March 1950], *NCZ*, 169.

—   "reared up . . . Hoards has become": LN to LZ [LZ: 27 February 1949], HRHRC.

100   "Good-bye to proof reading": "Switchboard Girl", *CW*, 335.

—   "No, *don't* send": LN to LZ [LZ: r'cd. 5 February 1951], *NCZ*, 176.

—   "I'd never get": "In the great snowfall before the bomb," *CW*, 142.

—   "Under the draconian": Phyllis Walsh, telephone interview with MP, 14 September 2010.

101   "gone off her rocker . . . Gert Runke helped": ÆM quoting LN to Glenna Breslin, 3 July 1988, GB. ÆM also told Breslin that LN considered her mother's madness no excuse for HN's philandering. But HN's involvement with Gertrude Runke began in the 1920s, implying that LN considered her mother deranged from that time.

—   "It was always amazing" and following quotations about the funeral: LN to LZ, 31 July [LZ: 1951], *NCZ*, 181.

—   "Old Mother turns blue": "Old Mother turns blue and from us," *T&G*, *MLBW*, and *CW*, 149.

102   "spent [her] life": "What horror to awake at night", in *T&G*, *MLBW*, and *CW*, 147–48.

—   "Dead / she now lay deaf": "Dead," *T&G*, *MLBW*, and *CW*, 150. For a variant version, see *CW*, 394.

Chapter 12. *For Paul*

103   "September dandelion": "Switchboard Girl", *CW*, 335–37. Thanks to Mary Gates, who identified the business LN fictionalizes as Wade Light in "Switchboard Girl." Gates says Moe Light was a Frank Lloyd Wright–type modern building, per LN's story.

—   "The elegant office girl . . . the street's bare-legged . . . little peet-tweet": "The elegant office girl," "Not feeling well, my wood uncut," "I lost you to water, summer" *CW*, 136, 95–96, 227.

—   "desperate" and following quotations: "The Evening's Automobiles," *CW*, 338–42. LZ suggested the title; Lorine appended notes to LZ (see *CW*, 457–58).

104   "a house of my own": "In moonlight lies," *CW*, 135.

—   "Henry had another": LN to LZ [LZ: 13 November 1951], HRHRC.

—   "all the neighbors": LN to LZ, postcard dated Thursday [1951], HRHRC.

—   "We've been washing": LN to LZ, 13 November 1952, HRHRC.

104　"Ah that A-12!": LN to LZ [LZ: 13 November 1951], HRHRC. LN had criticisms: LZ's use of the word "certain" in a line bothered her; she didn't understand the underlining in "Then it is Stainer"; she wondered at one point whether he was speaking of Confucius, etc.; but considering the difficulty of LZ's text they are minor and "I'm elated how little I have to use your notes for A-12—so far I recognize where things are from."

— "Paul with scarlet": LN to LZ [LZ: 25 April 1949], in *NCZ*, 158–59.

— "I can always": LN to LZ, fragment, [LZ: 27 July 1947], HRHRC.

— "Diddy 47": LN to LZ, fragment [LZ: 14 June 1949], HRHRC.

— "does he write": LN to LZ, fragment [LZ: 12 March 1948], HRHRC.

— "Play those little": an omitted stanza of LN's "My father said 'I remember,'" *CW*, 154, printed in *CW*, 402. The records were two singles the size of 45 rpms, without the wide hole. ÆM showed them to Glenna Breslin; they were recorded 31 October 1949. PZ concluded his recital with "Home on the Range."

105　"I mailed him": LN to LZ [LZ: 25 April 1949], *NCZ*, 159. The letter is dated "Monday at work, Sunday having been full of spading, raking, seeding and aching."

— "Dear fiddler": "Lugubre for a child," *CW*, 128–29. LN began her *For Paul* series in 1949. For the text of "You have power politics, Paul" see *CW*, 380–81. See also Penberthy's discussion of the *For Paul* poems, *NCZ*, 57–74.

— "beaming with pride": LN to LZ [LZ: 1949], *NCZ*, 157–58.

— "When I get a letter": LN to LZ, postmarked 12 February 1947, HRHRC.

106　"that little mainspring": LN to LZ [LZ: 28 December 1949], *NCZ*, 167.

— "Yes, we take": LN to LZ [LZ: 6 August 1951], *NCZ*, 184.

— "Child at your mountain-height": "High, lovely, light", *CW*, 131. See *NCZ*, 382, for variants.

— "to descend": LN to LZ, 12 August 1952, *NCZ*, 197. LZ's response was apparently destroyed.

— "The slip of a girl-announcer": ms. dated 22 October 1952, *CW*, 152.

107　"*If I were a bird*": undated ms., *CW*, 130. LZ wanted his paragraph to read: "I'd plunge with Zukofsky / all that means—stirred earth, / organ sounding, resounding / anew, anew." LN kept her version.

108　"I can't imagine": LN to LZ [LZ: 4 June 1952], HRHRC.

— "on top shelf": LN to LZ [LZ: r'cd. 5 February 1951], *NCZ*, 175.

— "I wake up": LN to LZ, 13 November 1952, *NCZ*, 199.

— "excitable children" and following quotations: LN to LZ, 15 March [LZ: 1951], HRHRC.

109　"I don't think": LN to LZ [undated, 1953], *NCZ*, 216.

— "I see they're": LN to LZ, postmarked 10 May 1950, HRHRC.

— "Have decided": LN to LZ [LZ: r'cd. February 5, 1951], *NCZ*, 176.

— "Let me see": LN to PZ, 7 February 1952, HRHRC.

110　"Of course, Zu" and following quotations: LN to LZ [LZ, 6 August 1951], *NCZ*, 184.

— "Well, Group III my god": LN to LZ, 2 September [LZ: 1951] and 15 March [LZ: 1951], *NCZ*, 184–85, 178.

— "*Don't* look at": LN to LZ [LZ: 28 September 1951], *NCZ*, 186.

110 "[t]ook my breath away": LN to LZ, Sunday [LZ: 9 December 1951], *NCZ*, 187.

— "only it's more": LN to LZ [LZ: 6 August 1952], *NCZ*, 197.

— "TERRIFIC—enchanting": LN to LZ, 12 August [LZ: 1952], *NCZ*, 197.

— "Oh Zu": LN to LZ [LZ: received 12 December 1952], *NCZ*, 202.

— "To be opened": LN wrote on a small card, "This I wrote hastily before I left for hospital—[ ] Keep or trow away." LZ transcribed information from the missing note and envelope, HRHRC. LN had suffered for years from menstrual problems caused, in part, by a fibroid tumor. After the hysterectomy she told LZ (with whom she frankly discussed all health problems) that she now believes it "when they say it takes 3 or 4 months before feeling well": fragment from 22 May [LZ: 1952], HRHRC.

Chapter 13. Æneas

111 "nice, amiable smile": ÆM, interview by Marilla Fuge and Mary Gates, 14 October 1994, CD transcribed by MP, DFPL.

— "were sort of keeping": ÆM to Glenna Breslin, 3 July 1988, a three-hour taped interview, GB. When Breslin first met him, she says, "I was anxious, as he had been hostile on the phone when I had called to ask for the interview. 'After she's dead, you intellectuals and poetesses jump on the bandwagon. Lemme ask you, where was you when she was alive, living in abject poverty? You ignored her. What are you trying to do now?'" He and Lorine "had a special thing going and he wanted to keep it private." Breslin won him over.

112 "People tell me": LN to LZ, 12 July [LZ, 1953], *NCZ*, 215.

— "Oh, do you like" and following quotations: ÆM, interview by Marilla Fugi and Mary Gates, 14 October 1994; CD transcribed my MP, DFPL. I have transposed reported dialogue into first person. In this interview, ÆM says LN entered the McAllister house without knocking. His version to Glenna Breslin in 1987 seems more plausible: ÆM "heard a light, rapid tap tap tap on the door" (Breslin, "Lorine Niedecker: The Poet," 201).

113 "I'm ashamed to say it": LN to LZ, 15 April [LZ: 1954], *NCZ*, 219. LZ, however, dated this fragment 15 March 1954, HRHRC.

— "A great deal . . . at once objective . . . more or less": LN, "The Poetry of Louis Zukofsky," 198–210.

— "'A' has never lived": LN to LZ, 17 October 1961, *NCZ*, 293. LN would type for GR a list of eleven quite different favorite LZ passages: LN Archives, Hoard.

114 "Yes, a cab": LN to LZ, 16 November [LZ: 1953], *NCZ*, 217.

— "Friday night": LN to LZ, 16 November [LZ: 1953], *NCZ*, 217–18.

— "a closing out of others": Mary Oppen to Glenna Breslin, 10 February 1986, GB.

— "Oh ivy green": "'Oh ivy green,'" *CW*, 159. See *CW*, 409, for drafts of this poem.

— "She was stagnant": ÆM to Glenna Breslin, "Lorine Niedecker: The Poet," 198.

115 "I've had two revolutions": LN to LZ, 15 April [LZ: 1954], *NCZ*, 218.

— "Cold!" and following quotations: ÆM to Glenna Breslin, 3 July 1988, GB.

— "To Aeneas": "To Aeneas who closed his piano," *CW*, 158.

116 "Lorine, you goddamn": ÆM to Glenna Breslin, 2 August 1987, GB.

116 "snookered up" and following quotations: ÆM to Glenna Breslin, n.d., but 1987, after her first interview with him.
— "I don't have any" and following quotations: Marilla Fuge and Mary Gates's interview with ÆM, 14 October 1994, DFPL.
— "I was a half-assed": from Glenna Breslin's interviews of ÆM, 2 and 4 August 1987, and ÆM's written answers to her questions, received 27 August 1990, GB.
— "How I wish": "So this was I", *CW*, 133.
— "Woman in middle life": "Woman in middle life," *CW*, 163.
117 "with a box of candy": LN to LZ [LZ: 12 May 1954], *NCZ*, 220.
— "Trash, terrible people . . . who couldn't believe": ÆM to Glenna Breslin, 3 July 1988, GB.
— "I found Henry": LN to LZ, 30 June [LZ: 1954], *NCZ*, 221. HN was buried next to his wife in Union Cemetery on 2 July 1954. Today only a bush separates his grave from that of Gertrude Runke; they are literally buried side by side. ÆM thought Henry's house cost him about $13,000 to build; LN sold it to Rowland Bennett for only $8,800 in 1954.
— "recalled that Niedecker entered": Mr. and Mrs. Carl Hausz to Lisa Pater Faranda, August 1981, introduction to *BYHM*, 3.
— "ticked off": ÆM to Glenna Breslin, December 1988, GB.
— "The graves": "The graves," *CW*, 175; revised for *For Paul and Other Poems* from a 1945 poem titled "The Graves and the Other Woman" in which LN calls her mother a peony bush.
— "The death of": "The death of my poor father," *CW*, 157–58.
118 "she was headstrong": ÆM to Glenna Breslin, 3 July 1988, GB.
— "hotly caring": "The graves", *CW*, 175.
— "gave a hoot . . . I showed him": ÆM to Glenna Breslin, "Lorine Niedecker: The Poet," 204; also Breslin's notes from an interview of 3 July 1988 and ÆM's letter to Breslin of December 1988, which differs slightly from the account in *RV*. The snobbery could have been felt both ways. The Zukofskys had known prejudice: refused housing, for instance, because they were Jews. In retaliation, they could be scornful lineally and intellectually. CZ once introduced Mary Oppen to a Jewish friend by saying "She is not one of us"; at music camp PZ called two Midwestern students stupid shmucks taught by their local butcher.
119 "Don't know what": LZ to LN, 19 July 1954, HRHRC.
120 "I don't know": "I don't know what wave he's on," *CW*, 405. Penberthy notes: "A single stanza attached to the above ["To Aeneas who closed his piano"] alludes to LN's friendship with her neighbor ÆM and to a proposal of marriage (there is no indication that the stanza was to be included with the Æneas poem)."

Chapter 14. Blows

121 "For Paul: Child Violinist": the accepted poems were "Your father to me in your eighth summer," "Dear Paul," "Paul / when the leaves," "'Oh ivy green,'" and "They live a

cool distance," *Quarterly Review of Literature* 8, no. 2 (1955): 117–19. T. and Renée Weiss edited the review at Bard College, Annandale-on-Hudson, N.Y.

121 "I'm almost overcome": LN to Edward Dahlberg, 2 October 1955, HRHRC.

— "had a good heart. . . . She *hated* mice": Doris Perkin, telephone interview with MP, 5 November 2009. Perkin's rental cottage was separated from LN's cabin "by a big white house."

— "You don't get": LN to LZ, 17 September [LZ: 1963], HRHRC.

122 "I'm all right. . . . Was going to copy": LN to LZ, 19 and 23 March [LZ: 1956], *NCZ*, 226–27.

— "He brought over": LN to LZ, 1 April [LZ: 1956], *NCZ*, 227–28.

— "[W]hat the hell is": WCW to LZ [March 1956], Ahearn, *Correspondence of William Carlos Williams and Louis Zukofsky*, 473. WCW was recommending poets for a new encyclopedia being "compiled by a group in NYC. More when I myself know more of it."

123 "Now Zu, the last poem": LN to LZ, "29 Septenber" [LZ: 1955?], *NCZ*, 223–24.

— "They live a cool distance": *CW*, 160–61. LN's explanation to LZ of her intent is rather vague: "Very difficult problem to state—I feel I haven't yet got it all, left out maybe: their love of this thing. The stoic enters in but is only one aspect. I hope the poem doesn't get over just the one idea that it's a principle. It's a compulsion to express thru difficulties, a love of the thing" (*NCZ*, 224); by which she seems to say that the Zukofskys are not ascetic on principle, but for the love of asceticism itself.

— "No red penciling": LN to LZ [LZ: December 1956], *NCZ*, 230. LN also says that she "destroyed 2 new ones [poems] and keep back one concerning Aen that I wouldn't want to print." An example of LN's frequently used "five-liners with 2 words rhyming": "July, waxwings / on the berries / have dyed red / the dead / branch" (*CW*, 174).

— "nice, nice letter": LN to LZ [LZ: rec'd 14 December 1956], *NCZ*, 231–32.

— "Louie and Celia": LN to JW, 11 and 24 December 1956, SUNY–Buffalo. On 24 December, LN lists nine poems she would remove if necessary to keep the cost down: "If he is of constant depth," "O Tannenbaum," "In the great snowfall," "Shut up in woods," "Old Mother turns blue," "The death of my poor father," "Energy glows at the lips," "We physicians," and "Woman in middle life." If six is sufficient, she wants to keep "If he is of constant depth," "In the great snowfall," and "Old Mother turns blue." With LZ she was diffident: "Actually, there are three poems in the book: July, the waxwings, Old man who seined, Paul / when the leaves"—judging these three poems for their sure, precise music. "If I destroyed all evidence of biographic story and saved only about 20 that I really feel must be saved, would such a one as Paul / when the leaves still stand?": [LZ: rec'd 14 December 1956], *NCZ*, 231–32. LN's three poems in *CW*: 174, 174, 156–57. Except for "Paul / when the leaves," these are later poems in the "For Paul" ms.

— "what I could unearth" and following quotations: The Jargon Society online at http://jargonbooks.com (no longer accessible). Williams died in 2008.

124 "logrolling . . . I feel that I shouldn't . . . the short Japanese-derived": LN to JW, 29 December [1956], SUNY–Buffalo.

124 "Beautiful book": LN to LZ, n.d. [probably early June 1957], *NCZ*, 235.

— "I'm involved . . . Poetry is the most": LN to JW, 10 January 1957, SUNY–Buffalo.

125 "Carnegie Hall, the great": "Violin Debut," unpublished in LN's lifetime, *CW*, 161. The music box metaphor reflects her birthday gift from the McAllisters and ÆM's coming over to show her "two tiny music box movements . . . and went out into the dark night with it to go home, a kind of musical firefly" (*NCZ*, 227), also commemorated in a poem "Peace": "Dark road home / from town—/ young neighbor as he walked / wound up tiny Swiss Works—/ a firefly music (*CW*, 290).

— "make me feel creepy": Barry Ahearn to MP, quoting PZ, telephone interview, 9 March 2009.

126 "Paul, hello": "Paul, hello," *CW*, 133.

— "I should draw": LN to LZ, 4 February [LZ: 1957], *NCZ*, 232–33.

— "I think they know": LN to LZ, "Zunday mit no zun" [LZ: 10 March 1958], *NCZ*, 244.

127 "James are . . . the one bright": LN to LZ [LZ: 18 April 1957], *NCZ*, 234.

— "its three moons": LN to LZ [LZ: 26 April 1957], *NCZ*, 234.

— "planted before me . . . just a": LN to LZ, n.d. [probably early June 1957], *NCZ*, 235–36. LN adds that her interest in music boxes extends only to "some highly polished beautiful little boxes I've seen," adding that, considering its garishness, it "undoubtedly came thru a Catholic organization."

— "so I get around": LN to LZ, 26 June [LZ, 1957], *NCZ*, 236.

— "When brown folk": "When brown folk lived a distance," *CW*, 136.

128 "[t]he proletariat *is*": LN had read Herbert Read in *Black Mountain Review* 7 (Autumn 1957), quoted in *NCZ*, 242.

— "I must have known": LN to LZ, Christmas Day [LZ: 1957], *NCZ*, 242.

— "The folk form": "In the great snowfall before the bomb", *CW*, 142.

— "Don't tell me property": "Don't tell me property is sacred!" *T&G*, *MLBW*, and *CW*, 172; for variants see *CW*, 416.

— "People, people": "People, people—" *CW*, 173.

129 "There is always": LN to LZ, 1 June [LZ: 1958], *NCZ*, 246. LN had unending trouble with her inherited property. The above letter goes on: "P.S. The lawyers + surveyor made out Henry's estate wrong when he died o I've heritied a mess—they included my cousin's [Lawrence Niedecker, Charles Jr.'s son] land in mine and I've spent some sleepless nights as I won't spend money to get it fixed up." An affidavit solved this problem.

— "The Bible they thumb": LN to LZ, 13 July [LZ: 1958], HRHRC.

— "For pure orneriness" and following flood quotations: *DJCU*, Hoard.

130 "Don't rip up my bushes": ÆM, interview by Marilla Fuge and Mary Gates, 14 October 1994, DFPL.

— "I was evacuated! . . . that have chicken": LN to LZ, Sunday night [LZ: 5 April 1959], *NCZ*, 249–50. Roland Hartel (1896–1964) was LN's first cousin, one of the sons of Theresa Kunz Niedecker's sister Ida Kunz (1866–1947), who married John Hartel in 1888. Roland married Maude Lezotte in 1915.

130 "[t]ook a man along": LN to LZ, Sunday [LZ: 19 April 1959], *NCZ*, 251.

— "who bailed boats . . . who knew how": "PAEAN TO PLACE," *CW*, 268.

131 "very precise . . . rather eccentric . . . a little bit flighty . . . Really, just a delightful": Fred Hobe, interview by GR, 27 January 1996, CD transcribed by MP, DFPL. On the original tape, Roub reads letters from LN to Hobe. Fred Hobe died in 2007. When I contacted Jean Hobe, his widow, to learn what happened to LN's originals, she said she didn't know: her husband kept his private and business lives strictly separate. Hobe must have seen land contracts as a win-win situation: if a buyer couldn't make payments, LN kept the property.

Chapter 15. Lorine in Love

132 "I dunno": LN to LZ, 16 October [1959], *NCZ*, 254.

— "Am I becoming": LN to LZ, 28 February 1960, *NCZ*, 260.

— "Nothing worth noting": "Linnaeus in Lapland," *T&G, MLBW*, and *CW*, 181. Originally printed as "In Exchange for Haiku" in *Neon* 4 (1959) with "July, the waxwings," "Old man who seined," "People, people—" and "Fog-thick morning."

133 "I hail the sun": LN to PZ [LZ: rec'd 15 October 1959], HRHRC, and "Letters to Celia and Paul Zukofsky, 1949–1959," *LNWP*, 62–63.

— "My friend tree": "My friend tree," *Origin* 2, no. 2 (July 1961): 27, *T&G, MLBW*, and *CW*, 186. "My friend tree" became the title of LN's second book of poetry, published in 1961.

— "mostly dull": LN to LZ [LZ: Xmas 1960], HRHRC.

— "without any doubt": LN to JW, 11 November 1957, SUNY–Buffalo.

— "You are so": LN to LZ, 29 November [LZ: 1959], *NCZ*, 258.

— "Rather than": WCW to LZ, 5 March 1958, Ahearn, *Correspondence of William Carlos Williams and Louis Zukofsky*, 490.

— "a lovely day . . . I have always": LN to LZ, 22 November [1959], *NCZ*, 257.

134 "cute and cozy . . . pretty happy": Nathalie Yackels, interview by GR and Jeanine Strunk, 21 August 1991, DFPL.

— "the damn shame": Dennis O'Connor to MP, 18 April 2009.

— "We nodded": James J. Nora, "We Knew Each Other," *Wisconsin Academy Review* 39 (Summer 1993): 52. Nora wrote novels and poetry, besides having a distinguished medical career. A less elevated encounter: a dummy called "Resusci-Annie" for CPR practice was left on a dining room table. LN entered, retreated: "There's some woman lying on one of the tables in there!" Her nearsighted mistake made the *JCU* in September 1962.

— "the flood gates": Betty Hampel Griffiths, interview by Marilla Fuge, 28 April 2001, DFPL.

— "The business of loneliness": LN to LZ, "Zunday mit no sun" [LZ: 10 March 1958], *NCZ*, 244.

134 "a small, thin": Harold Hein to Glenna Breslin, 27 June 1988, GB.

135 "climbed the hill": LN to LZ, 27 June [1960], *NCZ*, 264. LN is quoting from Hein's "letter of appreciation for Sunday June 19th on the hills."

— "I never laughed": LN to LZ, 12 October [LZ: 1961], *NCZ*, 293.

— "becoming warmer, gentler": Peter Jordan's notes on published and unpublished letters of LN to LZ, the latter of which he read at HRHRC. He detected "quite a striking change."

— "Well, I think it's going to be": LN to LZ and CZ, 21 June [LZ: 1960], *NCZ*, 263.

136 "Your letter—so nice": LN to LZ, 27 June 1960, *NCZ*, 263.

137 "3 fishes, bright blue" and following quotations: LN to LZ, an exuberant (and often pained) thirteen-page letter, 5 July 1960, HRHRC.

138 "never wore anything": Mary Rockenfield to MP, interview, 19 October 2009. Rockenfield is the granddaughter of George Neidecker, HN's brother; Mary's mother, Esther Neidecker, was a first cousin of LN. Rockenfield's paternal grandfather was A. J. Glover, LN's immediate supervisor at Hoard's and subject of "Regards to Mr. Glover." Rockenfield lived with George Neidecker in Janesville and would visit HN often in the 1930s and 1940s on Blackhawk Island. HN was "calm, always glad to see us," LN "calm." Daisy peeked out, greeted them, and disappeared.

— "o lovely day . . . Well, skies . . . his face black . . . His yard wonderful": LN to LZ, 22 July [LZ: 1960], *NCZ*, 264–65; complete letter at HRHRC. LZ constantly talked about his ailments and LN often matched him, in this letter expanding on Hein's consideration for the gall bladder diet she currently was on: "Harold advised me to let the cranberry sauce alone . . . I can't even eat prunes anymore"; he did permit her raspberries: 22 July 22 [LZ: 1960], HRHRC.

— "He said he": LN to LZ, July 1960, HRHRC. Harold Hein left his family papers to the Milwaukee Public Library, including his genealogical research. His obituary notice gives his daughter's name as Susan E. (Gerard) Fisher of Green Valley, AZ. When I telephoned the Gerard Fisher residence in Green Valley and stated my business, a woman slammed the phone in my ear; my subsequent letter was returned unopened.

139 "sprinkled a little rain . . . knotty-piney": LN to LZ, 22 August [LZ: 1960], *NCZ*, 266. Tibbic's, on the bank of the Rock River, was destroyed by fire. Today a park and taverns flank both banks of the Rock River. Quotations from Hein's notes on da Vinci from same source, as well as "I was so fascinated."

— "In Leonardo's light": "In Leonardo's light," *T&G*, *MLBW*, and *CW*, 189.

140 "You are my friend—": "You are my friend—" ms. dated 15 September 1960, *MFT*, *MLBW*, and *CW*, 189. See *CW*, 421, for a last stanza that LN wisely omitted: "it shore bothers me now, dead weight of that third stanza" (LN to LZ, 18 December [LZ: 1960], *NCZ*, 271); LN hoped that CC would let her revise it for *Origin*.

— "He told me": LN to LZ, Wednesday [LZ: 15 September 1960], *NCZ*, 269.

— "lovely soft fall": LN to LZ, 30 October [LZ: 1960], *NCZ*, 269.

141 "Nice house . . . show is not . . . with not a drop": LN to LZ, 27 November [LZ: 1960], HRHRC and *NCZ*, 270. In a letter of 5 August 1988, Hein told Glenna Breslin that

Frederick Hein "wrote the book 'Living' which put his three children through college. I usually visited them Easter & Thanksgiving" (GB).

141 "who hears Callas": LN to LZ [LZ: Christmas 1960], HRHRC.
— "At 57 I have:" LN to LZ, Sunday, 27 November [LZ: 1960], *NCZ*, 270.
— "A queer week end": LN to LZ, 18 December [LZ: 1960], *NCZ*, 271.
— "Education, kindness": "Glen Ellyn," first ms. dated "Xmas 1960," eventually titled "Come In," *FTC* and *CW*, 190. For variants see *CW*, 422. LN to LZ, Xmas 1960: "I enclose my latest which I think I won't ever send around anywhere" (HRHRC). On 15 January 1961 she wrote LZ: "I've got the Glen Ellyn—as much as I'll ever have— enclosed. Had some idea of sending it to Ladies Home Journal just for fun, in fact I have it in envelope and sealed but think better of it—wouldn't want my fellow workers to know I write poetry—just wouldn't do. So as I say on enclosed—a nomb de ploom" (LN to LZ, Sunday, 15 January [LZ: 1961], 273). LN's nom de plume (unused) was Lora Decker.

Chapter 16. *My Friend Tree*

143 "a large loosely organized": LN to LZ, 15 January [LZ: 1961], *NCZ*, 274.
— "I'd like to": LN to LZ, 19 February [LZ: 1962], *NCZ*, 302.
144 "Always north of him": part 1 of "Florida," ms. dated 18 February 1962, parts 1 and 4 published in Ian Hamilton Finlay's *P.O.T.H.* (*Poor. Old. Tired. Horse.*), *CW*, 192–93.
— "*I* review it?": LN to LZ [LZ: r'cd. 12 January 1961], *NCZ*, 272. Finlay's *The Dancers Inherit the Party* was published in pamphlet form in 1960.
— "Nothing in a": LN to CC, 5 January 1961, *BYHM*, 26. More difficult in its working-class Glaswegian dialect was Finlay's *Glasgow Beasts* (1961), which LN struggled to read.
— "He was so": LN to LZ, 15 January [LZ: 1961], *NCZ*, 273.
— "slight . . . too much written": LN quoting CC to LZ, Wednesday [LZ: 12 September 1960], *NCZ*, 267. "Why do I press it: are you my friend?" is an earlier version of "You are my friend"; on 23 January 1962 LN sent CC the revised poem: "Louie likes this new version better and I know that there were dead spots in the first one" (LN to CC, *BYHM*, 27).
— "It gives me": LN to CC, 19 September 1960, *BYHM*, 24.
145 "your quiet . . . Cid *is* poetry": LN to LZ, quoting CC, 7 November 1960, HRHRC.
— "You now inhabit": LN to CC, 18 February 1962, *BYHM*, 33. The contents of LN's bookshelf—Immortal Cupboard—where she kept her favorite books, changed through the years, though Dickinson, Thoreau, Marcus Aurelius, Lucretius, and LZ were staples.
— "the first time": LN to CC, 23 January 1961, *BYHM*, 27. LN sent the poems through Gael Turnbull, a Scottish poet and physician living in Ventura, California, where he managed the Migrant Press, asking him to forward them to Finlay.
— "fair bowled over": IHF to CC, *Origin* 2, no. 6 (July 1962): 1.
— "Read the enclosed": LN to LZ, Tuesday [n.d.], *NCZ*, 285–86. As usual, LN immediately thought of putting Jessie McGuffie in touch with LZ about publishing a selection of his poems, offering to copy them and send them to McGuffie herself.

145 "Don't they read": LN to LZ, Tuesday [n.d.], *NCZ*, 284.

146 "I smiled when you said": IHF to LN, "last of June 1961 and Friday, July 21" [1961], typed copy by LN for LZ, HRHRC. "I have shown [your poems] to a Glasgow writer, Elizabeth Clark," IHF told LN, "and she was so moved she almost cried—'So wise,' she said." During the publication of *My Friend Tree*, IHF (1925–2006) was hospitalized at Ross Clinic, Aberdeen, Scotland, presumably with agoraphobia: "I am hanging on to life by slender threads" (LN quoting to LZ, 26 August [LZ: 1961], *NCZ*, 290). IHF was made a Commander of the Order of the British Empire in 2002; Little Sparta was voted the most important work of Scottish art in 2004.

— "the sentence lies in wait": LN to CC, 18 February 1962, *BYHM*, 33.

— "because I cdn't": LN to LZ [LZ: 7 July 1961], *NCZ*, 284.

— "sentiment of the affections": LZ to CC, 15 July 1961, HRHRC. "Now go to the party," ms. dated 22 October 1952, *Origin* 2, no. 2 (July 1961): 30 and *CW*, 152. The concluding stanza, "What you don't know, / that even yet / players come dressed with shields / and spears," adds philosophical point to the description of Paul in costume: first, that the mind/pen is not always more powerful than the sword; second, that his fellow music students—"players"—will be fiercely competitive. Meadowmount School of Music is a seven-week summer school founded by PZ's teacher, Ivan Galamian, in Wesport, New York, for young violinists, cellists, and pianists planning professional careers.

— "Dear Louie: No": LN to LZ, 7 August 1961, *NCZ*, 287–88.

147 "[T]heir words and tone": LN to LZ, 26 August [1961], *NCZ*, 289. In 1962 IHF also brought out LZ's *16 Once Published* in brief pamphlet form with linocuts by James Gavin.

— "On the hill": LN to LZ [LZ: 10 May 1961], *NCZ*, 280–81. The hill was the Indian Mounds overlooking Lake Koshkonong.

— "Yes, Manitowish Waters . . . I told him . . . Dear Louie": LN to LZ, 2 July [LZ, 1961], *NCZ*, 282. LZ sent her "a nice letter" in response. Harold Hein died 10 August 1996, age ninety-one. Never remarried, he was survived by "a very special friend," Lorraine Sellhorn. Lorine, Lorrine, Dorraine, Lorraine: a haunting constellation of names.

148 "Queer about time having to pass . . . Lonesome . . . Dahlberg at his best . . . Poetry today . . . There is no hurt . . . *Use it*": LN to LZ [LZ: 7 July 1961], *NCZ*, 283–85. LN owned four books by Dahlberg: *Do These Bones Live*, *Epitaphs of our Times*, *The Sorrows of Priapus*, and *Truth Is More Sacred*. LN to JW, 6 November 1961: "Edw. Dahlberg— D. H. Lawrence advised him to cultivate a bitter style and lo, he did, with a vengeance" (SUNY–Buffalo).

149 "The men leave": "The men leave the car," *Origin* 2, no. 6 (July 1962): 24, *T&G*, *MLBW*, and *CW*, 190. Sending the poem to CC, she offered the titles "Calla of the Heart-Shaped Leaves" or "Calla."

— "have a way": LN to JW, 31 December 1961, SUNY–Buffalo.

— "I must inform you": LN to LZ, 31 December 1961, *NCZ*, 296. LN also complained of the omissions to JW: "Not that I'll be too happy" (31 December 1961, SUNY–Buffalo), and to CC: "terribly disappointed" (5 February 1962, *BYHM*, 31–32).

149 "Remember my little": "Remember my little granite pail?" *NG, MFT, T&G, MLBW*, and *CW*, 96.

150 "The wee bit of wit": LN to LZ, 26 August [LZ: 1961], *NCZ*, 290.

— "I don't 'understand'" and following quotations: Edward Dorn, "Introduction," insert in *My Friend Tree*; reprinted in *TFN*, 23.

— "I greatly appreciate . . . Suzz. If he doesn't": LN to LZ, quoting her letter to Dorn, 1 October [LZ: 1961], *NCZ*, 292.

— "Your visit to": LN to JW, 1 October 1961, SUNY–Buffalo.

— "I would have": LN to LZ, 6 November [LZ: 1961], *NCZ*, 294–95. Further LN quotes about JW's visit are from this source.

151 "She has never": review of *My Friend Tree, Kulchur* 2 (Autumn 1962): 87–88; reprinted in part in *BYHM*, 32n2.

— "He talks so well . . . Oh and your preface": LN to LZ, 6 November [1961], *NCZ*, 294, 295.

— "don't vibrate": LN to LZ, 18 February [LZ: 1962], *NCZ*, 302.

Chapter 17. Alone Again

152 "I can't get": LN to LZ [LZ: 10 May 1961], *NCZ*, 281.

— "black-marked": "J.F. Kennedy after the Bay of Pigs," *Origin* 3, no. 7 (October 1967): 53, and *CW*, 246.

— "Any sense to": LN to LZ, 17 October 1961, *NCZ*, 293–94.

— "Each person silently": LN to LZ, 24 October [1962], *NCZ*, 324–25. On 22 October Kennedy demanded withdrawal of the missiles; the Soviets capitulated 28 October.

153 "caused shock waves": Ginsberg, in a discussion with Robert Duncan, quoted in *BYHM*, 14.

154 "The poetry of . . . I'd like to see": LN to CC, 3 January 1963 and 11 February 1965, *BYHM*, 36, 51.

— "Too perfect": LN to JW, 9 March 1965, SUNY–Buffalo. *All in All* is in LN's personal library, DFPL.

— "much let down": LN to LZ, [LZ: 4 February 1962], *NCZ*, 300.

— "Not much ahead": LN to LZ, 31 December 1961, *NCZ*, 297.

— "My life": "My life is hung up," ms. dated 8 June 1962, *T&G, MLBW*, and *CW*, 193. JL considered the poem "echt Niedecker" (*The Way It Wasn't*, 336). Blackhawk Island flooded in spring 1962, though not nearly as seriously as in 1959: "I understand a megaton of water is coming down from the north" (LN to JW, 22 March 1962, SUNY–Buffalo).

155 "She always pointed": Terry Ganser, interview with MP, 23 September 2008. I'm grateful to Ganser, former Blackhawk Island resident, for driving me out to the island and, while I photographed and took notes, pointing out the places he had known as a boy in the 1950s. Ganser especially liked ÆM, "the normal one of the McAllisters, really good on piano, had an old upright in the garage, played boogie."

155 "[S]till daylight": LN to LZ, Sunday, 29 July [LZ: 1962], *NCZ*, 317. Club 26, torn down, had a plaque above the bar commemorating LN's visit and poem.

156 "Our talk": "Club 26," *T&G*, *MLBW*, and *CW*, 196; published in *Midwest* (Spring 1963) as "Place to Dine."

— "In a way": LN to LZ, 26 September 1962, *NCZ*, 322.

— "She wouldn't change": Darrell Prisk, interview with MP, 7 August 2009, at his Black-hawk Island home. Prisk forgot our first interview date, so I talked with his wife, Judy. She said, "Lorine wasn't weird, just different. She stayed to herself, but when you talked to her she was pleasant. She never asked for a lot of help from the Prisks, only something absolutely essential."

157 "I've got plumbing!": LN to LZ, 19 September [LZ: 1962], *NCZ*, 319–20. LN was reading Edward John Trelawny's *Recollections of the Last Days of Byron and Shelley* (1858); she also owned a 1959 biography of Mary Shelley by Eileen Bigland. These works inspired her poem "Who was Mary Shelley?" *CW*, 212. LN's water came from a neighbor's 275-foot-deep well across the road: "[T]hey dug under the road to get to me, very dramatic, a neighbor's big cat machine and men disappearing from view down the 7 ft. deep ditch" (*NCZ*, 320).

— "Now in one year": "Now in one year," *T&G*, *MLBW*, and *CW*, 195.

158 "I have discovered": Fred Hobe, interview with GR, 27 January 1996, transcribed from CD by MP, DFPL.

— "they are lovely . . . I *write*": LN to LZ, quoting IHF, 24 February 24 1963, *NCZ*, 329. LN had sent IHF "the irate or trouble ones": "That woman eyeing houses," "The museum man," "What a woman!" and "Grandpa's got his old age pension."

— "no layoff from this condensery": "Poet's work," *CW*, 194.

— "I've had a good summer . . . Nerves, that's it": LN to LZ, 26 August 1962, HRHRC.

— "because the poems . . . These poems are brief records": JW and Gilbert Sorrentino, *Kulchur* 7 (Autumn 1962): 88–89, 87.

159 "Tonight I read": LN to LZ, 26 September 1962, *NCZ*, 321.

— "I told the plumber . . . Anything mechanical": LN to LZ, 15 October [LZ: 1962], *NCZ*, 323.

— "sensitive pump . . . a proper balance": *H&SF* and *CW*, 285. LN wrote LZ oo 18 November 1962: "he cdn't have done better if he'd been 'the greatest plumber in all London' as [Leigh] Hunt's neighbors called the one that lived near 'em" (*NCZ*, 325–26). LN wrote two other pump poems: "To my small electric pump" and "To my pres-/ure pump," *CW*, 197, 201.

— "[T]o retain property": Plotinus, "Third Ennead, Second Tractate, On Providence, No. Fifteen." LN did not have Plotinus's work in her personal library; presumably she read Stephen MacKenna's translation, revised for the Encyclopedia Britannica by B. S. Page (1952).

— "Just wrote poem": LN to LZ, 1963 [LZ: rec'd 4 January 1963], *NCZ*, 327. LN had sent an earlier poem to LZ, "Property is poverty" (*CW*, 194), warning him not to confuse the poem with reality: she didn't really have to foreclose. By January 1963, however, she'd foreclosed. Whether the issue was unpaid money, race, or both is unclear; however. "To foreclose" (*CW*, 197) adapts lines from Catullus: "or care a kite / if the p-p / be yellow, black / or white."

159 "See Lorine Niedecker": JS to MP, 18 July 2008.

Chapter 18. Little Lorie, Happy at Last?

160 "sudden melting look": LN to LZ, 3 April 1963, *NCZ*, 331.

— "[I]f this relationship grows . . . I see there's": LN to LZ, 10 April 1963, *NCZ*, 331.

— Albert Omar Millen was born to Julia and Willard Millen. Willard was born in England, emigrated, and worked his way through Canada to Minnesota in lumber camps. AM had two brothers, Robert and Frank, and a sister, Mary. AM and Margaret Sheldon married in 1930 and had four children: Virginia (9 October 1931), George (6 August 1933), Alice (24 April 1935), and Juleen (Julie) (17 December 1938). They divorced in 1956.

161 "No, not *sure*": LN to LZ, n.d. [probably April 1963], *NCZ*, 332.

— "immanent marriage": LN to CC, 13 May 1963, *BYHM*, 39–40.

— "a couple . . . the tent guy . . . [A] queer mixture": LN to LZ, 15 May [LZ: 1963], fragment, HRHRC.

162 "Not important . . . not quite all": LN to LZ, 7 June 1963, HRHRC.

— "stood up for": Arvella Humbach and Adeline Garthwaite, interview by GR, 21 June 1991, transcribed from CD by MP, DFPL.

— "I shall skirt": LN to LZ, 3 July [LZ: 1963], HRHRC.

— "lucky enough": LN to LZ, 7 June 1963, HRHRC.

— "Those words": LN to LZ [LZ: 10 June 1963], misdated by LZ as 7 June 1963, HRHRC. Fragment of letter in *NCZ*, 333, misdated by LZ as rec'd 10 June 1963.

163 "My father spent": JS, interview by MP, 18 July 2008. "I was the pampered fourth child," says JS, "the only child to go away to college, Concordia. AM's favorite was Alice. Virginia, the oldest child, and AM didn't get along; she left home and married at sixteen."

— "3 bedrooms": LN to LZ, 7 June 1963, HRHRC. In the same letter, LN writes confusingly: "We'll probably sell the [house] Al bought of me. I'll eventually sell mine & that leaves us two. His is on the river & he want[s] it for his kids." But if they sold the house AM bought from LN, he couldn't keep it for his kids.

— "I have a box": LN to CC, 5 June 1964, *BYHM*, 46.

— "A . . . *what*?": JS to MP, 18 July 2008.

— "if we manage": LN to LZ, 7 June 1963, HRHRC.

164 "We talked about . . . I'm sure it's all . . . Last letter": LN to LZ, 10 June 1963, HRHRC.

— "on the stroke": LN to CC, 13 January 1963, *BYHM*, 38.

— "Return / the night women's": "Hospital Kitchen," *Origin* 3, no. 2 (July 1966): 21, *BC*, and *CW*, 205.

164 "We had our hoe-down": LN to LZ, Wednesday, 3 July [1963], HRHRC. The Hunt Club, renamed The Black Hawk Club, was owned by Richard Prisk; it subsequently burned down.

— "Lorine no longer": Fred Hobe, interview by GR, 27 January 1966, transcribed from CD by MP, DFPL.

— "Al Millen was": Darrel Prisk, interview by MP, 7 August 2009.

165 "I boycotted the wedding": ÆM to Glenna Breslin, 3 July 1988, GB.

— "I knew a clean man": "I knew a clean man," *T&G*, *MLBW*, and *CW*, 208. In a letter to LZ of 25 August 1964, LN explains "now I sew green aprons / over covered seats": "I'm putting slip covers over slips covers, a kind of apron over the regular covers so that when Al comes in from looking at a fish pole or cutting another tree he can sit down without my worrying" (*NCZ*, 348).

Chapter 19. Milwaukee

179 "We stood . . . We had a deer": LN's "Upper Mississippi River vacation, July 1963," written for Al's daughter JS and her husband Eugene Schoessow. They had previously stopped at Mille Lacs County in east central Minnesota, one thousand lakes to explore; after Swan River they went on to Duluth. LN prefaced her notes with the lines "Of Father / of waters / Of son / and daughters / whose sons / and daughters" and enclosed photos of AM at Wyalusing and the Swan River depot.

180 "Have I written": LN to LZ, 2 August 1963, *NCZ*, 334. LN wrote up her experiences in a six-page typescript, HRHRC.

— "I wish you'd ask me": LN to LZ, 15 August 1963, *NCZ*, 335. About the same time, LN offered her work to the Library of Congress, which replied that more fittingly she should offer her papers to her college alma mater: "Of course I am not an alumna" (LN to LZ, 17 September [LZ: 1963], HRHRC). She also unsuccessfully offered the Minnesota Historical Society her honeymoon travelog and AM's reminiscences.

— "Respectable at last! . . . We use *All* ": LN to LZ, 23 July [LZ: 1964], *NCZ*, 347.

181 "As to your letters": LN to LZ, 15 August 1963, *NCZ*, 335.

— "I've always abided": LN to CC, postmarked 8 June 1965, *BYHM*, 59.

— "dark and depressing": JS, interview with MP, 15 October 2008.

— "[T]he cleaning": LN to LZ, 13 December 1963, *NCZ*, 338.

— "I do think third shift" and following dialogue quotations: AM, recorded by LN in "Kooky Conversations," a handmade booklet given to "Julie & Gene [Schoessow] Christmas '65 from Lorine and Dad," LN Archives, Hoard.

182 "Casual, sudsy": "Laundromat," part of *Homemade/Handmade Poems*, *Origin* 3, no. 2 (July 1966): 21 and *CW*, 202.

— "a bit of Black Hawk Island . . . [t]he park saves my life": LN to LZ, 13 December 1963, *NCZ*, 340.

— "huge red ore boats": LN to CC, 12 March 1964, *BYHM*, 43–44.

182 "[t]he only way I'd": LN to LZ, 13 December 1963, *NCZ*, 338.

183 "[E]veryone uses words": LN to LZ, 30 October 1964, unpublished poem about LZ and CZ's translations of Catullus, HRHRC. The *New Statesman* called the translations "complete lunacy" (*TPAL*, 369). LN always spoke tactfully to LZ about the translation.

— "It's my trip to the moon! . . . Writing is toning down": LN to LZ, [11 November] 1964, HRHRC. "I seem to have written down 5 points relatin' to my paintin'."

— "huge glass mushroom . . . Here the taverns": LN to JW, 19 February 1964, SUNY–Buffalo.

184 "a domineering type": JS to Glenna Breslin, 5 August 1987 and 5 July 1998, GB.

— "said things": LN to LZ [LZ: 7 January 1964], *NCZ*, 342.

— "We have made": LN to LZ [LZ: 7 February 1964], *NCZ*, 343. LN's math is confusing: if AM went to the bank at 9 a.m. and had 3 hours of leisurely drinking, he'd have come home about noon, not 11 a.m. LN's tension is plain: it's 10 a.m. on the first Friday of the pact; she's washed her hair, done the dishes, taken a walk and is now watching the clock. Will he come home as promised?

— "Alcoholic dream": "Alcoholic dream," *Paris Review* 8, no. 32 (Summer/Fall 1964): 198, *T&G*, *MLBW*, and *CW*, 200. Other poems that refer to AM's drinking: "Some float off on chocolate bars," "I married/in the world's black night," and "Why can't I be happy" (*CW*, 207, 228, 230).

185 "My lovely husband": LN to LZ [7 January 1964], *NCZ*, 341.

— "never wore beads . . . move before . . . smooth-draped": "Truth" and "Sewing a Dress," *CW*, 218, 245.

— "You know Al": LN to LZ [LZ: 7 January 1964], *NCZ*, 342.

— "a shake of cayenne": Lorine Niedecker Millen's *A Cooking Book*, "Winter (1st married winter) in Milwaukee—1963–64," LN Archives, Hoard. During the Friends of Lorine Niedecker's 2009 Poetry Festival, the Café Carpe in Fort Atkinson offered a dinner buffet of LN recipes: her favorite Jell-O Salad, Corn and Cheese Fondue, Chicken Loaf, Swedish Meatballs, Bread Pudding, and Pumpkin Pie with Hard Sauce. Reviews were decidedly mixed.

— "The fact that I don't" and following quotations: LN, *A Cooking Book*, 1.

— "[A]ctually some things": LN to LZ, 13 December 1963, *NCZ*, 339.

186 "I had the impression": LN to CC, 18 June [1965], *BYHM*, 62.

— "[a]bout one poem": Jonathan Williams, "Think What's Got Away in My Life," *Kulchur* 2 (Autumn 1962): 87–88.

— "There is sumpn": LN to LZ [7 February 1964], *NCZ*, 343.

— "conversational—metaphysical . . . over and over": LN to CC, 5 June 1964, *BYHM*, 46.

— "The shiver / which is death": CC, "The Shiver," *in no time*. See Lisa Pater Faranda's note on the poem in *BYHM*, 47.

187 "Please don't mind": LN to CC, October 1964, *BYHM*, 19.

— "a form of poetic": LN to LZ [LZ: 2 July 1964], *NCZ*, 343.

— "In the transcendence": "In the transcendence," *CW*, 204.

— "We are reading": LN to LZ [29 September 1964], *NCZ*, 349.

187 "the Thames, St. Paul's": LN to CC, 11 February 1965, *BYHM*, 54.

188 "I'm afraid to ask": LN to CC, 27 March 1965, *BYHM*, 56.

— "Consider at the outset": "Consider at the outset," *Poetry* (August 1965), *T&G*, *MLBW*, and *CW*, 200.

— "My father and mother": JS to MP, 15 October 2008.

189 "I cooked, washed": LN to LZ [18 March 1964], *NCZ*, 344.

— "We aren't building": LN to LZ, 17 September [LZ: 1963], HRHRC.

— "[O]h how we work": LN to LZ, 13 October 1964, *NCZ*, 350.

190 "I gave my binoculars": LN to LZ, 11 May 1964, fragment, HRHRC.

Chapter 20. Husband to a Poet

191 "Don't ever marry": AM to JS, 17 January 1971, letter in possession of JS.

— "I get half a dozen": LN to CC, February 11, 1965, *BYHM*, 53.

— "even before I die!": LN to Fred Hobe, 9 January 1964, as reported by Hobe to GR, 27 January 1996, transcribed from CD by MP, DFPL.

— "time and space for poetry": LN to LZ, 10 April 1963, *NCZ*, 331–32. Since some poems probably written during the first years of LN's marriage were published posthumously, their dating is uncertain. The following poems can be assigned with a fair degree of certainty to post-marriage 1963–64: "To my small electric pump," "T. E. Lawrence," "As I paint the street," "Art Center," "Consider at the outset," "Ah your face," "Alcoholic dream," "To my pressure pump," "Laundromat," "March," "Something in the water," "Santayana," "Frog noise," "To whom," "Margaret Fuller," "Watching dancers on skates," "Hospital Kitchen," "Chicory flower," "Fall," "Some float off on chocolate bars," "I knew a clean man," "I visit the graves," "Obliteration," "Spring," "Who was Mary Shelley?" and "Wild strawberries."

— "Send 'em the typewriter": LN, "Kooky Conversations," LN Archives, Hoard.

192 "How impossible it is": "T. E. Lawrence," *Origin* 3, no. 2 (July 1966): 32, *MLBW*, and *CW*, 198.

— "in the center": LN to LZ, 26 December 1963, *NCZ*, 337.

— "I really don't think": JS e-mail to MP, 5 January 2010.

— "I somehow feel": LN to CC, October 1964, *BYHM*, 48.

— "I cd. do better": LN to CC, 12 December 1964, *BYHM*, 49.

— "Popcorn-can cover": "Popcorn-can cover," *Poor. Old. Tired. Horse.* 9 (undated, probably 1965), *T&G*, MYBW, and *CW*, 218.

— "[I] was thinking last night . . . go way back . . . We might let . . . It shouldn't be mentioned": LN to CC, 11 February 1965, *BYHM*, 51–54.

193 "I couldn't say": LN to CC, 8 June 1965, *BYHM*, 59.

— "Couldn't sleep last night": LN to CC, 18 June 1965, postscript to a letter of 17 June 1965, *BYHM*, 62. CC evidently wrote a strong letter to LN: "a tidal wave from Japan against an already icelandic—tho momentary—situation here at home—Cid!" but followed with a positive one (LN to CC, 2 July 1965, *BYHM*, 63).

193 "As I go": LN to CC, 2 July 1965, *BYHM*, 64. CC replied that he would be delighted to publish LZ's letters to LN.

— "just the essences . . . a chore tho": LN to CC, postmarked 8 June 1965, *BYHM*, 59.

194 "Why Black Hills? . . . I dunno": LN to CC, 2 July 1965, *BYHM*, 64.

— "always very luxurious": LN to CC, 28 July 1965, *BYHM*, 66–67. Unless noted otherwise, all descriptions of their vacation are from this source.

— "a cowboy on a horse": LN, "Kooky Conversations," LN Archives, Hoard.

— "The face wd. be": LN notes on Ziółkowski and Crazy Horse are the only ones that survive from the Black Hills vacation, LN Archives, Hoard.

195 "The Badlands": "The Badlands," *Origin* 3, no. 2 (July 1966): 14, *T&G*, *MLBW*, and *CW*, 220.

— "a letter from New York": LN to CC, 2 July 1965, *BYHM*, 63.

196 "Do you know": Bonnie and GR's talk for the Fort Atkinson Tuesday Club, 21 October 1986, transcribed from CD by MP, DFPL. The *Carmen* production, staged by the Fort Atkinson Mounds Players, had four performances, 21–25 March 1963 (*DJCU*). Hobe also directed. GR's Blackhawk Island house was at fire-number W7495, upstream from LN's.

— "I had no idea": LN to Fred Hobe, as reported by Hobe to GR, 27 January 1996, transcribed from CD by MP, DFPL. The meeting LN refers to took place on Saturday, 1 May 1965; what she seems to have talked too much about, from the letter, was Emerson's correspondence with Carlyle.

— "Lorine: *who are you?*": Bonnie and GR on LN for the Fort Atkinson Tuesday Club, 21 October 1986, transcribed from a CD by MP, DFPL. See also GR's account of events in *LNWP*, 68–69.

— "half in love": Linda Kreger Sawyer to MP, telephone interview, 2 November 2009. Linda knew Phoebe Sorenson and GR.

— "Bird singing": "Prothonotary Warbler," *T&G*, *MLBW*, and *CW*, 221. All three versions are reprinted in *FTC*, 224–25; the third version is titled "Warbler."

197 "I don't know if I can . . . He's left here . . . Why did you ever . . . He's the only": Bonnie and GR on LN for the Fort Atkinson Tuesday Club, 21 October 1986, transcribed from a CD by MP, DFPL.

— "Oh, darling . . . Is Lorine safe . . . Oh, well, Gail": Fred Hobe, interview with GR, 27 January 1996, transcribed from CD by MP, DFPL.

198 "I married": "I married," *Origin* 3, no. 9 (April 1968): 38, *BC*, and *CW*, 228.

Chapter 21. An End, an Experiment

199 "I'm so optimistic": LN to LZ [LZ: 15 August 1963], *NCZ*, 335.

— "Some people think": GR at a Wisconsin Library Association meeting, October 1986, transcribed from CD by MP, DFPL.

— "in a rapid": LN to CC, 27 August 1965, *BYHM*, 69.

— "fret not": JW, quoted by LN to CC, 14 September 1965, *BYHM*, 71.

— "I've typed for a Collected": LN to CC, 27 August 1965, *BYHM*, 70.

200 "not easy": LN to CC, 18 September 1965, *BYHM*, 72. Weill accepted "I've been away from poetry" for his Elizabeth Press publication.

— "Wonder what to call . . . I'm editing": LN to JW, 22 August 1965, SUNY–Buffalo. By 17 September 1965 LN had come up with the title "The Common Air" from part 17 of Walt Whitman's "Song of Myself": "This the common air that bathes the globe."

— "If sooner than that": LN to JW, 27 August 1965, SUNY–Buffalo.

— "[V]ery heavy . . . God! help me!": LN to CC, 18 and 14 September 1965, *BYHM*, 72, 71.

— "[T]he fact that": LN to CC, 7 October 1965, *BYHM*, 73.

— "A bit of": LN to JW, 8 December 1965, SUNY–Buffalo. "I've written [LZ] re his statement on the jacket of New Goose and on a 1951 To Whom It May Concern letter when I was applying for a Guggenheim—just a chance he'll not object to at least one of those in direct quote."

— "No go": LN to JW, 14 December 1965, SUNY–Buffalo.

201 "WHAT???—is that": LN to CC, quoting from her letter to LZ, 13 October 1966, *BYHM*, 101.

— "bitterly crushed . . . somewhat disingenuous": CC to Lisa Pater Faranda, 1 April 1982, *BYHM*, 61, 64.

— "Come quick": LN to KC, 11 June 1969, *TFN*, 38. The program was *Poetry: Louis Zukofsky*, National Education Television, Indiana University, Bloomington, Audiovisual Center, 1966, shown on Milwaukee Public TV.

— "but *there*, the same . . . And the talking": LN to CC, 20 August 1966, *BYHM*, 97–98. The Zukofskys moved in June 1964 to 77 Seventh Avenue in Manhattan; the film is shot in his Brooklyn Heights apartment, however, so the filming predates the move.

202 "you know": LN to CC, 7 October 1965, *BYHM*, 73.

— "A book larger": LN to CC, 16 December 1965, *BYHM*, 79.

— "I can honestly . . . but I fight shy": LN to CC, Thanksgiving, but postmarked 6 December 1965, *BYHM*, 77.

203 "Each man an empire . . . rain stops": LN, "The Poetry of Cid Corman," *Arts in Society* 3 (Summer 1966): 558–60. Though Gibson called the piece "perfect," LN deprecates her reviewing skills to CC, calling herself "a weak sister of Marianne Moore" (LN to CC, 4 November 1965, *BYHM*, 75).

— "how tiny my comments": LN to CC, postmarked 20 August 1966, *BYHM*, 96.

— "good, young face": LN to CC, postmarked 12 April 1966, *BYHM*, 82.

— "both happy and terrified . . . I share your views": LN to Morgan Gibson, 12 August and 6 October 1966, *LNWP*, 89, 90. Nine LN letters to Gibson are printed in *LNWP*.

— "Al, one stormy": LN, "Kooky Conversations," LN Archives, Hoard.

204 "Time to garden": "Tradition," *Origin* 3, no. 2 (July 1966): 29, *BC*, and *CW*, 224–25.

— "lisp and wisp," "I lost you": "Autumn Night" and "I lost you to water, summer," *Origin* 3, no. 2 (July 1966): 31, 36, and *CW*, 225, 227.

— "The issue received": LN to CC, 15 June 1966, *BYHM*, 86. Poems published in *Origin* 3, no. 2 (July 1966): 1–37 were: "Easter Greeting," "Audubon," "Van Gogh," "The museum man," "Mr. Van Ess," "Asa Gray wrote Increase Lapham," "To see the man who took care of our stock," "Depression years," "Brought the enemy down," "Two old men," "My father said I remember," "I am sick with the Time's buying sickness," "The Badlands," "The flower beds," "I'm good for people?" "As praiseworthy," "They've lost their leaves," "As I Paint the Street," "My mother saw the green tree toad," "Ah your face," "Laundromat," "Hospital Kitchen," "For best work," "Ian's," "Wild Strawberries," "Margaret Fuller," "To whom," "Watching dan-/cers on skates," "Tradition," "Sewing a dress," "Autumn Night," "T. E. Lawrence," "Sky," "Nothing to speak of," "Sweden-borg," "I lost you to water, summer," and "The eye." Corman also excerpted six LN letters in the issue.

204 "Well—Milwaukee had": LN to CC, 11 February 1965, *BYHM*, 53. For *Origin*, CC broke LN's words into a poem of three three-line stanzas.

205 "T&G coming out": LN to JW, 30 June 1966, SUNY–Buffalo.

— "Eagle Harbor . . . knobs of Archaen . . . French spoken . . . the shining big sea-water . . . What I didn't": LN's Lake Superor Trip notes, LN Archives, Hoard. Some 260 pages of these notes survive on varying sizes of paper, some pages bearing only a name or descriptive phrase. A few instances of uneven writing suggest that LN took notes in the moving car. Their itinerary: July 26: Green Bay, Escanaba, Gladstone, Manistique; July 27: St. Ignace, Sault Ste. Marie (Michigan); July 28: Sault Ste. Marie (Canada), Wawa, White River; July 29: Marathon, Lake Nipigon, Port Arthur; July 30: Fort William, Pigeon River, Schroeder, Grand Marais, Two Harbors, Duluth, Itasca, Winnibigoshish, Lake Bemidji, Walker, Leech Lake, Swan River; July 31: Brainard, Lake St. Croix, Pine City, Little Falls; August 1: return through Wisconsin to Blackhawk Island.

— "Traverse des Millens . . . [a] millenium": LN to CC, 20 August 1966, *BYHM*, 94.

206 "the heroes": Davie, "Lorine Niedecker," 64–73. Marilla Fuge did considerable research on Dr. George Frederick Kunz, a famous gemologist who worked for Tiffany. "In studying the life of Lorine Niedecker," Fuge wrote to an informant, "many of us feel she knew of her Grandfather Kunz's family in New York." Though it's interesting to speculate that LN inherited her interest in rocks—Fuge cited "The Granite Pail"—this is not very conclusive evidence.

— "Lorine: 'One could' . . . Lorine: 'Schoolcraft' . . . everything looks the same": LN's handmade booklet, "Christmas '66 To Julie and Gene from L. and Al," LN Archives, Hoard.

207 "a great delight": LN to CC, 20 August 1966, *BYHM*, 94, 93.

— "shows a working out . . . Between typographical errors": LN to Morgan Gibson, 12 August and 6 October 1966, *LNWP*, 89, 90. "I've finished the Lake Superior poem," she told Corman 13 October 1966, "—5 pages long—after much culling but I might just make a small book of it with a short poem on each page." The ms. of "Circle Tour" does not survive.

208 "a short poem": Wallace Stevens to Thomas McGreevy, 13 July 1949, Stevens, *Letters*, 640.

208 "short, sharp": LN's "LAKE SUPERIOR" notes, LN Archives, Hoard.

— "The leaf was once the stone": Herman and Nina Schneider, *Rocks, Rivers and the Changing Earth* (New York: W. R. Scott, 1952), 11. Schneider was a Carl Sagan–like popularizer of science, though he wrote chiefly for children.

— "You can see": LN's "Christmas '66 To Julie and Gene from L. and Al," LN Archives, Hoard. LN also remarked: "As H.G. Wells said, taking the world as a whole, including all matter: 'something is thinking here,'" a theme not developed in the poem that came to be known as "LAKE SUPERIOR."

— "wait with a good grace": Marcus Aurelius, *Meditations*, book 2, 51.

— "The smooth black stone": the penultimate stanza of "LAKE SUPERIOR," *CW*, 232–38 (stanza on 236). For the version published in *Arts in Society* 4, no. 3 (Fall/Winter 1967): 508–13, see *CW*, 434–38.

209 "Strange—we are": LN to CC, 16 July 1966, *BYHM*, 92.

— "cries of their occasions": CC's introduction to Bashō, *Origin* 2, no. 14 (July 1964): 2. LN prized that Bashō *Origin*: when LZ asked her to send it to Brown University because it also contained his poems, she refused.

— "[w]riting is toning down": LN to LZ [11 November] 1964, HRHRC.

— "by the way": LN to CC, 24 October 1967, *BYHM*, 133.

210 "Geology has done": LN to CC, 7 December 1967, *BYHM*, 137.

Chapter 22. *North Central*

211 "Cid had written": Nero, "Remembering Lorine," 136–40. All of Nero's comments about LN are from this source.

212 "I did meet Bob Nero": LN to CC, 13 October 1966, *BYHM*, 102.

— "I am not": LN to CC, 22 November 1966, *BYHM*, 106.

— "[I]t's commendable": LN to JW, 11 January 1967, SUNY–Buffalo.

213 "Jonathan Williams dug": LN to GR, 10 February [1967], GR Collection, Hoard. See Roub, "Getting to Know Lorine Niedecker," 82.

— "old, almost abandoned": LN to CC, 2 March 1967, *BYHM*, 113.

— "buzzing . . . but why must": LN to CC, 13 October 1966, *BYHM*, 101. LN called "Kaddish" "spiritual"; in fact the poem is based on a Jewish prayer.

214 "Al slept right": LN to GR, 10 February [1967], GR Collection, Hoard.

— "I've thought so much": LN to CC, 3 May 1967, *BYHM*, 121.

— "Thought you might": LN to GR, 10 February [1967], GR Collection, Hoard.

— "felt something like": LN to CC, 15 December 1966, *BYHM*, 108.

— "Sleep's dream": "SUBLIMINAL"; LN's typescript of "Harpsichord & Salt Fish" in the Boston University's Mugar Memorial Library contains this poem, published finally in *Origin* 4, no. 16 (July 1981): 32–33 and *CW*, 287.

215 "My life": "*My Life by Water*," *Origin* 3, no. 7 (October 1967): 55, *NC*, *MLBW*, and *CW*, 237–38.

216 "Niedecker's knife buried": Karl Gartung, poet and Niedecker authority, interview with MP, 26 March 2009.

— "Wild, wild praise": LN to CC, 13 October 1967, *BYHM*, 132.

— "like a brother": LN to JW, 26 October 1966, SUNY–Buffalo.

— "Overwhelming whatever he means . . . well, I suppose": LN to JW, 28 November 1966, SUNY–Buffalo. LN's letter is full of details for the anticipated publication by JW of *T&G*; it would not be published until 1969.

— "Lorine Niedecker's poems": KC, "The Poems of Lorine Niedecker," *Truck* 16 (Summer 1975): 94.

217 "I don't suppose": LN, quoting BB to CC, 12 July 1967, *BYHM*, 127.

— "painful hour . . . very bitter": BB to Tom Pickard, 30 March 1967, quoted in Makin, *Bunting: The Shaping of His Verse*, 324.

— "tough and lovely": LN to JW, 18 July 1967, SUNY–Buffalo. LN and BB did not appear together in *Poetry* for August 1967 ("LZ reigns alone": LN to CC, 13 September 1967, *BYHM*, 131).

— "[v]ery delicate": BB to Tom Pickard, 28 August 1967, quoted in Makin, *Bunting on Poetry*, 180n82.

— "And of course . . . his manner is timid": LN to CC, 12 July 1967, *BYHM*, 127.

— "a high point in my later life": LN to JW, 18 July 1967, SUNY–Buffalo.

— "how dark / how inconsiderate": "WINTERGREEN RIDGE," *CW*, 254.

— "nobody else has": BB to JW, 11 December 1966, quoted in Quartermain, "Take Oil/and Hum," 278.

— "a glorious time": LN to GR, 20 June 1967, GR Collection, Hoard.

— "she was not . . . Gene and the kids": JS to MP, 18 July 2008.

218 "Why didn't you call": JS, interview by Glenna Breslin, 5 August 1987 and 5 July 1988, GB.

— "They don't wait": LN to LZ, n.d. [probably 25 August 1964], HRHRC.

— "Captive in my own house": LN to GR, summer 1967, GR Collection, Hoard.

— "Why can't I": "Why can't I be happy," *Origin* 3, no. 7 (October 1967): 54 (one of eleven poems in a group titled "HEAR & SEE"), *BC*, and *CW*, 230.

— "sent out 16 poems": LN to GR, summer 1967, GR Collection, Hoard.

— "rather spontaneous": LN to CC, 20 July 1967, *BYHM*, 129.

— "I married": "I married," *Origin* 3, no. 9 (April 1968): 54, *BC*, and *CW*, 228. Significantly, LN did not want "I married" to be published in a group of her poems but to stand alone.

219 "define a way of writing poetry": LN to GR, 20 June 1967, GR Collection, Hoard; see Roub, "Getting to Know Lorine Niedecker," 86. LN said that Myron Turner came closest to talking about what she meant in his article "The Imagery of Wallace Stevens and Henry Green," *Wisconsin Studies in Contemporary Literature* 8, no. 1 (1967): 60–77, but she perhaps extracted more than Turner states. He claims that neither Stevens nor Green keep their eye on the object but instead "recreate it into something it both is and

is not. This accounts for the unreality of their imagery. . . . [F]or both of them a description of a tree must first be true to the perceiving mind and not to the tree" (62, 66).

219 "you know—that": LN to CC, 13 September 1967, *BYHM*, 130.

220 "extremely prejudiced": JS to MP, 15 October 2008.

— "Tense situation in Milwaukee": LN to JW, 13 September 1967, SUNY–Buffalo. James Groppi (1930–85) was Milwaukee advisor to the NAACP Youth Council (1965–68) and organizer of a black youth group called the Milwaukee Commandos, formed to help control violence during the revolt. The demonstrations against a number of racial issues lasted into 1969.

— "Holed damp": "*Shelter*," *Origin* 3, no. 7 (October 1967): 56, *NC*, *MLBW*, and *CW*, 246.

— "I'm hungry . . . I hope I haven't done the wrong thing": LN to CC, 24 October 1967, *BYHM*, 133–34. LN always apologized for not sending CC poems first; she also told him to "feel perfectly free to not print me—tho saying that I feel lost": LN to CC, 13 October 1967, *BYHM*, 132.

— "strange feeling": this comment from Fulcrum Press's Stuart Montgomery was printed as a lead-in to "TRACES OF LIVING THINGS," *CW*, 238. Further quotes from the poems in the series "TRACES OF LIVING THINGS" can be found in *CW*, 238–47.

— "Can't get to": LN to CC, 8 November 1967, *BYHM*, 135.

— "knocked out . . . something wild": LN to Clayton Eshleman, n.d. [February 1968], Fales. "Modern poetry is difficult. . . . I think it's going to be more difficult before it's over! No semblance of syntax after awhile, a confusion of words that seem to go together. . . . The glorification of the fragment and why not. I should have done something on this 'wild' order immediately following NC but I fell ill and it got knocked out of me."

— "I feel it won't": LN to CC, 15 and 29 December 1967, *BYHM*, 140, 141.

221 "Mebbe I offended . . . would not show": LN to GR, 8 November 1967, GR Collection, Hoard. LN grew to like GR's photos, using the one of her reading a book as a Christmas card. See Roub, "Getting to Know Lorine Niedecker," 83.

— "She had the figure": JS to MP, 8 January 2010.

Chapter 23. Full Flood

222 "Where the arrows . . . Lady's slipper's glue" and following quotations: "WINTER-GREEN RIDGE," *Caterpillar* 3, no. 4 (April–July 1968): 229–37, *NC*, *MLBW*, and *CW*, 247–57; for variants see *CW*, 441. For analyses of the poem, see especially *BYHM*, 137–40, and KC, "The Longer Poems." *LNWP* also contains Karl Gartung's excellent black-and-white photographs of Wintergreen Ridge, 295–302.

— "with the mystery of poetry . . . connect with": LN to CC, 10 January 1968, *BYHM*, 145. LN is reacting to CC and Kamaike Susumu's edition of Bashō's *Back Roads to Far*

Towns, sent to her by CC: "Here—I think this is it—the ultimate in poetry." Though expressing these sentiments after finishing "WINTERGREEN RIDGE," LN had long held these poetic ideals.

223 "The lady's-slippers . . . which manage to live": Eifert, *Journeys in Green Places*, 105, 35.

225 "I should have sent": LN to CC, 7 December 1967, *BYHM*, 136.

— "I've had an offer": LN to JW, 24 January 1968, SUNY–Buffalo. LN had written previously on 19 January 1968, also mentioning an offer to publish *T&G*; she wrote again fearing that letter misdirected.

— "if I can manage $500": LN to CC, 10 January 1968, *BYHM*, 146.

— "[N]ow even more": LN to JW, 5 March 1968, SUNY–Buffalo.

— "tiny design": LN to JW, 12 March 1968, SUNY–Buffalo.

226 "I think I'll": LN to JW, 15 March 1968, SUNY–Buffalo.

— "across many states": LN to CC, 14 February 1968, *BYHM*, 153.

— "sound and word patterns seethe": Clayton Eshleman to LN [15 December 1967], Fales.

— "We are still": Clayton Eshleman to LN, n.d., Fales.

227 "I can talk . . . tied to . . . movement, gist": LN to Clayton Eshleman, 27 December 1967 and 3 February 1968, Fales. LN continues: "It's in the province of natural history that imagination in the protoplasm of the mind is limited by actual experience, but it has the innate impulse to cross barriers. It is the nature of protoplasm in the cerebral cortex never to be satisfied but always to want more. (I take from science just what I want, like Bible readers taking only what they want from there) I begin to wonder if it isn't reality— natural—to be beautifully lost for a time and to me that's poetry. One thing I must be correct on—we now find ourselves in a deeper strata of the subconscious, not only that but we are somewhat driven into it by the horrible state of the conscious world."

— "I believe that": Clayton Eshleman to LN [18 January 1968], Fales.

— "I'm reading": LN to Fred Hobe, 23 October [1968], taped interview of Hobe by GR, 27 January 1996, LN Archives, Hoard.

— "this time he has": LN to CC, 21 May 1968, *BYHM*, 165. Scroggins in his biography of LZ says that LZ was "disgusted and enraged" by passages in "The Moistinsplendour" in which Eshleman "imagined Louis and Celia having sex" (*TPAL*, 413). These passages must have been encoded; they are not evident to a general reader, though Eshleman obliquely mentions LZ.

— "I'm caught up": LN to Clayton Eshleman, 14 February 1968, Fales. Letter quoted out of order, beginning with LN's "P.S."

228 "Art is cooler": LN to CC, 14 February 1968, *BYHM*, 153. LN's letter to CC is franker about "Walks" than hers to Eshleman: "Well now!"

— "It's true I'd like": LN to Clayton Eshleman, 20 February 1968, Fales.

— "Silly, but I've . . . W. H. Hudson": LN to CC, 30 January 1968, *BYHM*, 149.

— "I like rigor": Duncan, "From a Notebook," 210. LN's quote to CC is close to the original.

— "was amazed" and following quotations: GR to Michael Paul Vandre, 3 January 1968, courtesy Michael Vandre. Vandre (then using the name Paul) had been an indifferent student, but Connie Carlson, one of his English teachers, passed on his poems to GR, who took them to LN. "Lack of love": courtesy Michael Vandre, published in *Monk's Pond* (Summer 1968).

229 "Oh, you found me out" and following quotations: Ronald Ellis, interview by MP, 1 August 2008.

— "We are nothing": LN to Ronald Ellis, 2 December 1966, written on the envelope, Ellis. Some letters from LN to Ellis are published in *LNWP*, 94–99.

— "I live among": LN to Ronald Ellis, 26 October 1966, *LNWP*, 94.

— "I'm no critic": LN to Ronald Ellis, 30 November 1966, *LNWP*, 95.

— "Well, wasn't ever": LN to Ronald Ellis, 24 December 1966, *LNWP*, 97. With the letter LN enclosed her "Horse, hello," "Hi, Hot-and-Humid," "To Aeneas who closed his piano," and a Proletarian poem "I can't bear to think of now" (it was "We know him—Law and Order League").

230 "I think he": Thomas Merton to LN, 29 February 1968, Archives of the Thomas Merton Center, Bellarmine University, Louisville, Ky.

— "running down the scale": LN to CC, 10 January 1968, *BYHM*, 146.

231 "your senior citizen": LN to GR, "Last day of February" [1968], GR Collection, Hoard.

— "This strange winter": LN to CC, 7 March 1968, *BYHM*, 155–56. LN's troubles were not over. On 27 March 1968 she reported herself "ill with it all," that is, the contractual difficulties of the British publication of *T&G*: "Poets shouldn't have to be so involved. Where are my Marcus Aurelius meditations now?" (LN to CC, *BYHM*, 159).

— "three blocks up . . . where the people": LN to CC, 2 May 1968 [postmark] and 19 April 1968, *BYHM*, 163, 160. "Cleaned all surfaces" (*BC* and *CW*, 231) was written before the move in 1968 but indicative of the labor LN put into every place she lived, including her Blackhawk Island rentals. LN describes 539 Maple Street as part of a row of old houses. Today a newer two-story structure tops an old low brick building divided into two apartments, 539 and, side entry, 539A.

— "like the ancient": LN to CC, postmarked 2 May 1968, *BYHM*, 163.

— "A really sweet": George Millen to MP, telephone interview, 8 April 2010.

— "alluvial deposits": LN to JW, 2 May 1968, SUNY–Buffalo.

232 "Lovely day . . . his grey head": LN to CC, 21 May 1968, *BYHM*, 164–65.

— "Yes, well": LN to CC, 12 June 1968, *BYHM*, 167.

— "best and maybe": LN to CC, 12 June 1968, *BYHM*, 166. LN thought the funeral a "little lavish" but beautiful in parts. Senator Edward Kennedy read his brother's 1966 speech to the youth of South Africa.

— "I don't know": LN to CC, 4 October 1968, *BYHM*, 171. LN finished "PAEAN TO PLACE" in August 1968, when she gave a typed copy to GR, though the poem wasn't printed until 1969.

233 "When you're over sixty": LN to KC, 2 May 1969, *TFN*, 37.

— "a kind of": LN to Florence Dollase, postmarked 4 August 1969, DFPL; she sent Dollase a handwritten copy of "PAEAN TO PLACE." In the poem LN refers thirteen times to her father, eleven to her mother, thirteen directly to herself: her own "holy trinity." The last nine lines of "PAEAN TO PLACE" retrieve imagery of "Old man who seined."

233 "I was the solitary" and following quotations: "PAEAN TO PLACE," *Stony Brook* 3, no. 4 (1969): 32–35, *MLBW*, and *CW*, 261–69. My belief that "PAEAN" is LN's greatest poem contradicts a critic like KC, who calls it regressive, "a bundle of short poems . . . trying to pass itself off as one long one" ("The Longer Poems," 308).

— "lush, mush-music": LN to CC, n.d. [fall 1968], *BYHM*, 176.

— "Just home from . . . I think we never": LN to CC, 1 August 1968, *BYHM*, 168.

234 "Sometime I must": LN to JW, 29 October 1968, SUNY–Buffalo.

— "not beautiful . . . but this is": LN to CC, 1 August 1968, *BYHM*, 169.

— "I can't see how": LN to CC, 1 August 1968, *BYHM*, 169.

— "He walked—loped": "LZ," *Origin* 3, no. 12 (January 1969): 3, *BC*, and *CW*, 289–90.

235 "LZ doesn't even": LN to CC, 21 November 1968, *BYHM*, 179.

— "[Y]ou may know": LN to CC, 3 December 1968, *BYHM*, 181.

— "a rich sitter" and following quotes: LZ, *"A" 1–12*, 143, 171, 220–21, 252, 256.

— "And Stuart wormed . . . my day old . . . with disastrous": LN to CC, 22 October 1968, *BYHM*, 175.

— "know her": Bonnie Roub to MP, 14 July 2008.

236 "Oh, are you Bonnie's": Joan Jones to MP, 17 March 2010.

— "Doloroso . . . wondered if it . . . I don't feel": LN to CC, 27 December 1968, *BYHM*, 182.

— "I fainted one midnight": LN to CC, 4 February 1969, *BYHM*, 182.

— "he from work": LN to JW, 7 December 1968, SUNY–Buffalo.

— "Out home the beautiful": LN to CC, 28 May 1969, *BYHM*, 194.

Chapter 24. The Urgent Wave

237 "o Lord . . . Please answer": LN to JW, 26 February 1969, SUNY–Buffalo.

— "I maintain": LN to Morgan Gibson, 6 October 1966, *LNWP*, 90.

— "poetry should be": LN to KC, 3 May 1969, *TFN*, 37.

— "I know how": LN to CC, 7 May 1969, *BYHM*, 188. LN wrote JW that she'd give her life to see Morris's *Birds* woolen fabric design: 17 November 1969, SUNY–Buffalo.

— "the letters of": LN to KC, 2 May 1969, *TFN*, 37.

— "delightful deshabille": LN, quoting KC to CC, 15 May 1969, *BYHM*, 191.

238 "society's / corruption": "His Carpets Flowered," *CW*, 292.

— "Do you notice": LN to JW, 17 November 1969, SUNY–Buffalo.

— "absolutely cordial" and following quotations: Michael Vandre, interview by GR, 26 October 1989, CD, DFPL, and by MP, 2 February 2009.

— "why I don't": LN to JW, 2 July 1969, SUNY–Buffalo.

— "bridge to Winnipeg": LN scrapbooks, with some pictures, LN Archives, Hoard.

— "Canada—too tiring . . . only 8 . . . [N]o room of my own": LN to CC, 28 August [1969], *BYHM*, 198.

239 "Oh, didn't she": LN to JW, 4 September 1969, SUNY–Buffalo.

— "Well, my first . . . Millen care of": LN to JW, 24 September 1969, SUNY–Buffalo. LZ congratulated LN on *T&G*; poems he liked best were: "There's a better shine," "He built four houses," "Tell me a story about the war," "The young ones go away to school," "Paul / when the leaves," "Sorrow moves in wide waves," "Hear," "To foreclose," "River-marsh-drowse" and "Fall"—five from *For Paul and Other Poems*.

— "$350, maybe": Tom Meyer to MP, 24 May 2010. With a grant, those were the sums JW usually gave to authors.

— "The chief focus . . . but with the pulse": Tomlinson, "A Rich Sitter." He calls LN's poems "points of patience . . . fragments shored against long winters, spring floods and literary isolation."

240 "Tomlinson says I got": LN to KC, 2 July 1969, *TFN*, 38.

— "I sent University": LN to CC, 7 December 1969, *BYHM*, 208. In "The Milk Separator and the New Goose," Elizabeth Willis argues that LN belongs to an international group of writers "whose work, like hers, explores cultural conflict and an interest in folk forms" (1).

— "I rise to" and following quotations: LN to JW, 2 July 1969, SUNY–Buffalo.

— "This book, along . . . notations of isolation": Heller, "I've Seen It There," 444–45.

— "I'm so afraid": LN to CC, 4 May [1970], *BYHM*, 221.

241 "humiliated . . . When I took care . . . I feel like": Bonnie Roub at the "Remembering Lorine Niedecker Conference" in Appleton, Wis., 29 October 1986.

— "though a poet": LN to Frank and Annie Laurie Hoard Brewer, 19 January 1970, in *LNWP*, 100, and DFPL.

— "Al was the opposite": ÆM to Glenna Breslin, 3 July 1988, GB. In 1987 Æneas had been negative about AM; in 1988 he said, "I liked Al, I got along with him."

— "You are the man": "Wilderness," *CW*, 283. When she recorded for CC, she called the poem "Wild Man"; CC used that title in *BC*.

— "How upset she was": GR, "Getting to Know Lorine Niedecker," 82.

242 "a honey": quoted in Knox, *Lorine Niedecker*, 27.

— "In that dark": LN to KC, 15 July 1969, *TFN*, 38.

— "I'd very much": LN to KC, 15 July 1969, *TFN*, 38.

— "so fascinating": LN to LZ, "Almost Feb '61", *NCZ*, 275. LN's personal library contained *The Autobiography of Thomas Jefferson* (New York: Putnam, 1959), Karl Lehman Hartleboro, *Thomas Jefferson, American Humanist* (New York: Macmillan, 1947), Dumas Malone, *Jefferson the Virginian* (Boston: Little, Brown, 1948) and *Jefferson and the Rights of Man* (Boston: Little, Brown, 1951), and Saul K. Padover's edition of *Thomas Jefferson on Democracy* (New York: American Library, 1939).

— "For austere education": text on LN's season's greetings card sent to GR, n.d., *BYHM*, 37.

243 "splendid torments . . . To daughter Patsy": "Thomas Jefferson," *Origin* 3, no. 19 (October 1970): 57–64 and *CW*, 275–82. For an early version at Hoard see *CW*, 444–53, a poem of 235 lines that LN cut severely to 158.

243 "deft . . . I always feel": LN to CC, 24 August 1970, *BYHM*, 230–31. LN calls "Darwin" "good but not as deft as the Jefferson." LN had seven Pound books in her personal library. A note in the Cantos indicates what interested her: "Pisan Cantos—p. 451 ff, Adams—Jefferson—p. 357 ff, John Adams—p. 357 ff, Section Rock Drill—p. 371 ff, Thrones—p. 681." In *Personae* she noted poems on pp. 112, 113, 116, and 117 as favorites.

244 "Would you believe" and following quotations: note on a typed copy of "BULLETIN" dated 23 July 1970 and given to the Roubs. See *CW*, 452–53, for the version that became "John Adams is our man" (*CW*, 285–86).

— "My Thomas Jefferson": LN to KC, 2 February 1970, *TFN*, 40.

— "an undercurrent": LN to CC, 17 March 1970, *BYHM*, 221.

— "I look out": LN to CC, 7 March 1970, *BYHM*, 219.

— "I had some" and following quotations: Evans and Kleinzahler, "An Interview with Carl Rakosi," 74–75. LN revealed her opinion of Rakosi to CC: "not so strong as LZ of course & not so technically original as Williams—right?" (27 February 1970, *BYHM*, 217).

245 "I met her for the first time": Carl Rakosi to George Oppen, 18 January 1971, the George Oppen papers, University of California, San Diego, quoted in Rachel Blau DuPlessis, "Lorine Niedecker, the Anonymous," 115.

246 "I guess I": LN to CC, 4 February 1969, *BYHM*, 183.

— "dragged herself": LN to CC, 17 June 1970, *BYHM*, 226. LN tells CC she mourns the fact that Jefferson didn't get to meet Diderot before his death, the subject of the last (deleted) stanza of "BULLETIN": "Jefferson mourned: to arrive / in Paris just too late / to see Diderot / alive."

— "O too hot": LN to Bonnie and GR, n.d., written on notepaper with an embellished "M," GR Collection, Hoard.

— "in the same predicament . . . I am ill . . . Let each man hope": "Darwin," 124-line poem unpublished in LN's lifetime, later in *BC* and *CW*, 295–99. For variants and other publications see *CW*, 455–56.

— "a high gabbling": "Young in Fall I said: the birds," *CW*, 231.

247 "good . . . with no great hopes": LN to CC, 24 August 1970, *BYHM*, 231.

— "Wyalusing State Park": "Trip to Prairie du Chien, '70," notes, accompanying LN's photos, given to GR, GR Collection, Hoard.

— "Me new book": LN to JW, 4 November 1970, her last to JW.

— "an organ": LN to KC, 10 October 1970, *TFN*, 41.

— "Halfway thru *Little*": LN to LZ, 9 November 1970, *NCZ*, 360.

248 "I'd like to": LN to CC, 18 August 1970 and 2 November 1970, *BYHM*, 229–30, 236. CC was planning to pay his way in the States by giving lectures.

— "starred but not": LN to CC, 5 September 1970, *BYHM*, 233.

— "Reaching the age": LN to James Laughlin, 18 September 1970, Houghton, Harvard.

— "It was so good": JL to LN, 9 November 1970, Houghton, Harvard. JL suggested LN send him a six- to eight-page sequence of poems for the 1972 *ND*.

248 "Jonathan Williams, yes": LN to JL, 24 November 1970, Houghton, Harvard.

— "Yes, I can well": JL to LN, 28 December 1970, Houghton, Harvard. Hospitalized, LN never read the letter.

— "In Fort Atkinson": CC's 1970 notebook, Special Collections, Morris Library, University of Delaware, published in *Truck* 16 (1975): 73 and *BYHM*, 243.

249 "a day o": LN to Bonnie and GR, ca. 18 November 1970, GR Collection, Hoard.

— "Your father was funnier . . . When we took them back": LN to the Schoessows, 18 November 1970, letter in possession of JS.

250 "She made it clear . . . She read poorly": CC, in *Truck* 16 (1975): 73–74, and *BYHM*, 243–44.

— "calmly read!!": LN to Bonnie and GR [18 November 1970?], GR Collection, Hoard.

— "Two things I did": LN to KC, 32 November 1970, *TFN*, 41.

— "Do you think": LN to LZ, 9 November 1970, *NCZ*, 361.

— "I find myself": LN to JS, 4 November 1970, letter in possession of JS.

— "the kind of gilded": LN to LZ, 9 November 1970, *NCZ*, 361.

— "Honey, I feel" and following quotes: JS to MP, quoting AM.

251 "What I remember": Doris Perkin, telephone interview with MP, 5 November 2009.

Afterword

252 "Lorine died yesterday afternoon": Alice Millen to JS, 1 January 1971, letter in possession of JS.

— "I didn't know:" George Millen to MP, telephone interview, 8 April 2010. Bonnie Roub says that ÆM and others "signed the funeral book at GR's house." If so, it was not the official funeral book (Hoard), which states that LN is survived by twelve grandchildren and one great-grand child, organist was Mrs. Lawrence Becker, and cards accompanying flowers were from Blackhawk Island Neighbors and Friends; Mrs. Maude Hartel; Mrs. Arvella Humbach; Mr. and Mrs. Maurice McQuade; Mr. and Mrs. Ed Garthwaite; Gail, Bonnie, and Katharine Roub; Royal and Elizabeth Hayes; Julie and Gene Schoessow; Mrs. Edna Neidecker (Leon) Dodge; Mrs. Mary Ann Glover (Robert) Rockenfield; Mrs. Robert Marceick; Jack and Jule Christman; Mrs. Theron Vickerman (Emma Niedecker Carmody's daughter); and Mae K. Ward. Relatives and friends signing the guestbook were Avis Meyer, Alex Kohlman, Justine Aspinwall, Maude Hartel, A. Peter Ganser, Raymond Prisk, and Mr. and Mrs. Gail Roub. The "Service of Memory for Mrs. Albert Millen" card called LN a "well-known Wisconsin poet," quoting August Derleth ("her poems are arresting, compelling and admirably clear"), and Sister M. Therese ("Steeped in the History of the Lake region of Northern Wisconsin, her poetry gave evidence of the authors deep empathy for nature").

253 "she went hard": Carroll Trieloff to MP, telephone interview, 10 October 2008.

— "Hope you carry": LN to LZ, 23 November 1970, *NCZ*, 362. LZ addressed the condolence: "Dear Albert Millen."

253 "We went thru": Alice Millen Zenisek to the Schoessows, 13 January 1971, letter in the possession of JS. Alice notes that AM has "3 copies of her new book [*My Life By Water*] & 3 of T&G & 2 of North Central. I put them in a pile on the cedar chest. I think he will give 1 of each to Alice [Millen] & he said yesterday he would take some to the funeral director's wife. So there should be 1 copy left. I will tell him to save you a copy." She also notes that AM is "writing all his own checks out & typing things now"; LN had paid the bills.

— "Dear Sir": JW, unpublished letter to the *New York Times*, 26 January 1971. The letter was published in *Truck* 16 (1975): 141. JW was contemptuous of the brief obituary in the 2 January 1971 *Madison Capital Times*: "Pretty damn hopeless" (*Epitaphs for Lorine*, n.p.).

254 "Now this is": AM to JS, 17 January 1971, letter in possession of JS.

— "I won't be your housekeeper": JS to MP, 18 July 2008.

255 "My mother was": JS to MP, 29 June 2010.

— "Bill, I don't": JS to MP, 18 July 2008. AM's death at seventy-six was caused by "[c]ardiovascular collapse probable due to pulmonary embolus or aortic aneurysm" (death certificate). AM willed Margaret Millen $5,000.00 and the rest of his estate to his four children, "share and share alike" (Certificate and Will courtesy JS). AM's property left to him by LN was appraised at $37,909.78.

— "starkly the same": Terrell, *Louis Zukofsky*, 31.

— "Zukofsky had created": Penberthy quoting CC to her on CZ's letter of 1 March 1979, *NCZ*, 70.

— "Lorine was very important" and following quotes: Tom Meyer to MP, telephone interview, 9 December 2009.

256 "a distinctive literary event": Heller, "Silence Is Musical," 26 January 1986, 25.

— "The time is": *TFN*, 5.

— "her place in history": Larry A. Reed, Local Preservation Coordinator to GR, 27 March 1990, GR Collection, Hoard.

— "once-in-a-lifetime": *DJCU*, 23 July 1991.

— "Fish / fowl / flood": "PAEAN TO PLACE," *CW*, 261–69.

257 "My concern for": CC to GR, 2 January 1980, GR Collection, Hoard.

— "Her style was": CC, in *Truck* 16 (1975): 89–90.

258 "She is a poet": Herd, review of *The Objectivists*, 27.

Selected Bibliography

Ahearn, Barry. *The Correspondence of William Carlos Williams and Louis Zukofsky*. Middletown, Conn.: Wesleyan University Press, 2003.

———, ed. *Pound/Zukofsky: Selected Letters of Ezra Pound and Louis Zukofsky*. New York: New Directions, 1987.

———. "Two Conversations with Celia Zukofsky." *Sagetrieb* 2, no. 1 (Spring 1983): 113–31.

Allen, Donald M., ed. *The New American Poetry: 1945–1960*. New York: Grove Press, 1960.

Aurelius, Marcus. *Meditations*. London: Penguin, 1964.

Ballowe, James. "Little Press on the Prairie." *Chicago Reader*, 3 May 1996.

Breslin, Glenna. "Lorine Niedecker and Louis Zukofsky." *Pacific Coast Philology* 20, nos. 1–2 (November 1985): 25–32.

———. "Lorine Niedecker: Composing a Life." In *Revealing Lives: Autobiography, Biography and Gender*, edited by Susan Groag Bell and Marilyn Yalom, 141–53. Albany: State University of New York Press, 1990.

———. "Lorine Niedecker: The Poet in Her Homeplace." In *Radical Vernacular: Lorine Niedecker and the Poetics of Place*, edited by Elizabeth Willis, 189–206. Iowa City: University of Iowa Press, 2008.

Bunting, Basil. *Collected Poems*. London: Fulcrum Press, 1968.

Caddel, Ric. "A Poem in Its Place." *Sagetrieb* 3, no. 3 (Winter 1984): 115–22.

Carruth, Hayden. *The Voice That Is Great within Us: American Poetry of the Twentieth Century*. New York: Bantam Books, 1970.

Chester, Laura, and Sharon Barba, eds. *Rising Tides: Twentieth Century American Women Poets*. New York: Simon and Schuster, 1973.

Ciardi, John, and Miller Williams. *How Does a Poem Mean?* New York: Houghton Mifflin, 1960.

Conte, Joseph. "Sounding and Resounding Anew: Louis Zukofsky and Lorine Niedecker." In *Unending Design: The Forms of Postmodern Poetry*, 141–63. Ithaca, N.Y.: Cornell University Press, 1991.

Corman, Cid. "Caught in the Act: The Comedian as Social Worker in the Poetry of Carl Rakosi." In *Carl Rakosi: Man and Poet*, edited by Michael Heller, 325–50. Orono, Maine: National Poetry Foundation, 1993.

————, ed. *The Gist of Origin: An Anthology*. New York: Grossman Publishers, 1975.

————. "With Lorine." *Truck* 16 (Summer 1975): 59–90.

Court Green 2. "Dossier: Tribute to Lorine Niedecker." Chicago: Columbia College English Department, 2005.

Cox, Kenneth. "The Longer Poems." In *Lorine Niedecker: Woman and Poet*, edited by Jenny Penberthy, 303–10. Orono, Maine: National Poetry Foundation, 1996.

————. "The Poems of Lorine Niedecker." *Cambridge Quarterly* 4 (Spring 1969): 169–75.

Crase, Douglas. "Niedecker and the Evolutional Sublime." In *Lorine Niedecker: Woman and Poet*, edited by Jenny Penberthy, 327–44. Orono, Maine: National Poetry Foundation, 1996.

————. "On Lorine Niedecker." *Raritan* 12, no. 2 (Fall 1992): 47–70.

Dahlberg, Edward, and Herbert Read. *Truth Is More Sacred: A Critical Exchange on Modern Literature*. New York: Horizon Press, 1961.

Davie, Donald. "Lapidary Lucidity." In *Carl Rakosi: Man and Poet*, edited by Michael Heller, 233–37. Orono, Maine: National Poetry Foundation, 1993.

————. "Lorine Niedecker: Lyric Minimum and Epic Scope." In *The Full Note: Lorine Niedecker*, edited by Peter Dent, 64–73. Budleigh Salterton, Devon: Interim Press, 1983.

Dembo, L. S. "Louis Zukofsky: Objectivist Poetics and the Quest for Form." *American Literature* 44 (March 1972): 74–96.

————. "The 'Objectivist' Poet: Four Interviews." *Contemporary Literature* 10 (Spring 1969): 155–219.

Dent, Peter, ed. *The Full Note: Lorine Niedecker*. Budleigh Salterton, Devon: Interim Press, 1983.

Dent, Peter, and Peter Quartermain, eds. *The Objectivist Nexus: Essays in Cultural Poetics*. Tuscaloosa: University of Alabama Press, 1999.

Duncan, Robert. "From a Notebook." *Black Mountain Review* 5 (1955): 209–12.

DuPlessis, Rachel Blau. "Lorine Niedecker's 'Paean to Place' and Its Reflective Fusions." In *Radical Vernacular: Lorine Niedecker and the Poetics of Place*, edited by Elizabeth Willis, 151–79. Iowa City: University of Iowa Press, 2008.

Eaton, Edward Dwight. *Historical Sketches of Beloit College*. New York: A. S. Barnes and Company, 1935.

Eckman, Frederick. "Lorine Niedecker's Local: 'a woody speech/a marshy retainer.'" *Truck* 16 (Summer 1975): 110–15.

Eifert, Virginia S. *Journeys in Green Places: The Shores and Woods of Wisconsin's Door Peninsula*. Sister Bay, Wis.: Wm. Caxton Ltd, 1963.

Evans, George, ed. *Charles Olson & Cid Corman: Complete Correspondence, 1950–1964*. 2 vols. Orono, Maine: National Poetry Foundation, 1991.

Evans, George, and August Kleinzahler. "An Interview with Carl Rakosi." In *Carl Rakosi: Man and Poet*, edited by Michael Heller, 61–92. Orono, Maine: National Poetry Foundation, 1993.

Faranda, Lisa Pater. "Composing a Place: Two Versions of Lorine Niedecker's 'Lake Superior.'" *North Dakota Quarterly* 55, no. 4 (Fall 1987): 348–64.

———. "Lorine Niedecker." In *American Poets, 1880–1945: Second Series*, edited by Peter Quartermain, 305–19. Dictionary of Literary Biography 48. Detroit: Gale Research, 1986.

———. "'Seashells on Mountaintops': The Poetics of Aging." In *Lorine Niedecker: Woman and Poet*, edited by Jenny Penberthy, 377–88. Orono, Maine: National Poetry Foundation, 1996.

Finlay, Ian Hamilton. *The Dancers Inherit the Party: Selected Poems*. Worcester, England: Migrant Press, 1960.

———. *Glasgow Beasts, an a Burd, Haw, an Inseks, an, Aw, a Fush*. Edinburgh: Wild Hawthorn Press, 1961.

Gartung, Karl. "One by Herself: The Achievement of Lorine Niedecker." *Wisconsin Academy Review* 32, no. 3 (June 1986): 42–47.

Gibson, Morgan. "Lorine Niedecker, Alive and Well." *Truck* 16 (Summer 1975): 123.

Hatlen, Burton, ed. *George Oppen: Man and Poet*. Orono, Maine: National Poetry Foundation, 1981.

———. "Interview with Carl Rakosi." *Sagetrieb* 5, no. 2 (Fall 1986): 95–123.

Hatlen, Burton, and Tom Mandel. "Poetry and Politics: A Conversation with George and Mary Oppen." In *George Oppen: Man and Poet*, edited by Burton Hatlen, 23–47. Orono, Maine: National Poetry Foundation, 1981.

Hayes, Paul. "The Poet and the Painter." *Wisconsin, the Milwaukee Journal Magazine* (30 December 1990): 4–12, 19–21.

Heilbrun, Carolyn C. *Writing a Woman's Life*. New York: Norton, 1988.

Heller, Michael, ed. *Carl Rakosi: Man and Poet*. Orono, Maine: National Poetry Foundation, 1993.

———. "I've Seen It There." *The Nation*, 13 April 1970.

———. "Lorine Niedecker: Light and Silence." In *Conviction's Net of Branches: Essays on the Objectivist Poets and Poetry*, edited by Michael Heller, 48–57. Carbondale: Southern Illinois University Press, 1985.

———. "Silence Is Musical." *New York Times Book Review*, 26 January 1986.

Herd, David. Review of *The Objectivists*, ed. Andrew McAllister. *Times Literary Supplement*, 3 January 1997.

Honig, Edwin. "A Memory of Lorine Niedecker in the Late '30s." In *Lorine Niedecker: Woman and Poet*, edited by Jenny Penberthy, 43–47. Orono, Maine: National Poetry Foundation, 1996.

Ivry, Jonathan. "Rock/River: Lorine Niedecker's Objectivist Poetics of the Natural World." *MidAmerica* 23 (2006): 48–65.

Jenkins, G. Matthew. "Lorine Niedecker, Simone de Beauvoir, and the Sexual Ethics of Experience." *Tulsa Studies in Women's Literature* 23, no. 2 (Fall 2004): 311–37.

Knox, Jane. *Lorine Niedecker: An Original Biography*. Fort Atkinson: Dwight Foster Public Library, 1987.

Laughlin, James. *The Way It Wasn't*. Edited by Barbara Epler and Daniel Javich. New York: New Directions, 2006.

Lawrence, D. H. *Fantasia of the Unconscious, with Phychoanalysis and the Unconscious*. New York: Viking Press, 1961.

Lehman, David, ed. *The Oxford Book of American Poetry*. Oxford: Oxford University Press, 2006.

Lehman, John. *America's Greatest Unknown Poet: Lorine Niedecker Reminiscences, Photographs, Letters and Her Most Memorable Poems*. Cambridge, Wis.: Zelda Wilde Publishing, 2003.

Makin, Peter, ed. *Bunting on Poetry*. Baltimore: Johns Hopkins University Press, 1999.

———. *Bunting: The Shaping of His Verse*. Oxford: Clarendon, 1992.

McAllister, Andrew, ed. *The Objectivists*. Newcastle-upon-Tyne: Bloodaxe, 1996.

McMillan, Donald. *Transition 1927–1938: The History of a Literary Era*. New York: George Braziller, 1975.

Meyer, Wayne. "Lorine Niedecker: A Life by Water." Presentation to the Conference of Wisconsin Writers, Lawrence University, Appleton, Wisconsin, 12 September 1980.

Middleton, Peter. "The British Niedecker." In *Radical Vernacular: Lorine Niedecker and the Poetics of Place*, edited by Elizabeth Willis, 247–70. Iowa City: University of Iowa Press, 2008.

———. "Lorine Niedecker's 'Folk Base' and Her Challenge to the American Avant-Garde." *Journal of American Studies* 31, no. 2 (1997): 203–18.

Miracle, Faith. "She Rose from Marsh." *Wisconsin Trails* 35, no. 6 (December 1994): 50–53.

Nero, Bob. "Remembering Lorine." *Truck* 16 (Summer 1975): 136–40.

Niedecker, Lorine. *"Between Your House and Mine": The Letters of Lorine Niedecker to Cid Corman, 1960–1970*. Edited by Lisa Pater Faranda. Durham, NC: Duke University Press, 1986.

———. *Blue Chickory*. New Rochelle, N.Y.: Elizabeth Press, 1975.

———. "Christmas '66 To Julie and Gene from L. and Al." LN Archives, Hoard.

———. *Collected Works*. Edited by Jenny Penberthy. Berkeley: University of California Press, 2002.

———. *A Cooking Book*. Green River, Vt.: Longhouse Publishers, 1992.

———. "Extracts from Letters to Kenneth Cox." In *The Full Note*, edited by Peter Dent, 36–42. Budleigh Salterton, Devon: Interim Press, 1983.

———. *From This Condensery: The Complete Writing of Lorine Niedecker*. Edited by Robert J. Bertholf. Penland, N.C.: Jargon Society, 1985.

———. *The Granite Pail: The Selected Poems of Lorine Niedecker*. Edited by Cid Corman. San Francisco: North Point Press, 1985.

———. *Harpsichord & Salt Fish*. Edited by Jenny Penberthy. Durham, N.C.: Pig Press, 1991.

———. "Kooky Conversations." LN Archives, Hoard.

———. "Letters to Celia and Paul Zukofsky, 1949–1959." In *Lorine Niedecker: Woman and Poet*, edited by Jenny Penberthy, 48–63. Orono, Maine: National Poetry Foundation, 1996.

———. "Letters to *Poetry* Magazine, 1931–1937." In *Lorine Niedecker: Woman and Poet*, edited by Jenny Penberthy, 175–92. Orono, Maine: National Poetry Foundation, 1996.

———. "Local Letters." In *Lorine Niedecker: Woman and Poet*, edited by Jenny Penberthy, 87–107. Orono, Maine: National Poetry Foundation, 1996.

———. *My Friend Tree*. Edinburgh, Scotland: Wild Hawthorn Press, 1961.

———. *My Life by Water*. London: Fulcrum Press, 1969.

———. *New Goose*. Prairie City, Ill.: The Press of James A. Decker, 1946.

———. *New Goose*. Edited by Jenny Penberthy. Berkeley, Calif.: Rumor Books, 2002.

———. *Niedecker and the Correspondence with Zukofsky, 1931–1970*. Edited by Jenny Penberthy. New York: Cambridge University Press, 1993.

———. *North Central*. London: Fulcrum Press, 1969.

———. Notes from Books in Lorine Niedecker's Personal Library. Compiled by Tom Montag. http://www.lorineniedecker.org.

———. "Of Father/of waters." LN Archives, Hoard.

———. "The Poetry of Cid Corman." *Arts in Society* 3 (Summer 1966): 558–60.

———. "The Poetry of Louis Zukofsky." *Quarterly Review of Literature* 8 (1956): 198–210.

———. *T & G: The Collected Poems (1936–1966)*. Penland, N.C.: Jargon Society, 1969.

Oppen, George. *The Selected Letters of George Oppen*. Edited by Rachel Blau DuPlessis. Durham, N.C.: Duke University Press, 1990.

Oppen, Mary. *Meaning a Life: An Autobiography*. Santa Barbara: Black Sparrow Press, 1978.

Origin 16, 4th ser. (July 1981). Lorine Niedecker featured.

Penberthy, Jenny, ed. *Lorine Niedecker: Woman and Poet*. Orono, Maine: National Poetry Foundation, 1996.

———. *Niedecker and the Correspondence with Zukofsky, 1931–1970*. New York: Cambridge University Press, 1993.

———. "Poems from Letters: The Lorine Niedecker–Louis Zukosfky Correspondence." *Line* 6 (Fall 1985): 3–20.

———. Review of *From This Condensery: The Complete Writings of Lorine Niedecker* edited by Robert J. Bertholf. *Sagetrieb* 5, no. 2 (Fall 1986): 139–51.

———. "The Revolutionary Word: Lorine Niedecker's Early Writings 1928–1946." *West Coast Line: A Journal of Contemporary Writing and Criticism* 7 (Spring 1992): 75–98.

———. "'The Very Variant': Lorine Niedecker's Manuscript Collection." *The Library Chronicle of the University of Texas at Austin* 22 (1992): 113–47.

———. "Writing 'Lake Superior.'" In *Radical Vernacular: Lorine Niedecker and the Poetics of Place*, edited by Elizabeth Willis, 61–79. Iowa City: University of Iowa Press, 2008: 61–79.

Phillips, Rodney. *The Hand of the Poet: Poems and Papers in Manuscript*. New York: Rizzoli International Publications, 1997.

Pound, Ezra. *The Cantos of Ezra Pound*. New York: New Directions, 1998.

Quartermain, Peter. "Reading Niedecker." In *Lorine Niedecker: Woman and Poet*, edited by Jenny Penberthy, 219–27. Orono, Maine: National Poetry Foundation, 1996.

———. "Take Oil/and Hum: Niedecker/Bunting." In *Radical Vernacular: Lorine Niedecker and the Poetics of Place*, edited by Elizabeth Willis, 271–83. Iowa City: University of Iowa Press, 2008.

Rakosi, Carl. *The Collected Prose of Carl Rakosi*. Orono, Maine: National Poetry Foundation, 1983.

Ramazani, Jahan, Richard Ellmann, and Robert O'Clair, eds. *Norton Anthology of Modern and Contemporary Poetry*. New York: W.W. Norton, 2003.

Reisman, Jerry. "Lorine: Some Memories of a Friend." In *Lorine Niedecker: Woman and Poet*, edited by Jenny Penberthy, 35–38. Orono, Maine: National Poetry Foundation, 1996.

———. "On Some Conversations with Celia Zukofsky," *Sagetrieb* 10, no. 3 (Winter 1991): 139–50.

Reznikoff, Charles. *Poems: 1918–1936*. Edited by Seamus Cooney. Santa Barbara: Black Sparrow Press, 1976.

———. *Poems: 1937–1975*. Edited by Seamus Cooney. Santa Barbara: Black Sparrow Press, 1977.

Rosenthal, M. L. *The New Poets: American and British Poetry since World War II*. New York: Oxford University Press, 1967.

Roub, Gail. "Getting to Know Lorine Niedecker." *Wisconsin Academy Review* 32, no. 3 (June 1996): 37–41. Also published in *Lorine Niedecker: Woman and Poet*, edited by Jenny Penberthy, 79–86. Orono, Maine: National Poetry Foundation, 1996.

Scroggins, Mark. *Louis Zukofsky and the Poetry of Knowledge*. Tuscaloosa: University of Alabama Press, 1998.

———. "The Piety of Terror: Ian Hamilton Finlay, the Modernist Fragment, and the Neo-Classical Sublime." http://www.flashpointmag.com/ihfinlay.htm.

———. *The Poem of a Life: A Biography of Louis Zukofsky*. [Emeryville, Calif.]: Shoemaker & Hoard, 2007.

Sheeler, Jessie. *Little Sparta: The Garden of Ian Hamilton Finlay*. Photographs by Andrew Lawson. London: Francis Lincoln, 2003.

Smith, William Jay. "Patchen's Province and Other Landscapes." *Poetry: A Magazine of Verse* 70 (April–September 1947): 108–13.

Stevens, Wallace. *Letters of Wallace Stevens*. Edited by Holly Stevens. Berkeley: University of California Press, 1996.

Terrell, Carroll F., ed. *Louis Zukofsky: Man and Poet*. Orono, Maine: National Poetry Foundation, 1979.

Tomlinson, Charles. "Objectivists: Zukofsky and Oppen, a Memoir." In *Louis Zukofsky: Man and Poet*, edited by Carroll F. Terrell, 79–95. Orono, Maine: National Poetry Foundation, 1979.

———. "A Rich Sitter: The Poetry of Lorine Niedecker." *Agenda* 7 (Spring 1969): 65–67.

Tiffany, Daniel. "The Rhetoric of Materiality." *Sulfer* 22 (Spring 1988): 202–9.

Truck 16: Lorine Niedecker Issue (Summer 1975).

Walsh, Phyllis. *Lorine Niedecker: Solitary Plover*. LaCrosse, Wis.: Juniper Press, 1992.

Williams, Jonathan. *Amen, Huzza, Selah: Poems, Black Mountain*. With a preface by Louis Zukofsky. Highlands, N.C.: Jargon Society, 1960.

————. *Descant on Rawthey's Madrigal (Conversations with Basil Bunting)*. Lexington, Ky.: Gnomen Press, 1968.

————, ed. *Epitaphs for Lorine*. Penland, N.C.: Jargon Society, 1973.

Willis, Elizabeth. "The Milk Separator and the New Goose: Niedecker, Eisenstein, and the Poetics of Non-Indifference." HOW2: http://www.asu.edu/piperwcenter/how@journal/archive/online.

————. "The Poetics of Affinity: Niedecker, Morris and the Art of Work." In *Radical Vernacular: Lorine Niedecker and the Poetics of Place*, edited by Elizabeth Willis, 223–46. Iowa City: University of Iowa Press, 2008.

————. "Possessing Possession: Lorine Niedecker, Folk, and the Allegory of Making." *Cross Cultural Poetics* 9 (2001): 97–106.

————, ed. *Radical Vernacular: Lorine Niedecker and the Poetics of Place*. Iowa City: University of Iowa Press, 2008.

Zukofsky, Louis. *"A" 1–12*. Garden City, N.Y.: Doubleday, 1967.

————. *Anew: Poems*. Prairie City, Ill.: Press of James A. Decker, 1946.

————. *Catullus*. Translated by Louis and Celia Zukofsky. London: Cape Golliard, 1969.

————. *Complete Short Poetry*. Baltimore: Johns Hopkins University Press, 1991.

————, ed. "'Objectivists' 1931." Special issue of *Poetry: A Magazine of Verse* 37, no. 5 (February 1931).

————, ed. *An "Objectivists" Anthology*. Le Beausset, France: To Publishers, 1932.

————. "'Recencies' in Poetry." Preface to *An "Objectivists" Anthology*, edited by Louis Zukofsky, 9–25. Le Beausset, France: To Publishers, 1932.

————. "Sincerity and Objectification." *Poetry: A Magazine of Verse* 37, no. 5 (February 1931): 273–300.

————. *A Test of Poetry*. Hanover: University Press of New Hampshire, 2000. Originally published by Objectivist Press, 1948.

Films, Music, Plays

Birtwistle, Harrison. *Nine Settings of Lorine Niedecker for Soprano and Cello*. Claron McFadden, soprano, and the Nash Ensemble. London: Sanctuary Classics CD, 2001. ["There's a better shine," "My friend tree," "Along the river," "Hear," "How white the gulls," "*My Life by Water*," "Paul / when the leaves," "O late fall," and "Sleep's dream."]

Brown, Rae. *Renowned* (play). First performed at the Hoard Museum in Fort Atkinson, June 2008.

Cook, Cathy. *The Immortal Cupboard: In Search of Lorine Niedecker* (film, 73 minutes, 16 mm. to DV and DVD, color, sound). Sprocket Productions, 2009.

Langholff, Nick, and Brent Nothbohm. *My Life By Water* (10-minute film). Narrated by Sarah Day, 2004.

Thatcher, Kristine. *Niedecker* (play). First performed at the Court Theatre, Milwaukee, 1987.

Index

References to LN in subheadings refer to Lorine Niedecker. Page numbers in *italics* refer to illustrations. Titles not otherwise attributed are works of Lorine Niedecker.

Cooking Book, 185

Corman, Cid, 30, *172*; correspondence with, 4, 5, 6, 144–45, 191, 209, 225, 228, 239–40; editorial advice exchanged with, 186–87, 232–33; friendship with, 144–45, 161, 236; as literary executor, 253; on LN, 257–58; as poet, 154, 186–87, 203; as publisher, 5, 133, 144–45, 154, 192–93, 199–200, 202, 203–5, 216, 255; visit to Blackhawk Island, 248–50

correspondence: collected for publication, 180–81; as poetry, 204–5; published, 6, 180–81. *See also specific correspondents*

Cox, Kenneth, 216, 232, 237, 240, 242

Craig, Georgiana Ann, 31

Crawford, John, 57

Creeley, Robert, 121, 154

Cummings, E. E., 32, 108

Dahlberg, Edward, 121, 124, 148

Daive, Jean, 186, 227

The Dancers at the Party (Finlay), 144

"DARWIN," 246–47, 248

Darwin, Charles, poem about, 7, 246–47, 248, 250

death of LN, 250–51

Dechar, Edouard and Diane, 48

DeFrancisci, Josephine, 97

Dembo, L. S., 231–32

Dent, Peter, 256

Derleth, August, 53, 74, 146, 150–51

divorce from Frank Hartwig, 68–69

Dollase, Florence, 12–13, 20–21, 27, 30, 73, 77, *82*

Domestic and Unavoidable, 45, 53

"Don't tell me property is sacred," 128

Dorn, Edward, 150, 154, 159

drugs, psychoactive, 153, 224, 226, 228

du Bouchet, André, 186

DuPlessis, Rachel Blau, 6

Durrell, Lawrence, 200

education: at Beloit College, 21–25; elementary school, 12–14; high school, 15–16, 18–21; LN as avid reader and autodidact, 19, 26, 43, 75, 91, 140–41, 186, 205

Eifert, Virginia, 222–24

Elizabeth Press, 199–200

Ellis, Ron, 229–30

employment: babysitting, 108–9; as cleaning woman at Fort Atkinson Hospital, 126, 134, 150, 164; with Federal Writers' Project, 60, 62–63, 230; with Fort Atkinson Public Library, 27–29, 31–32; with *Hoard's Dairyman*, 73, 92–93, 98, 99–100; retirement, 181; vision disability and, 63, 73, 100; with Wisconsin Writers' Project, 62–63, 65–68, 230

Enslin, Theodore, 186

Epitaphs for Lorine, 254

Eshleman, Clayton, 186, 193, 225, 226–28

Evans, Robert Allison, 54

"The Evening's Automobiles," 103–4, 241

Federal Writers' Project, 60, 62–63

feminism, 153

finances: Artist's Relief Fund grant, 111; aversion to money, 12, 164; college tuition as expense, 23; disability payments, 100, 122; employment and, 100–102, 109, 122; inheritance from mother, 102; parental financial support, 39, 49; payments for poems, 36, 76, 124, 132, 158, 199, 202, 239; payments to presses for publication, 72, 111, 123, 134, 149–50, 188, 192; property management, 129, 159, 160, 163–64, 189, 195–96; support of small presses, 132, 199, 239; Zukofsky family as LN's heirs, 110

Finlay, Ian Hamilton, 143–46, 144, 145–50, 149–50, 192

Fisher, Susan and Gerard, 138–39

"Florida," 143–44

folk style, 47, 54–56, 106, 109, 192, 216, 218–19. See also *New Goose*

For Paul, 105–6, 132, 144–45; Zukofsky's objections to publication of, 109–10, 122–25, 146

"For Paul: Child Violinist," 121

Fort Atkinson, *168*

Foster, Alice, 67

From this Condensery: The Complete Writings of Lorine Niedecker, 255–56

Fuge, Marilla, 256

Fulcrum Press, 216–17, 220, 226, 234, 235, 240

Niedecker, Henry (father), 9–10, 78, *84*, *86*, 91–92; death of, 117; poems about, 17–18, 58, 117–18, 144

Niedecker, Lorine: abortion experience of, 49–50; antimaterialism of, 7, 75, 95, 119, 159, 233; aversion to money of, 12, 164; birds, interest in and identification with, 16, 65–66, 228, 230; centenary celebration for, 258; death of, 250–51; divorce from Frank Hartwig, 68–69; education of, 12–16, 15–16, 18–21, 21–25; employment of, 27–29, 31–32, 60, 62–63, 65–68, 73, 92–93, 98–100, 108–9, 126, 134, 150, 164, 230; father, Henry, poems about, 17–18, 58, 117–18, 144; father, Henry, relationship with, 9–10, 78, 91–92, 117; Harold Hein, relationship with, 134–39, 141, 147–48, 165, *170*, 182, 242; health problems of, 63, 73, 100, 110, 137, 220–21, 236, 250–51; Louis Zukofsky and (*see under* Zukofsky, Louis); and male poets as colleagues, 230; marriage to Al Millen, 160–65, 181–83, 191–02, 197–98, 239, 254; marriage to Frank Hartwig, 28–31, 68–69; mother, "Daisy," poems about, 17, 27, 58, 101, 102–3; mother, "Daisy," relationship with, 9–11, 78, 101; nature, relationship with, 7, 13, 74–75, 128, 207–10, 215–16, 220, 246–47 (*see also* birds *under this heading*); pictured, 3, *80–83*, *85–90*, *177–78*; as poet of place rather than regional poet, 6–7; political philosophy of, 15–16, 18, 54–55, 58, 62, 63–64, 76, 153; as reader and autodidact, 19, 26–27, 28, 43, 75, 91, 109, 127, 140–41, 186, 205, 230; as reclusive or introverted, 10, 12, 42, 48, 65, 218, 235–36, 249; retirement of, 181; as secularist, 7, 230; sex and sexuality of, 29–30, 62–63, 68–69, 116–17, 137–38; subconscious, interest in, 4, 38, 43, 46, 55, 233, 244; vision, nystagmus, and visual impairment of, 10, 12, 13, 15, 63, 66, 73, 100, 195, 250; women as resented by, 16, 103–4, 118; writing process of, 4, 38, 43, 46, 55, 157, 233, 242, 244 (*see also* poetics)

Niedecker, Theresa Henrietta Kunz "Daisy" (mother), 9–10, 11, 78, *79*, *82*, 99; deafness

and isolation of, 10–11; death of, 101; poems about, 17, 27, 58, 101, 102–3

Niedecker-Thompson Fish Company, 10

"Niedecker Weather," 204–5

Nora, James, 134

North Central, 5, 219, 221, 225, 230, 234, 239–40

Objectivism: emergence of school, 3–5; issue of *Poetry* devoted to, 5, 34–36, 41, 54; Objectivist creed, 36. *See also specific poets*

Objectivist Press, 41

O'Connor, Dennis, 134

"Old man who seined," 124, 144, 151

"Old Mother turns blue and from us," 101

"On Valentine's Day to Friends" (Zukofsky), 235

Oppen, George, 3–4, 34, 43–44, 46, 97, 114

Oppen, Mary, 4, 43–44, 46, 49, 61, 105–6, 114

Origin, 133, 154, 186, 192, 209; LN's works published in, 144–45, 146, 202–5, 216, 234–35, 238, 255; poems published in, 186, 234–35

Owen, Keith, 229

"PAEAN TO PLACE," 8, 220, 232–33, 235, 241, 256–57

painting, 183

Paris Review, 192

Penberthy, Jenny, 6, 256

Penny Poems (magazine), 132

Perkin, Chuck and Doris, 121, 251

personality: ambitions, 55, 199, 240; guilt and shame, 27–28, 31; political passions, 15–16, 18, 54–55, 58, 62, 63–64, 76, 153; reclusiveness or introversion, 10, 12, 42, 48, 65, 218, 235–36, 249. *See also* intellect

physical descriptions, 10, 15, 64, 116, 160, 212, 214, 221; of LN's voice, 250

Pickard, Tom, 235

Pig Press, 256

place, Niedecker as poet of, 6–7

poetics: concision, 132–33, 208; the "conversational metaphysical," 186–87; five-line stanza form, 140, 233, 237; folk style, 47, 54–56, 106, 109, 192, 216, 218–19 (see also *New Goose*); Japanese poets and forms as influences on, 132–33, 187, 209–10; long

Yackels, Donald, 94, *169*

Yackels, Nathalie Kaufman, 30, 94, 134, 162, 165, *169*, 242

Yasuda, Shoson, 133

"You are my friend—" 132, 140

Zenisek, Alice Millen, 162, 184, 252–53

Zukofsky, Celia Thaew, 51–52, 60–62, 71, 96, 105, 112, 114, 136, 163, 253; on LN's career, 255

Zukofsky, correspondence with, 3, 65–66; about Harold Hein, 135–36, 139; affectionate pet names and abbreviations in, 38, 42; LN as editor of letter collection, 180–81, 193–94, 195, 200, 201; Zukofsky and destruction of LN's letters, 60, 114, 180

Zukofsky, Louis, 3, *167*; archival collections of papers, 180; as controlling, 60, 97; correspondence with (*see* Zukofsky, correspondence with); editorial advice to LN, 41–42, 59, 71, 104, 109, 110, 123, 201; employment as technical writer, 92; as father, 71, 96–97; gifts and money exchanged with, 48, 100, 105–6, 109, 122, 124–25, 163; homosexuality and, 40, 61; as jealous or possessive, 106, 109–10, 146, 217; LN as editor of letter collection, 180–81, 193–94, 195, 200, 201; LN as overshadowed by, 6; LN as typist for, 46, 65, 71–72, 122; LN's critiques of works, 113, 133; LN's *Quarterly Review* article about, 113, 121, 124; LN's will and Zukofsky family as beneficiaries, 110; objections to publication of *For Paul*, 109–10, 122–23, 146; obscurity of poems, 72, 113, 133; poems about, 42, 108, 234–35; relationship with Celia, 51–52, 58, 60–62, 92, 97, 114, 202, 232; reluctance to support LN's work publicly, 124, 146–47, 151, 200; television appearance of, 201–2; visits to Wisconsin, 50–51, 118–19

Zukofsky, Paul, 71, 96–97, 105–7, 112–13, 118–19, 124–26, 133; LN's "Paul" poems, 105–7, 109, 122–26, 146, 208, 217